The
GERMAN
FLEET at
WAR,
1939–1945

The

GERMAN FLEET at WAR,

1939-1945

VINCENT P. O'HARA

Naval Institute Press
Annapolis, Maryland

Naval Institute Press
291 Wood Road
Annapolis, MD 21402

First Naval Institute Press paperback edition published 2011.
ISBN 978-1-59114-643-8

The Library of Congress has catalogued the hardcover edition as follows:
O'Hara, Vincent P.
    The German fleet at war, 1939–1945 / Vincent P. O'Hara
    p. cm.
    Includes bibliographical references and index.
    ISBN 1-59114-651-8 (alk. paper)
    1. Germany. Kriegsmarine—History—World War, 1939–1945. 2. World War,
1939–1945—Naval operations, German. I. Title.

D770.O38 2004
940.54'5—dc22

                                                        2004012716

Printed in the United States of America.

19 18 17 16 15 14 13   9 8 7 6 5 4 3 2

CONTENTS

PREFACE and ACKNOWLEDGMENTS

In naval warfare, success and failure are only a hairline apart. A wrong decision or one a minute late, the wrong interpretation of a message, a bad change in the weather, an unfortunate hit— any of these can change victory into defeat in a twinkling.

GROSSADMIRAL ERICH RAEDER

JUST BEFORE MIDNIGHT on 11 January 1945 off Norway's southwest coast a German convoy carrying coal and food-stuffs received word of British warships in the vicinity. The lookouts aboard *M273* focused their attention to port, toward the open sea from where danger seemed most likely to come. But the sudden twinkling of red lights appeared from dead ahead. There was a low whistling sound fol-lowed immediately by a muffled pop as the sky overhead exploded in harsh, yellow light. This scene—large German warships engaged with large enemy warships—occurred sixty-nine times during the Second World War. In a few cases involving famous ships like *Bismarck, Graf Spee,* or *Scharnhorst,* the details of the ensuing action are well known, but most of the surface battles the German navy fought have been relegated to asides or forgotten altogether.

Sea battles are a consequence of the tasks a navy faces during war. One task of the German navy was to disrupt Great Britain's trade and maritime lines of communication; for this the navy used submarines supported by surface warships. The navy also had vital trade routes to protect. It had to deny or dispute the Allies' ability to project power over the open seas and to protect the flanks of Fortress Europa; and occasionally the navy had to undertake power projections of its own. For these jobs the principal tools were surface warships. And, except for the brief Polish campaign, the fleet had to operate in the face of overwhelming Allied naval superiority. The German naval staff "contemplated no great Jutlands where (the) outnumbered surface forces would meet and destroy the enemy . . . (the) fundamental strategic concept was to obtain the most significant returns possible from its available forces but to avoid decisive battles with equal or superior enemy units."[1] But despite the naval staff's strategy, despite fuel shortages and inferior numbers, large warships of the German navy fought more sea battles than the Italian navy. They fought more than the Japanese navy. They even fought more than the United States Navy. This book is about these battles.

The details of these battles, both famous and forgotten, are interesting in themselves for illustrating how designs, doctrine, and leadership withstood the stress of combat. I unexpectedly discovered that the details fit together like a jigsaw puzzle to reveal a bigger picture. They reveal how the navy, its men, and its opponents evolved through six long years of warfare. They reveal that the German navy's war was not just a U-boat war, that the surface fleet was much more than a few doomed battleships. They reveal that the navy's contribution to Germany's war effort was greater and more crucial to her hopes for victory and later her survival than is commonly realized.

In this work I use the terms "surface engagement," "surface action," or "sea battle" interchangeably. They refer to an encounter between purpose-built surface warships displacing at least five hundred tons full load (which is how I define a "large" warship) where torpedoes and/or gunfire were exchanged. This definition excludes the many actions involving motor-torpedo boats, auxiliaries, and armed merchant cruisers or raiders where either opponent had only such ships engaged.

The German Fleet at War, 1939–1945 details each of the sixty-nine engagements fought by the German navy. A table summarizes the engagements discussed in each chapter. A header outlining the combat conditions and a brief background of the battle generally precedes each narrative. A table lists the participants, their nationality, the size, speed, and armament of the ships involved and damage suffered, if any. The reader is referred to the Appendix for a more detailed explanation of these matters. Finally, each chapter contains a map identifying the engagement's location and important geographic features in the vicinity or referenced in the narrative.

Language is standardized in the interest of precision. Instead of *Kriegsmarine,* Royal Navy, or *Polska Marynarka Wojenna,* the book

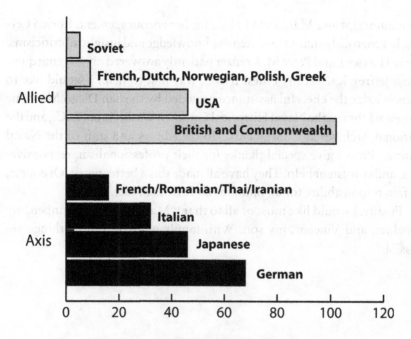

**Figure 1: Naval Surface Engagements
(by coalition and predominate participant)**

refers to these services as the German navy, British navy, and Polish navy. German ranks, however, remain in German because several have no English equivalent and because British and American ranks are not exactly equal. Similarly, *The German Fleet at War* retains German abbreviations for certain classes of warships: S-boat instead of motor-torpedo boat or E-boat, V-boat instead of patrol boat, and UJ-boat instead of subchaser or corvette. This is done because the English term is associated with the British navy ship types and does not necessarily describe the German equivalent. This book uses the English system of measurement with metric distances converted to yards and generally rounded off. The word "miles" always refers to nautical miles. The subject of this book is large; every effort has been made to present accurate information in an objective fashion. In cases where secondary sources disagree, I follow what I believe to be the most likely or reliable version.

Many people have supported my efforts to write *The German Fleet at War*. I would like to thank Vincent P. O'Hara Sr., for his careful scrutiny of the manuscript and Margaret O'Hara for her encouragement. Enrico Cernuschi generously shared his extensive knowledge and insightful criticisms. Pierre Hervieux and Peter M. Kreuzer patiently answered my nagging questions. Jeffrey Kacirk, my oldest friend, was first to help. I would like to acknowledge the cheerful assistance provided by the San Diego Maritime Museum Library, the Naval Historical Center in Washington, D.C., and the National Archives at College Park. To the editors and staff of the Naval Institute Press I give special thanks for their professionalism, responsiveness, and consistent help. They have all made this a better work. Of course, I retain responsibility for all opinions and errors of fact.

Finally, I would like most of all to thank Maria, my wife, Tunuen, my daughter, and Vincent, my son. With family and friends, all things are possible.

The
GERMAN
FLEET at
WAR,
1939–1945

1

OPENING ROUNDS

September 1939–January 1940

Things look different on the open ocean from the way they do
on the map at home.

GROSSADMIRAL ERICH RAEDER

GERMANY'S OBSOLETE BATTLESHIP *Schleswig-Holstein*
began World War II when her 11-inch guns opened fire on
Poland's Westerplatte base in Danzig. The navy that went to war in 1939
included 74 warships displacing five hundred tons or more (55 destroyer
types or larger) with another fifty-eight building or working up.[1] It faced the
British fleet of 275 such ships and the French navy with 106 more. This was
not the navy the German commander in chief, Grossadmiral Erich Raeder,
expected to deploy when he fought Great Britain. Only the year before Germany had adopted his ambitious Z-Plan, which called for a balanced fleet of
more than two hundred large surface warships by 1948.

Faced with such disparity in numbers, Raeder nonetheless adopted an
offensive posture wherever possible. In the opening months of the war
German warships instigated three sea battles against the Allies in the Baltic
Sea, the North Sea, and the South Atlantic.

Table 1.1. Opening Rounds

Date	Location	Name	Opponent	Type
3-Sep-39	Baltic Sea	Attack on Hel	Polish	Harbor attack
7-Dec-39	North Sea	Action off Cromer	British	Encounter
13-Dec-39	Atlantic	Battle of the River Plate	British/NZ	Interception

The German navy began the war with strong forces in the Baltic Sea to contain Poland's small, but modern, navy. Under the command of Naval Group East the German fleet included two obsolete battleships, three light cruisers, nine destroyers, one torpedo boat, eight S-boats, four escort ships, eight minesweepers, and ten submarines. To face this force the Poles, under Rear Admiral Józef Unrug, commander of the Coastal Defense Region, had a destroyer, *Wicher*, a minelayer, *Gryf*, two old torpedo boats, two gunboats, six small minesweepers, and five submarines. Their principal ships, the destroyers *Burza, Blyskawica,* and *Grom* were well on their way to Britain when *Schleswig-Holstein* fired the war's opening rounds.

The Polish invasion's short naval campaign mainly pitted Polish submarines against German submarine hunters. The submarines made five attacks, but *Zbik* registered the only success when one of her mines sank the minesweeper *M85* on 9 September. This was better than the Germans did; although their anti-sub forces reported definitely sinking seven boats, in fact, all five Polish submarines eventually escaped to Allied or neutral ports.[2] On the war's second day the Germans began moving ships out of the Baltic to counter the threat of an Anglo-French declaration of war. Before this redeployment was completed, however, large German and Polish warships exchanged fire on one occasion.

Attack on Hel, 3 September 1939

TIME   0630 to approximately 0735
TYPE: Harbor attack
WEATHER:
VISIBILITY: Hazy
SEA STATE: Calm
SURPRISE: None
MISSION: Poles—self defense; Germans—reconnaissance

A Polish fleet consisting of *Wicher* (Commander Stefan de Walden), *Gryf*, loaded with 300 mines, four minesweepers, and two gunboats sortied from Gdynia at 1600 hours on 1 September to lay a defensive minefield about twelve miles southeast of Hel. The destroyer went on ahead, but the mining flotilla was barely out of port when thirty-three Ju87Bs jumped them. The war's first air attack against ships under way lasted

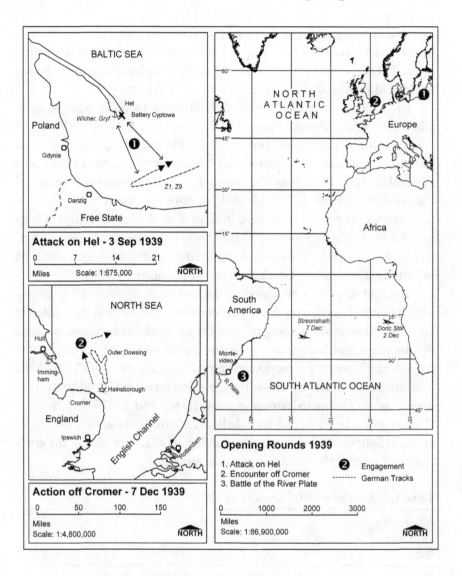

Attack on Hel - 3 Sep 1939

0   7   14   21

Miles   Scale: 1:675,000   NORTH

Action off Cromer - 7 Dec 1939

0   50   100   150

Miles
Scale: 1:4,800,000   NORTH

Opening Rounds 1939

1. Attack on Hel
2. Encounter off Cromer
3. Battle of the River Plate

Engagement
-------- German Tracks

0   1000   2000   3000

Miles
Scale: 1:86,900,000   NORTH

nearly three hours; the Poles successfully avoided direct hits, but near misses seriously damaged the minesweeper *Mewa,* and jammed *Gryf*'s rudder. Splinters killed twenty-one of *Gryf*'s men including her captain, Commander S. Kwiatkowski. The minelayers put into Hel although *Wicher,* not informed the mission was scrapped, continued on patrol. That night she observed enemy ships off Pillau, but "a unique opportunity for carrying out a night torpedo attack . . . was foregone since . . . *Wicher* was under strict orders not to jeopardize the primary mission of laying mines."[3] *Gryf*'s damage was so extensive, she was placed in a floating dock at Hel and sunk in shallow water as a permanent battery.

Early on the morning of the 3rd, Führer der Torpedoboote, Konteradmiral Günther Lütjens, ordered the destroyers Z1 *Leberecht Maass* and Z9 *Wolfgang Zenker* to reconnoiter Hel. This was an aggressive mission more easily and safely accomplished by the air force, but Lütjens was mindful that the navy's contribution to the campaign had been small and that victories had to be seized while opportunity lasted. The German destroyers found what they were looking for: *Wicher* and *Gryf* (Commander Stanislaw Hryniewiecki) sheltering under the protection of battery Cyplowa's four 6-inch guns, supported by a pair of 4.1-inch weapons in batteries Dunska and Grecka just up the peninsula.

The German ships appeared to the southeast of the harbor shortly after dawn and opened fire from fourteen thousand yards as they sailed in a west southwesterly heading toward Danzig. *Leberecht Maass* engaged the destroyer and *Wolfgang Zenker* the minelayer. The Poles outgunned the Germans and their marksmanship was better as well. With shells splashing uncomfortably close, the Germans increased speed to twenty-seven knots, conducted sharp evasive turns, and finally laid smoke. Despite these maneuvers a 6-inch shell hit *Leberecht Maass* near No. 2 gun at 0657. Splinters killed four and wounded another four men of the gun's crew and severed electrical power to the mount.

Table 1.2. Attack on Hel, 3 September 1939

Allied Ships and Shore Battery	TYP	YL	DFL	SPD	GUNS	TT	GF	DAM
Wicher	DD	28	1,920	33	4×5.1/40	6×21.7	5	
Gryf	ML	36	2,250	0	6×4.7/50		6	D2
Cyplowa	SB	n/a	n/a	n/a	4×6 & 4×4		6	
German Ships								
Leberecht Maass	DD	36	3,110	38	5×5/45	8×21	7	D2
Wolfgang Zenker	DD	37	3,190	38	5×5/45	8×21	7	

After this blow the adversaries exchanged fire for nearly forty minutes more. The German destroyers registered two hits on *Gryf,* damaging her antiaircraft weapons and killing four members of her crew; splinters damaged *Wicher* superficially and wounded two. Finally, at 0735 Lütjens terminated the action and proceeded to Pillau to refuel. *Leberecht Maass* shot a total of seventy-seven rounds in almost one hour, hardly a fast and furious rate of fire. She repaired her damage at Swinemunde and was completely battleworthy by 10 September. The German air force appeared over Hel later in the day. In several heavy raids they sank *Wicher, Gryf,* a gunboat, and some smaller auxiliaries, erasing any satisfaction the Poles may have enjoyed from their repulse of the German destroyers.

Action off Cromer, 7 December 1939

TIME: 0255–0318, G+1
TYPE: Encounter
WEATHER: Good
VISIBILITY: New moon, good, up to ten miles
SEA STATE:
SURPRISE: Germans
MISSION: British—patrol and sea security; Germans—offensive
               mining

Germany's destroyers spent the first month of the war helping lay the defensive West Wall mine barrage in the North Sea. After this task was accomplished they began sowing offensive minefields off Britain's east coast. Between 17 October 1939 and 10 February 1940, destroyers dropped 2,160 mines in eleven different fields in seven separate operations. The third operation involved more than just mines.

On the morning of 6 December 1939, Z12 *Erich Giese* and Z11 *Bernd von Arnim* departed the Jade loaded with 120 contact and magnetic mines to lay a field off Cromer. Z10 *Hans Lody* (Fregattenkapitän Erich Bey, flag 4th Destroyer Flotilla) provided the escort. Several hours into the mission *Bernd von Arnim,* displaying the unreliability of the high-pressure steam system used on most major German warships, blew a boiler tube. After that a generator failed so, at 1835, Bey ordered her back to port and continued with only *Erich Giese.*

At 0105 hours on 7 December a pair of vessels approached the inbound Germans and then turned away. Although the lookouts couldn't identify the dark shapes, they were British destroyers, *Juno* (senior officer Commander W. E. Wilson) and *Jersey* on a routine patrol out of Immingham.

At 0205 *Erich Giese* arrived at her destination just three miles off the Hainsborough lightship, square in the narrow shipping lane between Britain's east coast and the Outer Dowsing, the shoal waters farther offshore. Seven minutes later her crew, in teams of five or six men, began rolling the bulky mines off the stern while *Hans Lody* loitered some distance to the north. Within half an hour the dangerous job was done. Two premature detonations caused some commotion onshore, but British searchlights probed the sky, assuming German bombers were the cause of the blasts.

Erich Giese joined her sister and the two ships steered north to clear the Outer Dowsing before turning east for home. But, sixteen minutes later at 0255, they detected two darkened shapes about nine thousand yards away sailing at a high speed on nearly the same course bearing 325 degrees. Within several minutes lookouts identified them as British destroyers.

Bey decided to hazard a torpedo attack. With *Hans Lody* leading, he angled in on the contact. By 0310 the Germans, running west and slightly south of the British, had closed to about five thousand yards. At 0314 *Hans Lody* fired three torpedoes while *Erich Giese* launched four. They then turned east.

Hans Lody's salvo missed, perhaps because of the reliability problems German torpedoes suffered in the war's first year, but after three and three quarters minutes, one from *Erich Giese*'s salvo struck *Jersey* on her port

Table 1.3.   Action off Cromer, 7 December 1939

Allied Ships	TYP	YL	DFL	SPD	GUNS	TT	GF	DAM
Juno	DD	38	2,330	36	6×4.7/45	10×21	8	
Jersey	DD	38	2,330	36	6×4.7/45	10×21	8	D4
German Ships								
Hans Lody	DD	36	3,190	38	5×5/45	8×21	7	
Erich Giese	DD	37	3,190	38	5×5/45	8×21	7	

side abreast the after torpedo tubes. There was a violent explosion that ignited a large fire. *Juno* immediately turned and laid a smoke screen, uncertain whether the attack had come from mines, bombs, or a submarine. *Jersey* was fortunate on several counts—the torpedo caught her in a hard turn to port (the British had finally seen something and were turning to investigate) which blew the blast away from the ship, and escaping steam eventually helped douse the fire. She lost only nine men.

As he watched the welcome sight of the burning destroyer, Bey considered whether he should turn and attack with gunfire but instead he set a course for home. While his decision may have forfeited a more decisive tactical victory, it ensured the British remained unaware that enemy destroyers were laying minefields off their coast, a secret worth more than one or two destroyers. *Juno* eventually managed to tow *Jersey* near to Immingham, and the tug *Biddy* brought her into port. She was under repair until 23 September 1940.

Battle of the River Plate, 13 December 1939

TIME:	0614–0740
TYPE:	Interception
WEATHER:	Good, clear, slight breeze, no clouds
VISIBILITY:	Extreme
SEA STATE:	Slight from SE
SURPRISE:	None
MISSION:	British—patrol and sea security; German—offensive and sea superiority commerce raiding

The Battle of the River Plate was the war's first sea battle involving major warships. It was the first to be fought on the open sea and the only surface engagement of the war fought off the coast of South America. It was also the war's first Allied victory and so attracted tremendous attention in the English press and subsequent histories.

Grossadmiral Raeder had developed a strategy to deal with Great Britain's naval superiority. He envisioned Germany would conduct cruiser warfare against Britain's maritime lines of communication with specialized raiders supported by powerful surface groups. The surface groups would bring to battle elements of the divided British fleet as they chased the raiders. But when war broke out, he was seven years away from possessing the fleet required to implement his strategy. Germany did possess, however, some ships expressly designed for raiding or cruiser warfare, hybrid heavy cruisers the British press dubbed "pocket battleships." Two of these cruisers, *Admiral Graf Spee* and *Deutschland,* were at sea when Britain and France declared war.

On 25 September, when it became clear there would be no early peace, Raeder unleashed *Graf Spee* to begin raiding operations in a poor man's version of his strategy. (The raid was supported by the foray of *Scharnhorst* and *Gneisenau* that sank the armed merchant cruiser *Rawalpindi* on 23 November 1939. This raid was an attempt to "maintain strategic pressure on the enemy's North Atlantic sea routes and [to launch] successful strikes against inferior forces whenever the occasion offered.")[4]

Graf Spee subsequently destroyed nine vessels totaling more than 50,000 grt in waters ranging from the coast of Brazil to the Indian Ocean's Mozambique Channel. The tonnage destroyed was insignificant. However, the disruption caused was sensational. The Allies hunted the raider with eight surface groups that included four aircraft carriers, three battle cruisers, ten heavy cruisers, and five light cruisers.

The British Force G under the command of Commodore Henry Harwood was responsible for protecting the South Atlantic from the Falklands to Rio de Janeiro. To patrol this immense area Harwood had two heavy and two light cruisers. Based upon the distress call of *Graf Spee*'s third to last victim, *Doric Star,* made 2 December off the coast of Angola, Harwood considered *Graf Spee*'s range and calculated the heavily trafficked waters off the River Plate would make a fine stage for her next appearance. Accordingly, he called the heavy cruiser *Exeter* up from the Falklands and the light cruiser *Achilles* down from Rio de Janeiro to join *Ajax* patrolling these waters. He had *Ajax, Achilles,* and *Exeter* concentrated off the River Plate twenty-four hours before the German cruiser arrived "one of the most remarkable pieces of intelligent guesswork of the entire war."[5] Or at least one of the luckiest.

Kapitän zur See Hans Langsdorff had conducted a careful, successful, and bloodless raiding cruise, but his vessel's diesel engines needed overhaul and it was time to head for home. On the way, however, he did indeed plan to appear in the waters off the River Plate as part of a feint toward the Pacific. On 6–7 December he rendezvoused with his supply ship, *Altmark,* and then set course southwest for the Plate estuary some two thousand miles away.

On 13 December 1939 *Graf Spee* arrived at a point three hundred miles east and slightly north of the estuary's mouth, searching for a small convoy Langsdorff expected in the area, intelligence he had obtained from his final victim, *Streonshalh* (3,895 grt) sunk on 7 December. At 0552, four minutes before dawn in the growing light of a beautiful, late spring morning, lookouts reported masts dead ahead below the horizon. As these resolved into warships, Langsdorff interpreted them as a cruiser and two destroyers—probably the convoy's escort. At 0600 he altered course toward them and worked up to 24 knots. He knew of Force G's presence, and his aggressiveness, which was contrary to orders, is generally interpreted as arising from a desire to make a grand finale to his cruise by destroying a convoy.[6] It is also possible that avoiding action for so long had influenced Langsdorff's state of mind, making him eager for an open fight.

At 0608, sixteen minutes after she had been sighted, lookouts on *Ajax* reported smoke to the northwest. Harwood ordered *Exeter* to investigate. She sheered out of position at the rear of the British column and, eight minutes later Captain F.S. Bell reported: "I think it is a pocket-battleship."[7] Immediately the cruisers broke out their battle ensigns and Bell implemented Harwood's tactical plan. This called for the British cruisers to attack the enemy in two separate divisions, permitting them to report each other's fall of shot and to complicate *Graf Spee*'s fire control solutions by either forcing her to choose a target or to split the fire of her main turrets between the two divisions. Thus, while *Exeter* turned west-northwest toward the enemy *Ajax* and *Achilles* continued northeast.

Conditions favored battle. The swell was slight from the southeast; the breeze was moderate and the visibility about twenty miles.

At 0615 *Graf Spee* swung to port, brought her broadside to bear, and at 0618, fired a three-gun salvo at *Exeter* from more than twenty thousand yards.[8] She fired deliberately using armor-piercing (AP) shells to facilitate range finding, although she switched to high explosive (HE) shells once she began to register hits. *Exeter* replied with her forward turrets at 0620 at an estimated range of 18,700 yards. *Achilles* entered the action at 0621 and *Ajax* at 0623 from 19,000 yards. The two light cruisers then turned to port to close the range. *Graf Spee* returned the fire of Harwood's division with her 5.9-inch guns and concentrated her primary weapons on her

Table 1.4. Battle of the River Plate, 13 December 1939

Allied Ships	TYP	YL	DFL	SPD	GUNS	TT	GF	DAM
Exeter	CA	29	11,000	32	6×8/50 & 4×4/45	6×21	24	D4
Ajax	CL	33	9,280	32	8×6/50 & 8×4/45	8×21	20	D2
Achilles (NZ)	CL	31	9,000	32	8×6/50 & 4×4/45	8×21	16	D1
German Ship								
Graf Spee	CA	34	16,200	24	6×11/54 & 8×5.9/55	8×21	46	D2

more dangerous foe. She straddled with her third salvo, which arrived on target at 0623; the near miss threw splinters aboard killing Exeter's starboard torpedo crew, destroying the command relay center, and damaging the searchlights and the seaplanes. Exeter drew blood with her fifth or sixth salvo: an 8-inch shell struck Graf Spee's starboard 4.1-inch mounting, killed part of the crew, and then penetrated thirty-two feet before exploding, destroying the fresh water plant. At the same time, splinters from an 8-inch near miss perforated the pocket-battleship's hull.[9] Then one of Graf Spee's 11-inch rounds plunged through the heavy cruiser's forecastle and out her side without exploding, and, at 0624, just after Exeter had fired her eighth salvo, a heavy shell exploded upon impacting "B" turret's 1-inch armor. The two guns were knocked out and fragments of metal and debris blasted over the cruiser's bridge killing or wounding everyone there, including Captain Bell, and destroying the wheelhouse communications. Because he could no longer steer Exeter from the bridge, and despite his wound, Bell started for the aft conning position as his ship ran west, northwest. Two more 11-inch shells and several near misses added to her damage. From Graf Spee could be seen "as a column of fire rising almost as high as her mast."[10] When he arrived Bell found he couldn't communicate from the aft conning position; he had to use a chain of men to pass his orders to the steering flat.

As Graf Spee punished Exeter, the two light cruisers began firing in concentration from 0625 with Ajax controlling. They successfully chased salvos from the German's secondary battery (which was ineffective all day) as they closed to thirteen thousand yards. By 0628 they were straddling their target with sixteen-gun broadsides fired at the rate of four a minute; although they had not inflicted any significant damage, it was clearly a matter of time. At 0630, after his torpedo officer advised him the British light cruisers were gaining position for a torpedo attack, Langsdorff shifted his 11-inch turrets (firing three-gun ranging salvos) to *Ajax* and quickly straddled. But it was *Exeter* that launched torpedoes, firing her three starboard tubes at 0632 under local control.

At 0637 *Graf Spee* made smoke and turned sharply to port, coming to the west northwest. (She had not spotted *Exeter*'s torpedoes, but the effect of her maneuver ensured they missed astern.) This radical maneuver led Harwood to suppose his gunfire was hurting his enemy. In fact, Langsdorff wanted to prevent the light cruisers from crossing his T. Meanwhile, at 0637 *Ajax* catapulted her Faiery Seafox "a very fine evolution observing that 'X' and 'Y' turrets were at that time firing on a forward bearing."[11]

After the failure of her torpedo attack, *Exeter* came to starboard to unmask her port tubes. She emerged from the smoke, her four-gun broadsides churning up the water in *Graf Spee*'s vicinity. The German shifted fire once again, but *Exeter* struck first, landing two shells on her adversary. One hit at 0637, just as the German ship was coming about, penetrated the main armor belt, and exploded in a workshop amidships while the other passed through her tower mast. A near miss sent splinters through the German's hull on the port side. At 0638 *Graf Spee* got revenge: an 11-inch shell disabled *Exeter*'s "A" turret, leaving only "Y" turret's two 8-inch guns in action. However, by this time, the light cruisers were hitting as well. Seeing that *Exeter* was in a bad way, Langsdorff changed target once again; the main turrets rotated to bear on his smaller foes and at 0640 discharged a broadside in their direction. The first shells straddled *Achilles*. A crewman wrote: ". . . as we watch, columns of discoloured water and smoke rear out of our curling bow-wave just right of the bridge. Red-hot metal fragments crash through armourplate, spattering the Control and tearing through the flesh of men."[12] Splinters from the near miss killed or disabled four men on the New Zealander's bridge and fire control director, and slightly wounded Captain W. E. Parry. *Achilles* lost radio communications with *Ajax* and returned her guns to local control. However, until the dead and wounded were replaced, her accuracy deteriorated. Moreover, the Seafox's pilot was using the reconnaissance frequency, not the spotting frequency. As a result, there was no communication with the spotter aircraft until 0649. Then, unaware *Achilles* was firing under local control, he reported her salvos to *Ajax* as if they were her own so that *Ajax*'s shells were constantly over target. This combination of circumstances resulted in *Graf Spee* enjoying a respite from 6-inch shellfire for nearly thirty minutes. Moreover, the cruisers' failure to promptly respond to *Graf Spee*'s turn to port opened the range to seventeen thousand yards.

At 0643 *Exeter* launched three more torpedoes, which *Graf Spee* avoided. Several minutes later, the German registered another hit on *Exeter,* igniting a large fire amidships and disabling the fire control circuits and gyrocompass repeaters. Then another shell struck forward and caused flooding that gave the British cruiser a 7-degree list to starboard. By 0650 this was only one problem of many: fires were raging, her bow was down, and only one turret was still in action. *Exeter* was veering slightly south of west, slowly opening the range.

Ajax and *Achilles* did not reacquire *Graf Spee*'s range until 0708. Then they began to harass her from her starboard quarter firing rapidly and scoring hits although most of their 6-inch shells shattered against their opponent's armor. At 0715 *Exeter* turned to port under the cover of smoke. One minute later, *Graf Spee,* wrapped in her own smoke, mimicked this maneuver. Langsdorff was commanding his ship from the exposed flying bridge. At 0717 splinters wounded him in his shoulder and arms. Then the concussion from the explosion of a 6-inch shell just below his position knocked him unconscious. It took the executive officer several minutes to reach the flying bridge, during which time the ship was without a commander, but shortly after he arrived, Langsdorff regained consciousness and resumed command.

Harwood assumed *Graf Spee* intended to finish off *Exeter.* The light cruisers came to full speed and by 0720 they had closed to eleven thousand yards. They then turned to starboard to unmask their full batteries, "deluging" the German with shells, hitting and setting afire the remains of her seaplane. Under this attention Langsdorff came back to starboard and engaged Harwood's division with every gun that could fire. At 0724 *Ajax* swung to starboard and fired four torpedoes from nine thousand yards. *Graf Spee* turned to avoid these and attempted to fire torpedoes of her own, but her violent maneuver to port kept all but one from launching.

At 0725 *Graf Spee* finally hit *Ajax* with an 11-inch shell. The damage was fearsome and disabled her aft turrets. Another two 4.1-inch shells struck *Ajax*'s bridge. At 0729 flooding aboard *Exeter* caused a short circuit in "Y" turret's power supply. With this her guns fell silent and she withdrew from the battle. *Graf Spee,* however, was busy with the light cruisers. At 0738 another 11-inch shell hit *Ajax* from eight thousand yards, toppling her mainmast.

At this point Harwood decided that there was nothing to gain from continuing the engagement and much to lose. He had received a report that his ammunition supply was down to 20 percent (he didn't realize this only applied to "A" turret). "*Graf Spee*'s shooting was still very accurate and she did not appear to have suffered much damage. I therefore decided to break off the day action and try and close in again after dark."[13] At 0740 he turned away under cover of smoke. Contrary to expectations, Langsdorff continued on his westerly heading away from the Allied cruisers. At 0746 Harwood brought his two cruisers back around to follow from each quarter.

Langsdorff has been roundly criticized for his lack of aggression. (For example: "To fail . . . to finish off . . . the two heavily outgunned light cruisers, one of them damaged, displays a fatal want of judgment on Langsdorff's part, or perhaps of professional nerve.")[14] However, he was suffering from ammunition supply problems as well. The damage to his ship worried him, considering the long voyage home he faced. He had suffered thirty-six men killed and another fifty-nine wounded. His water and fuel oil purification plants were wrecked. Moreover, a six-foot hole in his bow rendered his ship unfit to navigate the strong seas he would expect in the stormy North Atlantic. Finally, "several of his subordinates remarked how he seemed affected by his wounds and became more erratic and less considered."[15] For these reasons he elected to break off the action and seek sanctuary in Montevideo, the capital of Uruguay.

As *Graf Spee* sailed west for Montevideo, Harwood's cruisers trailed along keeping a respectful distance; nonetheless, the adversaries exchanged fire several times. At 1005 *Graf Spee* fired three salvos at *Achilles* from twenty-three thousand yards. Nine hours later she fired two more at *Ajax* from twenty-six thousand yards. At 2048 *Achilles* was at the receiving end of three salvoes to which *Achilles* replied with five. At 2130 and 2145 *Graf Spee* fired single salvos at *Achilles* and at 2350 she finally made port.

Although hit by three 8-inch shells and seventeen 6-inch shells *Graf Spee* was capable of full speed and had enough fuel to cruise at that velocity for sixteen days. She had 306 rounds of 11-inch ammunition remaining, 43 percent of her original supply, 50 percent of her 5.9-inch ammunition, 2,477 rounds of 4.1-inch, and six torpedoes. *Exeter,* on the other hand, was a floating wreck while only half of *Ajax*'s guns were serviceable. *Achilles* was the only ship in Harwood's squadron still fully battleworthy. *Exeter* suffered sixty-one killed in action and twenty-three wounded while *Ajax* had seven killed and five wounded and *Achilles* four killed. *Ajax* expended 823 6-inch rounds, *Achilles* fired 1,242 rounds, and *Exeter* about 200 rounds.

Although he clearly dominated the tactical engagement with effective long-range fire, Langsdorff surrendered the initiative, was blockaded in a neutral port, and ultimately scuttled his ship there and committed suicide. Harwood had delivered the Allies their first major victory of the war and a grateful Admiralty promoted him to rear admiral.

2

THE INVASION OF NORWAY
April–June 1940

The critical moment is the penetration of the harbours while passing the coastal fortifications. . . . The most difficult operation for the ships is the return voyage.

GROSSADMIRAL ERICH RAEDER

In April 1940 Germany attacked the neutral nation of Norway. Whereas the Polish campaign had been all army and air force, Norway provided the German navy—especially the navy's surface forces—the opportunity to demonstrate their capability and utility in the greater war effort. The navy responded with a daring and brilliant performance. Nearly every major warship as well as many minor vessels and submarines sailed simultaneously in eleven groups to attack seven targets in Norway and six more in Denmark. Every attack succeeded, although the cost was extremely high. This three-month campaign resulted in seven surface engagements, including three on one day.

In the months prior to the invasion, Germany and the Allies pushed and tested Norway's neutrality. One incident in particular convinced both

Table 2.1. The Invasion of Norway

Date	Location	Name	Opponent	Type
8-Apr-40	Norway	Sinking of the *Glowworm*	British	Encounter
9-Apr-40	Norway	Engagement off Lofoten	British	Encounter
9-Apr-40	Norway	Narvik Harbor	Norway	Harbor attack
9-Apr-40	Norway	Horten Harbor	Norway	Harbor attack
10-Apr-40	Norway	First Battle of Narvik	British	Harbor attack
13-Apr-40	Norway	Second Battle of Narvik	British	Harbor attack
8-Jun-40	Norway	Sinking of the *Glorious*	British	Encounter

they could not respect the Scandinavian nation's sovereignty; this was the boarding of *Altmark*, loaded with prisoners taken by *Graf Spee*, and their liberation by the British destroyer *Cossack*, under Captain Philip Vian. Neither side was satisfied with the conduct of the Norwegians—Germany because the escort (a pair of antique one hundred–ton torpedo boats) did

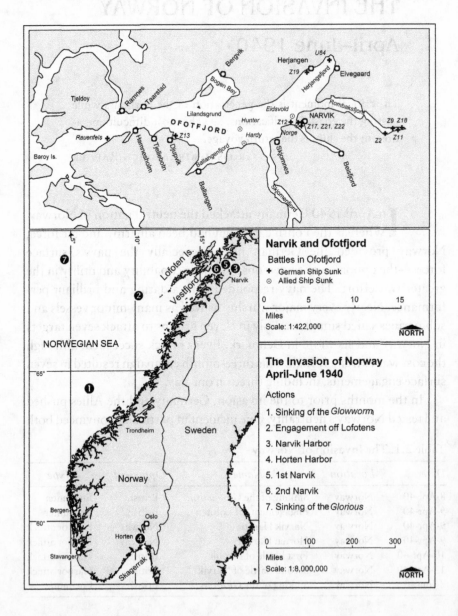

Narvik and Ofotfjord

Battles in Ofotfjord

+ German Ship Sunk
⊙ Allied Ship Sunk

0   5   10   15

Miles
Scale: 1:422,000   NORTH

**The Invasion of Norway
April–June 1940**

Actions

1. Sinking of the *Glowworm*
2. Engagement off Lofotens
3. Narvik Harbor
4. Horten Harbor
5. 1st Narvik
6. 2nd Narvik
7. Sinking of the *Glorious*

0   100   200   300

Miles
Scale: 1:8,000,000   NORTH

not fight to defend *Altmark* and Great Britain because *Altmark* had sup-
posedly been inspected at Bergen and declared free of weapons and con-
travened cargo (like prisoners of war). For these reasons Britain decided to
mine Norway's coastal waters and Germany decided to invade. It was one
of the ironies of war that both nations acted on their plans on the same day
and that the campaign's first engagement occurred when these forces
encountered each other at sea.

Sinking of the *Glowworm*, 8 April 1940

TIME:	0715–0924, Zone+1
TYPE:	Encounter
WEATHER:	Near gale, winds 30 knots
VISIBILITY:	Moderate
SEA STATE:	Large waves with crests
SURPRISE:	Both
MISSION:	British—transit; German—transit

On the morning of 8 April the most significant British group bound for
Norway consisted of the battle cruiser *Renown* (Vice Admiral William
Whitworth) screened by destroyers *Greyhound, Glowworm, Hyperion,*
and *Hero.* She sailed from Scapa Flow on 5 April for Vestfjord where, on
the next day, she joined the 20th Destroyer Flotilla (Captain J. G. Bickford)
with *Esk, Impulsive, Icarus,* and *Ivanhoe* (all fitted to lay mines) and their
close escort, the 2nd Destroyer Flotilla (Captain B. A. W. Warburton-Lee)
with *Hardy, Hotspur, Havock,* and *Hunter. Renown's* job was to provide
heavy support if Norway's ancient coastal defense ships stationed at
Narvik attempted to interfere with the operation. On the 6th *Glowworm*
(Lieutenant Commander G. B. Roope) lost a man overboard in wild seas
and, after turning to search, became separated from the rest of Whitworth's force. She was returning to Scapa Flow when the Admiralty
ordered her to join *Renown* (which in the meantime had sent *Hyperion*
and *Hero* to refuel and was left with only *Greyhound* in her screen).

As *Glowworm* plunged north, the German invasion was under way.
Groups 1 and 2 consisting of *Gneisenau, Scharnhorst, Admiral Hipper,* and
fourteen destroyers were sailing in company bound for their respective des-
tinations of Narvik and Trondheim. During the night the wind blew at

Table 2.2. Sinking of the *Glowworm*, 8 April 1940

Allied Ship	TYP	YL	DFL	SPD	GUNS	TT	GF	DAM
Glowworm	DD	35	1,890	36	4×4.7/45	10×21	6	Sunk
German Ships								
Bernd von Arnim	DD	36	3,190	38	5×5/45	8×21	7	
Admiral Hipper	CA	37	18,200	32	8×8/60 & 12×4.1/65	12×21	35	D2

moderate gale force with gusts up to hurricane strength, causing misery aboard the German destroyers (especially among the embarked mountain troops), which were taking green seas over their bridges. Z21 *Wilhelm Heidkamp* nearly foundered. The stormy dawn of 8 April found the German formation scattered and several ships separated from the fleet. At 0715 hours one of the lost ships, Z18 *Hans Ludemann*, encountered *Glowworm*. They exchanged signals and the German identified herself as the Swedish destroyer *Göteborg*. Roope did not believe this and, as *Hans Ludemann* turned into the mist, *Glowworm* fired two salvos that fell short. Shortly thereafter *Glowworm* encountered *Berndt von Arnim* (Korvettenkapitän C. Rechel) on a reciprocal course. *Glowworm* turned and came up on the German from astern. At 0802 *Bernd von Arnim* opened fire and *Glowworm* replied in kind. The destroyers were lively gun platforms in such a pitching, rolling sea, and neither did the other harm. Rechel signaled the fleet for support and increased speed in an attempt to draw away. At thirty knots, however, *Bernd von Arnim*'s bow submarined and waves swept two men from the forecastle, forcing Rechel to slow down.

Glowworm, aggressively maintaining contact with the enemy (and handling much better in the monstrous seas), chased *Bernd von Arnim* and attempted to gain position for a torpedo attack. At 0822 in response to *Bernd von Arnim*'s signal, Vizeadmiral Wilhelm Marschall ordered *Hipper* (Kapitän zur See H. Heye) to intervene. At 0850 *Hipper* sighted the two destroyers. Heye was not sure which was British until *Glowworm* signaled *Hipper* requesting her identification. Roope did not know German heavy units were at sea and believed the ship emerging from the mists to the north was *Renown* or a friendly cruiser. *Hipper*'s answer, a salvo fired at 0859 from ninety-two hundred yards, was a rude surprise.

Heye kept *Hipper* bow on toward the enemy, accepting a reduction in firepower to minimize the target for *Glowworm*'s torpedoes. *Glowworm* made a quarter turn toward the cruiser and closed range rapidly, returning fire. Conditions did not facilitate accurate marksmanship and there were long pauses between *Hipper*'s rounds. Nonetheless, a shell from her third or fourth salvo struck *Glowworm*'s superstructure forward and wrecked her wireless room; only a portion of the destroyer's enemy sighting report got through. After *Hipper*'s fifth salvo, *Glowworm* came hard to port and made smoke. She fired five of her ten torpedoes, but *Hipper* observed the launching and easily combed their tracks.

Glowworm's masthead was sticking up above her smokescreen and *Hipper* aimed salvos six and seven at this target; the last one hit near *Glowworm*'s fore-funnel on the starboard side. Shortly before 0907 *Hipper*'s secondary battery engaged and at least three 4.1-inch rounds struck the destroyer amidships, on No. 1 gun, and on the bridge. *Glowworm*'s return fire was ineffective; she registered only one hit on *Hipper*'s starboard bow. Then the British destroyer broke cover and launched her last torpedoes from three thousand yards. Two ran along *Hipper*'s port side, one nearly grazing her hull and another passing to starboard.

With her torpedoes expended, *Glowworm* turned away to port and plunged back into her curtain of smoke. After firing two salvos blind, Heye decided to chase his enemy down and closed to nine hundred yards, his antiaircraft guns raking *Glowworm*'s deck and superstructure. As *Hipper* broke through the smoke, Heye saw that *Glowworm* had altered course and was going to ram. *Hipper* couldn't respond to her helm in time to avoid the collision and at 0910 the British destroyer struck the cruiser just under her starboard anchor. The collision forced *Glowworm*'s bow under water; as she scraped along *Hipper*'s side, she peeled off one hundred thirty feet of armor plating back to the forward torpedo tubes (which were also destroyed).

The destroyer's guns were silent as she fell away aft, smoking and listing heavily. *Hipper* fired a few rounds from her Dora turret until it became clear the British ship was doomed. At 0924 *Glowworm* capsized and sank. In an operation lasting one hour *Hipper* rescued thirty-eight members of her crew. Roope reportedly made it to the side, but fell away before he could be hauled in. Five hundred thirty tons of water flooded *Hipper,* but this didn't impede her ability to fight or cruise. She expended 31 rounds of 8-inch, 104 rounds of 4.1-inch, 136 rounds of 37-mm, and 132 rounds of 20-mm ammunition.

Hipper anchored at Trondheim at 0425 hours the next day and sailed for Germany on 10 April. She passed unnoticed within thirty miles of the British fleet during the night of 10 and 11 April. After joining Vizeadmiral Günther Lütjens's battleships and avoiding a massed British air attack on 12 April, she anchored in the Jade that evening.

Roope's heroics might have been ill-advised and ineffective, but they have become part of the British navy's tradition. However, while his conduct was clearly aggressive, it is not certain he intended to ram *Hipper*. German interrogation of the only surviving officer indicated neither the helm nor the emergency rudders were manned when the collision occurred, presumably because of enemy fire. It could have been that *Glowworm*'s last defiant act was an accident. In any case, his country awarded Lieutenant Commander Roope a Victoria Cross when it learned of his action after the war.

Engagement off Lofoten, 9 April 1940

TIME: 0405–0630, Zone+1
TYPE: Encounter
WEATHER: Poor, snow and rain squalls, wind NNW twenty-five
              knots
VISIBILITY: Mixed, moderate to poor
SEA STATE: Heavy swell
SURPRISE: Allies
MISSION: British—offensive and sea superiority patrol; Germans—
              escort, transit and amphibious support

By the evening of 8 April the British knew the Germans were at sea in force and that an invasion of Norway was probably under way. Narvik was a port both sides wanted desperately to hold—it was ice-free year round and connected by rail to the Swedish iron mines. The British had a battalion standing by transports to occupy Narvik if Germany attacked, but Germany's 139th Mountain Regiment embarked aboard the ten destroyers of Group 1 was already closing the objective. To stop them, the British navy had, by fortunate coincidence, a powerful force—the modernized battle cruiser *Renown* and nine destroyers—in just the right place at just the right time.

At 1045 hours on 8 April the Admiralty ordered the eight destroyers of the mine-laying force to join Whitworth and at 1850 they further ordered Whitworth to prevent any German forces from sailing up Vestfjord to Narvik. Whitworth had accomplished his concentration by 1715 hours, but he followed the second order to deny entry to the Germans very loosely. He assumed the enemy had not yet arrived and that with rain mixed with snow squalls and wind gusting to fifty-five knots, they would not venture a night passage up Vestfjord. Accordingly, with nine destroyers he stood to seaward, abandoning the patrol line, intending to return at first light (the destroyers could ride out the heavy storm more comfortably by standing out to sea than by maintaining a patrol line).[1] Admiral Sir Charles Forbes, commander in chief of the Home Fleet, was at sea about three hundred miles southwest of Vestfjord. He later noted that the orders "which led to the Vest Fjord being left without any of our forces on patrol in it, had a very far-reaching effect."[2]

Command confusion crippled the British navy's response to Germany's invasion. The Admiralty issued orders that often contradicted the commander in chief, or worse. Thus, the 2nd Destroyer Flotilla received orders directly from London, bypassing Whitworth, its immediate commander and Forbes, his commander. Or, consider this:

> He (Vice Admiral G. Edwin-Collins) did not long maintain this course, however; first there came the Admiralty orders to act as a striking force . . . then the Commander-in-Chief's order for a cruiser patrol line, and finally, the Admiralty order for the cruisers to concentrate and steer to meet the fleet.[3]

Whitworth's force included *Greyhound* of *Renown*'s screen, the four mine-laying destroyers (all armed with two 4.7-inch guns and no torpedoes), and four destroyers of the 2nd Flotilla, *Hardy, Hotspur, Havock,* and *Hunter.* The German fleet, *Gneisenau* flying the flag of Vizeadmiral Lütjens, *Scharnhorst,* and the Narvik occupation force with nine destroyers (*Erich Giese* was trailing by some thirty miles) was only fifty miles behind *Renown.*

At 2000 hours on 8 April the German force arrived where the British had been concentrated just two-and-a-half hours before. Vestfjord was indeed a dangerous passage to navigate at night in heavy weather, but, notwithstanding Whitworth's assumptions, the Germans had a strict timetable to meet; they would not wait for dawn. While the destroyers entered the fjord, the battleships turned to the northwest and stood to sea, still following in Whitworth's wake.

At 0240 hours on 9 April the British Vice Admiral turned back for Vestfjord, intending to reestablish the patrol line by dawn. The battle cruiser led the destroyers, steaming 130 degrees at twelve knots. At 0337 *Renown* sighted the German battleships about ten miles off. They were emerging from a snow squall broad on her port bow proceeding at twelve knots on the opposite course. To the west visibility was intermittent with frequent rain squalls, but it was somewhat better to the east and south. The wind had abated to about twenty-five knots from the north northwest. There was a heavy sea and swell. *Renown*'s position was about fifty miles west of the southern tip of the Lofoten Islands.

Ten minutes after sighting the enemy, *Renown* turned 50 degrees to port to the east northeast and increased speed, eventually reaching twenty knots. The destroyers struggled along behind her. Whitworth believed he was facing a *Scharnhorst* class battleship and a *Hipper* class cruiser.

Table 2.3. Engagement off Lofoten, 9 April 1940

Allied Ships	TYP	YL	DFL	SPD	GUNS	TT	GF	DAM
Renown	BC	16	36,080	30	6×15/42 & 20×4.5/45		114	D1
Hardy	DD	36	2,053	36	5×4.7/45	8×21	7	
Hotspur	DD	36	1,890	36	4×4.7/45	8×21	6	
Havock	DD	36	1,890	36	4×4.7/45	8×21	6	
Hunter	DD	36	1,890	36	4×4.7/45	8×21	6	
Esk	DD	34	1,940	36	2×4.7/45		3	
Ivanhoe	DD	37	1,854	36	2×4.7/45		3	
Impulsive	DD	37	1,854	36	2×4.7/45		3	
Icarus	DD	36	1,854	36	2×4.7/45		3	
Greyhound	DD	35	1,890	36	4×4.7/45	8×21	6	
German Ships								
Scharnhorst	BB	36	38,900	32	9×11/54.5 & 12×5.9/55		79	
Gneisenau	BB	36	38,900	32	9×11/54.5 & 12×5.9/55		79	D2

At 0350 *Gneisenau*'s lookouts saw a shadow to the west. As the Germans studied this apparition, *Renown* brought her bow ponderously around to the northwest on course 305 degrees, roughly parallel to the Germans. Ten minutes later, at 0400 hours, *Gneisenau* decided she was seeing a *Nelson* class battleship and sounded the alarm. *Scharnhorst* didn't know why the commotion until 0405 when she saw six plumes of flame erupting from *Renown*'s heavy guns as she fired on *Gneisenau*. The initial range was 18,600 yards, according to *Renown*. Her opening salvoes fell short by 320 to 550 yards.

Gneisenau responded to *Renown*'s attack by increasing speed and, at 0408, adjusting course 40 degrees to starboard to course 350 degrees. *Scharnhorst* followed these evolutions. *Renown* was still building up speed although she was shipping heavy seas over her forecastle. Despite this difficulty, her 15-inch guns fired on *Gneisenau* regularly by battery divisions while her 4.5-inch guns engaged *Scharnhorst*. She straddled *Gneisenau* with her sixth salvo. The destroyers struggling behind were eager to join the action. Captain Warburton-Lee ordered his flotilla to engage in a "Divisional Concentration Shoot" in an attempt to increase their effectiveness. Plunging and bucking, their forward guns were underwater more often than not and *Hotspur*, for one, managed only one salvo in three. The range was too great and the weather too extreme for the Germans to see any splashes, but they did see the twinkling flashes of the destroyer's gunfire. This was enough evidence for Lütjens to conclude he was facing two battleships.

On the German side, *Scharnhorst* returned *Renown*'s fire at 0410 (she correctly identified the enemy as a *Renown* class battle cruiser). *Gneisenau* followed one minute later. For the next ten minutes the capital ships traded salvos at ranges that varied from fourteen thousand to sixteen thousand yards while the Germans, now on course 330 degrees, progressively increased speed (*Gneisenau* went from 15.5 knots at 0410 to twenty-four knots by 0416). *Renown* followed on the German's port quarter, building to full speed from twenty knots.

Scharnhorst obtained *Renown*'s range with her fifth salvo fired at 0413. However, heavy seas combined with higher speeds were causing problems. The forward 11-inch turrets were trained aft, their backs to the oncoming seas. When the ejection ports in the rear of the turrets opened to expel spent shells, water flooded in. This particularly hampered Anton turret. Moreover, sensitive training machinery and firing systems began to fail, requiring turrets to be trained and fired without centralized control. Nonetheless, the Germans hit *Renown* twice with heavy shells: the first hit aft in the gun-room head, but the shell passed through the ship without exploding. Another dud struck the foremast and disabled the radio aerials. At 0417 a 15-inch shell from *Renown*'s sixteenth salvo decided the further course of the battle. This hit *Gneisenau*'s foretop and detonated against her starboard forward bulkhead. The blast damaged the foretop range finder and director and caused splinter damage to a secondary battery director; it also killed six men and wounded nine.

Gneisenau hauled about 60 degrees to starboard, coming to the northeast. *Scharnhorst* crossed her stern, making smoke, and one minute later came to the same heading. *Renown* responded by also turning northeast and shifting her main guns to *Scharnhorst*. However, the pounding of the seas on her foredecks and the amount of water coming over her forward turrets forced Whitworth to reduce speed to twenty-three knots. The wind was rising and had shifted from north-northwest to north-northeast with a heavy swell and a great sea. Up to the time she turned away, *Scharnhorst* had fired twenty-one main-battery and twelve secondary-battery salvos. *Gneisenau*'s rate of fire was somewhat less and her secondary batteries never engaged.

The British destroyers tried vigorously to participate in the action, but they couldn't keep up (although German overs nearly hit *Hardy* and *Hunter*). As Whitworth began chasing the German battleships, the destroyers dropped farther back and so the admiral, recalling his primary mission, ordered them to return to Vestfjord and establish the patrol line.

The next phase of the battle lasted thirty-six minutes from the German turn away at 0419/0420 until *Renown* lost sight of her enemy in a rain squall at 0456. During this period, *Gneisenau* fired her Caesar turret while *Scharnhorst* occasionally yawed to fire broadsides. The British described the German fire as very ragged for range and line with a variable spread.[4] Visibility remained poor; *Renown* lost sight of her target on four occasions. Because *Renown* had dropped back to twenty knots and the Germans had increased speed to twenty-seven, the range opened. Seeing this Whitworth attempted to go to full speed, but it proved impossible to work the forward turrets so he eased to twenty-three knots, barely holding range. Concerned that the enemy was escaping, Whitworth ordered full broadsides at 0430, but after only five salvos, "Y" turret ceased to bear. Nonetheless, at 0434 and again shortly later *Renown* hit *Gneisenau* with 4.5-inch shells. The first did minimal damage, striking in the flak deck to port and aft, but the other hit Anton on the flap covering the range finder optic. This gave the icy seawater another point to pour into the turret.

By 0439 *Gneisenau* estimated the range was twenty thousand yards. She had turned to course 40 degrees two minutes before and was holding at twenty-seven knots. *Renown* had to reduce to twenty knots at 0440 to keep her forward turrets in action. The wind had freshened to a moderate gale, about thirty-five knots. *Renown* was now steering 10 degrees. Defects in *Scharnhorst*'s engines and in No. 1 and 3 boilers had periodically reduced the German ship's speed and this was the only reason the British battle cruiser was still in contact.

Gneisenau fired her last rounds at 0444. She lost sight of *Renown* at 0446 when she estimated the range was twenty-five thousand yards. As he was leaving *Scharnhorst* behind as well, Lütjens reduced speed to twenty-four knots and then to twenty. By 0455 repairs had restored *Scharnhorst* to twenty-six knots. *Renown*'s salvos were falling close off her port side when she disappeared into a squall and *Renown* had to check fire.

Whitworth had to guess where the Germans would reappear. He altered course to the east and increased speed to twenty-five knots. *Scharnhorst* would have escaped, but another breakdown in her starboard engine room reduced her speed to fifteen knots. At 0515 *Renown* spotted her; the British ship turned to bring the Germans fine on her bow and opened fire.

The third phase of the battle was an hour-long stern chase fought at extreme ranges. As *Scharnhorst*'s Caesar turret replied to *Renown*'s salvos she gradually managed to work back up to twenty-five knots altering course to avoid the fall of shot, but generally holding to the north northeast. At 0541 she ceased fire. *Renown* briefly came to twenty-nine knots at 0544 and turned her forward turrets away from the sea, but the range continued to open and additional squalls of rain and sleet periodically hid the Germans from her view. Her last sighting came at 0615; the German battleships were far ahead and out of range. *Renown* plunged ahead for another hour and forty-five minutes, but finally she broke off the pursuit and turned westward hoping to intercept the Germans if they should sail to the south. *Gneisenau* and *Scharnhorst* closed formation and reduced speed because of flooding in their forward turrets.

Despite their complaints that *Renown* fired fast and continuously while they were handicapped by the seas and machinery breakdowns, the Germans expended more large caliber shells, and the top heavy *Renown* labored harder in the heavy weather than the modern battleships.[5] *Renown* fired 230 15-inch rounds, mostly from "A" and "B" turrets, and 1,065 4.5-inch rounds. Severe blast damage allowed sea water to flood into her "A" and "Y" shell rooms. *Scharnhorst* fired 195 rounds of 11-inch (145 from Caesar) and 91 5.9-inch rounds. *Gneisenau* fired only 54 main battery rounds and nothing from her secondary batteries. German 11-inch shells struck *Renown* twice for a hit rate of 0.8 percent. *Renown* landed but one 15-inch shell, a hit rate of 0.4 percent. The Germans mounted eighteen heavy guns to *Renown*'s six and enjoyed vastly superior armor. Whitworth was lucky Lütjens chose to run rather than fight. It is questionable *Renown* would have otherwise survived.

The German battleships returned to Germany on 12 April after the British sank the ten destroyers they were at sea to support. The destroyers that had followed *Renown* returned to Vestfjord just one hour after the Germans had passed.

Action at Horten, 9 April 1940

TIME:	0330–1318
TYPE:	Harbor attack
WEATHER:	Calm
VISIBILITY:	Mixed, fog
SEA STATE:	Calm
SURPRISE:	Axis
MISSION:	Allies—self defense; Germans—amphibious attack

One of Germany's most important objectives in her invasion of Norway was Oslo, the capital. Naval Group 5 under Konteradmiral Oskar Kummetz, the armored cruiser *Lützow* and the heavy cruiser *Blücher* (on her first mission and still not completely worked up), the light cruiser *Emden*, the torpedo boats *Möwe*, *Kondor*, and *Albatros*, and the 1st Motor Minesweeper Flotilla with R-boats *R17* through *R24*, was responsible for capturing this objective. Group 5 made landfall at the entrance to Oslofjord at midnight on April 8/9. The Norwegian patrol boat *Pol III*, a converted whaler of 214 tons, challenged the Germans with her search-light. Kummetz sent *Albatros* to deal with her, but the Norwegian launched an alarm rocket and then opened fire with her 3-inch gun. *Albatros* sank this irritant at 0015. The patrol boat's crew abandoned ship, but the captain, Lief Welding Olsen, drowned. He was the first Norwegian killed in the invasion.

Next the German fleet passed between the shore batteries at Bolaerne and Rauoy ten miles up the fjord at high speed. Uncertain what was transpiring, the batteries illuminated *Blücher*, but only fired seven rounds which fell well short. At 0046 Kummetz paused and transferred soldiers from the cruisers to the R-boats. At 0330 he detached *Albatros* (Kapitän-leutnant Siegfried Strelow), *Kondor* (Kapitänleutnant H. Wilcke)—the decks of both crowded with soldiers—*R17*, and *R21* to Horten, the principal Norwegian naval base twenty-five miles up the fjord on the west bank. Their mission was to capture the port and clean up resistance behind the main landing.

At 0535 hours *R17* and *R21* sailed into the harbor past the moored minelayer *Olav Tryggvason*, which had taken station by the entrance channel at 0315 hours. At first *Olav Tryggvason* assumed the ships were friendly, but when the R-boats ignored her challenge, she fired on *R17* and sank her just as she reached the quay. The Norwegian minesweeper

Table 2.4. Action at Horton, 9 April 1940

Allied Ships	TYP	YL	DFL	SPD	GUNS	TT	GF	DAM
Olav Tryggvason	ML	34	1,924	23	4×4.7/45 &	4×18	6	
					1×3			
Rauma	MS	39	370	13	1×40-mm &		0	D?
					2×20-mm			
Otra	MS	39	370	13	1×40-mm &		0	
					2×20-mm			
Bolaern	SB				3x5.9		6	
German Ships								
Albatros	TB	25	1,290	33	3×4.1	6×21	3	Sunk
Kondor	TB	25	1,290	33	3×4.1	6×21	3	
R17	MMS	35	120	21	2×20-mm		0	Sunk
R21	MMS	37	124	23	2×20-mm		0	D?

Rauma opened up on *R21* with 40-mm and 20-mm guns. *R21* replied in kind and both ships suffered damage before breaking off. *R17's* depth charges exploded at 0617 inflicting further German casualties.

At 0730 hours *Albatros* attempted to restore the situation by sailing directly into the harbor, but while navigating the narrow channel she ran into *Olav Tryggvason's* 4.7-inch gunfire. The German torpedo boat could only reply with her forward 4.1-inch gun and that malfunctioned after just eight rounds. The coup de main repulsed, *Albatros* withdrew to more open waters. She continued to trade salvoes with *Olav Tryggvason*, but the Norwegian's fire was good; near misses showered the embarked troops with splinters and forced *Albatros* even farther off. She transshipped soldiers to *R21* so they could assault the Bolaerne shore batteries while she provided gunfire support. Shortly afterward a German delegation arrived at the naval base and its commanding officer, Admiral Smith Johansen, surrendered at 0835 hours.

Albatros had even worse luck with the 5.9-inch guns of the Bolaerne battery. When she approached the island early that afternoon the battery fired ten rounds from 8,750 yards. The torpedo boat turned away and, while maneuvering in the fog, she ran hard aground at 1318 hours southeast of Bolaerne Island and was a total loss.

Olav Tryggvason was subsequently taken into German service under the name of *Brummer*. Also captured were the old coast defense ships *Harald Haarfagre* and *Tordenskjold* (which played no part in the battle) and the incomplete torpedo boat *Balder*.

The rest of Group 5 also suffered heavily. Shore batteries and torpedoes severely damaged *Blücher* as she attempted to brazen her way past the second set of defenses at the narrows of Oslofjord; a partially trained crew and ineffective damage control finished the job. Oslo fell nonetheless, but the king of Norway and his government, with the nation's gold, escaped to Great Britain to serve as rallying points for Norwegian resistance.

Narvik Harbor, 9 April 1940

TIME:	0420–0455
TYPE:	Harbor attack
WEATHER:	Heavy intermittent snow
VISIBILITY:	Poor to limited
SEA STATE:	Calm

SURPRISE: None
MISSION: Allies—self defense; Germans—amphibious attack

At 0300 hours on 9 April the German destroyers of Group 1, under the command of Kommodore Friedrich Bonte aboard *Wilhelm Heidkamp,* began their dangerous passage up Vestfjord. They passed the pilot station at Tranoy (except for *Erich Giese,* which, because of sea damage, lagged fifty miles behind). The light was still burning. Ten minutes later they passed a Norwegian coast guard vessel. It did not challenge them. As they rounded Baroy Island and entered Ofotfjord the sea was calm, but a driving snowstorm limited visibility. The Germans encountered the Norwegian patrol vessels *Michael Sars* (226 tons, two 47-mm guns) and *Kelt* (376 tons, one 3-inch gun). Ignoring German warnings they radioed an alert to the old coast defense battleships at Narvik. This provoked Bonte to fire warning shots whereupon the Norwegians boats hove to and surrendered. The Germans continued up the fjord at twenty-seven knots. At the narrows, *Hans Ludemann* and Z22 *Anton Schmitt* split off to land two companies of mountain troops at Ramnes and Hamnes, to seize what proved to be empty gun emplacements. *Wolfgang Zenker,* Z13 *Erich Koellner,* and Z19 *Hermann Künne* entered Herjangsfjord to land more troops at Elvegaard, depot of the Norwegian 6th Infantry Division. Bonte sent Z17 *Diether von Roeder* to patrol the entrance to Ofotfjord while *Wilhelm Heidkamp,* Z2 *Georg Thiele,* and *Bernd von Arnim* continued on to Narvik.

The two largest ships in the Norwegian navy awaited them: coast defense battleships launched forty years before, possessing big guns, inadequate protection, and primitive fire control systems.

Table 2.5. Action at Narvik Harbor, 9 April 1940

Allied Ships	TYP	YL	DFL	SPD	GUNS	TT	GF	DAM
Norge	CB	00	4,165	16	2×8.2/44 & 6×5.9/46	2×18	4	Sunk
Eidsvold	CB	00	4,165	16	2×8.2/44 & 6×5.9/46	2×18	4	Sunk
German Ships								
Wilhelm Heidkamp	DD	38	3,415	38	5×5/45	8×21	7	
Bernd von Arnim	DD	36	3,190	38	5×5/45	8×21	7	
Georg Thiele	DD	35	3,156	38	5×5/45	8×21	7	

In heavy snow and mist, the three destroyers came upon *Eidsvold,* under Capitan Odd Isaksen Willoch, at 0415 hours loitering outside Narvik harbor. Forewarned by the patrol boats, she fired a shot across *Wilhelm Heidkamp*'s bow and ordered her to heave to. Bonte complied and signaled that he was sending an officer over. While *Wilhelm Heidkamp* lowered a boat *Georg Thiele* and *Bernd von Arnim* swung out of line and disappeared into the fog before *Eidsvold* could react. They continued stealthily toward the port.

A German officer boarded *Eidsvold* and read a curt demand for surrender. Willoch radioed his senior officer, Captain Per Askim aboard *Norge,* for instructions and received permission to fight. Willoch shouted to his men: "To the guns. We're going into action, men."[6] His weapons were trained and the range was under a thousand yards, but before he could open fire Willoch was obligated to let Bonte's envoy return. As the German pinnace pulled away the envoy fired a red flare to signal negotiations had failed. There was a brief debate on *Wilhelm Heidkamp*'s bridge between Bonte and Generalmajor Eduard Dietl, the army commander, with Dietl urging Bonte to open fire. *Eidsvold* was turning to the northeast. Finally Bonte nodded and *Wilhelm Heidkamp* launched four torpedoes. Two hit and detonated *Eidsvold*'s magazine. There was a tremendous explosion and the old ship broke in half; the forward section sank in just fifteen seconds, followed by the stern a few minutes later. One hundred seventy-five men died, including Willoch; there were only eight survivors. The time was 0437, twelve minutes after dawn.

Bernd von Arnim and *Georg Thiele* had entered Narvik harbor even as negotiations were under way. *Bernd von Arnim* edged her way through the press of merchant ships trying to locate the Post Pier. Visibility was worse than ever. *Norge* was in the middle of the broad anchorage; she caught a brief glimpse of the foreign ships, but reports that Vestfjord was full of British warships had confused Askim and he didn't react until *Bernd von Arnim* was nearly at the pier. Then, his challenge ignored, the Norwegian captain ordered his gunners to shoot. The range was only eight hundred yards, but their critical first salvo fell short. *Bernd von Arnim* replied with her 5-inch and 37-mm guns but concentrated on landing her troops. *Norge* ducked behind some merchantmen as the two ships traded shots across the crowded anchorage. Most of the Norwegian shells passed over their target and fell into the town. The old ship fired a total of four main

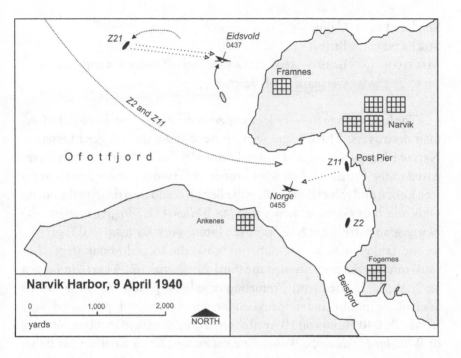

Narvik Harbor, 9 April 1940

battery salvos and five from her port side 5.9-inch guns. As *Bernd von Arnim* cast off from the pier she got a clear view of *Norge* and fired seven torpedoes; two ran on the surface and hit their target. There were twin explosions and *Norge* capsized to starboard at 0455, her propellers still turning. One hundred and one members of her crew perished in the icy waters. Boats rescued ninety men, including Captain Askim.

Georg Thiele proceeded to land her troops followed by *Wilhelm Heidkamp*. The military commander was pro-German and surrendered immediately; the town of Narvik passed into German possession without further struggle.

First Battle of Narvik, 10 April 1940

TIME: 0430–0700, Zone+1
TYPE: Harbor attack
WEATHER: Good, clear
VISIBILITY: Mixed poor to moderate

SEA STATE: Calm
SURPRISE: British
MISSION: British—reconnaissance and offensive sea superiority;
                Germans—self defense.

The long voyage to Narvik nearly emptied the fuel bunkers of the German destroyers. Three oilers were to meet these short-legged vessels at Narvik (they had a range of fifteen hundred miles at nineteen knots, compared to the British H class with a range of fifty-five hundred miles at fifteen knots) and refuel them before the British could trap them in the north. Only one, the ex–whale factory ship *Jan Wellem* (11,776 grt), made it. The Norwegian patrol boat *Nordkapp* (261 tons) sank *Kattegat* (6,031 grt) the second tanker with her 47-mm gun while the torpedo-boat *Stegg* (220 tons) intercepted and interned the third, *Skagerrak* (6,044 grt), in Bergen on 7 April.[7] Consequently, refueling relied completely on *Jan Wellem's* inadequate pump and improvised arrangements and proceeded very slowly. By 0400 hours on 10 April she had only managed to fill the bunkers of *Wilhelm Heidkamp*, *Wolfgang Zenker*, and *Erich Koellner*. As dawn approached on the second day of their occupation of Narvik, *Hermann Künne* and *Hans Ludemann* were alongside *Jan Wellem* slowly drawing their allotment of fuel oil. *Wilhelm Heidkamp* and *Anton Schmitt* were anchored in Narvik harbor. *Wolfgang Zenker*, *Erich Giese*, and *Erich Koellner* were at Elvegaard, *Georg Thiele* and *Bernd von Arnim* were in Ballangenfjord, and *Diether von Roeder* was on picket duty in Ofotfjord.

At this time the British were still uncertain what was happening in Norway. Vice Admiral Whitworth had sent Captain Warburton-Lee's 2nd Destroyer Flotilla to Vestfjord. Then, shortly after 0900 hours, he further ordered the flotilla to join him in a concentration of his forces at 1800 hours that evening in a position at sea some two hundred miles southwest of Narvik. However, this rendezvous was not to be. At 0952 Admiral Forbes ordered Warburton-Lee to "send some destroyers up to Narvik to make certain that no enemy troops land."[8] Then, at 1200 hours, the flotilla leader received orders direct from the Admiralty to sink or capture an enemy ship reported at Narvik. The higher commands ("Churchill in a high state of executive excitement in the map room") were clearly dissatisfied with Whitworth; however, directly issuing orders to his subordinates ruptured the chain of command and created confusion.[9]

Warburton-Lee may have welcomed this rupture. In any case, he seized the authority given him by the Admiralty's orders and took his entire flotilla up the fjord, leaving only three half-armed destroyers and one fleet destroyer patrolling Vestfjord.

When he stopped at the pilot station at Tranoy at 1600 hours on 9 April, he was surprised to hear that six German destroyers had passed the day before and that Narvik was in enemy hands. With only five destroyers, *Hardy*, the leader, *Hotspur*, *Havock*, *Hunter*, and *Hostile* (which had joined late) Warburton-Lee realized he would be outnumbered. Nonetheless, he made a signal at 1751 to the three levels of command who had been issuing him orders that day: "Norwegians report Germans holding Narvik in force also 6 destroyers and 1 submarine are there and channel is possibly mined. Intend attacking at high water."[10] Thereafter Warburton-Lee sought no direction. Whitworth received his signal in ample time to reinforce the 2nd Flotilla, but elected not to, fearful of causing confusion and interfering with an action already ordered by the Admiralty.

The British ventured up the fjord in a driving snowstorm that limited visibility to four hundred yards or less. Two submarines stationed along the way failed to spot the intruders in the dark and snow, although one

Table 2.6. First Battle of Narvik, 10 April 1940

Allied Ships	TYP	YL	DFL	SPD	GUNS	TT	GF	DAM
Hardy	DD	36	2,053	36	5×4.7/45	8×21	7	Sunk
Hotspur	DD	36	1,890	36	4×4.7/45	8×21	6	D3
Havock	DD	36	1,890	36	4×4.7/45	8×21	6	
Hunter	DD	36	1,890	36	4×4.7/45	8×21	6	Sunk
Hostile	DD	36	1,890	36	4×4.7/45	8×21	6	
German Ships								
Wilhelm Heidkamp	DD	38	3,415	38	5×5/45	8×21	7	Sunk
Anton Schmidt	DD	38	3,415	38	5×5/45	8×21	7	Sunk
Bernd von Arnim	DD	36	3,190	38	5×5/45	8×21	7	D2
Erich Giese	DD	37	3,190	38	5×5/45	8×21	7	
Erich Koellner	DD	37	3,190	38	5×5/45	8×21	7	
Diether von Roeder	DD	37	3,415	38	5×5/45	8×21	7	D3
Hans Ludemann	DD	37	3,415	38	5×5/45	8×21	7	D1
Hermann Künne	DD	37	3,415	38	5×5/45	8×21	7	D1
Georg Thiele	DD	35	3,156	38	5×5/45	8×21	7	D2
Wolfgang Zenker	DD	36	3,190	38	5×5/45	8×21	7	

reportedly felt their wake as they passed. Dawn came at 0420 hours. *Diether von Roeder* patrolled outside the harbor but her captain, Korvettenkapitän Erich Holtorf, interpreted his orders to mean he could quit his cold and uncomfortable duty at dawn.[11] He abandoned his post a little early and made for Narvik harbor. At the time *Hardy* was hidden in the fog only twenty-five hundred yards away. The British, unaware the enemy was so near, proceeded at six knots southwest of the Germans, conning by dead reckoning and waiting for sufficient light to commence action. A steady improvement in the weather expanded visibility to about a mile and the snow stopped falling, but it was still extremely hazy.

Anchored inside Narvik harbor were twenty-three merchant ships (five British, five Swedish, four Norwegian, one Dutch, and eight German) and five destroyers. *Diether von Roeder* was to the north; she had just dropped anchor at 0425. *Jan Wellem* was in the middle of the port with *Hermann Künne* and *Hans Ludemann* refueling on her port and starboard sides respectively. *Anton Schmitt* and *Wilhelm Heidkamp* were anchored about 250 and 500 yards south of the tanker, respectively. Bonte was sleeping aboard *Wilhelm Heidkamp*.

Warburton-Lee detached *Hostile* and *Hotspur* to engage a suspected shore battery at Framnes on the north arm of the harbor. Then, at 0430 hours, *Hardy* entered the broad harbor swinging inside the outermost merchant ship, completely silent, barely under way in the ghostly light of the arctic dawn. Her torpedo officer had four tubes trained to starboard, four to port, ready for anything. It was difficult to discern the German destroyers in the crowded roadstead; the lookouts spotted *Wilhelm Heidkamp* first and *Hardy* fired three of her starboard torpedoes. One missed, another sank a nearby merchantman and one hit its target, detonating the German flagship's after magazines and destroying the ship as far forward as No. 1 turbine room. Eighty-one men died in the blast, including Commodore Bonte. The time was 0435 hours. Ringing up twenty knots, *Hardy* swung around to port and commenced firing her 4.7-inch guns. Then she launched four more torpedoes at *Diether von Roeder,* but she couldn't train the tubes back to starboard in time, and her weapons struck the ore quay beyond their target. During these first minutes, the Germans believed they were under air attack and did not return fire.

Hunter attacked next making a circuit of the outer harbor with guns blazing. She fired eight torpedoes and hit *Anton Schmitt* in her No. 2 turbine room. She also landed at least one 4.7-inch shell on *Anton Schmitt*. German return fire increased to the point where *Hunter* felt the need to cover her exit with smoke. *Havock* entered the harbor third at 0446. She launched three torpedoes toward *Anton Schmitt*. All three found targets: two different merchantmen and *Anton Schmitt*'s No. 3 boiler room. The detonation broke the German destroyer in two and she sank in just a few moments; sixty-three men died.

Hermann Künne and *Hans Ludemann* were slipping their hoses and wire attachments to the oiler, a lengthy process undertaken in a hurry in the half-dark under fire. When *Anton Schmitt* exploded, *Hermann Künne* was only forty yards away, and the force of the blast seized her engines. Immobilized, she ineffectively targeted the British gun flashes. *Diether von Roeder* and *Hans Ludemann* also engaged *Havock* as she turned to leave the harbor. *Havock*, however, got the best of the exchange. She hit *Hans Ludemann* twice, wrecking her No. 1 gun, destroying her steering motor, and igniting a fire that forced her to flood her magazine.

Hotspur and *Hostile* found nothing at Framnes: "low visibility prevented a proper examination of Rombaks and Herjangs Fiords."[12] And, eager to get in the action, they only spent fifteen minutes looking, unfortunately as subsequent events would prove. They returned and *Hostile* lay off the harbor blindly firing grouped salvos at *Diether von Roeder* (and hitting her twice, inflicting significant damage) while *Hotspur* covered the retirement of her three sisters with a smoke screen. *Hotspur* then entered the harbor and fired four torpedoes, hitting two merchantmen.

The time was 0500 hours. Smoke pressed thick against the mountainsides that fell steeply into the fjord as ships burned in the harbor; the roar of the cannonade formed an echoing canopy. The flotilla lay several thousand yards off the harbor mouth, engaging when able, in no particular order as Warburton-Lee signaled his ships, trying to assess damage. The British destroyers finally assumed a counterclockwise movement, firing into the harbor as their guns bore. German return fire was heavy, but ineffective. *Diether von Roeder* was the closest target. Multiple hits wrecked her cable gear, damaged No. 3 gun, ignited serious fires in the portside oil bunker, in No. 2 boiler room, and No. 3 boiler room. Nonetheless, she managed to train her torpedoes and, at 0505 hours, fired a full salvo into the fjord. Had the depth setting on her weapons functioned, *Diether von Roeder* would have turned the tide of battle. *Havock* reported that "one torpedo appeared to pass underneath the ship."[13] Another ran under *Hardy* and a third under *Hunter.* Dragging her anchor, which she couldn't raise because she had lost electricity, *Diether von Roeder* managed to reach the Post Pier, there to be abandoned.

The British—aided by lazy security—accomplished at Narvik a rare thing: a surprise attack against anchored warships. In their initial assault they launched twenty-two torpedoes and sank two enemy destroyers (and five merchantmen). Their gunfire damaged two more destroyers while a third suffered collateral damage.

With the harbor completely enveloped in smoke, Warburton-Lee withdrew to reorganize and hold a brief war council with his captains. He was a "little uneasy" but, believing he had accounted for four of the six enemy ships, he decided to make another pass so *Hostile* could use her torpedoes.[14] It was during this respite that someone aboard *Hans Ludemann* thought to signal the five outlying destroyers and raise the alarm.

At 0514 Warburton-Lee signaled "Follow round" and the British came in again at fifteen knots in the following order: *Hardy, Havock, Hunter, Hotspur,* and *Hostile.* Their guns fired blind through the smoky haze as they bore, it being impossible to spot the fall of shot. *Hostile* penetrated the deepest, vainly seeking a target for her torpedoes. She fired four anyway, and then an enemy 5-inch shell struck under her forecastle. This was the only damage the British suffered in their attack on the harbor.

Aboard the British ships there was a euphoric feeling the battle was won. Some captains ordered landing parties to stand by. While German gunfire had slackened considerably, *Hans Ludemann,* in a parting shot, fired four torpedoes, one of which passed under *Hostile* without detonating.

At 0540 hours the head of the British column was passing Framnes heading northwest when lookouts aboard *Hardy* and *Havock* reported an unwelcome sight: *Wolfgang Zenker, Erich Koellner,* and *Erich Giese* under Fregattenkapitän Erich Bey, commander 4th Destroyer Flotilla, sailing down Herjangsfjord in port quarterline. (*Erich Giese* was almost out of fuel and running on only two boilers.) *Hardy* fired a five-gun salvo and the Germans replied with their forward mounts. The other British destroyers engaged as they completed their runs past the harbor mouth, but the range was long—seven to ten thousand yards and visibility poor. Neither side registered any hits. At 0551 Warburton-Lee reported the situation to the Admiralty, rang up thirty knots, and headed for the open sea. He believed

Bey's ships were pursuing hard in his wake, but they had encountered *Hans Ludemann*'s torpedoes still running hot and turned away 90 degrees to port to avoid them.

Warburton-Lee pressed his luck when he attacked the harbor a third time. It held up when *Hans Ludemann*'s torpedoes forced Bey to turn away; now fortune failed him utterly. *Georg Thiele* and *Bernd von Arnim* had weighed anchor at 0540, slowed down by heavy fog. Shortly after 0550, they emerged from Ballangenfjord, west of the British and directly astride their line of retreat. When the shapes of warships approaching bow on loomed through the mist Warburton-Lee vainly flashed recognition signals, logically hoping Whitworth or the Admiralty was sending him reinforcements. The captain of *Georg Thiele*, Korvettenkapitän Max-Eckhart Wolff, however, knew who the enemy was. At 0557 he swung to port to bring his broadside to bear; with smoke, flame, and thunder, his guns answered Warburton-Lee's signals. The range was only four thousand yards. *Hardy* also turned to port and attempted to return fire, but her gun director was still pointing astern toward Bey's ships. *Havock,* the only other 2nd Flotilla vessel to see this threat, engaged *Bernd von Arnim.* Smoke and lingering fog restricted the forward vision of the other three British destroyers.

Georg Thiele's fourth salvo straddled *Hardy* and then she began to register hits. Two 5-inch shells struck the flotilla leader's bridge with devastating effect, mortally wounding Captain Warburton-Lee. Additional rounds destroyed her steering control and forward guns. Antiaircraft rounds swept *Havock,* second in line, and ignited a fire in her forward ready-use cordite locker. In return *Havock* claimed a hit on *Bernd von Arnim.*

Out of control, *Hardy* careened south at thirty knots, her four consorts following. *Georg Thiele* fired two torpedoes, which *Havock* easily avoided as she turned to follow *Hardy.* The two German destroyers crossed ahead of the British line of advance. *Havock* fired five torpedoes at *Georg Thiele*, but miscalculated the target's speed, and all missed astern. The action now became general as the three trailing British destroyers came into view. The two columns traded a furious fire at ranges as close as three thousand yards, but did little damage. *Bernd von Arnim* fruitlessly fired one torpedo and *Hostile* four.

Bey, lagging far behind, brought his ships back to a northwesterly heading and finally crossed the harbor mouth. The gunners aboard the surviving German warships waited tensely by their weapons, unaware the British were finally on the run.

On *Hardy*'s bridge Warburton-Lee's secretary, the senior officer to survive, regained consciousness; he managed to bring his seriously damaged ship to a westerly course, but when another shell exploded in a boiler room he decided to run her aground. He swung *Hardy* out of line heading for the fjord's southern shore. The other four ships followed *Havock* west. Wolff brought *Georg Thiele* sharply around to the west and assumed a parallel course to the north. He incorrectly assumed Bey was pressing the British from behind. Instead, British firepower began to assert itself as a shell exploded in *Georg Thiele*'s boiler room. *Bernd von Arnim* followed *Georg Thiele* and began to weave and chase salvoes while *Hostile*'s torpedo salvo arrived and passed harmlessly between the German destroyers. The German gunners focused on *Hunter,* now the second ship in the British line, and registered several hits, igniting fires aboard their target.

Havock made a 180-degree turn to starboard to draw German fire and assess the situation. As he passed his own ships, *Havock*'s captain, Lieutenant Commander R. E. Courage, observed that *Hunter* was burning and appeared to be losing way and that *Hotspur,* behind her, was having trouble with her steering. He ordered his forward guns to fire on Bey's destroyers, about ten thousand yards east. But, learning they were out of action because of the cordite fire from an earlier hit, he came back about and took station on *Hostile*'s port quarter, shooting at Bey with "X" and "Y" mounts, causing yellow-green smoke to billow out with each shell discharged. It was only eight minutes since *Georg Thiele* had opened fire.

By 0605 Wolff was pulling ahead of the British, so he ordered starboard helm. As *Georg Thiele* heeled in her turn, three British shells struck in rapid succession, disabling No. 1 gun, damaging the fire control room and No. 2 boiler room, and igniting serious fires. Losing way, *Georg Thiele* continued to fire her four remaining guns under local control as *Bernd von Arnim* charged pass. *Hunter* was now leading the British column and the two German destroyers pounded her from ranges as near as seventeen hundred yards. Then *Georg Thiele* fired three torpedoes at her fiercely burning enemy. One finally ran true and detonated on target, blowing away *Hunter*'s forward torpedo tube and stopping her dead in the water. *Hotspur* was a half-mile behind. She had just launched a pair of torpedoes at *Georg Thiele* (which barely missed) when two 5-inch shells exploded on her bridge and wrecked her steering. Out of control, she swung to starboard and, steaming at 30 knots, she rammed *Hunter*. It was only seventeen minutes since *Georg Thiele* had opened fire.

Hostile and *Havock* veered around the pileup (in *Hostile*'s case just barely) and continued west. *Bernd von Arnim* lay a thousand yards off the tangled destroyers and poured on intense and accurate fire, hitting *Hotspur* at least seven times. Bey's flotilla finally drew nigh the scene of action and added the weight of their metal to *Hotspur*'s misery. *Erich Giese* fired a single torpedo from long range that passed her intended targets unnoticed. *Hotspur* and *Hunter* both returned fire over open sights hitting *Bernd von Arnim* and encouraging Bey to weave cautiously as he approached.

Aboard *Hotspur*, Commander H. Layman sent a runner to the engine room and tiller flat and ordered full steam astern. His ship slid off *Hunter*, bow torn and crumpled, but still able to steam. However, "the combined effects of the collision and the damage done by the enemy caused *Hunter* to sink." [15] As *Hotspur* escaped *Hunter*'s embrace she was the target of all five German destroyers. Hard on the rocks, even with her crew abandoning ship, *Hardy* supported her beleaguered sister firing her last gun and launching her last torpedo at either *Georg Thiele* or *Bernd von Arnim*.

Havock and *Hostile* turned back when they saw *Hotspur* emerge from the smoke two miles behind them, her ripped bow shooting fantastic plumes of water to either side. They were able to shepherd her down the fjord without interference because *Georg Thiele* and *Bernd von Arnim* had both been knocked out of action and Bey, uncertain of the enemy's strength, was advancing with extreme caution. *Erich Giese* was just about out of fuel in any case; she attempted to torpedo *Hardy*, but her weapon misfired. *Wolfgang Zenker* also turned to engage *Hardy* while *Erich Koellner* followed the retreating British for a short while. Finally, all three ships concentrated on rescuing *Hunter*'s crew, plucking forty-eight men from the frigid water.

While *Erich Giese*'s empty bunkers justified her withdrawal, *Wolfgang Zenker* and *Erich Koellner* had both refueled, making their failure to aggressively pursue the British especially unfortunate for the Germans inasmuch as the steamship *Rauenfels* (8,460 grt) was navigating up the fjord carrying much needed 5-inch destroyer shells (as well as vehicles, guns, and ammunition for the mountain troops). Shortly before 0650 hours, she ran into the three surviving British destroyers. One round from *Hostile* and she hove to. The senior officer ordered *Havock* to investigate.

She fired another round into the freighter's bow. This ignited a fire, and the crew quickly abandoned ship. After picking them up, *Havock* fired two more high effect rounds and "the result was certainly startling, as the German literally erupted and a column of flame and debris rose to over three thousand feet."[16] The huge blast slightly damaged *Havock*'s hull.

Greyhound, acting on her own initiative, met the British ships at 0930 hours near Tranoy. At 1100 hours *Penelope* joined them, belatedly ordered by Whitworth to their support.

Warburton-Lee's flotilla had inflicted severe damage on the German destroyers. *Wolfgang Zenker, Erich Giese,* and *Erich Koellner* were the only warships unharmed, although they were low on ammunition, and *Erich Giese*'s fuel bunkers were nearly dry. *Hermann Künne* lost 9 men and suffered extensive splinter damage. Five shells had pierced *Bernd von Arnim* at both her bow and stern and damaged a boiler. She had 2 dead. Seven shells struck *Georg Thiele*; she lost a gun and her fire control, her magazines were flooded, and her hull and machinery were damaged. Thirteen members of her crew perished. *Hans Ludemann* lost 2 men as well as No. 1 gun and a magazine. *Diether von Roeder* had taken five hits and was immobile. She lost 13 men. *Wilhelm Heidkamp* was sinking and *Anton Schmitt* was sunk. They suffered the greatest death tolls, 81 and 50 men, respectively. On the British side the two ships sunk, *Hunter* and *Hardy*, lost 108 and 19 men, respectively. *Hotspur* suffered 20 deaths, while *Hostile* and *Havock* escaped without injury.[17]

Second Battle of Narvik, 13 April 1940

TIME:	1230–1700
TYPE:	Harbor attack
WEATHER:	Mixed, snow flurries
VISIBILITY:	Mixed, fair to moderate
SEA STATE:	Calm
SURPRISE:	None
MISSION:	British—interception based upon specific intelligence; Germans—self defense

During the rest of the day the German destroyers regrouped and assessed their damage. While *Georg Thiele, Bernd von Arnim,* and *Hans*

Ludemann commenced emergency repairs, *Diether von Roeder*'s men wondered whether it was feasible to even attempt repairs, given the resources and time available. The crew of *Wilhelm Heidkamp* could only salvage guns and ammunition from their sinking ship. *Erich Giese*, at least, was able to refuel.

At 1812 hours Naval Group West ordered Bey to take *Wolfgang Zenker* and *Erich Giese* and break out as soon as it was dark. Their assessment that two battle cruisers were in the area and three battleships were on the way was a discouraging send-off. Nonetheless, the two destroyers cast off at 2040 hours and threaded their way between the wrecks and hulks that choked Narvik harbor. The sky was clear and visibility good, poor conditions for their purpose. Bey seemed skittish; he paused to examine *Hardy*'s beached wreck while the smoking remnants of *Rauenfels* triggered a false alarm.

At 2205 hours, while passing Baroy Island, the Germans saw three shadows, which they correctly interpreted as British destroyers and a cruiser (*Penelope, Bedouin,* and *Eskimo*). They had reached the point where the narrow waters opened, but Bey, after closing to seven thousand yards, made smoke and turned back to Narvik. The patrolling ships saw neither the Germans nor their smoke. Thus was lost Bey's only chance to salvage at least a small portion of his force.

By the late afternoon of 11 April, *Wolfgang Zenker, Erich Koellner, Hans Ludemann,* and *Hermann Künne* were fueled and operational, but the Germans had written off *Diether von Roeder.* Her crew landed the balance of the stores and equipment, sadly rigged her for demolition and left her tied to the Post Pier, her two forward guns to function as a floating battery. *Georg Thiele* and *Erich Giese* (which had developed mechanical problems upon returning from her aborted breakout attempt) lay alongside *Jan Wellem* using her workshop facilities to make repairs. Although his operational force was doubled and despite pressure from Group West and favorable weather conditions, Bey did not make another attempt to slip away. As if damning a faint heart, misfortune ravaged the remaining German force that night. Moving to their dispersal point at Ballangenfjord, *Erich Koellner* ran hard aground, ripping her bottom open as far as No. 3 boiler room and *Wolfgang Zenker* touched a submerged skerry, damaging her port screw.

The measure of disappointment and frustration felt by the German sailors may be imagined. *Erich Koellner*'s chief engineer wrote:

We decided that there was only one solution: dismount the guns and set up the battery ashore. . . . At about 1100 (on the 12th) Fregattenkapitän Bey appeared and looked with astonishment at what we were doing. The commander was sent for and had to explain. Bey ordered him to put absolutely everything back on board again. All this was incomprehensible to the ship's company. They had been through an indescribably hard voyage in a hurricane . . . and on top of all the physical exhaustion they knew . . . they wouldn't be going home. . . . Now this.[18]

By the end of the day, the German order of battle was as follows:

Hermann Künne: All guns and torpedoes and fully operational.
Wolfgang Zenker: All guns and torpedoes. A damaged propeller screw reduced her speed it was believed to twenty knots, but in the event not at all.
Erich Giese: All guns and torpedoes, but her machinery was still damaged from her breakout attempt.
Bernd von Arnim: All guns and six torpedoes. Capable of thirty-three knots.
Georg Thiele: Four guns, with local control only and six torpedoes. Capable of twenty-seven knots.
Hans Ludemann: Four guns and four torpedoes, otherwise fully operational.
Diether von Roeder: Two guns and no torpedoes. Docked as a floating battery.
Erich Koellner: All guns and two torpedoes. Only capable of seven knots, she could serve as a floating battery. Most of her oil and torpedoes were transferred to other ships.

The only action that day occurred at 1846 hours when two Swordfish squadrons from *Furious* attacked. *Erich Giese* suffered a few splinter casualties and a bomb landed near a party of sailors on the Ore Quay killing eight and wounding twenty. The Germans shot down two of the eight attackers. The strike delayed *Erich Koellner*'s departure to Taarstad where she was to set up an ambush for ships coming up the fjord.

On the morning of 13 April the brief lull ended.

After Warburton-Lee's gallant foray, the British mulled their options for dealing with a German force they believed included minefields, shore batteries, two cruisers, six destroyers, and one or two submarines; they didn't realize five U-boats, U25, U46, U48, U51, and U64 were concentrated in the fjord to repel their counterattack. The Admiralty signaled *Penelope* at 2012 on 10 April to attack that night or the next morning with available destroyers if she considered it a "justifiable operation." At 2219 hours on 10 April Whitworth complained to the Admiralty that it was ordering his ships to do three different things: prevent escape, repel reinforcements, and attack. He requested clarification. Churchill responded by telling *Penelope's* Captain D. G. Yates, that the Admiralty would back whatever decision he made (hoping to find another Warburton-Lee, perhaps). At 2310 Yates signaled that minefields and shore batteries make an attack inadvisable.[19] His caution went unrewarded as *Penelope* suffered damage fully equivalent to a mine at 1500 hours the next day when she tore her hull on a submerged rock near Bobo.

Then the British focused their expectations on *Furious* and her Swordfish. When these proved false, Admiral Forbes, under Admiralty orders, drafted a plan for a coordinated surface/air attack on 13 April. *Warspite,* supported by three destroyers in a minesweeping role (*Icarus, Foxhound,* and *Hero*) and six destroyers in an offensive role (*Kimberley, Forester, Cossack, Punjabi, Bedouin,* and *Eskimo*) would sail up the fjord and destroy all German ships in the Narvik area. The plan did not include a counterlanding to retake Narvik itself. Admiral Forbes gave command to Vice Admiral Whitworth who seemed grateful for the job. ("As I was unable to prevent the Germans entering Narvik, may I hoist my flag in *Warspite?*")[20]

By 0730 hours on 13 April, Whitworth had concentrated his ships in Vestfjord, with the exception of *Eskimo* patrolling near Tranoy Light sixty miles in from the assembly position. At 1010, only three hours later, Naval Group West code breakers informed Bey a British attack was coming and accurately listed the enemy force. Bey mulled this news for a half hour before ordering his ships to raise steam. Meanwhile, at 1030, *Erich Koellner* escorted by *Hermann Künne* set sail at seven knots for her ambush position at Taarstad.

As Whitworth's force swept up the outer fjord, the first enemy contact occurred at 1040 near Tranoy Light. U48 surfaced, but *Eskimo,* which was loitering there waiting to join Whitworth, spotted her. The U-boat crash dived as *Eskimo* charged over and began dropping depth charges, keeping her down as *Warspite* and her destroyers passed.

Table 2.7. Second Battle of Narvik, 13 April 1940

Allied Ships	TYP	YL	DFL	SPD	GUNS	TT	GF	DAM
Warspite	BB	13	36,450	23	8×15/42 & 8×6/45		111	
Bedouin	DD	37	2,519	36	8×4.7/45	4×21	11	
Cossack	DD	37	2,519	36	8×4.7/45	4×21	11	D4
Eskimo	DD	37	2,519	36	8×4.7/45	4×21	11	D3
Punjabi	DD	37	2,519	36	8×4.7/45	4×21	11	D3
Hero	DD	36	1,890	36	4×4.7/45	8×21	6	
Icarus	DD	36	1,854	36	2×4.7/45		3	
Kimberley	DD	39	2,330	36	6×4.7/45	10×21	8	
Forester	DD	34	1,940	36	4×4.7/45	8×21	6	
Foxhound	DD	34	1,940	36	4×4.7/45	8×21	6	
German Ships								
Bernd von Arnim	DD	36	3,190	33	5×5/45	6×21	7	Sunk
Erich Giese	DD	37	3,190	5	5×5/45	8×21	7	Sunk
Erich Koellner	DD	37	3,190	7	5×5/45	2×21	7	Sunk
Diether von Roeder	DD	37	3,415	0	2×5/45	8×21	3	Sunk
Hans Ludemann	DD	37	3,415	38	4×5/45	4×21	6	Sunk
Hermann Künne	DD	37	3,415	38	5×5/45	8×21	7	Sunk
Georg Thiele	DD	35	3,156	27	4×5/45	6×21	6	Sunk
Wolfgang Zenker	DD	36	3,190	5	5×5/45	8×21	7	Sunk

The British continued up the fjord with *Icarus* in the lead sweeping with bow paravanes and *Foxhound* and *Hero* with stern sweeps to either side, clearing the way. Starboard of *Warspite* sailed *Bedouin* (Commander J. A. McCoy, Senior Officer Destroyers), *Punjabi*, and *Eskimo*; to port proceeded *Cossack, Kimberley,* and *Forester.* The sky was heavily overcast with a light wind from the southwest; visibility extended as far as ten miles. The sea was calm.

At 1152 five miles west of Baroy Island *Warspite* launched her Swordfish spotter plane. The aircraft carried two 250-pound bombs, two 100-pound antisubmarine bombs, and eight 40-pound antipersonnel bombs. At 1156 *Hermann Künne* sighted the British vanguard and reported to Bey. He ordered all his destroyers to sail, but he failed to advise U64, at the head of Herjangsfjord, and U51 in Narvik harbor that the British were coming. U51 believed the alarm signified an air attack. She submerged inside the harbor and there she stayed. *Hans Ludemann, Wolfgang Zenker,* and *Bernd von Arnim,* however, were all under way by 1215.

At 1203 *Warspite*'s aircraft began radioing information. First it reported *Hermann Künne* off Tjellebotn then, at 1210, *Erich Koellner*'s position and finally at about 1220 it advised that *Hans Ludemann* was near the harbor entrance. After investigating Narvik harbor, the aircraft flew up Herjangsfjord and caught U64 lying anchored at its head. At 1230 it divebombed and hit its target with one 100-pound bomb and near missed with the other. This was enough to sink U64; eight men died, but thirty-eight used the escape apparatus to reach the surface. U64's return fire harmlessly punched holes in the aircraft's fabric body.

At the same time one submarine was sinking, U46 was stalking *Warspite* sailing steadily at fifteen knots as she left Baroy astern and entered the narrows of Ofotfjord. The range was only six hundred fifty yards, but seconds before she fired torpedoes, U46 hit an uncharted skerry and broke surface. If U46 had fired, there is no guarantee her weapons would have functioned correctly, or hit the battleship, but the odds favored this outcome. It is hard to imagine Whitworth continuing the operation with a flagship damaged just before battle. In the event, U46 backed off, went under, and lost her opportunity. On the British side lookouts missed U46's bow jump from the water to starboard because at the same time the alarm sounded round the fleet: "Enemy in sight!"

The enemy was *Hermann Künne*. The British finally picked her out of the mists when she turned beam on about twelve thousand yards from the lead British destroyers. *Cossack, Icarus, Punjabi,* and *Bedouin* all flung shells at this target as she turned back up the fjord toward Narvik, but the range was at the limits of visibility and after only a few salvos they checked fire. Hurrying along at her best speed of seven knots *Erich Koellner* clearly wasn't going to make it to Taarstad and so turned to port toward Djupvik, an inferior position, but better than being caught in the open water. Unfortunately for her, *Warspite*'s Swordfish was watching.

After the opening exchange of fire *Hans Ludemann* followed by *Wolfgang Zenker* with Bey aboard cleared Narvik harbor and were joined by *Bernd von Arnim*. The British attack caught *Georg Thiele* and *Erich Giese* with cold boilers; they remained in the harbor frantically raising steam. At 1245 *Hermann Künne* reached the area of Djupvik; she turned and laid a smoke screen across the fjord to cover the approach of her compatriots and to hide a torpedo attack. She briefly traded long-range salvos with *Cossack* and *Bedouin,* the lead destroyers of the two wings. As they nervously approached the narrows at Ramnes and Hamnes, the British were pleased to find false their intelligence about German shore batteries there.

At 1251 *Hans Ludemann* came into range from a position off the western end of Bogen Bay. There she turned south and engaged. *Wolfgang Zenker* found the range six minutes later and followed *Hans Ludemann* south. They straddled *Icarus*, but did not score any hits. The Germans proceeded to zigzag across the width of the fjord, with each turn being pressed ever east. This allowed them to use their entire batteries and the frequent changes in course complicated British fire solutions. The British, meanwhile, pushed forward, engaging with their forward mounts only. At 1259, when she was near Hamnesholm, *Warspite* opened fire on *Hermann Künne* from eighteen thousand five hundred yards. The booming echoes from the blast of her 15-inch guns caused avalanches on the steep mountains overhanging the fjord. Visibility quickly deteriorated as gun and funnel smoke, black, dirty-white, and yellow-green, mingled with mist and snow squalls blowing across the narrow waters.

At 1305 the steady British advance brought *Bedouin*, the leading destroyer on the starboard side, abreast Djupvik where *Erich Koellner* lay in ambush. Thanks to the warning broadcast by *Warspite's* aircraft *Bedouin's* guns and torpedo tubes were trained to starboard. Spotting *Erich Koellner*, as expected, about thirty-eight hundred yards away, she opened fire. *Punjabi* and *Eskimo* followed at two-minute intervals, likewise blasting the stationary warship as they cleared the point. *Erich Koellner* only had time to launch her two torpedoes and fire one salvo before British shells smothered her. *Bedouin* fired one torpedo and *Punjabi* and *Eskimo* two each and at least one found its target blowing off *Erich Koellner's* bow. After *Bedouin's* group passed, *Icarus* and *Cossack* also shot at *Erich Koellner*, which gamely replied with occasional rounds.

As her sister was being destroyed, *Bernd von Arnim* joined the action. The Germans kept up a heavy fire, particularly against the northern force (even though the southern force was the most advanced). The British replied with their forward guns and began weaving to spoil the Axis aim (except for the three minesweepers, which were bound to a steady course). The battleship maintained a deliberate fire from "A" and "B" turrets as she acquired targets.

The increasing smokiness combined with the difficulties of hitting small, fast moving targets at ranges up to fifteen thousand yards rendered all this shooting ineffective except for one man aboard *Foxhound* hit by a splinter. *Kimberley*, for example, sighted the German ships at 1232, but did not open fire until 1308. Her only close call came ten minutes later when a German salvo straddled. During this time *Wolfgang Zenker* fired four torpedoes at the northern British destroyers. *Warspite*'s faithful spotter saw the tracks and radioed a warning as *Cossack* swerved to avoid one and *Kimberley* observed two others passing down her port side.

At 1319 *U25* lying near Lilandsgrund fired two torpedoes at *Cossack* from eight hundred yards. These missed and passed down the fjord well to port of *Warspite*. At 1325 *Warspite* passed Djupvik and fired a pair of salvos at *Erich Koellner*. The German destroyer shuddered under the impact of at least two 15-inch shells. U25, realizing her torpedo attack had failed, withdrew down the fjord to ambush the British as they retired. At 1330 *Warspite* observed that men were still aboard *Erich Koellner*. She fired four more 15-inch salvos and finally sank the battered vessel. *Erich Koellner* suffered thirty-one men killed and thirty-nine wounded and for this sacrifice accomplished nothing.

As *Erich Koellner* sank, *Georg Thiele* finally joined the main German group, which had, by this time, been pressed back nearly all the way to Narvik harbor. *Georg Thiele* opened fire on *Bedouin*, the leader of the southern column from about thirteen thousand yards. By 1340 *Bedouin*'s group was approaching Skjomgrund shoal, more than five thousand yards ahead of the other British columns. They were in line abreast with *Bedouin*, the farthest south in the lead, followed by *Punjabi* in the middle, and *Eskimo* farthest north. The Germans concentrated their fire on this group. A near miss disabled *Bedouin*'s No. 1 gun. After more near misses, she sheered south of the shoal. *Punjabi*, under equally intense fire did the same, leaving *Eskimo* alone in the lead.

Warspite proceeded at ten knots and continued to engage, although "A" turret was filling with fumes due to constant dead-ahead fire. Between 1340 and 1350 her minesweepers dropped back and recovered their sweeps, glad to be done with their dangerous job and free to maneuver. *Hermann Künne* fired a spread of torpedoes straight back down the fjord at the battleship without effect.

With the Germans squeezed into Herjangsfjord, the battle's tempo accelerated. *Bernd von Arnim* made a large loop, first to the southwest and then to the northeast. As she came to her new heading, she fired two triple banks of torpedoes at *Warspite* and the northern destroyers. These were well aimed and one passed beneath *Cossack*. The British subjected *Bernd von Arnim* to a storm of fire, but twisting and jinking, the German emerged unharmed, although she did experience the excitement of being straddled by *Warspite*'s massive shells. *Georg Thiele* contributed two torpedoes as she headed north to join her compatriots.

At this point, ten Swordfish from *Furious* descended on the battle. At the cost of two of their number they managed to plant bombs near *Hermann Künne* and *Bernd von Arnim*.

At 1350 Bey ordered his ships to retire to Rombaksfjord, a finger of water that penetrated east into the mountains north of Narvik. *Bernd von Arnim* and *Wolfgang Zenker* were completely out of ammunition. In eighty minutes of intense action the British had destroyed *Erich Koellner* while *Bedouin, Foxhound,* and *Punjabi* all suffered varying degrees of splinter damage. *Hans Ludemann, Wolfgang Zenker, Bernd von Arnim,* and *Georg Thiele,* in that order, formed column and entered Rombaksfjord. *Hermann Künne,* however, missed Bey's instructions and headed by herself northeast up the broader and shorter Herjangsfjord. It was at this time that *Erich Giese* finally managed to get under way. However, as she approached the harbor entrance, her port engine failed.

At 1352 *Erich Giese* sighted *Eskimo, Bedouin,* and *Punjabi* approaching along the fjord's south shore and engaged them from six thousand yards. *Bedouin* and *Punjabi* saw *Erich Giese* and *Diether von Roeder* inside the harbor at the same time and returned fire. *Erich Giese* launched three torpedoes, but these were aimed at *Eskimo,* which was chasing *Hermann Künne* to the northeast, a very difficult retiring shot. *Eskimo* easily avoided the one torpedo that eventually caught up to her. *Bedouin* counterattacked with her three remaining torpedoes and *Punjabi* with her last two. Although their target was stationary, the only thing the five British torpedoes hit was the Post Pier near *Diether von Roeder.* The blast parted her mooring wires and shook the ship severely, but didn't damage her guns.

As the two British destroyers approached the harbor, the Germans focused their gunfire on *Punjabi,* the nearest; in the space of a few minutes they hit her five times destroying her fire control room, causing her to flood No. 4 magazine and igniting fires forward and abreast the after funnel. In return the British hit *Diether von Roeder* twice aft and a shell from *Bedouin* struck *Erich Giese,* but these blows did little damage. *Warspite* joined in against *Diether von Roeder* and her near misses caused spectacular collateral damage, but none on the target itself.

By 1400 Bey and four of his destroyers had withdrawn to Rombaks-fjord, temporarily shielded from the action; *Georg Thiele*, the last in, dropped smoke floats to cover their retreat. The undamaged *Hermann Künne*, out of ammunition and torpedoes, fled up Herjangsfjord, hurried along her way by *Eskimo*'s forward guns.

At 1405 *Erich Giese* finally brought her port engine back online and emerged from the harbor mouth at her maximum speed of twelve knots. She had enemies ahead, and her only visible friend lay immobile behind her. Her captain, Korvettenkapitän K. Smidt, might, by his maneuver, be accused of being careless with the lives of his men, but he had already crippled one enemy, and four torpedoes remained. Battered *Punjabi* remained his point of aim, but *Bedouin* suddenly bent on speed and closed rapidly. Her shells stuck *Erich Giese* almost immediately and most of the other British destroyers, even *Warspite*, fixed on this new target. Being hit repeatedly, the beleaguered *Erich Giese* fired her last four torpedoes at *Punjabi*. *Punjabi* avoided these with a violent turn west even as *Erich Giese*'s gunners struck her a sixth time. This was enough for *Punjabi*. She continued west and signaled Whitworth she was done.

Bedouin closed to a thousand yards, point-blank range, hitting hard and accepting splinter damage from near misses in return, while three of *Warspite*'s shells passed through the German destroyer's thin skin. *Erich Giese* returned fire while she was able, but this was not long. Listing, without power, taking water, and out of ammunition, Smidt ordered his crew to abandon ship. Eighty-three men died and many were wounded. The British had hammered *Erich Giese* with at least eighteen 4.7-inch and three 15-inch rounds. As *Erich Giese* was being shelled to death, U51 decided it was time to flee Narvik harbor, which she did without incident and without intervening in the action taking place above.

While most of the fleet bombarded *Erich Giese*, *Eskimo* and *Forester* chased *Hermann Künne*. Korvettenkapitän F. Kothe might have been surprised to find himself alone, but clear on his course of action he took his ship about halfway up the fjord to a position opposite Trollvik and there ran her aground with open seacocks and demolition charges triggered. *Hermann Künne*'s crew had been in action longest, but not one man had suffered a scratch from enemy action. *Eskimo* closed to about five thousand yards and at 1413 fired three torpedoes. *Forester* followed shortly after with two more. After a few minutes there was a tremendous explosion and *Hermann*

Künne was destroyed; whether by demolition charges or by torpedoes, the result was the same.

Whitworth made his first signal of the battle after 1400 specifying that *Warspite* would deal with shore batteries in the harbor while the destroyers went after the enemy ships. At 1412 *Warspite* commenced bombarding *Diether von Roeder* to which the immobile destroyer's two guns gamely replied. Whitworth's division of responsibilities made sense, but Commander R. St. V. Sherbrooke of *Cossack* decided his higher duty lay in Narvik harbor attacking *Diether von Roeder* and, even worse, he ordered *Kimberley* to follow. As the two destroyers turned into the harbor shortly after 1415 they fouled *Warspite*'s range, effectively forcing the battleship out of the action.

At 1420 *Cossack,* moving cautiously at twelve knots, cleared the obstructions of the outer harbor and came in sight of *Diether von Roeder.* Both ships opened fire simultaneously. *Cossack* was abeam on target while *Diether von Roeder* was end on. Although *Cossack* had more guns, *Diether von Roeder*'s first shots hit while *Cossack*'s missed short; moreover, *Diether von Roeder*'s shells struck *Cossack*'s fire control room forcing her guns to shift to local control at the worst possible moment. In the next two minutes the immobile destroyer gained a measure of revenge for all the harm inflicted by British guns, hitting *Cossack* six more times.

At 1422 *Cossack,* without steam or power, drifted ashore on the strand of Ankenes with nine dead and twenty-one wounded. She registered hits on *Diether von Roeder,* but not on the two guns, which was all that mattered. *Kimberley* then came around the bend and opened fire as did *Foxhound* from outside the harbor until smoke hid her target. *Diether von Roeder* fired back, although without the stunning results she achieved against *Cossack.* Then, ammunition exhausted, her gunnery crew of twenty-five fled the ship for the haven of the tunnels ashore where the captain and most of the crew sheltered. *Kimberley* then attempted to tow *Cossack* off the strand, but abandoned this effort when ordered to concentrate on Rombaksfjord.

At 1424 *Eskimo* and *Forester* entered Rombaksfjord. Commander St. J. Micklethwait in *Eskimo* flew the signal: "Enemy in sight," a slight exaggeration given the effectiveness of *Georg Thiele*'s smoke floats, but it attracted *Bedouin, Hero,* and *Icarus* nonetheless. Bey, meanwhile, sent the toothless *Wolfgang Zenker* and *Bernd von Arnim* to the far end of the fjord to rig for scuttling while *Hans Ludemann* and *Georg Thiele* prepared an ambush. Halfway down, the fjord's width narrowed to eight hundred yards and a bend hid the lower waters from view. *Hans Ludemann,* with four torpedoes and four guns, but little ammunition, and *Georg Thiele,* also with four guns and two torpedoes, took up position. *Hans Ludemann* was to the north about two and half miles east of the bend and the same distance from the end, stern facing the enemy, which permitted three guns to bear. *Georg Thiele* lay on the south shore, about three miles from the bend and two miles from the end.

Eskimo led the British column at fifteen knots through the gray, uncertain light, the fjord's steep, mountainous walls arching into the smoke overhead like a tunnel. At 1445 *Eskimo* came to the narrows at the midpoint knuckle and rounded the southern spit. Suddenly the roar of *Georg Thiele* and *Hans Ludemann*'s guns erupted, echoing up and down the narrow defile. The result was a curious reversal of the *Diether von Roeder/Cossack* encounter. Although the Germans knew the range, their aim was off while *Eskimo*'s accurate reply destroyed *Hans Ludemann*'s No. 3 gun. *Hans Ludemann* launched her last four torpedoes, and was almost immediately ripped by a salvo that disabled Nos. 4 and 5 guns. *Hans Ludemann*'s Korvettenkapitän Herbert Friedrichs decided he had done enough to uphold honor; he retreated toward the fjord's dead end to scuttle and save the balance of his crew. *Eskimo* hurried him on his way hitting *Hans Ludemann* in the stern several more times.

Forester rounded the bend next behind *Eskimo*. The two destroyers turned their guns on *Georg Thiele* and registered repeated hits. *Georg Thiele* fought back (albeit ineffectively) and Micklethwait impatiently decided a torpedo was required. He turned to port to launch his last one. Just as he committed to this maneuver, the four torpedoes launched a few minutes before by the already defeated *Hans Ludemann* were seen boiling up the fjord. By the greatest of exertions, including a near grounding on the north shore, Micklethwait just barely avoided the danger. The torpedoes continued on, one passing harmlessly under *Forester* and another running up on a spit of sand at the knuckle. *Hero,* poking around the bend decided there was insufficient room for her to join her mates, so she contented herself with using her forward guns against the enemy from that position.

Aboard *Georg Thiele* the torpedo officer waited by his last remaining weapon. Seeing *Eskimo*'s predicament, he fired. Micklethwait could do nothing when he saw this final threat. At 1451 *Georg Thiele*'s torpedo, the last of at least forty-four fired at the British that day, detonated below *Eskimo*'s No. 1 gun and ripped off her entire bow. In an outstanding exhibit of professionalism, No. 2 gun was back in action within thirty seconds and at 1452 *Eskimo* sent her final torpedo at *Georg Thiele*. It missed to starboard, but wasn't necessary in any case. *Hero* came up and passed *Eskimo*. *Forester, Hero,* and *Eskimo* bombarded *Georg Thiele* and hit repeatedly. She returned fire until her ammunition ran out. Then Korvettenkapitän Wolff turned his ship toward shore and, at 1500, ran her hard aground. He lost sixteen men killed and twenty-eight wounded.

The rest of the action was mopping up and anticlimax. By 1500 *Warspite* had entered the outer Rombaksfjord where she lay stopped. At the fjord's knuckle, the British destroyers withheld their final advance as *Eskimo* backed around the bend. In Narvik Harbor, *Foxhound* approached *Diether von Roeder*. A boarding party was standing by the boats, but upon seeing three men suddenly emerge and run from the deserted hulk, her captain sensed something wrong and backed off. His suspicions saved his ship because at 1520, *Diether von Roeder*'s demolition charges exploded cataclysmically. At 1520 demolition charges likewise destroyed *Bernd von Arnim* after her crew was safely ashore. *Wolfgang Zenker* and *Hans Ludemann*, however, remained aground, apparently undamaged. For all the British knew, they still had work to do and, at 1540, *Hero, Icarus,* and *Kimberley*, in that order, finally ventured cautiously past the knuckle, worried they were sailing into torpedo waters.

At 1545 *Hero* opened fire on *Wolfgang Zenker* and within five minutes the German warship rolled over and sank; the small party abroad (which included Bey) hastily evacuated in a motor boat. *Hans Ludemann* was farther east. *Hero* probed her with a couple of rounds and then she and *Icarus* sent armed parties to board. They hoisted the British ensign and considered towing the enemy destroyer off as a war prize, but Whitworth, concerned about German aerial strikes, ordered her sunk. This *Hero* did with a torpedo.

Cossack, meanwhile, worked on her damage. *Foxhound* offered a tow, but Sherbrooke declined, not sure if his ship would even float. The German army troops ashore lacked any weapons heavy enough to seriously damage the destroyer; they fired at her briefly with a mortar, but *Cossack*'s return salvos quickly silenced this nuisance. Her closest call came when *Hero*, returning from her exploits up the fjord, attempted to torpedo

Erich Giese's burning wreck. The weapon missed and exploded on the beach not far from *Cossack*. Then the anticipated German air attack arrived. It was conducted without enthusiasm and did no damage.

At 1755 *Warspite, Foxhound, Bedouin, Hero,* and *Icarus* withdrew west down the fjord. Whitworth had considered sending men ashore to seize the town, but he lacked orders and even if the first landing proved successful, holding Narvik against the mountain regiment would have been difficult without immediate reinforcement by regular troops.

Another German air attack at this time ignored the battleship and instead went after the destroyer *Ivanhoe*, which had come up the fjord after the battle and was rescuing *Hardy*'s stranded crew. The attack did her no harm. More serious was the U-boat danger. At 1840 U25 was in position to attack *Warspite* at the Tjellebotn narrows. However, *Foxhound* obtained contact and thwarted her attempt with depth charges. Korvettenkapitän V. Schutze, U25's commander, was an aggressive opponent. A half hour later he fired a torpedo at *Ivanhoe* from fifteen hundred yards, but without result—probably betrayed by a torpedo malfunction. U46, on the other hand, saw the British ships but was unable to obtain a firing position. U51 stayed under and saw nothing.

Whitworth was clearly ignorant of the submarine danger. At 2050 when his ship was back in Vestfjord, he reversed course and returned to Narvik to support *Cossack* and *Eskimo*. U25 attacked the battleship on her way back in, but missed. After towing attempts failed, *Cossack* managed to float off the shore at high tide, which took place at 0300 hours on 14 April and, steaming stern first, escaped the harbor. *Bedouin* towed *Eskimo* to safety. During their final passage down Ofotfjord, U46 almost got off an attack against the two destroyers, while U48 launched torpedoes at *Warspite*. Like all the efforts of the U-boat force that day, this attack was unsuccessful.

Kimberley remained in Narvik harbor to show the flag; shortly after 1500 hours on the 14th she sent a small party in her cutter to sink a flying boat moored in the harbor and lost five men when German soldiers opened fire. She returned fire and her cutting out party managed to sink their objective despite the casualties. These were the last shots of the battle.

The Second Battle of Narvik was an undoubted British victory, but flawed in several respects. The greatest flaw was strategic; the British made no provision to take the real prize: the town itself. Delaying the attack by a day or a week would not have materially changed the German position—their stock of torpedoes and ammunition would not have improved—and a battalion of Scots Guards could have landed under the umbrella of naval guns. Tactically, Sherbrooke's decision to enter the harbor against Whitworth's orders resulted in the near loss of his ship. The use of *Warspite* in such restricted, submarine-infested waters was dangerous and unnecessary. The battleship's greatest contribution was made by her spotter aircraft; she was fortunate none of the torpedo attacks against her succeeded.

In few surface engagements were submarines present in such numbers. A few well-placed torpedoes could have defeated the British the way Vichy submarines did at Dakar just five months later. But this didn't happen. Even though the German U-boat commanders operated in narrow waters, poorly charted and full of reefs and skerries, barely coordinating with surface forces, their failure to perform, despite numerous opportunities, is inexplicable. The northern conditions affected the behavior of German torpedoes in ways they did not understand, it is true, but they fired so few torpedoes, this problem was not apparent.

Sinking of the *Glorious*, 8 June 1940

TIME: 1546–1820
TYPE: Encounter
WEATHER: Wind WNW, moderate breeze 20 knots
VISIBILITY: Unlimited, 25+ miles
SEA STATE: Northwesterly swell, temperature 34° F.
SURPRISE: Germans obtain first sighting
MISSION: British—transit; Germans—offensive and sea superiority patrol without specific intelligence

One of the most unusual surface engagements of World War II occurred on the afternoon of 8 June 1940. Two German battleships encountered and sank the lightly escorted British aircraft carrier *Glorious*. This was the first time an aircraft carrier faced enemy surface gunfire, but the battle was noteworthy not only for its participants. In this battle, disadvantaged as she was, *Glorious* made every possible mistake. The gallant efforts of her small escort went for naught and more than fifteen hundred British sailors lost their lives. As American escort carriers demonstrated at Leyte Gulf four years and three months later, these results were not inevitable.

By the beginning of June 1940 the Norwegian Campaign was winding down. The Allies finally captured Narvik on 27 May, six weeks after Whitworth's victory and far too late considering the rush of events on the continent. Ten days later the evacuation began. Two convoys carrying nearly twenty-four thousand troops sailed on 7 June and 8 June escorted by ships of the Home Fleet. The fleet carrier *Glorious,* meanwhile, embarked two air force fighter squadrons from their base at Bardufoss. Ordered to abandon their aircraft, the pilots elected to land on *Glorious*'s flight deck, so they would be available to defend Britain should Germany invade. For everyone it would be their first carrier landing and the first carrier landing for the high-performance fighter the Hurricane, with no modifications other than slightly deflated tires. The German navy was sensitive to events in northern Norway. On 4 June it launched Operation Juno to relieve pressure on Narvik's defenders. This involved a sortie by the battleships *Gneisenau,* the flagship of Vizeadmiral Wilhelm Marschall, *Scharnhorst,* the heavy cruiser *Admiral Hipper* and the destroyers Z20 *Karl Galster,* Z10 *Hans Lody,* Z15 *Erich Steinbrinck,* and Z7 *Hermann Schoemann.*

Marschall sailed without a clear picture of the situation or a specific mission. He refueled *Hipper* and the destroyers at sea on 6 and 7 June. He then called a captain's conference aboard *Gneisenau.* Based on reconnaissance reports, they concluded the Allies were evacuating Norway. Although he was ordered to bombard Harstad, Marschall decided there was more profit going after the reported evacuation convoy.

During 8 June the fleet operated together and sank three British vessels: a navy oiler, *Oil Pioneer,* an armed trawler, *Juniper,* and an empty transport, *Orama.* Then at 1330 Marschall detached *Hipper* and the destroyers to refuel at Trondheim while the battleships continued alone. They swept north and then came to the northwest, steaming in line abreast at nineteen knots with *Gneisenau* leading. The conditions that afternoon favored the Germans—there were gentle swells, a light breeze from the northwest, and unlimited visibility. At 1546 hours lookouts atop *Scharnhorst*'s crow's nest sighted a wavering thread of smoke on the eastern horizon bearing 60 degrees. By 1600 they could see a mast at an estimated range of forty-four thousand yards. The German battleships increased speed and turned starboard to the northeast at 1606 hours. At 1610 lookouts reported the ship had a flight deck. They could also see a destroyer to the north and one to the south. Marschall had found an aircraft carrier sailing practically unescorted.

Table 2.8. Sinking of the *Glorious*, 8 June 1940

Allied Ships	TYP	YL	DFL	SPD	GUNS	TT	GF	DAM
Glorious	CV	30	27,400	30	16×4.7/40		20	Sunk
Ardent	DD	29	1,815	35	4×4.7/45	8×21	6	Sunk
Acasta	DD	29	1,815	35	4×4.7/45	8×21	6	Sunk
German Ships								
Scharnhorst	BB	36	38,900	32	9×11/54.5 &		79	D3
					12×5.9/55			
Gneisenau	BB	36	38,900	32	9×11/54.5 &		79	
					12×5.9/55			

Glorious under Captain Guy D'Oyly-Hughes and the destroyers *Ardent* (Lieutenant Commander J. F. Barker) and *Acasta* (Commander C. E. Glasfurd) were sailing southwest at seventeen knots with *Ardent* five hundred yards to the west off the starboard bow of *Glorious* and *Acasta* in the same position to port. The carrier was at cruising stations with no lookout aloft. There were no aircraft on deck and none in the air, although she was zigzagging in deference to the possibility of a submarine attack. Shortly after 1600 someone aboard noted two strange warships on the western horizon. D'Oyly-Hughes detached *Ardent* to investigate and continued on course. As a precaution he ordered aircraft ranged up from below.

How was such a valuable vessel exposed to enemy battleships with hardly any escort? The official history states that *Glorious*, originally scheduled to form a part of the escort for the second troop convoy, was ordered home early due to a shortage of fuel.[21] Unofficially, Captain D'Oyly-Hughes signaled Vice Admiral Air in *Ark Royal* and requested permission to proceed to Scapa Flow independently. He was eager to court martial his Commander (Air) who had disobeyed orders to conduct an attack during an earlier deployment. Although the British had no official indication German battleships were at sea—and even though *Glorious* had sailed between Scapa Flow and Harstad five times in May and June— her lack of ordinary wartime precautions was difficult to explain as were her subsequent maneuvers and reactions once she found herself in danger. Admiral Dudley Pound wrote: "*Glorious* seems to have forgotten that she was a Man o' War."[22] (The circumstances of *Glorious*'s voyage are still disputed. The British Ministry of Defense continues to maintain that the official history's version is correct although the history's author himself later recanted his account.)

Although two large unidentified warships were approaching, *Glorious* continued on course and did not go to action stations until 1620. One minute later the Germans turned 90 degrees to the southeast to close range. *Ardent*, flashing a challenge on her searchlight was about fifteen thousand yards west of the carrier while *Acasta* maintained position to the east. *Glorious* carried six Swordfish from Squadron 823; half had torpedo racks and her crew were bringing them on deck. She also carried ten Sea Gladiators of Fleet Air Arm Squadron 802, ten air force Hurricanes, and ten Gladiators she was evacuating, unavailable below.

By 1627 the Germans, sailing in echelon with *Gneisenau* on *Scharnhorst*'s port quarter, had worked up to twenty-nine knots. *Gneisenau* opened the action firing on *Ardent* with her secondary batteries. *Ardent* ceased challenging and turned away. Three minutes later *Scharnhorst*'s 5.9-inch guns opened fire, also targeting *Ardent*. The range was nearly sixteen thousand yards. All three British vessels commenced making smoke.

One of the ambiguities of this battle was *Glorious*'s failure to immediately radio an enemy contact report. Apparently she began broadcasting at 1620 on a discontinued frequency. Her first effective SOS did not go out until a half hour later and it was so weak the receiving ship, *Devonshire*, which was only about seventy miles west, was uncertain of its content. Neither destroyer signaled at all.[23]

At 1632 *Scharnhorst*'s 11-inch guns sent a salvo toward *Glorious* from a range of 28,400 yards. She ceased fire on *Ardent* one minute later as the secondary batteries interfered with the main guns. At 1638 *Scharnhorst*'s third salvo hit target from the incredible distance of 26,400 yards, penetrating the aircraft carrier's flight deck, exploding in the upper hangar, and igniting a large fire. This blast put an end to the strenuous efforts to arm the Swordfish, which were supposed to be on ten-minute call.[24]

Responding to this calamity, *Acasta* opened fire, although the range was too great. *Ardent* emerged from her smoke screen and at 1642 attacked *Scharnhorst* with torpedoes. *Scharnhorst* had her under fire from 1640. Her hydrophones picked up the approaching torpedoes and she turned 30 degrees to port for one minute to avoid them, although one passed close ahead.

At 1646 *Gneisenau* finally entered the action. She was steaming 1.5 knots faster than her sister, whose speed was affected by a split boiler tube, and was gradually reaching a position five thousand yards off *Scharnhorst*'s port quarter. One minute later *Glorious,* emitting a pillar of smoke and flame, but still moving at full speed, finally turned to the southeast. Up to this time, the range had been constantly closing. D'Oyly-Hughes's reasons for delaying his turn will forever be a mystery, because he had less than ten minutes to live. At 1656 a shell from *Gneisenau* struck *Glorious*'s homing beacon wrecking her bridge and killing the captain.

This was unfortunate because by 1658 *Glorious* was completely hidden by smoke, forcing the two German battleships to cease fire. Then *Ardent* emerged once again into the clear and at 1702 she fired a half salvo of torpedoes. *Scharnhorst* avoided these and, in return, her secondary batteries brought *Ardent* under a heavy fire, hitting the destroyer at 1704 and again at 1711 (even the 4.1-inch heavy antiaircraft guns came into action, earning an admonishment from Marschall about wasting ammunition). At 1713 *Scharnhorst* had *Glorious* back in sight (perhaps because *Ardent* was no longer adding to her smoke screen) and five minutes later her main batteries were again shooting at the carrier.

At 1720 *Gneisenau* hit *Glorious* in her center engine room. This was decisive; the carrier's speed fell off and she began to slowly circle to port, all the while developing a starboard list. At 1722 *Ardent*'s mast broke off and she capsized and sank. During her courageous counterattack, she registered one insignificant 4.7-inch hit on *Scharnhorst.*

Acasta was still undamaged. However, with the carrier clearly in serious trouble, she made a large loop to the west passing ahead of *Scharnhorst* to a position off the German's starboard beam. Glasfurd reportedly passed the message to his crew: "You may think we are running away from the enemy; we are not, our chummy ship has sunk, the *Glorious* is sinking, the least we can do is to make a show."[25] She made two attacks firing four torpedoes each time. *Scharnhorst* sighted the second salvo launched at 1732, but intent upon shooting at the retreating destroyer (and finally scoring hits) she terminated her evasive maneuvers too soon. At 1739 one torpedo blew a giant hole in her starboard side aft and forced the evacuation of Caesar turret due to smoke. The blast and subsequent flooding killed forty-eight men.

By 1740 the Germans ceased firing on *Glorious. Acasta* continued as a target for the secondary batteries of both ships until 1808. Then, at 1810, although clearly in a sinking condition, *Acasta* landed a 4.7-inch shell on *Scharnhorst's* Bruno turret's right barrel. This minor blow provoked renewed fire from *Scharnhorst's* secondary batteries. At 1810 *Glorious* sank. *Acasta* followed her under about ten minutes later.

Scharnhorst was the most heavily engaged during this action expending 212 11-inch shells in sixty-nine salvos, 842 rounds of 5.9-inch, and 136 of 4.1-inch. *Gneisenau* was more conservative, expending 175 rounds of 11-inch and 306 of 5.9-inch. Although many men were alive when the ships sank, it was several days before any rescue ships found them. Only 45 survived aboard the open floats and rafts in the frigid seas. Of the 1,245 men aboard *Glorious* there were 43 survivors. Only 1 man survived from *Acasta's* crew of 160 and 2 men from *Ardent's* crew of 152. One thousand five hundred and fifteen British sailors died.

This action was a disaster for the British, mitigated only by the skillful handling of the destroyers, particularly *Acasta*, and the damage done to *Scharnhorst*. If, however, this sacrifice prevented the German battleships from falling in with Troop Convoy II, which was only two hundred miles distant, it averted a much greater disaster.

3

THE ENGLISH CHANNEL AND THE HIGH SEAS 1940

In 1940–41, we (Germans) could do on our side more or less what we wanted.

VIZEADMIRAL FRIEDRICH RUGE

In the summer of 1940 the conquest of France and Norway transformed the German navy's missions and strategic options; it thrust on the navy responsibility for nearly six thousand additional miles of coastline, it opened several new theaters of operations, and provided excellent harbors on the high seas.[1] Initially, it seemed this tremendous gain merely provided a convenient staging area for the invasion of Great Britain. (Although Raeder believed that "a successful invasion of England was dependent on conditions which could scarcely be fulfilled.")[2] But beginning in September the French ports became more important as bases to exert control over the English Channel rather than places to accumulate invasion barges, even though, after the grievous losses suffered in the Norwegian campaign, there were few large warships available for the job.

Nowhere else did major naval forces face each other across such a narrow—and important—body of water for such a long time. From the beginning to the very end, the English Channel was a major arena of the naval war.

In September 1940 the 5th Torpedo Boat Flotilla moved to Cherbourg after escorting several minelaying expeditions in the North Sea. On 9 September 1940 the five destroyers of the 5th Destroyer Flotilla under Kapitän zur See Erich Bey left Germany for Brest to be on hand if the invasion should occur and to interdict British coastal traffic in the western Channel. On the 22nd the two ships of the 6th Destroyer Flotilla, Z5 *Paul Jacobi* and Z15 *Erich Steinbrinck* followed.

Table 3.1. The English Channel and the High Seas 1940

Date	Location	Name	Opponent	Type
12-Oct-40	English Channel	Chase off the Isle of Wight	British	Interception
17-Oct-40	English Channel	Action in the Western Approaches	British	Interception
29-Nov-40	English Channel	Action off Plymouth	British	Interception
25-Dec-40	North Atlantic	Christmas Convoy Action	British	Convoy attack

Bey's half-hearted performance at Narvik, his lack of aggression and failure to even attempt to save a few of his destroyers did not damage his career. In fact, Hitler awarded him the Ritterkreuz on 9 May 1940 and Raeder appointed him Führer der Zerstörer the following day, a post he held until his death three and a half years later. Bey was, in any case, the most battle experienced destroyer commander Germany had and his new assignment provided him with repeated opportunities to improve his résumé.

The German destroyers of the 5th and 6th Flotillas sortied on 28 September 1940 to mine Falmouth Bay. However, it was the torpedo boats, not the destroyers which first encountered British destroyers in the English Channel.

Chase off the Isle of Wight, 12 October 1940

TIME: 0325–0400
TYPE: Interception
WEATHER: Fair
VISIBILITY: Moon 85 percent, set at 0212
SEA STATE:
SURPRISE: None
MISSION: British—patrol and sea security; Germans—offensive and sea superiority patrol without specific intelligence

The five torpedo boats of the 5th Flotilla, *Greif, Kondor, Falke, Seeadler,* and *Wolf* sailed from Cherbourg at 1930 hours on the night of 11 October flying the flag of Korvettenkapitän Wolf Henne. Their mission was to harass English coastal shipping and repay a naval bombardment laid on their port the night before by the battleship *Revenge*. At 2327 hours on 11 October,

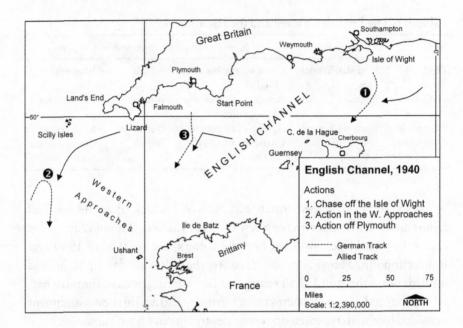

English Channel, 1940

Actions
1. Chase off the Isle of Wight
2. Action in the W. Approaches
3. Action off Plymouth

-------- German Track
———— Allied Track

0   25   50   75

Miles
Scale: 1:2,390,000   NORTH

thirteen miles southeast of the Isle of Wight, they encountered two armed trawlers, the French manned *Listrac*, (778 tons) and *Warwick Deeping* (445 tons), steaming west at five knots on anti-invasion patrol. The trawlers were surprised when gun flashes suddenly erupted to their port four thousand yards away. They even switched on identification lights. German 4.1-inch shells quickly struck *Listrac* and exploded in her boiler room. Then *Greif* torpedoed the trawler and she quickly sank. British ships rescued a few survivors the next day. *Warwick Deeping,* hit several times, attempted to escape to the north, but *Kondor* and *Falke* chased her down. *Kondor* fired a torpedo and missed, but concentrated gunfire from both torpedo boats quickly sank the unfortunate trawler with all hands.[3]

Shortly thereafter, the Germans encountered two Free French (Polish manned) submarine chasers, *CH6* and *CH7*. Displacing 137 tons fully loaded and armed with a 3-inch gun, they were no match for the torpedo boats. Henne closed to eleven hundred yards and, at 0111 hours on 12 October, his ships opened fire. After sinking both submarine chasers, the Germans rescued about forty survivors.

At 0220 hours Henne's ships formed up and turned for home but their return voyage proved eventful. The British 5th Destroyer Flotilla consisting of *Jackal, Jaguar, Jupiter, Kelvin,* and *Kipling* under Captain Lord Louis

Table 3.2. Chase off the Isle of Wight, 12 October 1940

Allied Ships	TYP	YL	DFL	SPD	GUNS	TT	GF	DAM
Jackal	DD	38	2,330	36	6×4.7/45 & 1×4/45	5×21	9	
Jupiter	DD	38	2,330	36	6×4.7/45 & 1×4/45	5×21	9	
Jaguar	DD	38	2,330	36	6×4.7/45 & 1×4/45	5×21	9	
Kelvin	DD	39	2,330	36	6×4.7/45 & 1×4/45	5×21	9	
Kipling	DD	39	2,330	36	6×4.7/45 & 1×4/45	5×21	9	
German Ships								
Greif	TB	26	1,290	33	3×4.1/45	6×21	3	
Kondor	TB	26	1,290	33	3×4.1/45	6×21	3	
Falke	TB	26	1,290	33	3×4.1/45	6×21	3	
Seeadler	TB	26	1,290	33	3×4.1/45	6×21	3	
Wolf	TB	27	1,290	33	3×4.1/45	6×21	3	

Mountbatten was at sea. Mountbatten had been sailing to intercept a reported enemy convoy, but upon receiving news of Henne's depredations, he turned in search of the German warships.

The Germans were in mid-Channel, about twenty-seven miles south-southwest of the Isle of Wight when lookouts spotted the British destroyers at fifty-four hundred yards bearing 140 degrees. The torpedo boats turned and increased speed, reaching twenty-eight knots at which point they began to lay smoke. Although Mountbatten was in position to cut the Germans off, he was late in reacting to the German turn and did not open fire until 0325, by which time his destroyers were following dead astern. The British first fired star shell, followed by ranging salvos that fell between Greif, Seeadler, and Kondor. One shell near-missed Kondor, but then British accuracy began to suffer as the smoke screen snuffed the illumination from their star shell. Henne withheld gunfire, but Falke and Wolf each aimed a torpedo at the flash of the British guns. Kondor dropped depth charges, hoping the British would mistake their detonations for mine explosions. These evasive maneuvers worked and by 0400 Henne's torpedo boats had eluded their pursuers. They turned for Cherbourg at 0550 hours and made port safely at 1025 hours that morning.

At this point in the war, British destroyers lacked radar and when operating at night, especially in an offensive capacity, their training and doctrine could not overcome the natural handicap that "at night, at sea, you don't see a damn."

Chase in the Western Approaches, 17 October 1940

TIME: 1707–1921
TYPE: Interception
WEATHER: Clear, fresh breeze
VISIBILITY: Extreme
SEA STATE: Moderate swells
SURPRISE: British
MISSION: British—interception based upon specific intelligence; German—offensive and sea superiority based on general intelligence

Encouraged by the positive results of the 5th Torpedo Boat Flotilla's raid of 11 and 12 October, Naval Group West ordered Bey to sea less than a week later to hunt for several British convoys German intelligence expected to pass near Brest. He sailed at 0403 hours on 17 October with Z10 *Hans Lody* (FS), Z6 *Theodor Riedel*, Z14 *Friedrich Ihn*, *Erich Steinbrinck*, and Z20 *Karl Galster*. Less than an hour into the mission *Theodor Riedel* experienced tube failures in her No. 1 boiler room that limited her speed to twenty-five knots and at 0548 hours she returned to port. At 0835 hours Bey's bad fortune continued when a British Blenheim sighted his force.

In response to the aircraft's report, Plymouth Command quickly diverted the three lightly escorted convoys, HG45, SL50, and OG44, away from danger. Moreover, sensitive to the threat presented by the German destroyer flotillas at Brest, the British navy retained at several hours' readiness a cruiser/destroyer force at Plymouth. Called Force F, these ships included the light cruisers *Newcastle* (Flag Rear Admiral A. Aylmer) and *Emerald*, and the 5th Destroyer Flotilla consisting of *Jackal* (flag of Captain Mountbatten), *Jupiter*, *Kashmir*, *Kelvin*, and *Kipling*. At 1035 hours these ships raised anchor, cleared the defensive mine barrages, and set course to the southwest to hunt the German destroyers.

As Force F steamed hard to intercept the enemy, Bey, joined by Henne's 5th Torpedo Boat Flotilla, swept an empty sea. The only event of significance was a blocked valve and a tube failure in *Erich Steinbrinck*'s turbines. For a time her top speed was only twenty-two knots. Nonetheless, the Germans pressed on to the north.

At 1433 hours Bey received a report that seven British destroyers were heading west at high speed. Nevertheless, he held his northern course until

Table 3.3. Chase in the Western Approaches, 17 October 1940

Allied Ships	TYP	YL	DFL	SPD	GUNS	TT	GF	DAM
Newcastle	CL	34	11,350	32	12×6/50 & 8×4/45	6×21	29	
Emerald	CL	20	9,106	33	7×6/45 & 4×4/45	16×21	13	
Jackal	DD	38	2,330	36	6×4.7/45 & 1×4/45	5×21	9	
Jupiter	DD	38	2,330	36	6×4.7/45 & 1×4/45	5×21	9	
Kashmir	DD	39	2,330	36	6×4.7/45 & 1×4/45	5×21	9	
Kelvin	DD	39	2,330	36	6×4.7/45 & 1×4/45	5×21	9	
Kipling	DD	39	2,330	36	6×4.7/45 & 1×4/45	5×21	9	
German Ships								
Hans Lody	DD	36	3,190	38	5×5/45	8×21	7	D1
Karl Galster	DD	38	3,415	38	5×5/45	8×21	7	D1
Friedrich Ihn	DD	36	3,165	38	5×5/45	8×21	7	
Erich Steinbrinck	DD	36	3,165	38	5×5/45	8×21	7	

1600 hours when he was about forty miles southwest of the Isles of Scilly. At this point he came about to course 190 degrees. The torpedo boats had gone their own way and the four destroyers were operating alone. The wind was light from the east northeast and visibility was extremely good. Bey did not know that lookouts aboard Newcastle had just sighted one of his ships hull down over the horizon to the southwest.

At 1607 hours five shells suddenly raised water geysers into the air astern of the German flagship. Newcastle, some twenty-five thousand yards to the north, was the agent of this unexpected attack. The Germans rushed to action stations. Bey altered course slightly to port, coming to a south-southeasterly heading, and his ships fled toward Brest at twenty-nine knots in line ahead formation, zigzagging and making smoke. The high-pressure hot steam boiler system of the German destroyers, normally a cause for complaint, showed to advantage in this situation with their ability to raise steam quickly. Aboard one of the ships, the turbines were running at full power only nine minutes after firing two cold boilers.

From the British perspective, the enemy ships came into view one by one, the last destroyer seen at 1624 crossing the stern of her flotilla mates emitting a dense and effective trail of smoke. Newcastle hoisted the general signal "chase" and every ship worked up to full speed, the cruisers firing at the enemy with their forward guns near full elevation.

Despite ineffective attacks by two German floatplanes at 1630 and a Dornier Do17 ten minutes later, the range steadily closed. By 1700 hours

Aylmer had cut the German lead to seventeen thousand five hundred yards and 6-inch shells were falling around the German ships. Even as she steamed at full speed through a brisk crosswind, engaged with enemy warships, *Newcastle* managed to launch her Walrus seaplane. The British destroyers, except for *Jupiter,* also opened fire, although, given the range and lively seas, a hit would have been pure coincidence. *Jupiter* had fallen back because of engine trouble. At 1720 hours she abandoned the chase altogether to investigate two sailing ships that had stumbled into the battle zone.

The British were able to close range because the need to take evasive action prevented the German destroyers from steering a straight course. Although it seemed to the British that they were mostly firing blind as enemy ships briefly appeared through the smoke, only to disappear again, Bey was feeling hard-pressed. By 1715 hours the Germans were steering south in starboard quarter-line formation with *Hans Lody* in the lead followed by *Friedrich Ihn* and *Karl Galster.* The rear ship, *Erich Steinbrinck,* which heretofore had been hidden, began to come under very accurate fire. Salvos bracketed her fore and aft, shells landing as close as ten yards away, their fragments showering onboard.

To force the British to do some defensive maneuvering of their own, *Hans Lody* and *Karl Galster* each launched three torpedoes dead astern at 1738 hours while *Erich Steinbrinck* turned to port and fired four more at an estimated range to target of fifteen thousand seven hundred yards. *Newcastle*'s Walrus radioed a warning and at 1741 the British cruisers turned to comb the tracks of the oncoming torpedoes. At 1801 a Dornier Do17 aircraft, one of several that had been shadowing Force F, dropped a stick of bombs at the British flagship. When they saw the water plumes thrown up by the bombs and the smoke from the antiaircraft fire, the German destroyer men cheered, thinking they had torpedoed *Newcastle*. This was not the case, but the torpedoes and the bombs slowed the British sufficiently to permit Bey to open range. Dusk was falling and a haze coming off the sea degraded visibility. Moreover, the German aircraft were becoming more aggressive making five attacks against *Emerald* and others against *Newcastle* and the destroyers. Aylmer abandoned the pursuit at 1821 hours and the ships of both sides returned to port without additional damage. Two British shells struck *Hans Lody* during this engagement, but caused only light damage.

The British were not satisfied with the results of this chase. *Newcastle* fired off 750 rounds of 6-inch and 300 rounds of 4-inch. *Emerald* fired 78 6-inch rounds and 118 rounds of 4-inch. Perhaps if Aylmer had held his finger off the trigger for a few minutes, Force F could have closed another thousand yards or more before the Germans began to run. Bey, on the other hand, surprised by a superior force, managed to extract his flotilla without suffering any consequential damage.

Action off Plymouth, 29 November 1940

TIME:	0643–0900
TYPE:	Interception
WEATHER:	Clear, calm
VISIBILITY:	Poor
SEA STATE:	Slight swell
SURPRISE:	None
MISSION:	British—patrol and sea security; Germans—offensive and sea superiority patrol without specific intelligence

On 22 October Z4 *Richard Beitzen* arrived at Brest, increasing the strength of Bey's 5th and 6th Flotillas to eight ships—the most German destroyers concentrated in one port since Narvik. However, when it became clear there would be no invasion of Great Britain, at least in 1940, *Paul Jacobi, Theodor Riedel, Friedrich Ihn, Erich Steinbrinck,* and *Friedrich Eckholdt* rotated back to home waters for repair and refit.

Richard Beitzen, Hans Lody, and *Karl Galster* continued to operate from Brest, although bad weather and delicate turbines limited their activities. On the night of 24 November Bey's next operation took him into the waters south of Plymouth. The three destroyers unsuccessfully attacked a fishing fleet twelve miles southwest of Wolf Rock, then located a convoy of three small freighters, a tug, and two barges. With gunfire and torpedoes they sank *Appolonia* (2,156 grt) and heavily damaged *Stadion II*, but the rest escaped into the dark. Mountbatten's 5th Destroyer Flotilla was at sea. He saw the distant gun flashes from the attack on the fishing fleet, but assumed they were over land; after seeing flashes again during the convoy attack, Mountbatten finally deduced there were German warships about. He turned his flotilla to intercept, but Bey was already gone and there was no contact that night.

Table 3.4. Action off Plymouth, 29 November 1940

Allied Ships	TYP	YL	DFL	SPD	GUNS	TT	GF	DAM
Javelin	DD	38	2,330	36	6×4.7/45 & 1×4/45	5×21	9	D4
Jupiter	DD	38	2,330	36	6×4.7/45 & 1×4/45	5×21	9	
Kashmir	DD	38	2,330	36	6×4.7/45 & 1×4/45	5×21	9	
Jackal	DD	38	2,330	36	6×4.7/45 & 1×4/45	5×21	9	
Jersey	DD	38	2,330	36	6×4.7/45 & 1×4/45	5×21	9	
German Ships								
Richard Beitzen	DD	35	3,156	38	5×5/45		8×21	7
Hans Lody	DD	36	3,190	38	5×5/45		8×21	7
Karl Galster	DD	38	3,415	38	5×5/45		8×21	7

The three German destroyers conducted another sweep off Plymouth four nights later under good conditions with clear weather and a light swell. At 0339 about twenty miles south of Eddystone reef lighthouse (fourteen miles south of Plymouth), Bey's destroyers encountered two tugs pulling a lighter. They came to a parallel course and closed to point-blank range, but still required thirty-five minutes to sink the lighter, *BHC10*, and the tug *Aid* (424 tons combined), while merely damaging the other tug. One tug captain described German marksmanship as "disgracefully bad."[4] About an hour later they encountered a pilot boat and expended fifty to sixty rounds sinking her. After these very small successes, Bey turned south and rang up twenty-nine knots for the return to Brest. However, Mountbatten's 5th Destroyer Flotilla (*Javelin, Jupiter, Kashmir, Jackal,* and *Jersey*) had received an alert and *Kashmir* saw the gun flashes in the northwestern sky. They turned at speed to intercept, determined the Germans would not escape them a third time.

At 0530 hours *Hans Lody* received a broadcast from German shore radar warning of unidentified ships approaching rapidly from the east southeast. When British lookouts spotted the enemy at 0542 hours, Mountbatten believed he had achieved surprise but this wasn't the case. *Karl Galster,* the leading German ship, altered to starboard and, beginning at 0542, each of the German ships fired four torpedoes. At 0544 Mountbatten swung his column to course 220 degrees to parallel the Germans from their port quarter, "a rather disastrous move as the directors swung off and lost target."[5] And far worse, a move that turned them beam on to

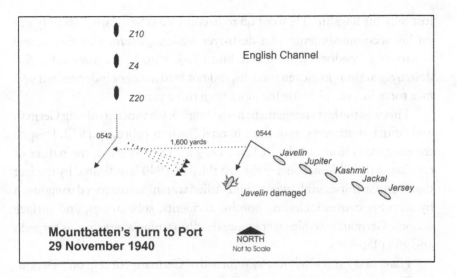

Z10

Z4

Z20

English Channel

0542   0544
                    1,600 yards
                                        Javelin
                                        Jupiter
                                        Kashmir
                                        Jackal
                                        Jersey
                    Javelin damaged

Mountbatten's Turn to Port   NORTH
29 November 1940   Not to Scale

the torpedo barrage. The British opened fire at 0545 and the Germans replied. Initial salvos were long as the range was only sixteen hundred yards, closer than either side estimated. The second British salvo was in the air when an enormous flash lit the darkness. Two torpedoes had slammed into *Javelin*, lifting her out of the water and blowing off both bow and stern.

The Germans made smoke and fled at thirty-five knots as the British destroyers steamed past their stricken flagship, their forward guns firing rapidly. During a long chase they straddled *Hans Lody*, the rear ship, several times and near misses peppered her superstructure with splinters, but the only hits the British registered came from several 2-pdr shells early in the action.

Slowly the superior speed of the German destroyers opened the range. At 0900 hours the British came about, fearing to venture too far into waters dominated by the German air force. Although *Javelin* had her length reduced from 356 feet to 155 feet, effective damage control, sturdy bulkheads, and very good luck saved her; the tug *Caroline Moller* towed the wreck back to Plymouth at two knots where she was under repair for thirteen months. Forty-eight men died in the attack. The Germans had no casualties.

This was the second time Bey bested Mountbatten. Admiralty staff criticized the British leader's turn to port as conveying no advantage and putting his ships in considerable danger. Mountbatten was fortunate he lost only his flagship. He went on to become First Sea Lord, certainly not on his accomplishments as a destroyer leader. (*Javelin* was the second destroyer torpedoed from under him.) Bey, who had commanded five destroyer actions in eleven months, did not lead another independent surface force in a naval battle for more than three years.

This was the last engagement in the English Channel involving German and British destroyers until the Channel Dash in February 1942. Despite the energetic efforts of the British to engage the Germans, the nature of combat in the Channel during the last third of 1940 is indicated by the fact that German mines sank twenty-nine Allied warships compared to eighteen by all other causes including bombs, accidents, submarines, and surface actions. German warships were more deadly as minelayers than as torpedo and gun platforms.

Hans Lody and *Karl Galster* returned to Germany for refit on 5 December. Torpedo boats undertook three mining operations in December 1940, but only four in all of 1941. And, while motor torpedo boats attacked British convoys several times during the winter of 1940–41, the tempo of war in the English Channel moderated during the balance of 1941 as the German navy turned its attention to the Baltic and Arctic theaters and to commerce warfare in the open Atlantic.

Christmas Convoy Action, 25 December 1940

TIME: 0639–0714
TYPE: Convoy attack
WEATHER: Rain squalls, strong SSE wind
VISIBILITY: Mixed, bad to poor
SEA STATE: Heavy swell, high seas
SURPRISE: Germans
MISSION: British—escort and transit; Germans—offensive and sea superiority commerce raiding

As it became clear Great Britain would not sue for peace, attacks against her oceanic lines of communications by both surface ships and submarines became a heightened priority for the German navy. The navy's principal limitation was a lack of ships. *Bismarck* and *Prinz Eugen* were fitting out; *Scharnhorst, Gneisenau,* and *Lützow* were under repair. This left only the heavy cruisers *Admiral Hipper* and *Admiral Scheer* available for cruiser warfare. *Scheer* broke out into the broad Atlantic in late October 1940, the first heavy warship to penetrate beyond the Norwegian Sea since *Graf Spee*. *Hipper* followed her six weeks later.

Hipper (Kapitän zur See Wilhelm Meisel) used bad weather to hide her passage through the Denmark Strait into the north Atlantic on the night of December 6–7. For two weeks she cruised the Halifax route undiscovered, finding nothing to attack, but enduring two storms of hurricane force and a failure in her starboard engine. She ran dangerously short of fuel for her thirsty turbines before rendezvousing with a pre-positioned tanker. Finally, on the 20th Meisel turned his ship east toward Brest, ready to call it quits.

At 2045 hours on Christmas Eve about 700 miles west of Cape Finisterre, *Hipper*'s luck abruptly changed when her radar reported multiple contacts. In fact, she had stumbled upon convoy WS5A, loaded with forty thousand troops sailing for the Middle East. Such an important convoy had a powerful escort: the heavy cruiser *Berwick*, the light cruisers *Bonaventure* and *Dunedin*, and the aircraft carrier *Furious* (serving as an aircraft transport and unable to operate even one plane for reconnaissance or defense).

Assuming the convoy was lightly escorted, Meisel decided to engage at first light. His only aggressive action that night came at 0153 hours when he fired three torpedoes from about five thousand yards, hoping if one hit, the British would blame a submarine. When this tactic failed, Meisel stood off to wait for dawn.

Hipper was running parallel to the convoy. As dim, gray light began to replace the dark she turned to close. The time was 0608 hours on Christmas morning. Rain squalls moved across the seascape degrading visibility and the wind blew strong from the south southeast. Peering through this

Table 3.5. Christmas Convoy Action, 25 December 1940

Allied Ships	TYP	YL	DFL	SPD	GUNS	TT	GF	DAM
Berwick	CA	26	13,400	31	6×8/50 & 8×4/45	8×21	32	D3
Bonaventure	CL	39	6,850	32	8×5.25/50	6×21	11	
Dunedin	CL	18	5,800	29	6×6/45 & 2×4/45	12×21	12	
German Ship								
Admiral Hipper	CA	37	18,200	32	8×8/60 & 12×4.1/65	12×21	35	

murk *Hipper*'s lookouts saw an unexpected and unwelcome sight: a three-funneled heavy cruiser. Meisel ordered his six starboard torpedoes to engage, but then he countermanded his order as more escorts hove into view. He turned toward *Berwick* and, still unsighted by the British cruiser, opened fire at 0639 hours, foregoing the opportunity to launch a surprise torpedo attack. Smoke, spray, and the intermittent visibility hindered accuracy. Moreover, when her 8-inch guns fired the blast effects disabled *Hipper*'s torpedo-training gear. At first *Hipper* engaged *Berwick* with all guns, but she quickly shifted her secondary batteries against the convoy, damaging *Empire Trooper* (13,994 grt) and *Arabistan* (5,874 grt).

Berwick was already at action stations and responded immediately to *Hipper*'s attack, turning toward the German and returning fire within two minutes. The light cruisers also altered course to engage. Meisel thought they were destroyers and, afraid of a torpedo attack, he sheered the cruiser to port, firing on *Berwick* with the aft turrets and keeping the other cruisers at a distance with his secondary battery. Mindful of his orders to refuse battle against an equal or superior enemy, he used the murky conditions to break contact.

At 0651 *Hipper* spotted *Berwick* once again about eight thousand yards off her port bow on a parallel course. *Hipper* opened fire; *Berwick* turned to bring her broadside to bear and replied at 0700. In a running fire-fight neither side registered any hits until 0705 when an 8-inch shell struck and disabled *Berwick*'s "X" turret. *Hipper* hit *Berwick* again at 0708 below the waterline abreast "B" turret, causing flooding. Two more shells found their target and caused more flooding. *Berwick*'s salvos were tightly grouped but failed to hit the mark, although *Hipper*'s crew found splinters aboard after the action. At this point rain squalls moved between the cruisers allowing *Hipper* to disengage to the northwest. The time was 0714. The convoy had scattered, and more concerned with regrouping than pursuit, *Berwick* did not follow. *Hipper* fired 185 8-inch rounds and 113 4.1-inch rounds, hitting *Berwick* four times (only two rounds exploded) and damaging *Empire Trooper* and *Arabistan*. When she returned to Great Britain *Berwick* went into dock and stayed there for six months.

Short of fuel and with her finicky turbines acting up, *Hipper* headed for Brest. She encountered and sank the cargo ship *Jumna* (6,078 tons) at 1000 hours that morning and made Brest on the 27th, evading British air patrols along the way. This cruise, unsatisfying to the Germans, frightened the British Admiralty. Confronted by the specter of a convoy carrying forty thousand precious lives ravaged by a battleship or heavy cruiser, the Admiralty hurried to assign heavy warships to convoy duty.

These escorts got the opportunity to show their utility during a flurry of activity by German raiders that lasted from October 1940 to May 1941. On 12 February *Hipper*, at sea once again, encountered an unescorted convoy of nineteen ships seven hundred sixty miles west of Gibraltar and sank seven totaling 32,806 tons. However, a greater menace was astride the sea lanes to the north. *Gneisenau* and *Scharnhorst* sailed from Germany on 23 January 1941 under the command of Admiral Günther Lütjens. With luck and skill Lütjens narrowly avoided the British Home Fleet and broke out into the North Atlantic. On 8 February *Gneisenau* sighted convoy HX106, forty-one ships strong. The German warships were steaming to conduct a head-on pincher attack against this rich prize when the British battleship *Ramillies* hove into view. Rejecting the plea of his captains to attack anyway, Lütjens retreated south at high speed. *Ramillies* only glimpsed *Scharnhorst* and from such a distance, she wasn't sure what she saw. Twice more during this long cruise that went from the Baltic to Greenland's west coast, from the Arctic Ocean to the Cape Verde Islands, Lütjens's squadron encountered convoys protected by British battleships. On 7 and 8 March *Malaya* and two cruisers prevented an attack on the fifty-four ships of SL67. The battleships came within range, but did not exchange salvos (although the German battleships did vector in U-boats, which sank five vessels from this convoy and damaged *Malaya*). On 15 and 16 March, however, Lütjens was finally able to justify his cruise when he steamed right into the path of a dispersed convoy of unescorted tankers. The battleships sank or captured six tankers totaling 40,079 tons on 15 March and ten more of 42,371 tons on 16 March. In fact, *Gneisenau* was in the process of picking up survivors from a burning vessel that evening when her radar detected a large contact. This was *Rodney*, armed with the biggest guns afloat in the Atlantic. When challenged, *Gneisenau* identified herself as HMS *Emerald* and, while *Rodney* considered this reply, she fled south at thirty-two knots, keeping the sinking tanker between herself and the British battleship.

Gneisenau and *Scharnhorst* made Brest on 22 March 1941 after a successful cruise. However, British dispositions combined with German caution saved at least two convoys from a powerful surface attack. Only one escorted convoy lost ships to a German warship when *Scheer* sank the armed merchant cruiser *Jervis Bay* and five ships of HX84's thirty-seven ships on 5 November 1940. And in this case the escort was not a purpose-built warship. Although the winter of 1941 was the acme of cruiser warfare in the Atlantic, Germany shied away from attacking escorted convoys. The only surface actions pitting convoy escorts against German warships would all occur in the Arctic Ocean, not the Atlantic.

4

THE *BISMARCK* CYCLE OF BATTLES
May 1941

The naval situation was both obscure and tense, and the Admiralty . . . became conscious of something coming, and also, acutely, of our full-spread target of merchant shipping.

WINSTON CHURCHILL

The pursuit and destruction of *Bismarck* was one of the most famous and dramatic naval events of World War II. During the German battleship's brief voyage, the German and British navies fought three distinct actions that ended in *Bismarck*'s destruction, a victory that came at a critical juncture in the war and helped offset the severe losses the British navy was suffering in the Mediterranean off Crete.

By April 1941 Grossadmiral Raeder's strategy of using heavy ships for cruiser warfare was proving successful and "it seemed that timid spirits who had cautioned against exposing the nucleus fleet, and who were reluctant to test the efficiency of British containment, had been proved wrong."[1] *Admiral Scheer* and *Admiral Hipper* had just returned from productive North Atlantic forays where they sank twenty-five freighters totaling 144,275 tons; German raiders were active on Allied sea lanes in three oceans and *Gneisenau* and *Scharnhorst* were harbored in Brest after a

Table 4.1. Engagements with *Bismarck*

Date	Location	Name	Opponent	Type
24-May-41	North Atlantic	Denmark Strait	British	Interception
26/27-May-41	North Atlantic	Destroyer Action	British/PO	Interception
27-May-41	North Atlantic	Sinking of the *Bismarck*	British	Interception

two-month rampage through the North Atlantic. They sank 115,622 tons of shipping despite restrictive rules of engagement and cautious handling and completely disrupted the British convoy system. *Bismarck* and *Prinz Eugen* were nearly ready for action. Raeder was putting the final touches on an operation that would deliver the heaviest strike of all against Britain's beleaguered Atlantic supply line: simultaneous sorties by three battleships and a cruiser.

Raeder's hammer blow did not fall, however, at the time or with the force planned because a successful air attack against *Gneisenau* and engine problems on *Scharnhorst* rendered these valuable ships unavailable. Then there was a month's delay when *Prinz Eugen* struck a mine returning from training maneuvers with *Bismarck*. The operation entitled Rheinübung finally commenced on 18 May with only *Bismarck* and *Prinz Eugen*, commanded by Admiral Günther Lütjens who led *Gneisenau* and *Scharnhorst* on their successful cruise. Lütjens wasn't even out of the Baltic, however, before the British had news of his sailing. Surprise was critical to Rheinübung's success, but Lütjens regained some advantage when he slipped away from Bergen, Norway, unseen on the evening of 21 May after having been photographed by a British Spitfire some hours earlier. There were only three exits into the broad reaches of the North Atlantic; against the advice of Naval Group North Lütjens elected the most distant and narrow, the Denmark Strait. It had served him well several months before.

The next day in Scapa Flow Admiral John C. Tovey, commander of the Home Fleet flying his flag aboard *King George V*, learned *Bismarck* had vanished from Norwegian waters. He had already sent Vice Admiral Lancelot Holland's Battle Cruiser Squadron consisting of *Hood*, *Prince of Wales* (Captain J. C. Leach), and six destroyers toward Iceland. He deployed his other forces based upon the enemy's possible routes, the most likely of which he considered to be the Denmark Strait. He then led *King George V*, the aircraft carrier *Victorious*, four cruisers, and seven destroyers to sea to await events.

Battle of Denmark Strait, 24 May 1941

TIME: 0552–0609 British Double Standard Time, 0152–0209 Local Time. Sunset 0151, sunrise 0637

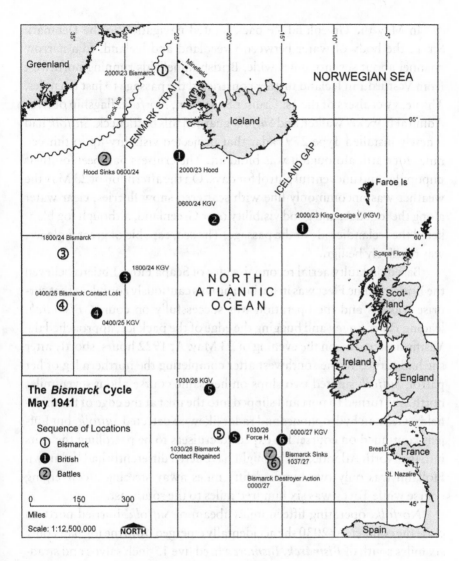

The *Bismarck* Cycle
May 1941

Sequence of Locations
① Bismarck
❶ British
② Battles

0   150   300
Miles
Scale: 1:12,500,000   NORTH

TYPE:	Interception
WEATHER:	Overcast, moderate north-westerly wind
VISIBILITY:	Excellent, about 30,000 yards
SEA STATE:	Moderate swells
SURPRISE:	None
MISSION:	British—interception based upon general intelligence; German—offensive and sea superiority commerce raiding

In May the Greenland ice pack limited navigation in the Denmark Strait, the body of water between Greenland and Iceland, to a narrow channel about seventy miles wide. British minefields running northwest from Vestfirdir in Iceland further constricted the passage to just ten miles. The heavy cruisers of the 1st Cruiser Squadron, *Norfolk*, flagship of Rear Admiral F. Wake-Walker, and *Suffolk* guarded this bottleneck. *Suffolk* had a newly installed Type 279 radar that projected visibility up to thirteen miles forward, although it was blind aft. The cruisers had been on their unpopular and uneventful patrol for days. On the afternoon of 23 May the weather was uncommonly fine with scattered snow flurries, clear water along the ice edge, and good visibility over Greenland, although fog blanketed the Icelandic side of the passage. The sea, capable of great violence, was relatively benign.

Based on faulty aerial reconnaissance of Scapa Flow, Lütjens believed the British Home Fleet was in harbor; he was cautiously confident that surprise was his and the operation was successfully on course. *Bismarck*, leading *Prinz Eugen* and hugging the edge of the pack ice, approached the Vestfirdir narrows on the evening of 23 May. At 1922 hours, shortly after she had turned to the southwest after completing the northern leg of her patrol, *Suffolk* sighted two ships on her same course about seven miles north. She turned to port and slipped into the mist at the edge of the minefields. German hydrophones and radar likewise detected *Suffolk*, but Lütjens continued on course. He expected cruisers to be patrolling the exits into the North Atlantic, but he might have acted differently had he known Holland was only two hundred fifty miles away steering a converging course while Tovey was six hundred miles to the southeast.

Norfolk, operating fifteen miles abeam of *Suffolk*, hurried north to close the contact. At 2030 she accidentally emerged from the fog bank only six miles south of *Bismarck*. *Bismarck* fired five 15-inch salvos and straddled the cruiser throwing splinters aboard. *Norfolk* came hard about and regained the safety of the fog. The blast from her heavy guns disabled *Bismarck*'s forward radar set. For this reason, and because he wanted *Bismarck*'s guns to cover the cruisers which were now trailing astern, Lütjens ordered *Prinz Eugen* to take the lead. The Germans steamed south at thirty knots, followed by the British ten to fourteen miles behind.

At 0012 hours on the 24th Vice Admiral Holland, leading the *Hood*, *Prince of Wales*, and four destroyers altered course from northwest to north-northwest. He hoped to cross in front of the enemy in two hours, just after sunset. This would silhouette the German ships against the setting sun, giving him the advantage of light. Moreover, by crossing the enemy's T his full broadside would bear while the Germans would be limited to their forward turrets. However, shortly before his change of course, *Suffolk* lost contact with *Bismarck* in a snowstorm. When he received this news, Holland could no longer depend on his point of interception. At 0017 he altered to due north and reduced speed to twenty-five knots. Still hoping to obtain surprise, he maintained radio silence.

By luck or instinct, Holland's new course would have resulted in the interception he desired. At 0140 his destroyers passed only ten miles southeast of *Bismarck,* which had altered course a little to the west keeping to the edge of the pack ice. But at this time the visibility was three miles and the forces passed unseen. At 0205 Holland turned back to the south southwest fearing the Germans had altered course to the southeast and that *Bismarck* might pass astern, although he instructed his destroyers to continue searching to the north. "Holland's guess was wrong . . . (his) action had the unhappy result of causing his squadron to lose bearing on the enemy—or, less technically expressed, to drop behind."[2]

At 0247 *Suffolk* regained contact. *Bismarck* had never deviated substantially from her original course; Holland had lost his lead and his destroyers were scattered. For the next three hours the British admiral maneuvered to undo the damage. At 0321 he came to course 220 degrees and at 0342 to 240 degrees, speed twenty-eight knots. By 0400 *Bismarck* was only twenty miles northwest of *Hood* on a parallel, slightly converging course. Visibility had improved to twelve miles. At 0440 Holland further modified course 40 degrees to starboard in order to close range. His destroyers trailed thirty miles behind. Although he intended to have the cruisers engage *Prinz Eugen* while he fought *Bismarck,* he never told Wake-Walker he was approaching and they were too far north to intervene when he appeared.

All of Holland's efforts and sacrifices to achieve surprise, however, were meaningless. *Prinz Eugen*'s hydrophones had caught the sounds of the two British heavy units long before. At 0535 when *Prince of Wales* established visual contact the two forces were about twenty-nine thousand yards apart, steering on slightly converging courses, the British on 240 degrees and the Germans on 220 degrees.

Table 4.2. Battle of Denmark Strait, 24 May 1941

Allied Ships	TYP	YL	DFL	SPD	GUNS	TT	GF	DAM
Hood	BC	18	48,360	31	8×15/42 & 14×4/45		116	Sunk
Prince of Wales	BB	39	42,076	28	10×14/45 & 16×5.25/50		117	D2
Norfolk	CA	28	13,425	32	8×8/50 & 8×4/45	8×21	32	
Suffolk	CA	26	13,540	31	8×8/50 & 8×4/45	8×21	32	
German Ships								
Bismarck	BB	39	50,900	30	8×15/47 & 12×5.9/55		125	D2
Prinz Eugen	CA	38	19,042	32	8×8/60 & 12×4.1/65	12×21	35	

Bismarck, Prinz Eugen, and *Prince of Wales* were all facing action for the first time. Both *Bismarck* and *Prinz Eugen*—completed in August 1940—were thoroughly worked up while the builders had delivered *Prince of Wales* a scant seven weeks before, hardly time to correct mechanical problems and train a battleship's crew.[3] Moreover, she sailed with a hundred Vickers-Armstrong workers fixing last-minute defects. *Hood,* a more experienced ship, was old, unmodernized, and had an inadequate fire control system. She was particularly vulnerable to long-range shell fire.

Weather and visibility had improved, although the northern twilight was not due to end for another hour. Holland altered course at 0537 turning 40 degrees toward the Germans. Lütjens responded two minutes later, turning 45 degrees away from the British, coming to course 265 degrees. This alteration decreased the rate of closing and caused the rear turrets of the British ships to lose bearing. Holland maintained his heading until 0549. With the range at nearly twenty-six thousand yards he altered 20 degrees to starboard to course 300 degrees. This resulted in an angle of convergence of 35 degrees and a rate of closure of about five hundred twenty yards per minute. *Prince of Wales* followed the flag twenty-four hundred yards off her starboard quarter. Holland knew well *Hood*'s vulnerability to long-range fire and it seemed his intention to close as rapidly as possible. However, he had "in effect allowed the enemy to cross his T by his own course alterations."[4] Lütjens was still uncertain what he was facing, but the enemy's speed told him that they were not old battleships he could outmaneuver.

The battle began at 0552 when *Hood* opened fire at *Prinz Eugen* from about twenty-five thousand yards. Her shots fell well wide. Despite Holland's signal to target the lead vessel, *Prince of Wales* fired a five-gun salvo a minute later at *Bismarck* from approximately twenty-six thousand yards. Her shells splashed beyond *Bismarck,* hanging giant columns of water two hundred feet in the air. Now Lütjens knew he was facing fast battleships. At 0553/54 he ordered his column to bend 65 degrees to port to course 200 degrees in order to open his arcs of fire.

The British had fired four or five times before *Bismarck* and *Prinz Eugen* settled on their new course and replied at 0555, both firing four-gun blasts at *Hood.* The range from *Bismarck* was approximately twenty-one thousand five hundred yards and from *Prinz Eugen* twenty-three thousand yards. Apparently Lütjens delayed giving the order to open fire and Captain E. Lindemann took the initiative, saying: "I won't let my ship get shot out from under my arse."[5] At the same time Holland responded to the German maneuver—and to the fact Lütjens was crossing his T—by ordering a turn 20 degrees to port, back to 280 degrees.

Between 0555 and 0559 *Prinz Eugen* fired six four-gun salvos. A high-explosive round from the third struck *Hood* and started a massive fire aft in her ready-use ammunition on the boat deck, near one of her twin 4-inch antiaircraft mountings. *Prinz Eugen* then shifted fire to *Prince of Wales* adhering to the principle that no enemy should be permitted to fire unengaged. *Bismarck* obtained straddles against *Hood* with her second and third volleys; the fourth fell short and very close.

The initial shooting by the British ships was not as good. Up to 0600 *Prince of Wales* fired nine times, but turret problems—the bane of her class—limited these to five-, and then three-gun salvos (of the six guns in her two forward turrets). She straddled with her sixth, but the fine angle and high speed of the approach prevented the British from obtaining accurate ranges. Moreover, the Germans enjoyed the weather gage, and sea and spray affected the British forward range finders. ("The 42 foot R/F in A was largely underwater.")[6] Another disadvantage suffered by the British was their diagonal angle of approach, which increased the probability of shells from a German volley striking them while the German parallel angle decreased the likelihood of a British hit.

At 0559 *Prinz Eugen* fired a full eight-gun salvo at *Prince of Wales* and claimed two hits on her port side. The decisive moment of the battle came one minute later. Holland had just ordered a 20-degree turn to port, so all eight guns would bear, when *Bismarck*'s fifth salvo arrived. The range was seventeen thousand yards. One or more shells struck *Hood* near her mainmast. Captain Leach recalled: "There was a very fierce upward rush of flame the shape of a funnel . . . and almost instantaneously the ship was enveloped in smoke from one end to the other."[7] A tremendous explosion followed. One of her crew saw "the whole forward section of *Hood* rear up from the water like the spire of a cathedral, towering above the upper deck of *Prince of Wales* as she steamed by."[8] *Prince of Wales* turned hard to starboard to avoid the wreckage.

Two official inquiries concluded that a shell from *Bismarck* penetrated *Hood*'s deck and detonated her main magazines. Other theories exist including the bursting of a 15-inch shell in the after 4-inch magazines or the detonation of these magazines by the fire from *Prinz Eugen*'s initial hit. The forward section of the ship sank at about 0603. By 0602 *Prince of Wales* had returned to course 260 degrees and resumed fire. The distance between her and *Bismarck* was down to fifteen thousand five hundred yards.

With *Hood* gone, it took *Bismarck* only a minute to shift fire and she quickly found the range. At 0602 a 15-inch shell passed through *Prince of Wale*'s bridge without exploding, although splinters killed or wounded everyone present except Captain Leach and one other man. At 0603 *Bismarck* began passing *Prinz Eugen,* forcing the cruiser to hold fire for several minutes. Also at 0603 Leach turned sharply to port assuming a course parallel to the Germans. During the next several minutes the German ships pummeled *Prince of Wales* and hit her six more times. An 8-inch shell glanced off the base of the forward 5.25-inch director without exploding, but knocking both directors out of action. A 15-inch shell struck the starboard aircraft crane and exploded abaft the after funnel, blasting splinters across the boat deck and perforating the Walrus seaplane. An 8-inch shell hit a motor launch on the boat deck and plowed through the upper part of the ship without exploding. The crew threw it overboard after it came to rest in a shell handling room. Hit number five, a 15-inch shell, pierced the hull below the waterline without exploding, but providing entry to four hundred tons of water. Finally, two 8-inch shells hit and exploded below *Prince of Wales*'s waterline, adding to the flooding.

At 0605 with the range down to fourteen thousand five hundred yards, Leach made another sharp turn to port, steering away from the Germans who continued on course. At 0609 when the range was seventeen thousand yards, Leach made smoke and broke contact. By so doing he risked court martial, but he was losing the battle and he knew that Tovey was closing as quickly as he could. It would not profit his nation to needlessly suffer the loss of another capital ship. The last shots of the action came ten minutes later at 0619 when *Suffolk* mistook an aircraft's radar shadow for *Bismarck*. She fired six salvos that fell far short.

Prince of Wales turned in a credible performance for a new ship that, by the end of the action, was limited to only two functioning guns (both of her four gun turrets broke down). She fired eighteen main battery salvos and five from her dual-purpose guns and hit *Bismarck* three times. A 14-inch shell struck amidships without exploding, damaging the aircraft launching gear and carrying away a boat. Another heavy shell penetrated the armor belt below the waterline, disabling two boilers and destroying a dynamo. The last hit was a 14-inch shell, which failed to explode as it passed through the ship below the bow-wave. This round pierced two tanks and cut off a thousand tons of fuel. Leaks left *Bismarck* trailing a long, iridescent ribbon of oil. Her top speed was twenty-eight knots and two thousand tons of water in the forecastle had her down 3 degrees by the bow and listing 9 degrees to port.

Bismarck fired 93 15-inch shells and an unknown number of 5.9-inch. *Prinz Eugen* fired 178 rounds of 8-inch and 78 rounds of 4.1-inch. Aboard *Prinz Eugen*, an after-action inspection revealed a metal fragment from *Prince of Wales*, apparently the result of an "over" fired at the time *Bismarck* passed her. This was the nearest she came to suffering any damage.

There was a disagreement between Lütjens and Lindemann whether *Bismarck* should chase down and sink *Prince of Wales*.[9] The fact Lütjens let the damaged ship go accorded with his instructions and is not remarkable. The results of this famous duel are commonly explained in terms of British errors rather than German skill. Stephen Roskill, the official British historian, assembled a damning collection, most of which he laid at the feet of Vice Admiral Holland.

First, he noted that the converging approach elected by Holland was an unhappy compromise that did not close range quickly but served to reduce the fighting power of the British ships to forward turrets only. Moreover, the "diagonal approach produced just the conditions of changing rate of change of range that *Hood*'s old and flawed Dreyer fire control computer could not cope with."

The second mistake was leading the column with the venerable and vulnerable *Hood*, rather than the modern and much better armored *Prince of Wales*. Tovey almost ordered Holland to let *Prince of Wales* lead, but he didn't want to tell such a senior officer what to do.

Third, Holland never ordered Wake-Walker's cruisers to engage, although he intended they do so. He kept radio silence far too long and made no effort to coordinate his forces.

Fourth, Holland didn't permit *Prince of Wales* freedom of maneuver: "The British squadron went into battle in close order and was maneuvered throughout by the Admiral. Individual captains thus had no freedom to adjust their courses to the best advantage of their own ships."

Holland failed to properly identify his principal target, wasting several salvos on *Prinz Eugen* and he stripped himself of his destroyers for insufficient reason. Finally, he failed to utilize his technological advantages: "Search radar in the *Prince of Wales* should have been used, at least intermittently, well before action was joined."[10]

Not all of these criticisms ring completely true. For example, the close-order battle line was British practice and Holland would have risked censure if he had permitted Leach to maneuver independently. In retrospect, he was a gunnery expert; he put his trust in the big gun and by the big gun he died. Making Holland the scapegoat ignores what sank *Hood*: superior shooting and luck. The shooting of both German ships—particularly *Bismarck*—was outstanding. However, it is one thing to hit a target and another to damage it. Of seven large caliber shells that struck their targets, four failed to explode. *Bismarck* hit *Hood* in the worst possible place at the worst possible time with a shell that functioned properly, and with this single blow the British lost the battle.

Wake-Walker, the senior officer present, was now in command. He wisely decided conditions did not justify a resumption of battle and settled back to shadow the German ships. Initially Lütjens tried to shake his pursuers with frequent alterations of course and speed, but *Suffolk*'s radar defeated these maneuvers. At 1240 Lütjens turned south on a steady course at twenty-four knots. He had the whole Atlantic before him in which to vanish, but he decided that *Bismarck*'s steady loss of fuel required him to set course for St. Nazaire by the shortest possible route while *Prinz Eugen* hunted alone.

At 1839 *Bismarck* came about while in a rain squall. *Suffolk* saw her coming on radar and was turning away when *Bismarck* emerged from the mist. The battleship fired at *Suffolk* from about ten miles; near misses loosened rivets aft, but did no other damage. *Suffolk* replied with nine salvos, but these fell short. *Prince of Wales* and *Norfolk*, seeing *Suffolk* under attack, altered course toward the enemy. At 1847 *Prince of Wales* opened fire from about twenty-six thousand yards followed by *Norfolk* at 1853. However, Lütjens only intended to divert the British ships so that *Prinz Eugen* could break free for independent operations. The brief exchange of fire was over by 1856 hours, although it was long enough for two of *Prince of Wales*'s guns to malfunction.

After *Prinz Eugen* went her way Wake-Walker continued to follow. Seven capital ships, two aircraft carriers, and twelve cruisers were converging on *Bismarck* from all directions. Her eventual destruction seemed a certainty if Wake-Walker could just maintain contact.

At midnight on 24 May (2000 hours local), nine Swordfish torpedo bombers launched by *Victorious* nearly two hours before delivered an attack on *Bismarck* under very difficult conditions and hit her once. However, the battleship's violent evasive maneuvers probably did more damage as leaks sprang open in No. 2 boiler room, which flooded and had to be abandoned. Then, at 0130 hours on 25 May, *Norfolk* suddenly came into view of *Bismarck* only fourteen thousand yards distant and another short action ensued. *Prince of Wales* fired two radar-directed salvos from twenty-five thousand yards to which *Bismarck* replied. Neither force suffered damage.

Overconfidence on the part of *Suffolk*'s radar operators combined with a skillful maneuver by Lütjens caused a crisis in the pursuit at 0306 hours on 25 May. Wake-Walker was worried *Bismarck* might be luring him toward a U-boat ambush and so ordered his ships to zigzag. On the far end of each outer leg, *Suffolk* would routinely lose radar contact with *Bismarck* for ten minutes and then regain it coming back on the inner leg. Using his ship's excellent hydrophones, Lütjens deduced this pattern. During the short period when she was off scope, *Bismarck* made a wide turn to starboard. She slipped behind her pursuers and vanished into the open Atlantic. Tovey was only one hundred miles to the southeast at the time and closing rapidly.

The British did not sight *Bismarck* again until 1030 hours on 26 May, thirty-one and a half very nervous hours later. Lütjens broke radio silence and transmitted a wordy message which allowed the Admiralty to fix his approximate position. ("A retransmission of four messages the fleet commander had attempted to send the previous night.")[11] They passed this information to *King George V,* but the flagship plotted the fix on the opposite bearing. This gave the impression *Bismarck* was heading for the North Sea; Tovey came about and steamed in the wrong direction. When the error was discovered, it seemed that *Bismarck* had sailed beyond the reach of any ship capable of stopping her.

Destroyer Action, 26/27 May 1941

TIME: 2130 26 May–0610 27 May
TYPE: Interception
WEATHER: Deteriorating, high winds, rain squalls
VISIBILITY: Dark, new moon
SEA STATE: Heavy swells
SURPRISE: None
MISSION: Allies—interception based upon general intelligence, maintain contact, inflict damage; German—transit, self defense

By the morning of 26 May the British knew *Bismarck* was bound for France. She was steaming southwest one hundred fifty miles ahead of *King George V.* At 1030 hours on 26 May a Catalina flying boat, acting on Ultra information, sighted the German battleship and the chase was on once again. The Admiralty had many forces at sea converging on *Bismarck. Prince of Wales* and *Suffolk* had been forced to return to port to refuel, but the Admiralty had diverted *Rodney* (on passage to the United States for refit, loaded with five hundred passengers and with "her upper deck stacked with crated stores for the refit.")[12] She was the best ship in terms of guns and armor to fight the German battleship, especially if *Bismarck*'s speed advantage could be negated. The Admiralty had also detached the destroyers of the 4th Flotilla under Captain Philip Vian from the escort of troop convoy WS8B. As he sailed north to join Tovey, Vian picked up the Catalina's contact report and decided to steer toward the enemy instead. Admiral James Somerville, commander of Force H, was even closer, steaming from Gibraltar to interpose his ships, the battle cruiser *Renown,* the aircraft carrier *Ark Royal,* and the light cruiser *Sheffield,* between *Bis-*

marck and the safety of French waters. However, after losing *Hood,* the Admiralty was not about to match *Renown* against *Bismarck* (an interesting contrast to the practice of a year earlier when *Renown* did not hesitate to engage *Scharnhorst* and *Gneisenau* off Norway). Force H and the 4th Flotilla were all Britain had to slow *Bismarck* down and force an engagement with Tovey and his two battleships.

Somerville made contact first. At 1315 hours on 26 May he sent *Sheffield* to shadow *Bismarck* while *Ark Royal* ranged her Swordfish for an air strike. The first attack mistakenly targeted *Sheffield,* but fortunately all torpedoes missed. The second strike, lasting from 2047 until 2127, succeeded in hitting *Bismarck* with two or three torpedoes. One struck the rudders and jammed them 12 degrees to port. As a result, *Bismarck* could only steer head to the wind in a northerly direction, straight at Tovey. At 2140 before properly assessing the damage Lütjens, wrapped in a private Götterdämmerung, signaled: "Ship no longer maneuverable. We fight to the last shell. Long live the Führer."

The surface action began even as Lütjens was signaling; *Bismarck* turned and fired six accurate salvos at *Sheffield* from sixteen thousand yards and came close enough to spray the cruiser with splinters, killing three men and wounding another eight. *Sheffield* backed off and spotting Vian's destroyers, she directed them toward the enemy. Although *Sheffield* reported *Bismarck's* course as north, the British did not appreciate the extent of her damage.

Conditions were difficult for the small warships—a northwest gale was blowing with high seas and frequent rain squalls. The destroyers

Table 4.3. Destroyer Action, 26–27 May 1941

Allied Ships	TYP	YL	DFL	SPD	GUNS	TT	GF	DAM
Sheffield	CL	35	11,350	32	12×6/50 & 8×4/45	6×21	29	D1
Piorun (PO)	DD	40	2,330	36	6×4.7/45 & 1×4/45	5×21	9	
Cossack	DD	37	2,519	36	6×4.7/45 & 2×4/45	4×21	11	D1
Zulu	DD	37	2,519	36	6×4.7/45 & 2×4/45	4×21	11	D1
Maori	DD	37	2,519	36	6×4.7/45 & 2×4/45	4×21	11	
Sikh	DD	37	2,519	36	6×4.7/45 & 2×4/45	4×21	11	
German Ship								
Bismarck	BB	39	50,900	10	8×15/47 & 12×5.9/55		125	

approached *Bismarck* in the dying light of the day from the northwest in line abreast forty-four hundred yards apart with Vian's flagship, *Cossack*, in the center, flanked to the northeast by *Maori* and *Piorun* and to the southwest by *Sikh* and *Zulu*. *Piorun* made first contact at 2238, reporting *Bismarck* about sixteen thousand yards distant bearing 145 degrees and steering southeastward. At 2242 *Bismarck*'s guns targeted *Piorun* and *Maori*. *Piorun* approached the battleship while *Maori* attempted to maneuver to the north. At 2248 Vian signaled his ships to shadow and attack only if serious risk could be avoided. Meanwhile, at 2306 Tovey altered course and decided to defer his engagement with *Bismarck* until dawn. This left Vian the task of maintaining contact throughout the night and ensuring the prize was properly delivered.

The four British Tribals maneuvered in a southeasterly direction ending up astern and to the west of *Bismarck*. From the northwest *Piorun* closed to thirteen thousand five hundred yards and opened fire, but after three salvos, a 15-inch shell missed her by only twenty yards whereupon she made smoke and turned away to port. She worked around to the northeast of *Bismarck*, but lost touch after 2355 having been under sporadic fire for nearly an hour.

At about 2300 *Bismarck* came to a northwesterly course, which she held for the remainder of the engagement. At this point she was engaging *Piorun* to the northwest. *Maori* was still to the northwest as well while *Cossack* was trailing her to the west-northwest. *Zulu* was to the southwest and *Sikh*, which had crossed *Zulu*'s stern, was farther to the west. At 2342 *Bismarck* straddled *Cossack*, then some seven thousand yards to the south southwest, inflicting splinter damage and shooting away her aerials. *Cossack* turned away under smoke. Eight minutes later the battleship straddled *Zulu* as well, damaging her gunnery director and wounding three men. *Zulu* likewise took evasive action. *Bismarck*, making the first combat use of night radar ranging, was an extremely dangerous opponent.

During the next hour and a half *Bismarck* steered erratically to the northwest, strenuously trying to fix the damage *Ark Royal*'s Swordfish had inflicted on her rudder and using her engine to change course. She had no idea how many destroyers were attacking her. By 0000 hours on 27 May *Cossack* was about ten thousand five hundred yards southeast of *Bismarck* with *Zulu* thirteen thousand and *Sikh* sixteen thousand yards off strung out in the same direction. *Maori* was about twelve thousand yards south, about five thousand yards west and slightly south of *Cossack*. *Piorun* was somewhere to the north, out of touch. At 0020 hours on 27 May *Bismarck* fired on *Sikh* and then altered course with her engines, temporarily breaking contact. The wind continued to blow harder. Seas were breaking green over the destroyers and spray reached as high as their bridges. At 0040 Vian, fretting whether he could reestablish contact and maintain it all night, ordered his ships to take any opportunity to attack with torpedoes. At approximately 0100 Tovey, also nervous, ordered star shell fired. Then, at 0110 hours, *Zulu* found *Bismarck* once again. She fired her full load of four torpedoes at 0121 from a position five thousand yards off *Bismarck*'s port beam. *Bismarck* replied with gunfire, but neither ship hit the other.

While the battleship's attention was thus distracted, *Maori* launched two torpedoes at 0137 from four thousand yards fine off the battleship's port quarter, followed closely by *Cossack* three minutes later, which fired three more from six thousand yards at *Bismarck*'s starboard beam, her target silhouetted by the broadside she was firing at *Maori*. *Maori* fled to ten thousand yards, bracketed by straddling columns of water. *Maori* claimed two hits and *Cossack* one.

At 0148 *Zulu* reported that *Bismarck* had stopped. *Sikh* came up and at 0218 fired all four of her torpedoes from seven thousand yards south and astern of the stationary ship. Her lookouts reported one hit. However, at 0240, *Bismarck* was under way once more. The destroyers continued to shadow. At 0325 *Cossack* launched her last torpedo from four thousand yards to the north, but it missed and *Bismarck* drove her off with heavy fire.

At 0400 the destroyers lost contact once again and, for two anxious hours, *Bismarck* remained hidden. Then, as dawn approached, *Maori* found her again. She fired her last two torpedoes at 0656 from nine thousand yards. *Bismarck* straddled her as *Maori* escaped at high speed. Then, with *Bismarck* in the bag, the destroyers settled back to await Tovey's battleships.

The British Tribal class destroyers were designed for gun actions, carrying only half the torpedo complement of the typical British Fleet destroyer. The extreme weather made it difficult for the destroyers to coordinate their actions and although they claimed four hits from the sixteen torpedoes fired, the battleship's survivors asserted that no torpedoes struck the ship that night. It is likely that the destroyers' only contribution was to deprive *Bismarck*'s crew of a night's rest.

Sinking of the *Bismarck*, 27 May 1941

TIME: 0842–1040
TYPE: Interception
WEATHER: Northwest gale, wind force 6–7
VISIBILITY: Low clouds, leaden sky, and some haze
SEA STATE: Heavy swells
SURPRISE: None
MISSION: British—interception based upon specific intelligence;
               German—transit, self defense.

A nasty day dawned on 27 May. A gale from the northwest blew spume from heavy seas. Low clouds and a heavy gray sky closed over the crippled *Bismarck* much like the trap the British had drawn around her. At first light Vian's four destroyers hove in sight, shadowing at a safe distance; then, just before 0800 hours, *Norfolk*, at the end of a long and bitterly sustained chase, came into view from the northeast. (There is the impression Wake-Walker was trying to offset some failure of duty because he had been out of place when *Bismarck* sank *Hood*; because he pursued rather than engaged *Bismarck*; and because *Suffolk* lost contact, even though the first and third events were beyond his control and he made the correct decision in the second case.)

Sheffield remained in the vicinity and *Dorsetshire* was at hand having steamed six hundred miles from the south into a heavy sea. At 0810 hours *Renown* turned south to leave the battle sea clear for the force de main, *King George V* and *Rodney* sweeping in from the west northwest. *Rodney*, commanded by Captain F. H. G. Dalrymple-Hamilton, was capable of twenty, perhaps twenty-one, knots. *King George V*, under Captain W. R. Patterson, had been in service since 1939, but this would be her first (and only) surface action. Fuel was a matter of grave concern with *King George V* at less than 30 percent capacity, while *Rodney* had indicated she would be forced to break off by 0800 hours on 27 May.

King George V and *Rodney* sailed in open order at nineteen knots with *Rodney* twelve hundred yards off *King George V*'s port quarter. (Tovey had resolved to let *Rodney* maneuver independently after the events at Denmark Strait.) At 0842 an officer aboard *King George V* spotted *Bismarck* against the rising sun thirty thousand yards off, fine on her starboard bow,

Table 4.4. Sinking of the *Bismarck*, 27 May 1941

Allied Ships	TYP	YL	DFL	SPD	GUNS	TT	GF	DAM
King George V	BB	39	42,076	28	10×14/45 & 16×5.25/50		117	
Rodney	BB	25	41,250	21	9×16/45 & 12×6/50	2×24.5	117	D1
Dorsetshire	CA	29	13,425	32	8×8/50 & 8×4/45	8×21	32	
Norfolk	CA	28	13,425	32	8×8/50 & 8×4/45	8×21	32	

German Ship

Bismarck	BB	39	50,900	10	8×15/47 & 12×5.9/55		125	Sunk

"veiled in distant rainfall a thick squat ghost of a ship . . . coming straight toward us, end on."[13] Sailing at six knots and steering with her engines *Bismarck* turned slightly to starboard to bring her broadside to bear. By this time there was no miracle Lütjens could envision that would result in *Bismarck*'s survival; all he could hope was that his ship would sell herself dearly, hardly a mission to inspire his young and inexperienced crew.

The battle's first salvo thundered from *Rodney*'s "A" and "B" turrets at 0847 at a range of twenty-five thousand yards followed a minute later by another from *King George V*. At those distances the shells took nearly a minute to reach their target, flying clearly visible across the sky. At 0850 *Bismarck* returned *Rodney*'s fire. Her first salvo was a thousand yards short and her second a thousand yards over. Her third salvo fired at 0851 straddled; one shell missed by only twenty yards, peppering *Rodney*'s anti-aircraft director with hot metal fragments and lightly wounding one man. This was good shooting and it forced *Rodney* to maneuver, costing her the range. Meanwhile, *King George V* controlled her shooting with her Type 284 radar because *Bismarck*'s head-on approach and a rain squall confounded her range finders. Moreover, the operator confused the fall of *Rodney*'s shot with his own and didn't figure out his mistake until 0853. Then the battleship fired two six-gun salvos from a range of twenty thousand five hundred yards. One shell from the second exploded in the base of *Bismarck*'s fore superstructure, igniting a large fire. At the same time *Norfolk* joined the action from twenty-two thousand yards.

At 0859 with the range at sixteen thousand yards Tovey ordered both battleships to turn to starboard on a course opposite and roughly parallel to *Bismarck* so all guns could bear. *Rodney* had fired overs from salvos five through seventeen but a shell from her eighteenth salvo exploded near *Bismarck*'s forward turrets and disabled both Anton and Bruno. This forced *Bismarck* to switch targets as *Rodney* was too far north for Caesar and Dora to bear. Two minutes later, the heavy cruiser *Dorsetshire* appeared from the southeast twenty thousand yards off. At this time the secondary batteries of both battleships also entered action, although briefly in the case of *King George V* because their smoke compounded her spotting problems.

By 0908 *Rodney* had closed to eleven thousand yards and had launched six torpedoes. *Norfolk* fired four more from sixteen thousand yards. These were long ranges and although *Bismarck* was maneuvering only in broad arcs in a constant northwesterly direction, no torpedoes hit. At this time, *King George V* was fourteen thousand yards west of *Bismarck*. The German was using her after director to control fire against *King George V*, but a 14-inch shell disabled it after only four salvos. The gun passed to local control and accuracy dropped off rapidly. At 0913 *King George V*, which had been shooting well (she recorded fourteen straddles in twenty-two salvos fired), lost her 284 radar to shock damage.

Rodney passed astern of *Bismarck* on a southerly heading and began to experience problems with the direction of the swells and wind blowing smoke forward over her guns. At 0916 she altered course 180 degrees to starboard, closing range to eight thousand yards. At 0920 *Bismarck* shifted fire to this nearer threat, but one minute later a premature explosion wracked Dora's starboard gun. The port barrel fired two more rounds before damage forced Dora to cease fire altogether.

At 0920 *King George V* also came around back to a northerly heading. The accuracy of her fire suffered when she switched to her Type 279 radar for ranging; then, at 0922, a jammed loading mechanism knocked the four guns of "A" turret out of commission for thirty minutes. Turret problems continued and at one point, she was reduced to firing two-gun broadsides. *Rodney*, however, continued to hit with her main and secondary batteries. One of *Bismarck*'s last salvos near-missed *Rodney* and jammed a torpedo sluice. Then, at 0931 a hit on Caesar silenced *Bismarck*'s big guns. The British battleships closed range rapidly thereafter, pounding the German with both their main and secondary batteries. The scene was spectral. "About this time, the coppery glow of our secondary armament shells striking the armoured upper works became more and more frequent and one fierce flame shot up from the base of the bridge structure, enveloping it as high as . . . the spotting top for a flickering second."[14]

Aboard *Bismarck* conditions were frightful. One survivor remembered escaping from his battle station into the open:

> I was horrified at what I saw in the forward conning tower. All of the fire- and ship-control equipment was demolished, and debris was pushed forward and aft of the tube opening in two piles. The intermediate deck that supported the fire-control position was gone, and the deck of the conning tower was cracked. A fine red dust was all around the deck. . . . British shells continued to hit the *Bismarck* and created such a noise that I could hardly think.[15]

Between 0952 and 1003 *Rodney* fired broadsides at maximum depression, hitting repeatedly, but the blast from her guns buckled her wooden decks. *King George V* stood three thousand yards off, firing as rapidly as possible in Tovey's haste to sink his stoutly constructed opponent. At 0958 *Rodney* fired four more torpedoes and claimed a hit on the starboard side. Given that they were shooting from point-blank range at a large target that couldn't maneuver or fire back, British gunnery was poor. Tovey at one point reportedly complained he would have a better chance of hitting *Bismarck* by throwing his binoculars than with *King George V*'s guns. Even though she had been in service a year and a half longer than *Prince of Wales*, the flagship suffered many of the same problems: one turret was out of action for thirty minutes and the other two for shorter periods. For seven minutes both four-gun turrets were inoperable leaving her to fight with only two guns.

Rodney ceased fire at 1014 having expended 375 rounds of 16-inch, 716 rounds of 6-inch, and 12 torpedoes; as many as 40 of her 2,048-pound shells hit their target. *King George V* ceased fire at 1021. She fired 339 14-inch shells and 660 5.25-inch. *Norfolk* contributed 527 8-inch rounds and *Dorsetshire* 254. This tremendous expenditure of ammunition resulted in three to four hundred hits, which shredded *Bismarck*'s superstructure. However, few, if any, shells penetrated the armored citadel. *Bismarck*'s honeycomb of watertight compartments made her extremely difficult to sink with gunfire alone.

Tovey was then faced with three problems: little fuel remained on his battleships; the threat of U-boats, which he could safely assume had been ordered to the area en masse, and the fact that *Bismarck* was still afloat. *Norfolk* tried to solve the third problem with her last four torpedoes. Although she registered one hit, there was no noticeable effect. At 1020 *Dorsetshire* fired two torpedoes on *Bismarck*'s starboard side from thirty-two hundred yards and observed two impacts. She then hove around to port and at 1036 launched a final torpedo from twenty-six thousand yards, the last of seventy-one fired at *Bismarck* over the past three days. This one was enough.

The crew was in the process of abandoning ship, carefully timing their leaps so the twenty-foot waves would not throw them back aboard or crush them against the hull. From the water the destruction was appalling.

> As I was swept along the port side of the battleship, I saw . . . gun barrels pointed in every direction, and some of the smaller gun mounts were destroyed totally. One of the 380-mm guns in turret Dora was shredded by what appeared to have been an internal explosion in the barrel. The *Bismarck* was slowly capsizing and sinking by the stern.[16]

At 1040 *Bismarck* finally sank. Whether British torpedoes or German scuttling charges were the catalyst is only a matter of pride. British ships lingered long enough to pull 110 oil soaked men from the frigid water before hauling off. Two small German auxiliary vessels arrived on the scene hours later and rescued 5 more men. More than 2,000 perished.

This victory came at a time of desperate British need and the government exaggerated their navy's accomplishment for propaganda reasons. In the month of May 1941, excluding *Hood* and damage sustained fighting *Bismarck*, the British navy lost three cruisers, eight destroyers, three minesweepers, a gunboat, and a sloop. An additional three battleships, five cruisers, one aircraft carrier, and five destroyers were damaged. It was not remarkable the British navy sank *Bismarck*; it was remarkable, given the resources deployed against her, that *Bismarck* so nearly escaped. In fact, to sink one battleship, the British required three surface actions and two air attacks and in the process lost one battle cruiser, suffered moderate damage to one battleship, light damage to another, light damage to two cruisers, and light damage to three destroyers. But *Bismarck*'s true impact was not the damage she inflicted.

Bismarck cast a long shadow over future British operations. The threat of encore by *Tirpitz* or even *Scharnhorst* acted like a chain around the neck of the British navy. The exaggerated measures to contain *Tirpitz* and the undertaking of operations like the raid on St. Nazaire (just a month after Germany went to such pains to withdraw her heavy surface units from the Atlantic coast) demonstrated that *Bismarck* had established a threat that Great Britain feared. In some respects Germany actually won a strategic victory in May 1941, but it was a victory her leaders never realized, and so it was one her navy never fully exploited.

5

ACTIONS IN SOVIET WATERS
1941

Even when Soviet major surface forces, mostly destroyers, met
on a few occasions much inferior Axis forces, they always broke
off the engagement after a few salvoes.

JÜRG MEISTER

The Soviet Union possessed a large navy at the start of World
War II. Even though they operated in four separate theaters
(the Baltic Sea, the Arctic Ocean, the Black Sea, and the Pacific Ocean) the
Soviets were the superior power in the Black Sea and a match for the Germans in the Baltic and Arctic. In June 1941 the navy deployed the following major warships, although not all were operational:

Table 5.1. Deployment of Major Soviet Naval Warships

Type	Baltic	Black	Arctic	Pacific	Total
Old Battleships	2	1	0	0	3
Heavy Cruisers	2	3	0	0	5
Light Cruisers	1	3	0	0	4
Destroyers	14	11	5	12	42
Old Destroyers	7	5	3	2	17
Torpedo Boats	7	2	3	6	18
Total	33	25	11	20	89

German, Finnish, Italian, and Romanian forces sank forty-one major
Soviet warships, but only one during a surface battle (and that by mines).
Destroyers were the largest Soviet vessels to face large Axis warships.
However, on three of the four occasions this happened, the Soviets disengaged in the face of inferior German forces, leaving their enemy unharmed.

Table 5.2. Actions in Soviet Waters

Date	Location	Name	Opponent	Type
26-Jun-41	Black Sea	Constanza Harbor	Soviet	Harbor Attack
6-Jul-41	Baltic Sea	Kolka Lighthouse	Soviet	Encounter
1-Aug-41	Baltic Sea	Cape Domesnäs	Soviet	Interception
7-Sep-41	Arctic Ocean	Porsanger Fjord	British	Convoy Attack
17-Dec-41	Arctic Ocean	Cape Gorodeski	British	Interception

Early mining and raiding forays in the Baltic and Black Seas with major warships were costly and achieved little, as when the cruiser *Maxim Gorky* and the destroyer *Gnevnyi* ran into a German minefield on 23 June or when S-boats torpedoed the destroyer *Storozhevoi* on 26 June.

Several factors explain the Soviet failure to successfully use their large warships. The Baltic Fleet was blockaded for much of the war; maintenance, training, and sea experience were all below German standards; naval crews were consistently drafted to form ground combat units; and the officer corps had been decimated and demoralized in the purges of the late 1930s. The Soviets employed their large submarine force and their light coastal units with greater energy. These units were better suited to Soviet capabilities and were sufficient to meet many of their requirements.

In the Black Sea the Royal Romanian Navy provided the Axis naval muscle. It deployed two modern and two old destroyers, three ex-Austro-Hungarian torpedo boats (two without torpedo tubes), along with one submarine and various antisubmarine escorts and auxiliaries. It was no match for the Soviet Black Sea Fleet. But the job of the Romanian navy, at least during the summer of 1941, was minelaying and escort duty on the oil and grain route to the Mediterranean Sea. There was no requirement to fight the Soviets on open waters and, except for one occasion at the beginning of the war, large Soviet units did not attempt to engage Romanian warships.

Bombardment of Constanza, 26 June 1941

TIME: 0400–0430
TYPE: Harbor attack
WEATHER: Fair
VISIBILITY: Good
SEA STATE: Calm

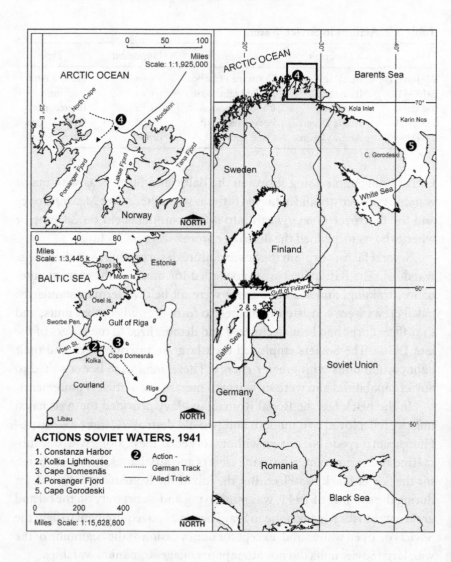

Actions Soviet Waters, 1941

1. Constanza Harbor
2. Kolka Lighthouse
3. Cape Domesnäs
4. Porsanger Fjord
5. Cape Gorodeski

SURPRISE: Soviets

MISSION: Soviets—reconnaissance and shore bombardment;
              Axis—self defense

On the evening of 25 June a Soviet task force of two large destroyers,
Kharkov and *Moskva,* covered by the heavy cruiser *Voroshilov* and the
destroyers *Smyshlennyi* and *Soobrazitelnyi* (Admiral T. A. Novikov) departed
Sevastopol "to reconnoiter by force the defensive system of the Romanian

naval base and to destroy the supplies of gasoline and oil stored there."[1] They were sixty miles east of their target when, at 0030 hours on 26 June, the Romanian submarine *Delfinul* spotted them and broadcast an alert. The Romanian warships at Constanza began to raise steam while the coastal defenses braced for an attack.

The Soviet flotilla arrived off Constanza shortly before 0400 hours. *Kharkov* and *Moskva* began a bombardment run heading south-southwest while the other warships stood off to provide support. In ten minutes the two destroyers fired 350 rounds from extreme range—twenty-one thousand to twenty-two thousand yards. They damaged the port facilities, started fires, and blew up an ammunition train at the Palas railroad station; however, they missed the oil storage tanks, their principal target.

Romanian warships in the area that morning included *Regina Maria*, one of their two modern destroyers, *Marasti* (a veteran of World War I, but still a significant unit), the minelayer *Murgescu*, and a pair of motor torpedo boats. Shore batteries included the German 11-inch "Tirpitz" to the south and the railroad battery "Bismarck" north of the city.

Regina Maria and *Marasti* lay south of the city off the cliffs of Cape Tuzla. They got under way shortly after the bombardment began while *Murgescu* sheltered beneath "Tirpitz" battery's 11-inch gun. The Romanian warships gained some offing and then turned north toward the Soviet destroyers. At 0407 a Soviet air group ineffectively attacked the harbor and the ships at sea. *Murgescu* claimed two planes shot down while *Regina Maria* claimed another.

The air attack was over when *Marasti* opened fire on the Soviet destroyers at 0412 followed by *Regina Maria* four minutes later. The range

Table 5.3. Bombardment of Constanza, 26 June 1941

Allied Ships	TYP	YL	DFL	SPD	GUNS	TT	GF	DAM
Moskva	DD	35	2,582	36	5×5.1/55 & 2×3/55	8×21	9	Sunk
Kharkov	DD	36	2,582	36	5×5.1/55 & 2×3/55	8×21	9	D1

Axis Ships and Shore Batteries								
Regina Maria	DD	28	1,850	35	5×4.7/50	8×21	7	
Marasti	DD	17	1,753	34	4×4.7/45	4×18	6	
"Tirpitz"(GE)	SB	n/a	n/a	n/a	1×11		14	
"Bismarck"(GE)	SB	n/a	n/a	n/a	1×8.26		8	

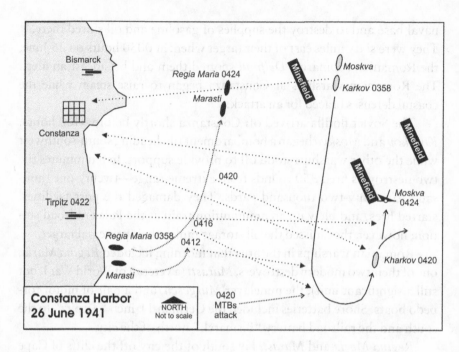

Bismarck

Regia Maria 0424

Marasti

Moskva

Karkov 0358

Minefield

Minefield

Minefield

Constanza

0420

Moskva
0424

Tirpitz 0422

Regia Maria 0358

0416

0412

Marasti

Kharkov 0420

Kharkov 0420

**Constanza Harbor
26 June 1941**

NORTH
Not to scale

0420
MTBs
attack

between the two forces was initially about eleven thousand yards, but rapidly opened to seventeen thousand. The Romanian destroyers had an advantage as they were difficult to see against the dark coast while the Soviets were silhouetted against the rising sun. They fired only twelve salvos, but with some effect, straddling *Moskva* and then hitting and toppling her main mast.

Moskva came to full speed and at 0415 she turned to port to run north-northeast. At 0420 a Romanian shell struck and lightly damaged *Kharkov*. Meanwhile, two MTBs, *Viforul* and *Vijelia,* thirty-nine-ton British built boats capable of forty knots and armed with two 21-inch torpedoes, began a run east toward the Soviet destroyers. At 0422 the pressure against the Soviets increased as the "Tirpitz" battery joined the battle (she only got off five shots before *Kharkov* passed out of range). As they sailed north, the Soviets unwittingly entered a protective minefield the Romanians had laid off the coast in the weeks leading up to war.

At 0424 *Moskva* suddenly exploded and broke in two, sinking in only five minutes. Although the explosion may have resulted from a torpedo attack by a trigger-happy Soviet submarine, a mine was the more likely cause. *Kharkov* turned east toward the protection of her covering force which frustrated the MTB attack. German float planes and the two MTBs subsequently rescued sixty-nine men from *Moskva*'s crew of 250.

Although this action represented a poor beginning, the major units of the Black Sea Fleet went on to play a decisive role in the defense and the evacuation of Odessa and Sevastopol. The Soviet Union maintained its dominance of the Black Sea throughout 1941 and 1942, although it reserved its major surface units for amphibious operations and ground support and used submarines to attack Axis shipping.

The first encounter between surface warships of the German and Soviet navies occurred two weeks into the campaign in the confined waters of the Gulf of Riga. The German navy had *Tirpitz,* two destroyers, and five torpedo boats available in the Baltic on 22 June, but didn't use these ships in the campaign, remembering the experiences of World War I when mines and submarines made the narrow waters such a perilous place for large warships to venture. Instead, the navy employed ten minelayers, about twenty M-class minesweepers, twenty-eight S-boats, sixteen R-boats, thirty trawlers as patrol boats and auxiliary minesweepers, and five U-boats to counter the strength of the Soviet Baltic Fleet.[2]

The German army advanced rapidly up the Baltic coast and on 2 July captured Riga, capital of Latvia and the principal port on the southern Baltic shore between Konigsberg and Kronstadt. The navy quickly began sweeping mines so they could use Riga to supply Army Group North.

Encounter off Kolka Lighthouse, 6 July 1941

TIME: 1200–1415
TYPE: Encounter
WEATHER: Fair
VISIBILITY: Extreme
SEA STATE: Calm
SURPRISE: None
MISSION: Soviets—offensive mining and patrol; Germans—escort
              and transit

On July 5 Naval Group East ordered the depot ship *MRS11* (*Minenraumschiff-11*), a former merchant ship equipped with twelve motor launches for sweeping shallow mines, to clear Riga harbor. The minesweepers *M23* and *M31* of the 5th Flotilla provided her escort. Early on the morning of 6 July, Soviet aircraft unsuccessfully bombed this little task force. At 1025, the senior German officer aboard *MRS11* received orders to wait at the entrance of Irben Strait for a convoy of four motor barges carrying army supplies. In view of the danger of further air attacks, he elected to proceed with *M31*, leaving *M23* to meet the barges. That same morning, a Soviet force under Commander G. S. Abaschwili consisting of the destroyers *Serdityi* and *Silnyi* with two smaller vessels, probably *Tral* class minesweepers, was mining the waters off the Sworbe Peninsula. At 1200 hours they spotted the German ships to their south.

The Soviets quickly dropped their dangerous cargo and approached, one destroyer with the two smaller ships steering east, the other southwest to block the German line of retreat. The Germans were heading east-northeast at the time. The group of three Soviet warships opened fire at nineteen thousand five hundred yards and their first salvos straddled *MRS11*. The Germans returned fire when the distance closed to sixteen thousand yards, the maximum range of their 4.1-inch guns, and Soviet marksmanship deteriorated appreciably. Appropriately concerned by the size of the force facing her, *M31* attempted to make smoke, but her apparatus malfunctioned. However, as she took up position off *MRS11*'s port bow, the Soviets turned away apparently mistaking the minesweeper for a destroyer launching torpedoes. The single Soviet destroyer then assumed a parallel course and all four Soviet ships began shooting once again. In the exchange *M31* hit *Silnyi* and the Soviets made smoke and turned away. From 1255 to 1330 there was a lull in the action as *MRS11* rounded Cape Domesnäs and entered the Gulf of Riga heading south. At 1330 five Soviet planes attacked and

Table 5.4. Encounter off Kolka Lighthouse, 6 July 1941

Allied Ships	TYP	YL	DFL	SPD	GUNS	TT	GF	DAM
Serdityi	DD	39	2,282	37	5×5.1/55 & 2×3/55	6×21	9	
Silnyi	DD	38	2,282	37	5×5.1/55 & 2×3/55	6×21	9	D1
Axis Ships								
MRS11	MRS	?	5,180 grt	12	3×4.1/45		3	
M31	MS	40	878	18	2×4.1/45		2	

dropped fourteen bombs. The Germans were unharmed and claimed they shot down one attacker. At 1335 the two destroyers opened fire again across Cape Domesnäs from the absurd range of twenty-seven thousand yards. Their opening salvos were very short, but they approached at high speed and the geysers from their misses drew closer. Then at 1415 the Soviet warships abruptly turned away and departed to the northwest. The Germans expended 198 4.1-inch shells and observed 120 rounds fall in their vicinity during the two-hour engagement.

Serdityi and Silnyi were both modern ships and should have been able to overwhelm a depot ship and a single minesweeper. The German commander wrote: "It is my opinion that the enemy had no clear picture of the type of ship he was confronted with. Probably he was deceived by the quick succession of our salvoes."[3] This action foretold how Soviet destroyers would fight during the remainder of the short Baltic campaign: at long ranges and in fear of torpedoes.

Attack Off Cape Domesnäs, 1 August 1941

TIME: Night
TYPE: Interception
WEATHER:
VISIBILITY: Moon 57 percent, set 0058
SEA STATE:
SURPRISE:
MISSION: Soviets—patrol and sea security; Germans—escort and
              transit

Once cleared of mines, Riga became an important destination for German coastal convoys; the Soviet navy attempted to blockade this valuable supply-head with a special unit of destroyers, torpedo cutters, and patrol boats under Rear Admiral W. P. Drozd. The route through the Irben Strait, around Cape Domesnäs and into the Gulf of Riga, saw many actions between Drozd's flotilla and German minesweepers, R-boats, and S-boats. The German navy ran its first convoy from Libau to Riga on 9 July; others followed on 12 July, 18 July, 26 July, 1 August, 17 August, 21 August, and 27 August. Soviet attacks forced the Germans to suspend operations or delay convoys several times, but they never stopped the traffic altogether.

Up through the end of August the navy delivered fifty thousand tons of supplies without loss to surface attack and very little damage.

On the night of 12–13 July seven destroyers and two torpedo boats attacked a large, slow convoy of barges, Siebel ferries, and coastal steamers escorted only by R-boats. The Germans drove the attackers off by feinting torpedo attacks. The Soviets claimed twelve transports sunk, but the worst the German ships suffered was splinter damage. On 1 August near Cape Domesnäs units of the 1st Minesweeper Flotilla repelled without loss an attack by six Soviet motor torpedo boats covered by two destroyers. The minesweepers sank the MTB *TKA 122* as the destroyers limited their participation to long-range fire.[4] When they returned to base the Soviet commander claimed his ships sank one German destroyer and two minelayers.

On the night of 28 August the Soviet navy had to abandon Revel, its last mainland base east of the Gulf of Finland. More than twenty transports and 120 warships, from heavy cruiser to motor minesweeper, set out for Kronstadt in six convoys; mines and German aircraft exacted a heavy toll, sinking five destroyers and three patrol ships and heavily damaging three more. Seeing the naval campaign in the Baltic was reaching a climax, the German navy assembled a powerful fleet under Vizeadmiral Otto Ciliax in case the Soviet fleet sought to fight or seek interment in Sweden. By September this force included the battleship *Tirpitz*, the armored cruiser *Admiral Scheer*, the light cruisers *Köln, Nürnberg, Emden*, and *Leipzig*, the destroyers *Z25, Z26*, and *Z27*, and the torpedo boats *T2, T5, T7*, and *T8* along with various smaller craft. However, the Soviet fleet focused on the defense of Leningrad, and the Germans wisely refrained from deploying their heavy ships in the confined waters of the Gulf of Finland. And so, the two fleets never met. In September Germany occupied the Estonian islands of Moon, Ösel, and Dagö and with that the Baltic Sea passed under German domination until 1944: a place to train cadets and work up new ships.

When Germany invaded the Soviet Union, the Arctic front, dormant since Great Britain's expulsion from Norway, became active once again. The ice-free port of Murmansk, the Soviet Arctic Fleet's main base, lay barely sixty miles east of the front line. The elite German XIX Mountain Corp under Generalmajor Eduard Dietl expected to quickly advance over the rocky tundra, seize Murmansk, and secure the northern front. Instead, the Arctic Fleet stymied Dietl with shore bombardments and timely amphibious landings behind German lines and brought the Germans to a halt only halfway to their objective.

Grossadmiral Raeder had warned Hitler of the need for a strong naval presence along the polar coast on 4 February and 30 March 1941, but Hitler believed Murmansk would quickly fall to a land attack and the navy would have nothing to do. Consequently, on 22 June 1941, the Admiral of the Polar Coast in Kirkenes, Vizeadmiral Otto Schenk, could only deploy nineteen patrol boats (mostly armed trawlers), two submarine chasers, eleven R-boats of the 5th Flotilla, three auxiliaries, and a small minelayer.[5] He could not dispute the Arctic Fleet's domination of the waters along the front lines. Distance and scarcity of roads forced Germany to ship most of the polar army's supplies to the Norwegian port of Kirkenes eighty miles west of Murmansk. Schenk's little fleet was hardly enough to protect this port and the shipping lanes leading to it.

In June the German command recognized they had a problem and ordered the 6th Destroyer Flotilla under Kapitän zur See Alfred Schulze-Hinrichs to Kirkenes. This unit consisted of five destroyers: Z20 *Karl Galster*, Z7 *Hermann Schoemann*, Z16 *Friedrich Echoldt*, Z4 *Richard Beitzen*, and Z10 *Hans Lody*. Their mission was to

> attack the Russian destroyers and surface craft supporting the various Soviet forces in the Litsa Bay area and to hinder any landings by the Red Army; in addition, flank attacks were to be made in support of the German Army in its advance to Murmansk.[6]

Operational elements of the flotilla (it always happened that one or more ships was suffering from some type of defect) sortied four times in 1941: 12 July, 22 July, 29 July, and 9 August. Their accomplishments fell far short of their objectives.

On their first foray the German destroyers sank two trawlers out of a convoy of three, shooting off nearly a thousand rounds in the process. On the second mission, after a sterile run all the way to the White Sea, *Hermann Schoemann* sank a naval survey ship, *Meridian* (three hundred tons), with three salvos; and on the fourth, *Richard Beitzen, Hans Lody,* and *Friedrich Echoldt* expended 270 5-inch rounds and dispatched the auxiliary trawler *Tuman/SKR12* (574 tons) in ten minutes. The flotilla failed to intervene against Soviet amphibious landings (supported by destroyers) conducted on 14 and 16 July, which were instrumental in repulsing German ground attacks out of the Litsa bridgehead, or in interfering with the evacuation of these troops on 3 August. Schenk also refused Dietl's requests for direct gunfire support, arguing the valuable destroyers couldn't be risked so close inshore.

By the middle of August only three destroyers were still operational, *Hans Lody, Karl Galster,* and *Friedrich Echoldt,* and they concentrated on escorting convoys. By November accidents, along with normal wear and tear, had reduced the 6th Destroyer Flotilla's strength to just *Karl Galster.* The flotilla was not a factor when British warships made a night raid into their area of operation.

Action off Porsanger Fjord, 7 September 1941

TIME: 0129–0144
TYPE: Interception
WEATHER: Northeasterly gale
VISIBILITY: Poor, low clouds and drizzle
SEA STATE: Heavy swells
SURPRISE: Allied
MISSION: Allied—interception based upon general intelligence;
                 German—escort and transit

The British Admiralty dispatched the light cruisers *Aurora* and *Nigeria,* the destroyers *Icarus, Antelope,* and *Anthony,* and the passenger liner *Empress of Canada* under the command of Rear Admiral Philip L. Vian to evacuate the Soviet and Norwegian colonies on Spitzbergen and destroy the island's installations. This force arrived off the polar island on 25 August and by 3 September 1941 the British had loaded its thirty-two hundred inhabitants aboard the liner and demolished all weather, radio, and power stations. *Empress of Canada* and the destroyers then sailed for home. Vian, however, acting on intelligence, turned his two cruisers toward the Norwegian coast four hundred miles south navigating to arrive at a specific point west of Nordkyn at 0030 hours on 7 September.

After a rough passage at twenty-nine knots through heavy swells and a raising northeasterly gale, Vian made his landfall and turned to the southwest at twenty knots to sweep the thirty-five-mile-wide sound between North Cape and Nordkyn. At 0126 hours Vian's flagship, *Nige-*

Table 5.5. Action off Porsanger Fjord, 7 September 1941

Allied Ships	TYP	YL	DFL	SPD	GUNS	TT	GF	DAM
Nigeria	CL	39	11,090	31	12×6/50 & 8×4/45	6×21	29	D1
Aurora	CL	36	7,400	32	6×6/50 & 8×4/45	6×21	20	
Axis Ships								
Bremse	GB	31	1,870	27	4×5/45		6	Sunk
UJ1701	DC	40	1,140	12	1×4.1 & 1×3.5		2	
V6103	PB	?	?	?	?		?	

ria, which was leading *Aurora* by a thousand yards, made radar contact with an enemy convoy sailing from Hammerfest to Kirkenes.

The convoy consisted of two transports, *Barcelona* (3,101 grt) and *Trautenfels* (6,418 grt) carrying fifteen hundred troops of the 6th Mountain Division escorted by the gunnery training ship *Bremse* (Korvettenkapitän H. von Brosy-Steinberg), the trawlers *V6103* (*Nordlicht*) and *UJ1701,* and the motor minesweeper *R162.*

Initially, *Nigeria* mistook her contact for land and Vian began a starboard turn to clear the coast. At that point, through the dark, the low, hanging clouds and a misty drizzle, lookouts reported one shadow off the port bow; then more shadows. Vian had found a convoy.

The German ships were sailing with *UJ1701* in the van followed by *Trautenfels* and *Barcelona. V6103* sailed on *Trautenfel's* port beam while *R162* was on *Barcelona's* starboard beam. *Bremse* zigzagged to port of *Barcelona* on the convoy's open flank.

Nigeria opened fire at 0129 hours. The transports and smaller escorts immediately turned to starboard at full speed hurrying toward the safety of the inner fjords. *Nigeria* had portions of the convoy in sight, but before she could acquire a solid target *Bremse* loomed up on her port bow. The cruisers thought a destroyer was attacking and turned their guns to counter this danger. *Bremse* increased speed to twenty-four knots and began making smoke; she returned fire as she crossed *Nigeria's* bow to starboard. The cruiser, fearing torpedoes, turned away to port as *Bremse* disappeared into the smoke, heading in an easterly direction. In this brief engagement both cruisers hit the German warship repeatedly with 6-inch down to 2-pdr pompom rounds, knocking her center gun out of action.

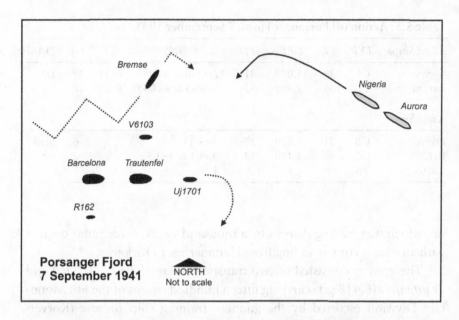

Vian came about in pursuit, but he had hardly steadied on an easterly heading before there was *Bremse* coming as if to ram. The time was 0134 hours. She passed between the two cruisers forcing *Aurora* to avoid a collision by turning sharply to starboard. *Nigeria* raked the enemy with three broadsides and *Aurora* claimed multiple light and medium hits on the German's bridge. Then, only three minutes after regaining contact, *Bremse*'s smoke screen enveloped *Nigeria*. Immediately, the cruiser shuddered from a sudden and severe impact to her bow. The damage control parties scrambled to their stations and, as reports rapidly came in, Vian found, to his relief, *Nigeria* could still steam and fight and no one had been hurt. The cruiser retreated from the smoke to find *Aurora* and *Bremse* trading broadsides. At 0140 a shell from *Aurora* exploded amidships on *Bremse*. She altered course and then experienced another, larger explosion aft, which seemed like a torpedo detonation to British observers and German survivors. This blow wrecked her steering and left only her forward gun in action. The German ship turned away listing and heavily damaged.

At 0144 the British cruisers aimed their guns on a target identified as a trawler. Then *Aurora* encountered *Bremse* once again. She fired five more broadsides into the unfortunate ship. As *Bremse* drifted away to the north, the cruisers engaged another unidentified target. They then hauled off through thickening weather to the northwest and home as the short polar night was ending. Beside *Nigeria*'s collision, both cruisers had splinter damage but were otherwise unharmed.

Bremse slowly foundered, and although five patrol boats mounted a rescue effort they saved only 37 men. Korvettenkapitän von Brosy-Steinberg and 159 others perished in this action. British claims are summarized in their daily war situation telegram to President Roosevelt.

IN FOUL WEATHER AT 08.30/7 NIGERIA AND AURORA ENGAGED ENEMY FORCE IN INLET EAST NORTH CAPE; RESULT OBSCURE BUT SEEMS CERTAIN THAT SMALL DESTROYER, ONE TRAWLER AND ANOTHER SHIP SUNK. GERMAN BREMSE AND ANOTHER SHIP WERE HARD HIT AND OUR SIDE MAY HAVE TORPEDOED FORMER. WE SUFFERED NO CASUALTIES BUT NIGERIA DAMAGED HER BOW BY RAMMING A WRECK IN A SMOKE SCREEN.[7]

The poor visibility and the frenetic pace of the action contributed to these exaggerated claims. *Bremse*, for example, was sequentially identified as a destroyer, an F class escort, and then as herself. In fact she was the only ship hit by British gunfire. Given that Vian's cruisers were between her and the convoy when action commenced, she conducted a skillful defense. If a transport had been sunk, hundreds more would have died in the icy water. The source of *Nigeria*'s damage is something of a mystery. The waters where the engagement took place were deep and there have been suggestions a Soviet submarine, which was subsequently lost, torpedoed both her and *Bremse*. It is more likely in the dark, smoke, and confusion she accidentally rammed *Bremse*.[8]

This action influenced the subsequent movements of the 6th Mountain Division. On 15 September Germany decided to suspend troop movements by sea. The fifteen hundred men from the *Bremse* convoy ended up walking 160 miles to the front instead of the fifty-five they would have marched from Kirkenes and subsequent reinforcements debarked at the head of the Gulf of Bothnia, a full 275 miles from the front. If indeed it is true that "in consequence, the land attack on Murmansk was repulsed,"[9] then Vian's foray along the Arctic coast had immense strategic consequences.

Encounter off Cape Gorodeski, 17 December 1941

TIME: 1732–1747
TYPE: Encounter

WEATHER: Fog and snow squalls
VISIBILITY: Poor
SEA STATE:
SURPRISE: Germans
MISSION: British—transit; Germans—offensive and sea superior-
              ity patrol without specific intelligence

With the depletion of the 6th Destroyer Flotilla, the German command ordered the large, but untested ships of the 8th Destroyer Flotilla
under Kapitän zur See Gottfried Pönitz north to the polar coast. Consisting of Z23, Z24, Z25, Z26, and Z27, the flotilla had gathered at Kirkenes
by 13 December. Although the 8th had been operational for more than a
year, Pönitz did not consider his ships fully combat ready. He was also worried about the shortage of torpedoes, it being his intention to use them as
his principal weapon. Nonetheless, Pönitz conducted his first combat mission four days later with his entire flotilla save Z26, which was down with
machinery problems.

At 1830 hours on 16 December, Pönitz led his ships out Kirkenes's ten-
mile-long fjord to the open waters of the Barents Sea. He stood well off the
coast, reaching a point about eighty-five miles north of Murmansk before
heading due east to the waters north of Cape Kanin, the eastern limit of the
White Sea. At 0947 hours on 17 December the Germans swept south nearing the vicinity of Cape Kanin by 1427 hours. From here they proceeded
south-southwest across the entrance of the White Sea. Nearing Cape
Gorodeski on the western shore Z25's radar detected two ships bearing
240 degrees at a range of forty-one hundred yards. Evening was coming

Table 5.6. Encounter off Cape Gorodeski, 17 December 1941

Allied Ships	TYP	YL	DFL	SPD	GUNS	TT	GF	DAM
Speedy	MS	38	1,330	17	2×4/45		2	
Hazard	MS	37	1,330	17	2×4/45		2	D3
Axis Ships								
Z23	DD	39	3,605	38	4×5.9/50	8×21	8	
Z24	DD	40	3,605	38	4×5.9/50	8×21	8	
Z25	DD	40	3,543	38	4×5.9/50	8×21	8	
Z27	DD	40	3,543	38	4×5.9/50	8×21	8	

on and visibility was poor—fog mixed with snow squalls. The Germans believed they had found two Russian destroyers, but the ships were actually the British minesweepers *Speedy* and *Hazard,* sailing at eleven knots to meet convoy PQ6.

The Germans closed range and opened fire at 1732. Three minutes later *Z25* launched three torpedoes (only one of which actually functioned) while *Z27* attempted to discharge her whole load of eight, but only got five into the water. All the torpedoes missed while the gun battle lasted only until 1748 with the targets "appearing and disappearing in the murky weather." The Germans shot off a "prodigious" amount of ordnance, but only managed to hit *Hazard* four times, disabling both her guns.[10] She was under repair for eight weeks. *Speedy* escaped untouched, and British return fire did no damage.

At 1915 hours the heavy cruiser *Kent* escorted by the Soviet destroyers *Groznyi* and *Sokrushitelnyi* departed Kola Inlet and sailed to a point north of Murmansk astride the German line of retreat. However, Pönitz's ships slipped by shortly before the Allied ships arrived and returned to Tromsö safely.

This action was symbolic of the German navy's failure to exploit its capabilities in arctic waters. It was the Soviets, not the Germans, who used their fleet to support the army and maintain sea superiority at the vital point of contact along the front. This was a major reason why Murmansk was the only original objective that never fell to the German onslaught. Had the Germans captured Murmansk, much of the valuable material support the Soviet Union received from the Western Allies would have never arrived (or taken much longer to arrive) and the consequences to their total war effort may have been enough to result in a German, not a Soviet, victory.

6

THE ENGLISH CHANNEL AND THE FRENCH COAST 1942

The two main duties of the Western Security Forces were getting our submarines, war vessels, and blockade runners into and out of their bases on the coast of the Bay of Biscay, and getting a constant stream of vessels in both directions through the Channel.

VIZEADMIRAL FRIEDRICH RUGE

The English Channel was the most contested waterway in northern Europe during World War II. After passing through a period of German domination and relative quiet in 1941, the tempo of conflict accelerated in 1942 as each side attempted to employ the Channel more and deny its waters to the enemy.

The German navy mobilized its largest fleet, if not its most powerful, in 1942 to cover the withdrawal of the battleships *Scharnhorst* and *Gneisenau* and the heavy cruiser *Prinz Eugen* from Brest to home waters. Given the risk of breaking the British North Sea blockade and gaining the open waters of the Atlantic, it would seem Brest was the ideal base for the High Seas Fleet. While this was true geographically, there were other problems with the French harbor as became apparent after *Scharnhorst* and

Table 6.1. Actions off the French Coast 1942.

Date	Location	Name	Opponent	Type
12-Feb-42	English Channel	Channel Dash	British	Interception
14-Mar-42	English Channel	Attack on *Michel*	British	Convoy attack
28-Mar-42	Bay of Biscay	St. Nazaire	British	Interception
14-Oct-42	English Channel	Attack on *Komet*	British/Polish	Convoy attack

Gneisenau made port there on 22 March 1941, followed by *Prinz Eugen* on 1 June 1941. First, the city was only 140 air miles from Plymouth, an easy flight for a modern bomber. The British air force succeeded in keeping at least one of the three ships out of action for the best part of a year. While the port enjoyed excellent repair and support facilities, it was occupied territory; espionage and the potential for sabotage were constant problems. And when the damaged ships were under repair, work never progressed as fast or as well as it would have in Germany.

The true value of a heavy flotilla based at Brest was as a fleet in being; as a diversion of limited British resources. Hitler, however, did not appreciate this and felt that the ships, or at least their guns, would better serve German interests by defending Norway against an invasion he believed imminent. Early in 1942 he ordered they either be transferred to Norway, or stripped of their armament so the guns could be shipped there. This directive left Grossadmiral Raeder little choice. By late January 1942 all three heavy ships were, for the first time, simultaneously operational. With this opportunity they had to undertake a mission that was, by its very nature, an admission of defeat.

The decision to undertake the Channel passage home, as opposed to the longer route round the north of Britain, was not as dangerous as a glance at the map might indicate. On the oceanic passage there was the hazard of interception by the battleships of the Home Fleet. Careful planning and organization, which could function during a two-day operation in the close waters of the Channel, would not serve so well in the distant extremes of the perilous North Atlantic. Moreover, the crews of the three ships had been culled several times to provide personnel for the submarines, torpedo boats, and other units. The new replacements were hardly worked up. A dash through coastal waters better suited their capabilities than an oceanic voyage.

Air power was Britain's main means of blocking the Channel to large warships, but this weapon's edge was dulled by poor coordination, lack of experience attacking ships at sea, and the strength of German countermeasures which included continuous coverage by flights of at least sixteen fighters. The only naval forces available were two small detachments of MTBs and an ad hoc collection of old destroyers, even though the British had a good idea both where and approximately when the Germans would be going.

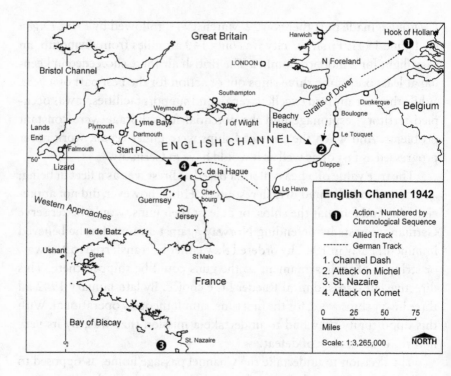

Channel Dash, 12 February 1942

TIME:	1542–1600 (surface action)
TYPE:	Interception
WEATHER:	Rain squalls
VISIBILITY:	Poor, under seven thousand yards
SEA STATE:	Heavy swell from the west
SURPRISE:	British
MISSION:	British—interception based upon specific intelligence; Germans—transit

The German force, led by Vizeadmiral Felix Ciliax, flying his flag in *Scharnhorst,* departed Brest late on the night of 11 February. The 5th Destroyer Flotilla (*Richard Beitzen, Paul Jacobi, Hermann Schuemann, Friedrich Ihn,* Z25, and Z29 [F]) under Führer der Zerstörer, Kapitän zur See Erich Bey formed the immediate escort. The 2nd Torpedo Boat Flotilla (*T2, T4, T5, T11,* and *T12* under Korvettenkapitän Heinrich Erdmann) from Le Havre and the 3rd Torpedo Boat Flotilla (*T13, T15, T16,* and *T17* under

Korvettenkapitän Hans Wilcke) from Dunkirk joined Ciliax at 0900 hours. The heavy units of the escort were rounded out by the 5th Torpedo Boat Flotilla (*Seeadler, Falke, Kondor, Iltis,* and *Jaguar* under Fregattenkapitän Moritz Schmidt), which rendezvoused off Cape Gris Nez in the narrowest portion of the Channel. Three MTB flotillas, the 2nd, 4th, and 6th with ten S-boats, joined the armada near the Straits of Dover.

Because of a series of missteps, the British failed to detect the German fleet for eleven hours after it cleared Brest, and their first challenge at 1210 was an ineffectual bombardment by the 9.2-inch battery at South Fore-land on the Dover Straits, which fired thirty-three rounds from an initial range of twenty-seven thousand yards. All fell well short. Four MTBs supported by a pair of MGBs attacked shortly after. Although they managed to get several torpedoes into the water from as near as three thousand yards, the German fleet passed unharmed.

British air attacks commenced at 1245 when six Swordfish of 825 Squadron flew to their doom, followed by a series of fruitless attacks by air force and Coastal Command squadrons: "They often did not know where they were going and what they would be firing at. Coordination was a joke, communications a farce and fighter cover unavailable."[1] The British delivered a hundred attacks involving six hundred aircraft, but only sank the patrol boat *V1302* and damaged *T13* and *Jaguar*. These meager results came at the cost of forty-two aircraft shot down.

The first check to Ciliax's progress came at 1432 when *Scharnhorst* struck a mine off Ostend, but by 1450 she had repaired the worst of her damage and was steaming hard to catch up with the rest of the fleet, unmolested the entire time by British forces.

The German fleet had sailed largely unharmed through everything the British had flung at it; the last unit available to contest their passage was an amalgamation of the 21st and 16th Destroyer Flotillas: *Campbell* (flag of Captain C. T. M. Pizey), *Vivacious, Walpole, Worcester, Mackay,* and *Whitshed*. Of all the British units deployed that day, Pizey's destroyers were the most prepared. He had sailed from Harwich at 0600 hours, long before the British knew the Germans were coming, and exercised his ships with an escort of six Hunt destroyer escorts, thinking he would be more available in an emergency at sea than in port. However, Dover Command underestimated the German fleet's speed and by the time he realized the actual situation, Pizey could intercept only by steaming at twenty-eight

Table 6.2. The Channel Dash, 12 February 1942 (only ships participating in the surface action)

Allied Ships	TYP	YL	DFL	SPD	GUNS	TT	GF	DAM
Campbell	DD	18	2,055	36	4×4.7/45 & 1×3	6×21	6	D2
Vivacious	DD	17	1,523	34	3×4/45 & 1×3	3×21	3	
Worcester	DD	19	1,523	34	4×4.7/45 & 1×3	6×21	6	D4
Mackay	DD	18	2,055	36	5×4.7/45 & 1×3	6×21	7	
Whitshed	DD	19	1,523	34	4×4.7/45 & 1×3	6×21	6	
German Ships								
Gneisenau	BB	36	38,900	32	9×11/54.5 & 12× 5.9/55		79	
Prinz Eugen	CA	38	19,042	32	8×8/60 & 12×4.1/60	12×21	35	
Richard Beitzen	DD	35	3,156	38	5×5/45	8×21	7	
Z5 Paul Jacobi	DD	36	3,110	38	5×5/45	8×21	7	

knots across a presumed minefield directly for the estuary of the River Scheldt in Holland. The Hunts could not participate as they were too slow to reach the contact point in time.

During their five hour run across the North Sea to the Dutch coast, the destroyers suffered first the loss of *Walpole,* which stripped her main bearing and dropped out after 1320, and then a series of air attacks delivered by both German and British aircraft. Pizey pressed on undaunted. As the two flotillas neared the continental mainland, *Campbell,* the only ship equipped with modern T271 radar, acquired two large contacts sixteen thousand five hundred yards ahead. The time was 1517 hours and conditions were deteriorating with a heavy swell from the west and a rising gale; visibility had dropped to four miles. The thick weather favored Pizey. An air attack was under way at the same time. He wrote: "Great numbers of aircraft— friendly and hostile—were observed. Low down were large numbers of Me.109s and an occasional Beaufort; higher up were Hampdens, Dorniers and Me.110s while still higher a few Halifaxes were to be seen."[2] The aerial show helped him penetrate the German outer screen undetected.

At 1542 the British destroyers turned to attack in two divisions: Pizey led *Campbell, Vivacious,* and *Worcester* against *Gneisenau,* while *Mackay* and *Whitshed* sailing to starboard of Pizey tried to obtain a firing position on *Gneisenau*'s bow. Pizey's three ships swung parallel to the battleship when the range was down to four thousand yards. One minute later *Richard Beitzen* finally noticed the intruders and broadcast an enemy contact alarm. She fired her guns and launched four torpedoes at *Campbell's* column, one of which *Vivacious* barely avoided. *Paul Jacobi* came up and shot six salvos and straddled her target; then both German destroyers cleared the range for the battleship and cruiser. *Gneisenau's* large guns erupted with flame and smoke, but Pizey continued to close. His ship twisted between towering columns of water from 11-inch straddles until 1547 when, from a range of thirty-three hundred yards, *Campbell* turned and fired six torpedoes; *Vivacious* on her starboard quarter fired three more. After their weapons were away *Campbell* (her bow damaged during her run in) fled to the northeast, shooting at enemy destroyers until 1553; *Vivacious* turned northwest. Both found shelter in a rain squall. *Worcester* had been following about sixteen hundred yards back and missed her leader's turn; she pressed on for another three minutes. Pizey claimed two of his torpedoes hit, but in fact all missed. Meanwhile at 1543 *Mackay* and *Whitshed* saw *Prinz Eugen* steering toward them while avoiding a Beaufort's torpedo. At 1545 the cruiser realized the two ships were enemies and immediately opened fire. The range was less than four thousand yards. Smoke and the following wind forced the cruiser to pass gunnery control from the foretop to the forward director and the gun crews could only snatch glimpses of their targets as they appeared and vanished in the murk. *Mackay* launched torpedoes as soon as *Prinz Eugen* opened fire. *Whitshed* had trouble training her tubes because of heavy beam-on seas that were washing over her deck. She did not launch until 1547, when the range was down to three thousand yards. *Prinz Eugen's* lookouts observed the British weapons entering the water and she swung south allowing the bubbling wakes to pass ahead. Both British destroyers retired into a rain squall and returned to Harwich independently.

Worcester was the last ship to fire torpedoes. Her captain, Lieutenant Commander E. C. Coates, was determined to register a hit even though he was now in the crosshairs of both *Gneisenau* and *Prinz Eugen*. At 1550 with the range just twenty-four hundred yards the destroyer swung to launch torpedoes. At just that moment two large shells struck *Worcester's* boiler room. As the destroyer lost power she emptied her tubes under local control and drifted to a halt. Coates observed his torpedoes passing well behind the battleship and ahead of the cruiser. The cost of his unrequited boldness was heavy. During the next ten minutes at least two 11-inch, seven 8-inch, and many smaller projectiles pummeled the helpless destroyer and she took on a heavy list as fires raged from stem to stern. The German fleet swept by. *Prinz Eugen* checked fire rather than waste ordnance on a ship obviously doomed while a jammed shell case temporarily silenced *Gneisenau*'s guns.

At 1558 *Campbell,* which had turned back, encountered *Worcester* lying stopped, "badly on fire forward and amidships, with smoke and steam pouring from the funnels, rafts and floats adrift clear of her and men in the water."[3] However, after the Germans had disappeared to the north, her crew (those that had remained aboard) extinguished her fires and worked up to six knots using salt water in the boilers. *Worcester* eventually returned to port under her own power, having suffered twenty-seven dead and many wounded. She was out of action for several months while *Campbell*'s damage required five weeks to repair. None of the other destroyers suffered harm even though the friendly air attacks continued as they returned to base.

Both *Scharnhorst* and *Gneisenau* struck mines along the Dutch coast, but made harbor safely. It was ironic that the strongest force the British navy could muster to attack enemy battleships passing within gunshot of Dover was five second-line destroyers. Nonetheless, the failure of the twenty-three torpedoes they launched to find a target was more a comment on the miserable luck the British had that day than on the skill and determination of their attack.

Attack on *Michel*, 14 March 1942

TIME:	Morning
TYPE:	Interception
WEATHER:	
VISIBILITY:	
SEA STATE:	
SURPRISE:	None
MISSIONS:	British—interception based upon specific intelligence; German—escort and transit

Scharnhorst and *Gneisenau*'s "dash" was a dramatic event, but it only represented, writ large, what the Germans did routinely. One British historian bitterly complained: "The Germans continued to make use of the Channel as they pleased. No less than twenty-nine major ships and eleven destroyers passed through the Straits between April and June 1941 without loss or hindrance."[4] In 1941 the English Channel was the major route for German *Hilfskreuzer,* or disguised raiders breaking out into the open sea or returning to Germany. They received escorts proportional to their value, but the first major engagement to result from this traffic didn't occur until March 1942.

On the evening of 13 March, the 5th Torpedo Boat Flotilla, *Seeadler, Falke, Kondor, Iltis,* and *Jaguar* under Fregattenkapitän Schmidt with eight minesweepers from the 1st and 2nd Flotillas and nine R-boats of the 2nd Flotilla sailed from Vlissingen, Holland, in company with the new auxiliary cruiser *Michel,* commanded by Kapitän zur See Helmut von Ruckteschell. The large minesweeping force would clear the way during her hazardous journey down the heavily mined Channel while the torpedo boats would protect her if British surface forces intervened, which seemed certain as the British, still smarting from the sting of German success in the Channel Dash, desperately wanted to deny *Michel* passage.

Michel sailed close inshore with the minesweepers ahead and the torpedo boats protecting her starboard flank. Radio intelligence advised Schmidt of British movements and greatly assisted the ordering of his defense. He easily repulsed several probing attacks by British MTBs as well as the first serious assault, delivered at 0400 hours by six MTBs and three MGBs out of Dover. German shore batteries illuminated the attackers with star shell while the escort laid down a wall of fire the MTBs couldn't penetrate. At 0700 hours the British made another fruitless attack when the German flotilla was off Le Touquet. The third and final attack developed that morning when a mixed group of Hunt I and II class destroyer escorts and converted World War I destroyers arrived from their patrol zone off Beachy Head.

This force, consisting of the old destroyers *Walpole* and *Windsor* and the Hunts *Blencathra, Fernie,* and *Calpe* attacked in an engagement so fierce even *Michel* dropped her disguise and opened fire. The two destroyers each launched their total load of three torpedoes, and although they claimed that they inflicted serious harm on the auxiliary cruiser and several of her escorts, in fact *Michel* was the only target hit and just by splinters and antiaircraft rounds. (She suffered eight men killed.) The German escort's

Table 6.3. Attack on *Michel*, 14 March 1942

Allied Ships	TYP	YL	DFL	SPD	GUNS	TT	GF	DAM
Fernie	DE	40	1,450	28	4×4/45		4	D1
Walpole	DD	19	1,523	34	3×4/45 & 1×3	3×21	3	D1
Windsor	DD	18	1,523	34	3×4/45 & 1×3	3×21	3	D3
Blencathra	DE	40	1,450	28	4×4/45		4	D1
Calpe	DE	41	1,625	27	6×4/45		6	
German Ships								
Seeadler	TB	26	1,290	33	3×4.1/45	6×21	3	
Iltis	TB	27	1,320	34	3×4.1/45	6×21	3	
Jaguar	TB	28	1,320	34	3×4.1/45	6×21	3	
Falke	TB	26	1,290	33	3×4.1/45	6×21	3	
Kondor	TB	26	1,290	33	3×4.1/45	6×21	3	
1st & 2nd Flot	MS×8	37	874	18	2×4.1/45		16	
2nd Flot	MMS×9		120	19–23	2×20-mm			
Michel	HK	41	10,900	16	6×5.9/45 & 1×4.1/45	6×21	10	D1

intense return fire damaged nearly the entire British force. A 4.1-inch shell put *Windsor* into the dock for two months while the Germans lightly injured *Fernie* and *Walpole*. Splinter damage to *Blencathra* required three weeks to fix.

The German flotilla continued and reached Le Havre a few hours later that afternoon. This success demonstrated that the lessons of the Channel Dash had yet to sink in; the British still needed to improve their coordination of forces and their determination at the point of attack. But, they were learning. The disguised raider *Stier* made a successful passage down Channel two months later, but at the cost of two large escorts, *Iltis* and *Seeadler*, sunk in an MTB torpedo attack.

St. Nazaire, 28 March 1942

TIME:	0630–0645
TYPE:	Encounter
WEATHER:	Good
VISIBILITY:	Good
SEA STATE:	Calm

SURPRISE: Germans
MISSION: British—escort; Germans—offensive and sea superiority
              patrol without specific intelligence

Even after Hitler evacuated his heavy surface flotilla from the French
Atlantic coast, the British remained possessed by the fear that German battleships, particularly *Tirpitz,* would return to threaten their sea-lanes. And
"should she do so there was only one place where she could be docked-in the
great lock at St. Nazaire."[5] This preoccupation demonstrated the impact
Bismarck's cruise had had upon Britain's assessment of the threats facing
her. To eliminate the possibility of *Tirpitz* using the dry dock, the British con-
cocted a scheme to attack the port with commandos and to ram the dock's
gate with an old explosive-laden destroyer. This attack duly occurred on the
night of 27–28 March 1942. It succeeded in its grand purpose, although
most of the participants ended up dead or taken prisoner. The fleet which
carried the 268 commandos over four hundred miles of open water consisted of *Campbeltown,* the explosive ram, sixteen motor launches,
MGB314, and *MTB74.* The Hunt class destroyer escorts *Atherstone* (Lieutenant Commander R. F. Jenks) and *Tynedale* (Lieutenant-Commander
H. E. F. Tweedie) provided the "heavy" support.

The German navy had the experienced 5th Torpedo Boat Flotilla,
Seeadler, Falke, Kondor, Iltis, and *Jaguar* under Fregattenkapitän Schmidt
at St. Nazaire. Fortunately for the commandos in their flimsy motor
launches, Schmidt was at sea when the British arrived off the river estuary
at 2200 hours on 27 March, thanks to an encounter with U593 earlier that
day. *Tynedale* attacked the submarine and believed she sank her, but U593
survived to surface and radio a sighting report. Based upon this information, Naval Group West ordered Schmidt to conduct a night sweep off the
coast. Schmidt did not receive word of the commando attack until 0250
hours the next morning when he was a hundred miles offshore.

While the British raiders fought a desperate and heroic battle, *Atherstone* and *Tynedale* loitered in the offing, waiting for the survivors (eight
of the eighteen boats that went in finally came out). They had set the initial rendezvous for 0630 hours at Point "Y" twenty miles off the estuary
mouth, but events disrupted the timetable and the motor launches began
debouching from the river far sooner than expected. *ML306* was first and
rather than wait near shore at Point "Y," her skipper preferred to head to

Table 6.4. St. Nazaire, 28 March 1942

Allied Ships	TYP	YL	DFL	SPD	GUNS	TT	GF	DAM
Atherstone	DE	39	1,450	28	4×4/45		4	
Tynedale	DE	40	1,450	28	4×4/45		4	D1
German Ships								
Seeadler	TB	26	1,290	33	3×4.1/45	6×21	3	
Falke	TB	26	1,290	33	3×4.1/45	6×21	3	
Kondor	TB	26	1,290	33	3×4.1/45	6×21	3	
Iltis	TB	27	1,320	34	3×4.1/45	6×21	3	
Jaguar	TB	28	1,320	34	3×4.1/45	6×21	3	

sea for the second point seventy miles farther out. However, at 0530, it was his misfortune to encounter the 5th Torpedo Boat Flotilla sailing hard for St. Nazaire. Schmidt detached *Jaguar* to deal with the contact while he continued with his other four ships, not certain what was happening or what he would face when he arrived. *Jaguar* forced *ML306*'s surrender after a spirited resistance that left most of her complement killed or wounded and took the British boat in tow.

    Atherstone and *Tynedale* had been patrolling between Île d'Yeu and the rendezvous point. At 0530 hours they came to Point "Y" and turned southwest in line abreast to sweep the route the MLs were to follow during their escape, *Tynedale* five thousand yards north of *Atherstone*. Schmidt's four ships were sailing for the estuary at full speed in line ahead with *Seeadler* leading followed by *Iltis, Falke,* and *Kondor.* At daybreak, shortly before 0630 hours, *Seeadler*'s lookout saw a shadow about eight thousand yards off against the growing light of the eastern horizon. The Germans were turning to starboard when *Tynedale* saw the danger.

    Tynedale came to port intending to close *Atherstone*, but Jenks, the senior officer, turned *Atherstone* to port as well, thinking to lure the Germans away from any friendly motor launches that might be in the area. As the German column came up astern of *Tynedale* crossing from her starboard to her port quarter, Schmidt blinkered a challenge to which *Tynedale* replied, trying to gain sea room before action commenced. At 0631 Schmidt felt assured he was facing the enemy and opened fire. The first salvos straddled *Atherstone* at a range of about fourteen thousand yards. *Atherstone* made smoke and the Germans shifted their fire to *Tynedale* only fifty-five hundred

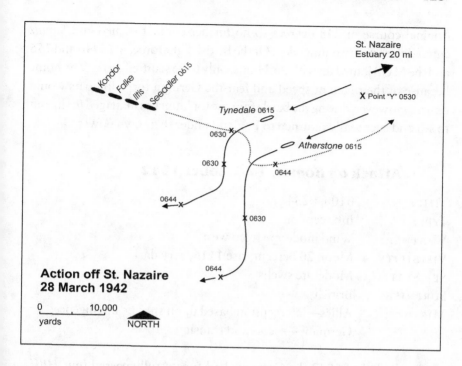

Kondor Falke Iltis

Seeadler 0615

Tynedale 0615

0630

0630

0644

0630

St. Nazaire
Estuary 20 mi

X Point "Y" 0530

Atherstone 0615

0644

0644

**Action off St. Nazaire
28 March 1942**

0   10,000
yards

NORTH

yards to their southwest. *Tynedale* replied with her stern mount while *Atherstone* did not fire at all, being masked by *Tynedale* and her own smoke.

Tynedale initially engaged *Seeadler* and then shifted fire to *Iltis*. However, she had trouble observing the fall of her shot against the dark horizon. For their part, the Germans all fired on *Tynedale* independently, making it nearly impossible for them to correct their aim onto target in a coordinated fashion. "We appeared to be in the middle of a cone of enemy fall of shot, rather than being straddled."[6] The torpedo boats registered two hits on *Tynedale* causing light damage. Then, with the range down to four thousand yards, *Seeadler* and *Iltis* each launched salvos of three torpedoes. At 0644 *Tynedale* made smoke and turned west, seeking to disengage, or better, to lead the Germans toward the two Hunts, *Cleveland* and *Brocklesby,* then eighty miles off and coming on fast. Schmidt didn't fall for the bait; instead he turned north toward St. Nazaire. *Tynedale* fired fifty-two shells from her after gun and estimated the Germans fired 240 to 360 rounds in return.

Some miles to the northwest, *Jaguar* saw the flashes from this encounter. After Schmidt had turned north the British came back to their original course of 248 degrees so no further contact ensued and *Jaguar* entered the estuary unimpeded. Of the British light force, *MLs446* and *156* and the MGB joined up with the Hunts, only to be scuttled on the way home because of their lack of speed and fear the German torpedo boats would return. However, during the battle four motor launches managed to slip out to sea and eventually returned to England under their own power.

Attack on *Komet*, 14 October 1942

TIME: 0100–0234
TYPE: Interception
WEATHER: Wind moderate from west
VISIBILITY: Moon 20 percent, rise 1116, very dark
SEA STATE: Moderate swells
SURPRISE: British
MISSION: Allies—interception based upon specific intelligence;
              Germans—escort and transit

By the fall of 1942 the Germans had successfully passed four *Hilfs-kreuzer* through the English Channel. The raider *Komet*, setting out on her second cruise under a new captain, Kapitän zur See Ulrich Brocksien, was scheduled to be number five. Group West allotted her a small escort compared to the protection lavished on *Michel* and *Stier*. It consisted of the 3rd Torpedo Boat Flotilla (*T14*, flag of Korvettenkapitän Wilcke, *T10*, *T4*, and *T19*) and the 2nd Motor Minesweeper Flotilla with only six R-boats. Unlike her sisters, *Komet* had a difficult passage to Le Havre: bad weather delayed her departure and she lost most of her minesweepers (*R77*, *R78*, *R82*, and *R86*) off Dunkirk to moored acoustic mines in waters that had been swept only hours before. Moreover, the British Admiralty was aware of the operation and had learned from past failures. They dispatched five Hunts and eight MTBs from Dartmouth: *Cottesmore* (flag of Lieutenant Commander J. C. A. Ingram), *Quorn*, *Glaisdale*, *Eskdale*, and *Albrighton* with MTBs *49*, *55*, *56*, *84*, *95*, *203*, *229*, and *236*. These were to patrol off Cap de la Hague and another four Hunts (*Brocklesby*, *Fernie*, *Tynedale*, and the Polish *Krakowiak*) from Plymouth were to loiter near the Channel Islands, in case the Germans broke through the first group.

Table 6.5. Attack on *Komet*, 14 October 1942

Allied Ships	TYP	YL	DFL	SPD	GUNS	TT	GF	DAM
Cottesmore	DE	40	1,450	28	4×4/45		4	
Quorn	DE	40	1,450	28	4×4/45		4	
Glaisdale (NO)	DE	42	1,545	27	4×4/45	2×21	4	
Eskdale	DE	42	1,545	27	4×4/45	2×21	4	
Albrighton	DE	41	1,545	27	4×4/45	2×21	4	
Brocklesby	DE	40	1,450	28	4×4/45		4	D1
Fernie	DE	40	1,450	28	4×4/45		4	
Tynedale	DE	40	1,450	28	4×4/45		4	
Krakowiak (PO)	DE	40	1,580	27	6×4/45		6	
MTB236	MTB	41	44	42		2×21	0	
German Ships								
Komet	HK	38	7,500	14.8	6×5.9/45	6×21	9	Sunk
T4	TB	38	1,088	35	1×4.1/45	6×21	1	D1
T10	TB	38	1,082	35	1×4.1/45	6×21	1	D3
T14	TB	40	1,098	35	1×4.1/45	6×21	1	D1
T19	TB	40	1,098	35	1×4.1/45	6×21	1	D1
2nd Flot	MMSx2		120	19–23	2×20-mm		0	

The Germans departed Le Havre at 1900 hours on 13 October, sailing at thirteen knots in a diamond formation around *Komet*, five hundred fifty yards between ships with *T14* in the van, *T10* to seaward, *T4* inshore, and *T19* astern. Off Barfleur, only two hours into their voyage, the convoy heard the unwelcome sound of airplane engines; then harsh, bright aerial flares floated down around the ships. Despite this unsettling attention, Brocksien rejected Wilcke's suggestion they put into Cherbourg, and ordered his little fleet to press ahead.

The British Dartmouth force sailed in three groups: the Hunts first, followed by a slow division of MTBs *49, 55, 56,* and *203,* and then a fast division consisting of MTBs *84, 95, 229,* and *236.* The wind was moderate from the west and it was very dark. The slow MTBs could not keep pace with the Hunts and lost contact, ensuring that the fast group following behind them lost contact as well. The tail end of the column, *MTB236,* lost contact with everyone. As it happened, she was the only boat to find the battle.

Shortly before 0100, on 14 October, Ingram's ships spotted the German convoy off Cap de la Hague. This time radio intelligence let the Germans down and the attack came by surprise. Proceeding in column led by *Cottesmore*, the British fired star shell, swung to port on an opposite heading, and discharged broadsides from four thousand yards. The British ships concentrated on *Komet*, the largest target, but hit *T10*, the nearest ship, twice in her turbine room, cutting her speed to eight knots. *T10* turned toward shore and made smoke. Her captain intended to launch a torpedo attack, but her tubes were trained in the wrong direction. As she swung her stern toward the British column, a shell struck the depth charge rack and touched off a series of large secondary explosions that set ablaze the torpedo boat's stern.

In contrast to the heavy defensive fire that had protected *Michel* from harm, the British managed several unanswered broadsides. The German torpedo boats had but one gun apiece and *T10* lost hers in the first minutes while *Komet* blocked *T4*'s line of sight. *Komet* opened fire to starboard with her 6-inch guns, but from panic, inexperience, or most likely both, her machine gun crews began spraying flak on all sides, hitting *T4*, *T19*, and *T14* and killing several of their crew, including Korvettenkapitän Wilcke.

T10 had worked back up to twenty-four knots when a 4-inch shell struck her starboard engine reducing speed once again. Hit one more time, and with all but a few flak guns out of action, she withdrew close inshore, badly damaged with eleven men killed. Meanwhile both *Cottesmore* and *T4* reported avoiding enemy torpedo attacks. German shore batteries opened fire, contributing to the confusion. By 0115 *Komet* was burning fiercely.

Meanwhile, aboard *MTB236* Sub-Lieutenant R. Drayson, a temporary replacement on his first command, displayed an initiative that was strangely lacking in all the other MTB captains. He proceeded to Cap de la Hague independently and then homed in on the star shells bursting to the south. Approaching close inshore, he saw *Komet* aflame and silhouetted by the hanging pyrotechnics. The MTB stalked her at low speed and, shortly before 0115, fired both torpedoes from five hundred yards.

At 0115/0116 *Komet* blew up. Ingram reported: "A violent explosion took place, followed a fraction of a second later by another which dwarfed the previous one. Flames shot up at least four hundred feet, the ship blew completely to pieces and burning oil spread over about a square mile of sea."[7] Kapitän zur See Brocksien and all three hundred fifty members of his crew perished. Most sources attribute the fatal blow to *MTB236*, although German post-action analysis concluded that fires ignited by British shells cooked off *Komet*'s store of aviation spirits, which in turn detonated her forward magazines. The Dartmouth Hunts continued firing on the German torpedo boats and claimed they set two afire, although all the damage suffered by *T4*, *T14*, and *T19* was minor and mainly inflicted by *Komet*.

The Plymouth Hunts, abeam of Sark about thirty miles south of the action, observed the explosion and hastened to join the battle. At 0215 they came into contact with the four German torpedo boats and a sharp engagement at close range ensued. However, German shore batteries intervened and hit *Brocklesby* lightly, wounding two of her crew. At 0234 hours the British broke off, satisfied with their night's work. The German torpedo boats made their escape without further molestation.

The destruction of *Komet* was the first clear victory won by Britain's destroyers in the English Channel. Although the British would suffer many more setbacks and defeats, increasingly it was Germany that found herself on the defensive, fending off increasingly skilled and effective British coastal forces.

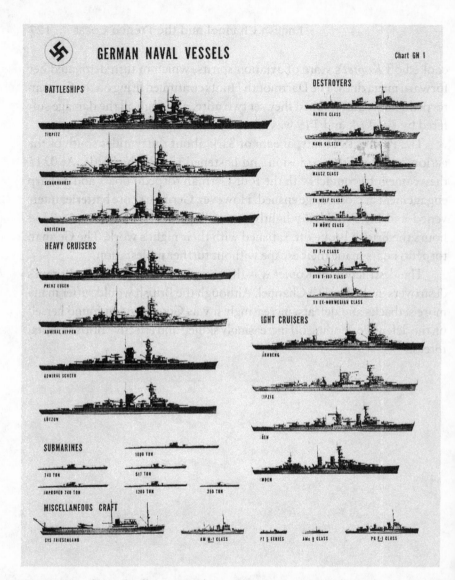

German Naval Vessels silhouettes. This was not the navy the German commander in chief, Grossadmiral Erich Raeder, expected to deploy when he fought Great Britain. *U.S. Naval Historical Center 173099*

Admiral Hipper engaging *Glowworm* 8 April 1940. Copied from a German book published during the war. Heye kept *Hipper* bow on toward the enemy, accepting a reduction in firepower to minimize the target for *Glowworm*'s torpedoes. *U.S. Naval Historical Center NH 61836*

Narvik harbor after the British attack. The British—aided by lazy security—
accomplished at Narvik a rare thing: a surprise attack against anchored warships.
In their initial assault they launched twenty-two torpedoes and sank two enemy
destroyers (and five merchantmen). Their gunfire damaged two more destroyers
while a third suffered collateral damage.
Naval Institute Photographic Library

The Second Battle of Narvik, 13 April 1940. *Warspite* preceded by three destroyers firing on Z13 *Erich Koellner.* At 1330 *Warspite* observed that men were still aboard *Erich Koellner.* She fired four more 15-inch salvos and finally sank the battered vessel.
Naval Institute Photographic Library

"The Heroic Struggle of our Destroyers before Narvik." Copied from a German book published during the war. The Germans proceeded to zigzag across the width of the fjord, with each turn being pressed ever east. This allowed them to use their entire batteries, and the frequent changes in course complicated British fire solutions.
Naval Institute Photographic Library

Z2 *Georg Thiele* aground at Rombaksfjord 13 April 1940. She returned fire until her ammunition ran out. Then Korvettenkapitän Wolff turned his ship toward shore and at 1500 ran her hard aground. He lost sixteen men killed and twenty-eight wounded.
Naval Institute Photographic Library

Scharnhorst in action against *Glorious*, 8 June 1940. At 1638 *Scharnhorst*'s third salvo hit target from the incredible distance of 26,400 yards, penetrating the aircraft carrier's flight deck, exploding in the upper hangar, and igniting a large fire.
U.S. Naval Historical Center NH 83981

Newcastle in action against Bey's 5th Flotilla 17 October 1940. *Newcastle* hoisted the general signal "chase" and every ship worked up to full speed, the cruisers firing at the enemy with their forward guns near full elevation.
Imperial War Museum A1380

Hood sinking, 24 May 1941. Painting from the Time-Life Collection. The whole forward section of *Hood* reared up from the water like the spire of a cathedral, towering above the upper deck of *Prince of Wales* as she steamed by.
U.S. Naval Historical Center NH 50741

Splashes from *Prince of Wales* landing astern of *Bismarck* 21 May 1941. *Bismarck* has been hit and is down by the bow. *Prince of Wales* turned in a credible performance for a new ship that, by the end of the action, was limited to only two functioning guns (both of her four gun turrets broke down). She fired eighteen main-battery salvos and five from her dual-purpose guns and hit *Bismarck* three times.   *U.S. Naval Historical Center NH 69728*

German destroyers with close air cover in the English Channel, 1941. After passing through a period of German domination and relative quiet in 1941, the tempo of conflict accelerated in 1942 as each side attempted to employ the Channel more and deny its waters to the enemy.
Naval Institute Photographic Library

Edinburgh's crew boarding *Gossamer,* 2 May 1942. The torpedoes *Z25* had launched some minutes before were approaching the end of their run. The cruiser's rotation converged with their deadly track and then an explosion ripped her hull opposite the earlier damage and nearly broke the ship in two.
Imperial War Museum MH 23867

Detail of *TA39* (ex-Italian torpedo boat *Daga*) under way. Lange's flotilla completed their odyssey (the transfer was codenamed Odysseus) on the afternoon of 24 September 1944, when they dropped anchor at Piraeus. There, the real work would begin and the new torpedo boats were quick to prove their worth, escorting convoys and sowing mines. . . . *TA38* and *TA39* even fought a minor surface action on 6 October, when they sank the British motor-launch *ML1227*.
Storia Militare

UJ204 (ex-Italian *Gabbiano*-class corvette *Euridice*). Her sisters, including *UJ201*, fought several surface engagements. *Le Malin* continued northwest and encountered *UJ201*. She hit the escort several times with her 90-pound shells and then fired torpedoes. One struck and detonated the corvette's magazine. The unfortunate ship exploded and quickly sank with all hands.
Storia Militare

TA20 (ex-*Audace*) being overflown by a Arado Ar. 196 A-3. Again their first salvos hit, this time on *TA20*'s bridge, slaughtering her officers and destroying the fire control systems. *TA20* sank at 2230, close inshore off Pag Island.
Storia Militare

Unidentified trawlers, either V-boats or UJ-boats, in a French Channel port. The right vessel has a bow socket for mounting a minesweeper's paravanes. The destroyers duly set *M4611* afire and, after maneuvering around and investigating a false contact, returned to finish off the two patrol boats. But *V213*, whose heaviest weapon was an 88-mm gun, fought back. She hit *Eskimo* twice. The powerful destroyer lost steering power and could only steam in circles at a top speed of six knots.

U.S. Naval Historical Center SCH 596776 30321-A

Mauritius in a night action, 23 August 1944. When star shell exploded overhead, the Germans knew exactly what they were in for.
Imperial War Museum A25321

Another view of *Mauritius* in the same action, silhouetted by flashes from her after 6-inch guns. They sank *V702* (ex-*Memel,* 444 tons), *V717* (ex–*Alfred III,* 1,000 tons), *V720, V729* (ex–*Marie Simone,* 282 tons), and *V730* (ex–*Michel Francois,* 535 tons). This was the last naval action of any significance to occur in French waters during the war.
Imperial War Museum A27270

German convoy off the North Cape, screened by destroyers. Germany relied on shipping along the coastal waters of Norway's deeply indented arctic shoreline to sustain its divisions struggling to advance on Murmansk and, after their drive stalled, for the exploitation of the area's valuable nickel and iron ore resources. In the first six months of 1942 alone, 872 transports carrying 2,608,057 tons of supplies plied the route between Kirkenes and Narvik.
U.S. Naval Historical Center NR&L 30321-A

Action off La Ciotat, 17 August 1944: *Endicott* engaging *UJ6073, ex–Nimet Allah.* She challenged with a flashing light and then engaged *UJ6073*, much the bigger target. In the first minutes two 5-inch shells detonated in the ex-yacht's engine room and she quickly lost way.
U.S. Naval Historical Center NH54382

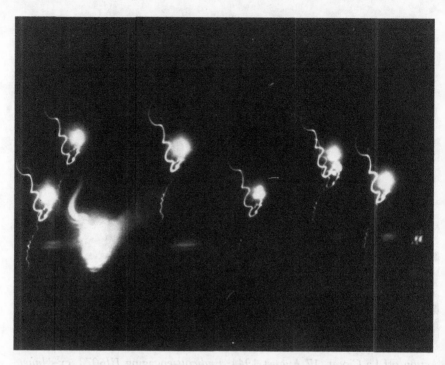

Night action off Listerfjord, 12–13 November 1944. Picture was taken from *Kent*. The large light to the left is an explosion while the points of light to the right are ships on fire. The circular lights are falling star shell. At 2313, with the nearest enemy ships only five thousand yards away, *Bellona* and *Algonquin* filled the sky with star shell. The drifting pyrotechnics were very effective in the clear air, and the Allied ships could easily see their targets.

Imperial War Museum A27101

Spoils of war: *T35* under the American flag. There were also fourteen destroyers and fourteen torpedo boats in service on 1 April 1945. To these larger units can be added hundreds of minesweepers, UJ-boats, V-boats, and S-boats still in action.
Naval Institute Photographic Library

7

BATTLES OF THE POLAR SEA
1942–43

I would never take a convoy anywhere near ice, accepting
almost any other risk in preference.

CAPTAIN M. M. DENNY OF HMS *KENYA*

After the destruction of *Bismarck*, the German navy's largest
warships saw little activity for nearly a year. In a series of con-
ferences lasting from September 1941 to January 1942 the Navy and the
government slowly (and acrimoniously) evolved a strategy to govern the
High Seas Fleet's future employment. The Navy favored an Atlantic role
for *Scheer* and the squadron at Brest, *Scharnhorst, Gneisenau,* and *Prinz
Eugen.* Hitler disagreed. He wanted the fleet in Norway. Other issues complicated the debate. First, the termination of Soviet supply and the
demands of the armies on the Eastern front (and the Italian navy) created
a shortage of fuel oil for the thirsty battleships and cruisers. The fact that
the Soviet Union would not be destroyed in the first year's campaign and
the entry of the United States into the war raised other concerns.

In August 1941 the British began sailing convoys through the Arctic
Ocean into the Soviet ports of Murmansk and Archangel. Renewed British
commando raids against the Norwegian coast in December reinforced
Hitler's concern about the security of his northern flank. By January 1942,
Grossadmiral Raeder had lost the debate. The Channel Dash was the
result and the price was high. On 1 March 1942 the German navy was a
shadow of what it had been just one month before.

Of the navy's three battleships, eight cruisers, and seventeen destroyers, only one battleship, two cruisers, and five destroyers were operational.
With the exception of *Hipper,* all operational ships were in Norway.

Table 7.1. Status German Navy 1 March 1942

Name	Type	Status	Location	Comment
Tirpitz	BB	Operational	Trondheim	
Scharnhorst	BB	Under repair	Kiel	Until January 1943
Gneisenau	BB	Severe damage	Kiel	Never returned
Admiral Scheer	CA	Operational	Trondheim	
Lützow	CA	Under repair	Swinemunde	Until 10 May
Admiral Hipper	CA	Operational	Kiel	
Prinz Eugen	CA	Under repair	Trondheim	Until 6 January 1943
Emden	CL	Training duty	Baltic	
Köln	CL	Refit	Wilhelmshaven	Until 23 May
Leipzig	CL	Training duty	Baltic	
Nurnberg	CL	Training duty	Baltic	
Richard Beitzen	DD	Operational	Trondheim	Refit 14 March
Paul Jacobi	DD	Operational	Trondheim	
Theodor Riedel	DD	Under repair	Kiel	Until 10 May
Hermann Schoemann	DD	Operational	Trondheim	
Hans Lody	DD	Under repair	Wesermunde	
Friedrich Ihn	DD	Operational	Trondheim	
Erich Steinbrinck	DD	Under repair	Hamburg	Until 5 August
Friedrich Eckholdt	DD	Under repair	Kiel	Until 15 April
Karl Galster	DD	Under repair	Kiel	Until 5 May
Z23	DD	Under repair	Trondheim	Until August
Z24	DD	Under repair	Kiel	Until early March
Z25	DD	Operational	Trondheim	
Z26	DD	Refit	Germany	Until early March
Z27	DD	Refit	Germany	Until May
Z28	DD	Working up	Aarhus, Denmark	Until April
Z29	DD	Under repair	Wesermunde	Repairs
Z30	DD	Working up	Germany	Until mid March

Through March 1942 Germany sank only one Allied ship sailing in an arctic convoy, but the transfer of heavy warships to Norway told the British they would no longer enjoy uncontested passage. In 1942 and 1943 the German navy repeatedly attacked the arctic convoys, provoking some of the largest surface naval battles fought outside the Pacific and Mediterranean.

Tirpitz and three destroyers made the first foray on 6 March 1942 to attack PQ12. Alerted by Ultra, the British attempted to intercept with *King George V, Duke of York,* and *Renown,* but the fleets missed each other in atrocious weather. *Tirpitz* escaped an attack by carrier Albacore biplanes and returned safely to port.

Table 7.2. Battles in the Polar Sea

Date	Location	Name	Opponent	Type
29-Mar-42	Arctic	Action against PQ13	British/SO	Convoy attack
1-May-42	Arctic	Action off Bear Island	British	Convoy attack
2-May-42	Arctic	Attack on *Edinburgh*	British	Interception
31-Dec-42	Arctic	Barents Sea	British	Convoy attack
21-Jan-43	Arctic	Action off Syltefjord	Soviet	Interception
26-Dec-43	Arctic	North Cape	British	Interception

Attack on PQ13, 29 March 1942

TIME: 0950–1130 hours
TYPE: Convoy attack
WEATHER: Strong wind, variable to heavy snow
VISIBILITY: Variable, between 500 to 10,000 yards
SEA STATE: Strong swells
SURPRISE: None (both)
MISSION: British—escort and transit; Germans—interception
                 based upon general intelligence

The next convoy, PQ13 with nineteen merchantmen, sailed from Reykjavik, Iceland, on 20 March 1942. The escort consisted of the light cruiser *Trinidad,* the destroyers *Eclipse* and *Fury,* and assorted minesweepers and sloops. On 24 March an especially violent gale scattered the ships across 150 miles of sea, some all the way to the pack ice that still enclosed Bear Island. By 27 March, when the weather moderated, not a single merchantman was in contact with an escort. That same day German reconnaissance aircraft spotted some of the isolated ships. Naval Group North saw this as a golden opportunity to strike with the surface fleet, although after *Tirpitz*'s close call they decided to use destroyers only.

On the afternoon of 28 March three destroyers of the 8th Flotilla, *Z24, Z25,* and *Z26* (FS) under Kapitän zur See Gottfried Pönitz sortied from Kirkenes. These ships were all polar sea veterans, but *Z25* had gone to France to participate in the Channel Dash while *Z24* and *Z26* had just finished repairs and a refit in Germany. They had returned to Kirkenes only the day before.

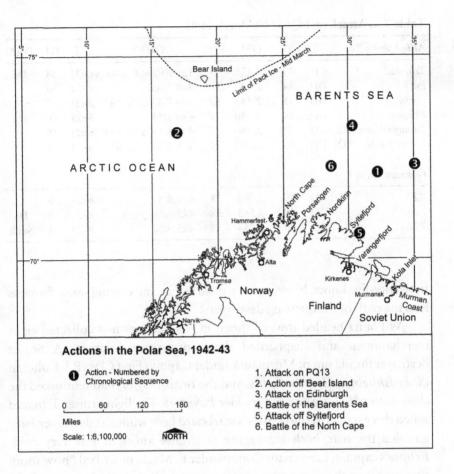

Actions in the Polar Sea, 1942-43

⬤ Action - Numbered by
   Chronological Sequence

0   60   120   180
Miles
Scale: 1:6,100,000   NORTH

1. Attack on PQ13
2. Action off Bear Island
3. Attack on Edinburgh
4. Battle of the Barents Sea
5. Attack off Syltefjord
6. Battle of the North Cape

Pönitz led his ships north through a calm sea. At 2338 hours on 28 March he encountered lifeboats from the freighter *Empire Ranger,* sunk in an aerial attack three hours earlier. The Germans rescued sixty-one seamen and, based upon their information, Pönitz turned his flotilla to the northwest, sailing in an extended line-abreast search formation. At 0143 hours they came upon a PQ13 straggler, the Soviet freighter *Bateau* (4,687 tons). Z26 sank her in five minutes with gunfire and a torpedo and, helped by Z24, she rescued seven crew members.

Encouraged by this success, the destroyers continued their search, but the weather deteriorated and they plunged north for three hours without seeing a thing. Then Pönitz received a position report from a U-boat trailing the convoy. On this intelligence he turned west. The wind had increased

Table 7.3. Attack on PQ13, 29 March 1942

Allied Ships	TYP	YL	DFL	SPD	GUNS	TT	GF	DAM
Trinidad	CL	40	10,450	31	12×6/50 & 8×4/45	6×21	33	D4
Fury	DD	34	2,025	36	4×4.7/45	8×21	6	
Oribi	DD	41	2,365	37	4×4.7/45 & 1×4/45	4×21	7	
Eclipse	DD	34	1,940	37	4×4.7/45	8×21	6	D3
Gremyashchiy (SO)	DD	37	2,380	37	4×5.1/50 & 2×3/55	6×21	8	
Sokrushitelnyi (SO)	DD	36	2,380	37	4×5.1/50 & 2×3/55	6×21	8	
German Ships								
Z24	DD	40	3,605	38	4×5.9/50	8×21	8	
Z25	DD	40	3,543	38	4×5.9/50	8×21	8	D1
Z26	DD	40	3,543	38	4×5.9/50	8×21	8	Sunk

to twenty-five knots, blowing from dead astern and driving snow showers into the path of the questing destroyers.

As Pönitz headed toward them, PQ13's escorts had collected eight merchantmen and shepherded them into three columns. A Soviet destroyer flotilla out of Murmansk under Captain First Class P. I. Koltchin (*Sokrushitelnyi, Gremyashchiy,* and the British *Oribi*) had reinforced the close escort (*Eclipse* and the trawler *Paynter*). The light cruiser *Trinidad* sailed three miles off the convoy's starboard bow while the destroyer *Fury* guarded the rear, both zigzagging at twenty knots. It was very cold. *Eclipse*'s captain, Lieutenant Commander E. Mack, described "how spray sweeping over the guns and bridge froze instantly; how the gun wells filled with sea water and ice. It was almost impossible to use binoculars because frozen spray immediately obscured the lenses."[1] The British had intelligence that a destroyer attack was possible, but it did not seem that conditions favored contact, much less a sea battle.

At 0940 hours on the morning of 29 March, with visibility less than two miles, contact did occur almost simultaneously. Pönitz's destroyers had unwittingly worked north of *Trinidad*; at 0946 hours the cruiser loomed out of the snow and mist only thirty-five hundred yards west and slightly south of Z26. Pönitz gave his units permission to fire torpedoes and guns as they bore, but *Trinidad* was first off the trigger. Ranging her forward turrets with radar, her initial salvo fell short, while the German reply straddled. But the cruiser's next brace of shells hit and devastated

Z26, disabling the German flagship's port engine, Nos. 2 and 3 guns, and igniting a large fire amidships.

After five salvos, Trinidad shifted fire to Z25, the next in line, firing three more times, including one complete broadside and claiming hits. In reply, the German destroyers landed two shells on their adversary, smashing Trinidad's admiral's office, some cabins aft, and causing light flooding. Then Z26 followed by Z25 discharged their full load of torpedoes (seven in the case of Z26 because she had already expended one sinking the Soviet freighter the night before). The Germans turned north, hard to starboard, as Trinidad also came to starboard (south) to avoid the torpedoes surging her way. Z24, the rear ship, fired four more torpedoes as she turned, unable to deploy her last set of four due to a training error.

Once the German torpedo barrage had passed, some torpedoes coming uncomfortably close, Trinidad circled north in pursuit of the enemy. She had lost contact, but at 0956 her radar found Z26 once again. Unfortunately for the flagship, she had become separated from her flotilla mates and had no support as the cruiser followed the black smoke roiling up from her fires and closed to thirty-four hundred yards. Trinidad ducked behind her enemy and opened fire with her forward turrets. Z26's forward gun was her only operational weapon and this didn't bear, so she made no reply. Trinidad continued in to point-blank range, firing with her aft turrets, 4-inch secondary battery, and pom-poms and registering repeated hits. Z26 seemed doomed as she lost headway and fell to starboard, finally able to open fire with her solitary gun over open sights. Trinidad had fired twenty-four salvos from her "A" and "B" turrets and a further thirteen from "X" and "Y." The time was 1022 hours when she launched three torpedoes to finish the job. Two failed to deploy and the third malfunctioned. It circled back and exploded against the cruiser. The intense cold had solidified the weapon's engine oil provoking a circular run. The unexpected impact caused serious flooding and a 17-degree list, forcing Trinidad to disengage.

With this reprieve, Z26 regained a chance for survival. Although she had but one gun left and her speed was reduced, she could still maneuver. When a destroyer appeared off her port bow, Pönitz optimistically flashed his call sign, assuming the newcomer was friendly. She was not.

Eclipse's aggressive captain, Mack, had left the convoy looking for action and thanks to his Type 286P radar he found it, even though the snow was blowing harder and visibility was under a thousand yards. As Eclipse's forward guns opened rapid fire against her Z26 turned to starboard and increased speed, attempting to lose this new foe by working south under cover of smoke. In a running fight that saw the British destroyer register repeated hits, Z26 increased speed from fifteen to twenty-five knots, but trailing oil and faced with British radar, she was unable to disappear into the murk. Finally, at 1120, *Eclipse* landed a flurry of six shells. "By this time [Z26] had her stern awash, clouds of smoke and steam were issuing from amidships and black smoke was pouring from her fore funnel. Listing to port, with the icy seas sluicing over her upper deck, Z26 could no longer fight or run."[2] *Eclipse* closed for the kill.

Then the snow stopped and visibility cleared dramatically revealing Z24 and Z25 steaming to succor their flagship. They hit *Eclipse* three times from long range, causing serious damage with their 100-pound shells, although only two rounds detonated. Z24 also fired her last three torpedoes. However, salvation came too late for Z26; all they could do was rescue survivors, and there were only 88 of these (including Pönitz); 243 men perished.

Z24 and Z25 returned to Kirkenes that evening. *Trinidad* limped into Murmansk on 30 March. The convoy had escaped the surface threat, but U-boats and aircraft took their toll. Of the nineteen ships that left Reykjavik, only fourteen arrived at their destination. Despite their losses (a minesweeper from the inbound convoy's escort sank U655 while a floating mine claimed U585), the Germans claimed a "notable success."[3]

Action off Bear Island, 1 May 1942

TIME: 1405–1730 hours
TYPE: Convoy attack
WEATHER: Strong wind
VISIBILITY: Sleeting snow
SEA STATE: Swells, obstructed by many ice floes
SURPRISE: None
MISSION: British—escort and transit; Germans—interception based upon general intelligence

The Arctic Destroyer Group continued to serve as the German surface strike force with Z7 *Hermann Schoemann* replacing Z26 on 9 April 1942.

Just two days later the group set forth to attack PQ14 under a new commander, Kapitän zur See Fritz Berger, commander of the 5th Destroyer Flotilla. However, snow, low visibility, and winds reaching sixty knots plagued the mission and the group failed to find any targets, much to the displeasure of Naval Group North, which felt Berger gave up too soon.

The next convoy pair, PQ15/QP11 with twenty-five and thirteen ships, respectively, sailed from Iceland and Murmansk at the end of April. The strength of QP11's escort—the light cruiser *Edinburgh*, six destroyers, four corvettes, and a trawler as well as a pair of Soviet destroyers and four British minesweepers for the initial portion of its run—demonstrated the respect the British had developed for the German menace. (Although *Edinburgh*'s cargo of 465 twelve-inch ingots of Soviet gold may have also played a part in the escort's size.) Nonetheless, this convoy ran into serious trouble.

At 1618 hours on 30 April *Edinburgh* was zigzagging ahead of the convoy. Suddenly there were two explosions aft. U456 had ambushed the cruiser and torpedoed her twice. *Edinburgh* had major flooding and lost her stern abaft "Y" turret. Within hours Generaladmiral Hubert Schmundt, commander of Naval Group North, issued orders for Destroyer Group Arctic, now under the command of Kapitän zur See Alfred Schulze-Hinrichs, to strike the convoy and then double back to sink the damaged cruiser, which was being towed toward Murmansk. At 2330 hours they weighed anchor, made the dog-leg around the North Cape, and set course northwest.

By the afternoon of 1 May QP11 was sailing at the edge of the pack ice east, southeast of Bear Island. The blow to *Edinburgh* had left it with an escort of only four old and under-armed destroyers, *Bulldog* (Commander Maxwell Richmond), *Beagle*, *Amazon*, and *Beverley*, the corvettes *Oxlip*, *Saxafrage*, *Campanula*, and *Snowflake*, and the armed trawler *Lord Middleton*. The escort had successfully repelled an attack by torpedo-armed Heinkel 111s that morning. The time was 1340 hours. The open waters were strewn with drifting ice and large floes. It was very cold with intermittent visibility amid snow flurries and showers. The aptly named *Snowflake* on the convoy's port beam reported three radar contacts to the south. *Beverley* turned to investigate. She flashed a challenge as unidentified ships hove into view and when this wasn't answered, she hoisted the signal: "Enemy in sight."

Schulze-Hinrichs had found the lightly protected convoy and seemed to possess every advantage. At 1405 *Hermann Schoemann* opened fire at

Table 7.4. Action off Bear Island, 1 May 1942

Allied Ships	TYP	YL	DFL	SPD	GUNS	TT	GF	DAM
Bulldog	DD	30	1,815	35	2×4.7/45	4×21	3	D1
Amazon	DD	26	1,812	37	2×4.7/45 & 1×3	3×21	3	D3
Beagle	DD	30	1,815	35	2×4.7/45	4×21	3	D1
Beverley	DD	19	1,308	35	3×4/50	6×21	3	
Oxlip	DC	41	1,245	16	1×4/45		1	
Saxafrage	DC	41	1,245	16	1×4/45		1	
Campanula	DC	40	1,245	16	1×4/45		1	
Snowflake	DC	41	1,245	16	1×4/45		1	
German Ships								
Hermann Schoemann	DD	36	3,110	38	5×5/45	8×21	7	
Z24	DD	40	3,605	38	4×5.9/50	8×21	8	
Z25	DD	40	3,543	38	4×5.9/50	8×21	8	

the nearest destroyer. Richmond ordered *Amazon*, *Beverley*, and *Beagle* to form up behind him as he steamed across the front of the convoy and came between the German destroyers and their target on a parallel course. Meanwhile, the merchant ships huddled against the pack ice; some even discovered channels inside.

The two lines of battle traded shots as they headed west at high speed, approximately ten thousand yards apart. Then a salvo fired by *Hermann Schoemann* caught *Amazon*, the second ship in line. Two 5-inch shells disabled both her 4.7-inch mounts, her 3-inch gun amidships, her wheelhouse, and destroyed her main and auxiliary steering positions. The only thing the destroyer could still do was steam at full speed. When the British column came about, she continued straight ahead. Only by steering with her engine was *Amazon* able to finally take position at the rear of the British line. After this short gun action, Schulze-Hinrichs saw that an attempt to rush the convoy could be costly and so he broke off. Richmond used the respite to lay a thick smoke screen.

At 1430 hours Schulze-Hinrichs made another lunge from the southeast. In response, *Bulldog* led her column straight at the German line. The Germans turned while *Z24* and *Z25* fired three and one torpedoes, respectively, toward the convoy. The British destroyers replied in kind. After some minutes, German hydrophones detected three explosions; at least one of their torpedoes struck and sank the Soviet freighter *Tsiolkovski*

(2,847 grt). The British salvo missed, although crewmen aboard the German ships saw a torpedo explode against a nearby iceberg.

A third attack developed at 1530 hours from the east. The convoy was strung out in a single file nearly seven miles long, threading its way through a convenient channel in the ice pack. *Bulldog* raced to the formation's rear leading the British column toward the enemy once again. This time German shells were nearly on target as the British destroyer was suddenly surrounded by geysers of icy water, her hull and upper works rang with sharp pings as splinters rattled aboard. But once again, Schulze-Hinrichs declined the challenge implicit in Richmond's aggressive maneuver and turned away.

Three times more that afternoon Schulze-Hinrichs probed the convoy hoping to catch the escorts out of position or to sneak up behind a favorable snowstorm. Three times more Richmond's destroyers gathered and forced him to turn away, feinting torpedo attacks, skillfully weaving smoke screens, and maintaining an intense counterfire.

Finally, at 1750 hours Schmundt ordered Schulze-Hinrichs to disengage and go after the British cruiser. Although the German destroyers had shot off up to 60 percent of their ammunition (*Hermann Schoemann* 380 rounds and *Z24* 204 rounds), and the British had been just as lavish in their use of ordnance, *Amazon* was the only ship significantly damaged during this prolonged engagement. (*Bulldog* and *Beagle* had their fighting ability slightly impaired by splinter damage and the concussive impact of near misses.) As the German destroyers disappeared to the southeast, Commander Richmond signaled congratulations to his fellow captains. One replied: "I should hate to play poker with you."[4]

Attack on *Edinburgh*, 2 May 1942

TIME	0617–0830
TYPE:	Interception
WEATHER:	Dense snow
VISIBILITY:	Mixed, bad to poor, three to eight miles
SEA STATE:	
SURPRISE:	Germans
MISSION:	British—escort and transit; Germans—interception based upon specific intelligence

When Schulze-Hinrichs abandoned his attack on QP11, the severely damaged *Edinburgh* was six hundred miles east, limping southeast at two knots toward Kola Inlet, steering with her engines. When Rear Admiral S. S. Bonham-Carter heard of *Bulldog*'s pugnacious defense of the convoy, he realized it would be his turn next. He instructed his escorts, *Foresight* and *Forester*, to act independently in the event of an attack. It seemed they could do little to protect the cruiser.

As the day wore on, a Soviet guardship, *Rubin*, joined Bonham-Carter's little force; then around midnight on 1 May four minesweepers from Murmansk appeared, *Hussar, Harrier, Gossamer,* and *Niger*. By 0530 hours on 2 May *Rubin* and *Gossamer* had attached tow lines to *Edinburgh*. Although her speed was still little better than two knots, at least these kept her on a steady course. *Foresight* and *Forester* proceeded on either beam while the other three minesweepers sailed astern. U456 was also attending, although periscope damage prevented her from attacking again.

As the British flotilla struggled to keep the cruiser under way and pointed in the right direction, Schulze-Hinrichs was rushing southeast at thirty-five knots. He was frustrated by his failure to harm QP11 and planned to execute the cruiser quickly by attacking in extended line abreast from the north with the advantages of light and wind. His destroyers would launch their remaining torpedoes simultaneously and then turn away. With *Edinburgh* unable to maneuver, this tactic seemed to guarantee success.

Table 7.5. Attack on *Edinburgh*, 2 May 1942

Allied Ships	TYP	YL	DFL	SPD	GUNS	TT	GF	DAM
Edinburgh	CL	38	13,175	32	12×6/50 & 12×4/45	6×21	33	Sunk
Foresight	DD	34	1,940	36	4×4/7/45	8×21	6	D3
Forester	DD	34	1,940	36	4×4/7/45	8×21	6	D3
Harrier	MS	34	1,330	16	2×4/45	2		
Niger	MS	36	1,330	16	2×4/45	2		
Gossamer	MS	37	1,330	16	2×4/45	2		
Hussar	MS	34	1,330	16	2×4/45	2		
Rubin (SO)	DC	36	550	17	1×4/60	1		
German Ships								
Hermann Schoemann	DD	36	3,110	38	5×5/45	8×21	7	Sunk
Z24	DD	40	3,605	38	4×5.9/50	8×21	8	
Z25	DD	40	3,543	38	4×5.9/50	8×21	8	D2

That was the plan. In the arctic, however, conditions of weather and sea had a way of dictating their own outcomes. At 0617 *Hermann Schoemann* sighted *Edinburgh* and the minesweeper *Hussar* (identified as a Tribal Class destroyer!) eight miles away. *Hermann Schoemann* closed at twenty-one knots, followed by *Z25* and *Z24*, driving off the minesweeper with gunfire as they maneuvered to obtain a favorable position to launch torpedoes. *Edinburgh* cast off her tow lines and Bonham-Carter ordered full speed—eight knots—even though the cruiser could only steam in a circle. *Hermann Schoemann*'s torpedo crew rushed to change the setting on their tubes to short range. At 0634 Schulze-Hinrichs ordered all ships to turn and fire. At that moment a local snow shower suddenly descended between *Hermann Schoemann* and the destroyers following her, masking them from view.

Hermann Schoemann was only four thousand yards from the British ship. She turned and slowed, intent on the target as *Edinburgh*'s bow slowly swung to port. The cruiser's fire director was inoperable and there was no power to train her turrets. Nonetheless, as the destroyer crossed the cruiser's line of fire, flame erupted from her "B" turret and 6-inch shells fell one hundred yards wide. *Hermann Schoemann* immediately increased speed and heeled over in a hard turn to starboard, but it was too late. The second salvo, directed by the turret officer standing halfway out the upper hatch, was on its way. One shell fell forty yards short, but the other two each landed in one of *Hermann Schoemann*'s turbine rooms, immediately stalling her engines and disrupting electricity supply. Only one torpedo was away when this blow struck. The destroyer dropped smoke floats as she drifted to a stop.

Foresight, with *Forester* two hundred yards behind, sailed toward the engaged side to challenge the attackers. The action was confused as the ships steamed at high speed, adding their yellow-green smoke to the mist and sheeting snow, groping for the enemy. Then the British destroyers encountered *Hermann Schoemann* and attacked. One 4.7-inch shell ignited a fire on the German's mess deck, another flooded the Nos. 1 and 2 magazines, and a third entered the boiler room. *Hermann Schoemann* could only defend herself with single shots over open sights and although she did manage to launch four more torpedoes at one of the British destroyers, these all missed. Her only positive accomplishment was to alert her flotilla mates to her plight using a reserve shortwave set.

At 0645 *Z24* and *Z25* found their flagship and made smoke to screen her from the British destroyers. At 0648 the mist around *Z25* suddenly opened like a curtain, giving view of *Edinburgh* beyond the battle. At the same moment *Foresight* and *Forester* were attempting to fire torpedoes. *Foresight* lost her target in a cloud of smoke and mist and just as *Forester* was about to empty her tubes, a 5.9-inch shell from *Z25* ran the course of her hull, devastating the forward and after boiler rooms. A second shell struck "X" gun and a third exploded against the shield of "B" gun near the bridge. A splinter killed the captain, Lieutenant Commander George Huddart, as he was leaning over the bridge railing, exhorting his men. Five minutes later two more shells found *Forester*. She drifted, dead in the water less than four thousand yards from the enemy. *Z25* fired four torpedoes to finish her off.

Foresight rushed to the assistance of *Forester* sailing between her and the Germans and paid the price. *Z25*'s gunners had found a rhythm; they landed one shell in *Foresight*'s forward boiler room and another aft. The damage left *Foresight* with only one gun in action and all she could do was fall back on *Edinburgh* at fifteen knots. *Forester* managed to restore some power and she slowly followed her mate, zigzagging to avoid the shells straddling her on all sides. The cruiser continued to yaw to port, firing her guns as they bore. The torpedoes *Z25* had launched some minutes before were approaching the end of their run. The cruiser's rotation converged with their deadly track and then an explosion ripped her hull opposite the earlier damage and nearly broke the ship in two.[5]

The destroyer battle did not last long after that. *Forester* turned back and managed to hit *Z25* in her radio room, killing four and wounding seven. The minesweepers kept their distance, but the flashes from their 4-inch guns and their gray forms emerging and vanishing in the smoke and mist gave the impression that the British were stronger than they really were. As *Forester* made smoke to screen the doomed cruiser, the Germans unexpectedly broke off the action.

Aboard *Hermann Schoemann* the fires were now under control, but her engines remained useless. *Z24* attempted to come alongside while *Z25* stood by, but for an hour the surging sea stymied these efforts. Finally at 0815 *Z24* secured herself to *Hermann Schoemann* and rescued 244 men. The scuttling charges exploded at 0830 and *Hermann Schoemann* quickly sank. Another 56 men from her crew remained behind aboard her cutter, but *U88* subsequently rescued them.

The final toll aboard *Hermann Schoemann* was remarkably small: eight dead and forty-five wounded. Criticisms of the Germans for failing to sink the crippled British destroyers ("another German case of not engaging the enemy more closely")[6] seem unjustified given the German situation. They were out of torpedoes and very short on ammunition and, mistaking the minesweepers for destroyers, they magnified their opposition. Both British destroyers managed to get under way at slow speed after the Germans withdrew while the minesweepers rescued *Edinburgh*'s crew, less fifty-seven men who went down with their ship. Finally *Foresight* dispatched *Edinburgh* with a torpedo and the entire force returned to Murmansk. Schulze-Hinrichs had led a successful sortie, sinking a cruiser and a merchant ship and inflicting heavy damage on three destroyers at the cost of one of his own.

The Battle of the Barents Sea, 31 December 1942

TIME: 0830–1215
TYPE: Convoy attack
WEATHER: Clear, snow squalls, very cold
VISIBILITY: Variable, 7–10 miles initially
SEA STATE: Small swells
SURPRISE: Germans
MISSION: British—escort and transit; Germans—interception
                based upon general intelligence

Germany's efforts to halt the Russian convoys intensified after the narrow victory over QP11. The onset of arctic summer brought never-ending daylight and better weather (relatively). These conditions favored the Germans; the Allies gained meager compensation in the more northerly route their convoys could take due to the summer retreat of the pack ice. Convoys PQ16/QP12 departed Reykjavik and Kola Inlet respectively on 21 May. QP12 had an uneventful voyage, but submarines and air attacks sank nearly a quarter of the PQ16. Surface forces did not intervene, influenced by false intelligence that the British would attempt a landing somewhere in Norway.

PQ17/QP13 sailed at the height of summer. German armies were rampaging deep into the Soviet Union toward the Volga River and the Caucasus Mountains; Stalin was pressuring the British to open a second front—something they had no intention of doing. Continuing the arctic convoys despite the intensifying German threat was their barely acceptable alternative. Grossadmiral Raeder and Navy Group North intended to smash this convoy with the full force of the High Seas Fleet: one battleship, three heavy cruisers, ten destroyers, and two torpedo boats. The stage was set for a decisive battle, and this is exactly what happened. A portion of the German armada—including *Tirpitz*—did sail, but were quickly recalled. But just the threat of a sortie was enough. Before *Tirpitz* even weighed anchor, Britain's First Sea Lord, Admiral Dudley Pound ordered the escort to retreat and the convoy to scatter. It was a reckless test of an unproven tactic which the commander in chief of the Home Fleet, Admiral Tovey, predicted would result in "sheer bloody murder."[7] Of PQ17's thirty-six merchant ships and one tanker, three turned back while U-boats and aircraft made Tovey a prophet, sinking twenty-four.

PQ18 with thirty-nine freighters and three tankers sailed on 2 September. This time the escort stuck to the convoy and, although subjected to massive air strikes and constant submarine harassment, they fought through with a loss of thirteen ships, destroying three U-boats and forty-one aircraft in the process. German forces also attacked the return convoy, QP14 of fifteen ships, sinking three freighters, a tanker, and two escorts. Inadequate reconnaissance resulted in the cancellation of an operation against QP14 by *Hipper* and the 8th Destroyer Flotilla. This was the last arctic convoy operation until the end of the year.

The activity log of Germany's High Seas Fleet during the summer of 1942 made a thin volume. The capital ships shifted from anchorage to anchorage to confuse British attacks; the shortage of fuel oil limited their training and the enforced idleness degraded both morale and effectiveness. Moreover, Hitler had decreed that before he would sanction a convoy attack by the fleet there had to be a weak escort with no aircraft carrier or heavy ships and a U-boat shadowing. These were tough conditions to meet.

There were only two operations that summer. In August *Scheer* briefly cruised into the Kara Sea. She missed a nine ship convoy, but on 25 August sank the Soviet icebreaker *Alexander Sibiriakoff* (1,384 tons and three 76.2-mm guns) after "heroic resistance,"[8] and shelled the port of Novy Dikson, damaging the icebreaker *Dezhnev* and the steamer *Revolutsioner*. On 24–28 September *Hipper* and five destroyers successfully mined the lonely waters off Novaya Zemyla. Between October and December 1942 thirteen Allied freighters sailed to the Soviet Union independently. Only four arrived. On 5 November *Hipper* with *Richard Beitzen, Friedrich Echoldt, Z27,* and *Z30* searched the Barents Sea for this traffic and enjoyed a small success when *Z27* sank the Soviet trawler *SKR23/Musson* and the tanker *Donbass* (8,000 grt) on 7 November.

After the Battle of Stalingrad it was clear the Soviet Union had survived another year. With the resources freed up after the North African landing, the British began planning another arctic convoy operation.

At 0300 hours, 30 December U354 reported a lightly guarded convoy of six to ten ships 50 miles south of Bear Island. She had found JW51B, which originally consisted of fourteen freighters escorted by the destroyers *Onslow* (flag Captain Robert St. Vincent Sherbrooke of Narvik fame), *Oribi* (which lost contact before the battle and did not participate), *Obedient, Obdurate, Orwell, Achates,* the minesweeper *Bramble,* the corvettes *Hyderabad* and *Rhododendron,* and two trawlers, *Ocean Gem* and *Vizalma.* JW51B was a test of Tovey's theory that two small convoys would be easier to protect than a single large one (borrowing a system introduced by the Italians to fight their convoys through to Libya a year before). JW51A had sailed a week earlier and arrived in Soviet waters unnoticed; so far so good, but JW51B had a rougher time. On Christmas Eve a powerful storm scattered the ships and, one week later, there were still stragglers.

U354's report excited Naval Group North. At last a target that seemed to meet all the Führer's prerequisites. That same morning they ordered the polar fleet to stand by. Initially, only *Hipper* and six destroyers of the 5th Destroyer Flotilla, under Kapitän zur See Alfred Schemmel, *Richard Beitzen, Theodor Riedel, Friedrich Echoldt, Z29, Z30,* and *Z31* were to participate in the planned action, but Berlin gave permission for *Lützow* to join the force at the last moment (she received the final confirmation of her orders after she was already under way).

The plan of Vizeadmiral Oskar Kummetz, Befehlshaber der Kreuzer, called for *Hipper* and three destroyers, *Friedrich Echoldt, Richard Beitzen,* and *Z29,* to approach from the northwest, attack at dawn (0840 hours), and attract the convoy's escorts to them. He assumed the convoy would turn south where *Lützow, Theodor Riedel, Z30,* and *Z31,* would be waiting to snap it up. Daylight at that latitude and time of year consisted of four hours of twilight. For all ships to arrive at the right place at the right time would require careful coordination and good luck. After the engagement *Lützow* was to continue on a raiding cruise in the Arctic Ocean.

(Kapitän zur See Rudolf Stange, *Lützow*'s captain, only learned of this mission after he was at sea!) Kummetz's orders were typically restrictive— he was to avoid action with equal or superior forces and not risk his heavy ships in a night action.

Leaving the sheltered waters of Altenfjord the fleet encountered a heavy swell that laid many low with seasickness. *Lützow*, for example, was two hours decoding instructions from Kummetz because everyone in the signals staff was sick. To ensure he found his target in plenty of time, Kummetz sailed in an extended line of search eighty-five miles long, with *Hipper* at the northern end and *Lützow* at the south. Between the cruisers, in order from north to south, sailed *Friedrich Echoldt, Z29, Richard Beitzen, Z31, Z30,* and *Theodor Riedel*.

The British had four groups of ships scattered in the vicinity, none of which knew for certain the exact position of the others. The convoy—now twelve ships with eight escorts—was heading east. Forty-five miles north

Table 7.6. The Battle of the Barents Sea, 31 December 1942

Allied Ships	TYP	YL	DFL	SPD	GUNS	TT	GF	DAM
Sheffield	CL	36	12,190	32	12×6/50 & 8×4/45	6×21	29	
Jamaica	CL	40	11,090	31	12×6/50 & 8×4/45	6×21	29	
Onslow	DD	41	2,365	37	4×4.7/45 & 1×4/45	4×21	7	D4
Obdurate	DD	42	2,365	37	4×4/45	8×21	5	D2
Obedient	DD	42	2,365	37	4×4/45	8×21	5	D1
Orwell	DD	42	2,365	37	4×4/45	8×21	5	
Achates	DD	29	1,815	35	2×4.7/45	4×21	3	Sunk
Bramble	MS	38	1,330	17	2×4/45		2	Sunk
Hyderabad	DC	41	1,245	16	1×4/45		1	
Rhododendron	DC	40	1,245	16	1×4/45		1	
German Ships								
Admiral Hipper	CA	37	18,200	32	8×8/60 & 12×4.1/65	12×21	35	D3
Lützow	CA	31	16,200	28	6×11/54 & 8×5.9/55	8×21	46	
Friedrich Eckoldt	DD	37	3,165	38	5×5/45	8×21	7	Sunk
Richard Beitzen	DD	35	3,156	38	5×5/45	8×21	7	
Theodor Riedel	DD	36	3,110	38	5×5/45	8×21	7	
Z29	DD	40	3,597	38	4×5.9/50	8×21	8	
Z30	DD	40	3,597	38	4×5.9/50	8×21	8	
Z31	DD	41	3,691	38	5×5.9/50	8×21	9	

the trawler *Vizalma* was shepherding one straggler while *Bramble,* fifteen miles northeast of the convoy, was searching for the other. Finally, Force R, *Sheffield* and *Jamaica,* commanded by Rear Admiral Robert Burnett, sailed fifteen miles southeast of *Vizalma. Hipper* and her destroyers were rushing north toward their attack position while *Lützow* and her destroyers were fifty miles south and closing. There was a low overcast, scattered snow squalls, a calm sea and good visibility seven miles to the north and ten miles to the south. A gentle breeze blew west-northwest at 16 knots.

Fortune initially favored the Germans. At 0718 hours, in the arctic pre-dawn darkness, *Hipper* detected shadows to starboard. She pulled back and sent *Friedrich Echoldt* to investigate. More shadows emerged. Kummetz had found the convoy. Dawn was an hour away. His ships were in perfect position. Operation Regenbogen was off to an excellent start.

At 0820 *Hyderabad,* sailing on the convoy's starboard quarter, sighted two vessels, but did not report them, assuming Soviet ships had joined the escort. At 0830 *Obdurate* on the starboard beam saw the same two ships bearing 210 degrees. She informed Captain Sherbrooke, who sent her to investigate. *Obdurate* followed the contacts (*Friedrich Echoldt, Richard Beitzen,* and *Z29*) around the stern of the convoy and off to the northwest. Then, at 0929 hours, by which time the British destroyer had approached to eight thousand yards, *Friedrich Echoldt* opened fire. *Obdurate* retreated, radioing the alarm. Sherbrooke ordered *Obedient* and *Orwell* to concentrate on his flag while *Achates* and the smaller escorts began to lay smoke.

At 0930 the *Lützow* group sighted the British convoy, but Stange, displaying caution above and beyond the call of duty, recalled his destroyers to await better information.

At 0939 *Onslow* followed by *Orwell* was steaming northwest to close both *Obdurate* and the German destroyers when a larger shape hove into view fine on her starboard bow. It was *Hipper.* At 0941 the cruiser opened fire and Sherbrooke broadcast the first definitive enemy report. Burnett received this report, but he kept his cruisers sailing northeast until 0955 to investigate a radar contact, which proved to be *Vizalma.* (He believed the convoy was north, not south, of his position.)

Onslow and *Orwell* opened fire at *Hipper* from nine thousand yards and played a cat-and-mouse game for half an hour, simulating torpedo attacks as they dodged in and out of the smoke. As in all arctic battles, the cold played an important role. On *Onslow,* for example, a thin sheet of ice behind the extractors disabled "A" and "X" mountings while iced range finders and binoculars degraded the accuracy of the guns that could fire. First *Hipper* fired five salvos at *Achates*, easily distinguished by a thick, rolling trail of smoke. One seaman recalled: "The enemy picked us out for his early fire. We must have been conspicuous. The German cruiser got us the first time."[9] Actually a series of very near misses inflicted extensive splinter damage and fractures in her hull plates, forcing the old destroyer to reduce speed.

At 0945 hours the convoy turned southeast. At the same time *Hipper* made a sharp alteration to the northeast in response to a feinted torpedo attack. She then returned to her generally easterly course, firing for the next fifteen minutes at the destroyers paralleling her course to the south at ranges between thirteen thousand to nineteen thousand yards. By this time Sherbrooke had collected his four O class vessels, but, uncertain about the location of the German destroyers, he sent *Obedient* and *Obdurate* back to the convoy. He did not need to worry. Kummetz was more concerned about *Hipper*'s lines of fire than the potential mayhem his destroyers were capable of inflicting. He kept them on a tight rein behind the cruiser.

Between 1001 and 1016 *Hipper* fired only one salvo. The uncertain visibility whereby sea and cloud merged into a uniform silver-gray affected her aim. With their camouflage, the British ships were hard to see. Kummetz complained: "The light conditions were exceptionally unfavorable, reducing even further the little brightness we could otherwise expect. Everything looked as if covered by a gray veil, which distorted all outlines and merged them together."[10] *Hipper* finally acquired a good fix on *Onslow* at 1016. Geysers erupted into the sky on either side of the British flagship, spraying splinters over her deck and wounding Captain Sherbrooke in the face. Then successive salvos toppled the destroyer's funnel and aerials and hit her superstructure under "B" turret and on the forecastle. Severe fires erupted throughout *Onslow*'s forward half as she put up a protective smokescreen and turned to starboard. Sherbrooke remained at his post until his ship was out of danger and then transferred command of the flotilla to Lieutenant Commander D. C. Kinlock of *Obedient*. He received the Victoria Cross for this action. *Hipper* expended forty-eight 8-inch and seventy-two 4.1-inch rounds to hit the flagship three times and knock her out of the fight.

At 1030 hours Kummetz stood on the verge of victory. *Hipper* had just altered course to slightly north of east and was sixteen miles east-northeast of the convoy (sailing southeast at nine knots). All the destroyers were on the engaged flank between eight to nine miles from the German cruiser. Two of the five were significantly damaged. Meanwhile *Lützow*, trailed by her three destroyers, was a scant five miles south of the convoy, which was unwittingly sailing straight toward her. *Sheffield* and *Jamaica* were fifteen miles northwest of *Hipper*. Burnett could see gun flashes to the south, but he adjusted course from a southerly to an easterly heading, wanting to clarify his radar contacts before he blundered into a surface action.

At 1045 *Rhododendron* reported unidentified ships to the south—*Lützow* and her destroyers. Instead of attacking, Stange altered course and passed ahead of the convoy; although his radar was reporting contacts as near as three miles, he couldn't tell what they were because a snow squall providentially (for the British) hid them from his sight. He kept his destroyers astern and came to a parallel course to the north to "wait for the weather to clear."[11] Aboard *Onslow* the weather was clear enough: "Into view silently slid the huge silhouette of the German pocket battleship . . . we simply stopped breathing and waited for the first broadside. But nothing happened! As quietly as she came into view she slid out—a ghost ship if ever there was."[12] Raeder wrote: "A favorable opportunity to score a success and possibly finish the appointed job at one blow was not here exploited."[13] Stange had been *Lützow*'s captain for nearly a year, but this was his first mission and he had never seen action. One can imagine how an aggressive commander, a Philip Vian or a Max-Eckart Wolff, would have reacted.

At 1030 hours *Bramble* appeared from the northeast. She signaled: "One cruiser bearing 300°."[14] The cruiser was *Hipper*. The minesweeper engaged the cruiser's attention for a critical half hour from 1036 to 1106. *Hipper* expended fifty-one 8-inch and thirty-eight 4.1-inch shells, battering the unfortunate ship and leaving her all but sunk. Having run far north in the process, Kummetz detached *Richard Beitzen* and *Friedrich Echoldt* to finish off the cripple while he hurried south at thirty-one knots to regain contact. Because the entire German force was now north of the convoy, the escort could concentrate on that side, maintaining smoke and standing ready to counter any lunge toward the merchantmen.

At 1115 hours *Achates* had just cleared her own smoke when *Hipper* reappeared to northeast. The cruiser opened fire from fourteen thousand yards and hit with her first broadside. The 269-pound shell smashed *Achates*'s bridge, killing her captain, Lieutenant Commander A. H. T. Johns;

other shells struck the destroyer's boiler room and forecastle, causing flooding. Her speed dropped to twelve knots; forty men died. Nonetheless, she fell behind the convoy and continued to weave, contributing her only remaining weapon—black funnel smoke—to the defense. Meanwhile Stange was still waiting. He could see *Hipper*'s gun-flashes behind him to the north so at 1126 he came about to the northwest on a reciprocal heading. At the exact same time *Hipper* shifted fire to *Obedient*, flag of Sherbrooke's replacement, Lieutenant Commander D. C. Kinloch. The cruiser's gunners continued to shoot effectively, straddling the destroyer from eighty-five hundred yards and destroying her wireless. This forced Kinloch to rotate command to Lieutenant Commander C. E. L. Sclater of *Obdurate*. Regardless of who ordered the defense, however, the tactics remained the same. The destroyers feinted a torpedo attack causing *Hipper* to turn sharply to starboard at 1130.

That same minute *Sheffield* and *Jamaica* finally entered action. Burnett was following his radar, aware he was rapidly closing a contact larger than a destroyer and faster than a merchant ship. Then *Hipper*, heading northeast avoiding imaginary torpedoes, appeared eight miles to the southwest. Burnett turned to a parallel course and at 1131 hours *Sheffield* and then *Jamaica* opened fire. Completely surprised by the columns of water that spouted on either side, *Hipper*'s captain, Kapitän zur See Hans Hartmann ordered a hard 270-degree turn to starboard. His ship was heeled steeply to port when a 6-inch shell struck her hull eleven feet below the waterline, severely damaging the No. 3 boiler room. One thousand tons of water flooded in, knocking No. 2 boiler room off-line and temporarily reducing speed to fifteen knots. At 1135 a second shell struck *Hipper*'s hull amidships on the starboard side and passed through, failing to explode. A third shell detonated in her aircraft hangar, igniting a fire. At just that moment Kummetz received a message from the Admiral Polar Coast: "No unnecessary risk." Uncertain about the damage just sustained and the identity of his new opponents, he signaled "Break off, turn away to the west."[15] The time was 1137.

The British cruisers pursued, but *Hipper* vanished into a snow squall. Then, at 1143 *Friedrich Echoldt* and *Richard Beitzen,* trying to find their flag after sinking *Bramble* with all hands, stumbled upon Burnett's cruisers only four thousand yards to the north. *Sheffield* turned toward *Friedrich Echoldt* the nearer one and flames erupted from all twelve of her guns. Unaware there were English cruisers in action, Schemmel signaled *Hipper* to stop shooting at him. *Richard Beitzen,* realizing the awful truth, warned it was the enemy. But it was too late for *Friedrich Echoldt.* *Sheffield* hit with her first salvo and badly damaged the destroyer with her third. She checked fire after sixteen broadsides. An observer wrote: "This dark grey wreck of a vessel (passed) down our ship's side. The upper deck short-range weapons raked the burning deck with gun fire as she drifted astern of us into the darkness and oblivion."[16] *Friedrich Echoldt* perished with her entire crew of 340 men. *Jamaica* failed to engage *Richard Beitzen,* which was lucky to escape.

After loitering for more than two hours Stange finally obtained a satisfactorily clear view of the convoy at 1138 as it emerged from the snow squall eight miles to his south. Four minutes later, the thunder of *Lützow's* 11-inch guns finally erupted across the battle sea. She straddled the freighter *Calobre* and splinter damage forced the merchant ship to drop out of line. Sclater responded by leading his destroyers to the threatened flank, laying heavy smoke, while the convoy made an emergency turn to starboard. Stange continued to the northwest, fighting a leisurely battle, periodically engaging targets with his main and secondary batteries. (His ship only expended eighty-six 11-inch and seventy-six 5.9-inch rounds the entire battle.)

Following behind, *Theodor Riedel* and *Z30* managed to snap off a few rounds and some torpedoes as well (the frustration of the destroyer captains can be imagined), but, except for severe splinter damage *Lützow* inflicted on *Obdurate* at 1200 hours (which required five weeks in dock to repair), the Germans did no further harm. When *Hipper* briefly appeared to the west of *Lützow* Sclater turned toward her and came under fire, but at 1149 Kummetz ordered the fleet to withdraw. Dark was drawing near and his orders forbade night combat. At 1203 Stange received this order and immediately complied.

At 1230 there was a brief engagement between the British and German cruisers. The shooting of both forces was good with *Lützow* straddling Burnett's ships and being straddled in turn. But neither side appeared to have the heart for a slugfest and Burnett (wisely) altered course to the northwest at 1236. *Achates* finally capsized and sank at 0115 hours.

That a German "pocket battleship," heavy cruiser, and five destroyers would flee from a pair of light cruisers was a powerful indication of how the nature of the surface war had changed since December 1939 and the Battle of the River Plate. In fact, the Battle of the Barents Sea was one of the decisive naval battles of World War II because of the impact it had on the future use of the German navy's large warships. Berlin expected success and the initial reports only heightened that anticipation. Then Führer headquarters heard nothing until the BBC announced a great victory. The consequences of Hitler's disappointment led to the downfall of Grossadmiral Raeder and an order to pay off every surface warship larger than a destroyer. While this order was never carried out as originally delivered, it nonetheless gutted the surface fleet as a fighting force. Before Barents Sea, the Germany Navy fought twenty-nine surface actions and a third involved cruisers or larger ships. After Barents Sea, the navy fought thirty-seven actions and only one involved a heavy unit.

Action Off Syltefjord, 21 January 1943

TIME: 2123–2230
TYPE: Interception
WEATHER: Full moon, winds SW force 4 to 5
VISIBILITY: three to five miles
SEA STATE: Calm, sea state 1 to 2
SURPRISE: Soviet
MISSION: Soviets—interception based upon general intelligence;
               Germans—escort and transit

Even as Germany's capital ships swung at anchor in the northern fjords, protected by torpedo nets, fog machines, and heavy antiaircraft batteries, her light forces were at sea every day engaged in the mundane tasks that are the foundation of sea power. Germany relied on shipping along the coastal waters of Norway's deeply indented arctic shoreline to sustain its divisions struggling to advance on Murmansk and, after their drive stalled, for the exploitation of the area's valuable nickel and iron ore resources. In the first six months of 1942 alone, 872 transports carrying 2,608,057 tons of supplies plied the route between Kirkenes and Narvik. The Soviets attacked this traffic with submarines, aircraft, and motor torpedo-boats; they used heavier units much more rarely, but their destroyers did conduct several surface sweeps and once they attacked a German convoy.

Destroyers were the largest units in the Soviet Northern Fleet up through 1944. The Soviet Union began the war with five modern and three old destroyers. They were supported by three larger torpedo boats, two minelayers, seven guardships, fifteen submarines, and fifteen sub-chasers/patrol boats.[17] During 1942 a flotilla leader, *Baku,* and three destroyers (*Razumnyi, Razyaryonnyi,* and *Revnostnyi*) transferred from the Pacific Fleet (the voyage took exactly three months, 15 July to 14 October) raising the destroyer force stationed at Murmansk to eight modern units and one destroyer leader after one of the original ships, *Sokrushitelny,* foundered in the Barents Sea during a storm. The fleet commander, Admiral A. G. Golovko, defined the mission of these destroyers to be interdiction of enemy traffic by raids, laying offensive minefields, and day or night torpedo or gunfire attacks (but not protection of Allied convoys). The opportunity for two units of this force to carry out a mission came just three weeks after the German defeat in the Battle of the Barents Sea. On 19 January 1943 Soviet radio interception units learned of a German convoy sailing for Kirkenes. On 20 January *Baku* and *Razumnyi* under Captain First Class P. I. Koltchin stood out from Kola Inlet to search for this convoy, proceeding west at twenty knots four miles off the coast.

The German minelayer *Skagerrak,* accompanied by *M322* and *M303* had sailed from Hammerfest at 1700 hours on 20 January to lay an anti-submarine mine barrage off North Cape. After she successfully discharged her load of 130 mines, the submarine hunters *UJ1104* and *UJ1105* joined *Skagerrak's* flotilla; together they continued east for Kirkenes to pick up a new load of mines. *M322* led the formation followed by *M303* with the minelayer six hundred fifty yards astern. *UJ1105* was sixteen hundred yards to seaward of *Skagerrak* following *UJ1104,* a little closer to shore guarding against any threats that might appear out of the offing. They were sailing at eleven knots roughly one mile off the shore's steep, snowy cliffs.

The Germans were just passing Makkaur at 2100 hours on 21 January when *UJ1105's* lookouts peering through the clear, relatively mild night air (the temperature was 28 degrees Fahrenheit) saw two silhouettes ahead to port, bow on, and sailing too fast to be anything but warships. *UJ1104* queried *Skagerrak* if she was aware of any friendly vessels in the area, but when the unknown ships increased speed and came to 320 degrees the sub-hunters sounded the alarm, and at 2118 hours they began to flash a challenge.

Table 7.7. Action Off Syltefjord, 21 January 1943

Allied Ships	TYP	YL	DFL	SPD	GUNS	TT	GF	DAM
Baku	DD	38	2,680	36	5×5.1/55 & 2×3/55	8×21	9	
Razumnyi	DD	40	2,380	37	4×5.1/55 & 2×3/55	6×21	8	D1
German Ships								
Skagerrak	ML	n/a	1,280	17	2×37-mm		0	
M303	MS	41	775	18	1×4.1/45		1	
M322	MS	41	775	18	1×4.1/45		1	
UJ1104	DC	37	1,100	12	1×88-mm		1	
UJ1105	DC	36	1,075	12	1×88-mm		1	

Captain Koltchin's two ships, *Baku* leading *Razumnyi* by a thousand yards, saw the German force at the same time *UJ1105* spotted them. The Soviets judged they were facing two transports and several escorts. They came to twenty-eight knots and changed course slightly to the northwest in order to pass the German formation on an opposite bearing. They held fire as the range closed, ignoring German challenges until 2123 hours. At that point *Baku* fired four torpedoes at what she believed was the lead transport from an estimated range of fifty-five hundred yards while *Razumnyi* targeted the follow-up ship. As they swept past the Germans at high speed, lookouts on *Baku* reported explosions. Believing she sank her target, *Baku* shifted fire to one of the escorts.

When *Baku* opened fire, all the German ships were fully alert. *Skagerrak* immediately came to starboard and made for the coast while the UJ-boats made smoke. Ahead the two minesweepers cut their sweeps and began to zigzag. All of the German ships returned fire. Because of the close range even their 20-mm guns could join in.

For six minutes heavy gunfire and the streaking tracers crisscrossed the sky; the roar of gunfire echoed off the cliffs. The Soviets drew abreast of the German ships and then passed to the northwest. During this time, the Germans counted twenty heavy salvos that fell around them, but not a single shell hit. They observed two explosions on their unengaged side and assumed these were Soviet torpedoes detonating ashore. At 2230 the Soviet destroyers disappeared behind a smoke screen and, just like that, the action was over.

UJ1104 was the most heavily engaged of the German ships firing 28 88-mm rounds, 125 37-mm, and 222 20-mm. The four other ships

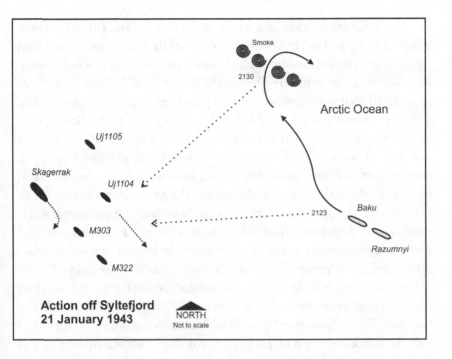

fired 13 88-mm, 182 37-mm, and 370 20-mm rounds, collectively. The two minesweepers, particularly *M322* in front of the formation, were lightly engaged and didn't use their 4.1-inch guns. *Razumnyi* was the only ship damaged; one shell ignited a small fire in the vicinity of her No. 2 mount.

Skagerrak and the minesweepers turned into Syltefjord and anchored. The UJ-boats lingered off the fjord's mouth in case the Soviets returned and then joined the rest of their flotilla. The destroyers returned triumphantly to port claiming one transport of nine thousand tons sunk and another damaged. Koltchin's report gave concern over German minefields and fire from German shore batteries as the reasons he terminated action so quickly; but, although the Germans had a battery of six 5.7-inch guns on the cliffs above the fjord, these never opened fire.

The Soviet destroyers enjoyed every advantage in this action—firepower, speed, surprise, and light—but their rapid approach and hasty exit prevented them from achieving results. Although Admiral Golovko concluded the destroyers should have been more aggressive, the fleet's political commissar was happy to celebrate a victory.

The Allies ran pairs of arctic convoys in January and February 1943, which U-boats and aircraft contested only lightly. But Grossadmiral Karl Dönitz, the new commander in chief of the German navy, was not content to let this situation continue. Despite the fallout from the Barents Sea battle and Hitler's irrevocable order to scrap the large ships, Germany still had a powerful battlegroup assembled in the vicinity of Narvik: *Tirpitz,* flagship of Vizeadmiral Oskar Kummetz, who, from February, assumed the new role of Battlegroup Commander (Befehlshaber der Kampfgruppe), *Scharnhorst, Lützow,* seven destroyers, and two torpedo boats. Naval Group North, anxious to erase the stain of the Barents Sea, devised a realistic plan for an April convoy attack using the entire force and giving Kummetz increased operational freedom. The trouble was the Allies suspended convoy operations as soon as they learned of the battlegroup's formation. A raid on Spitzbergen, really more of a training exercise involving *Tirpitz, Scharnhorst,* and nine destroyers, was the only action Germany could find for her capital ships during 1943. However, action was not required. The threat of *Tirpitz* "in view of what it had taken to trap and sink her sistership *Bismarck* became a major preoccupation . . . for the Admiralty and the government."[18] This threat was one of Germany's most effective uses of sea power in the war; it was enough to close the seaway to the Soviet Union and deny the British use of an entire ocean. Even if Hitler and most of the naval command did not recognize this, the British did.

On the night of 21–22 September, British midget submarines successfully attacked *Tirpitz,* putting her out of action for six months. On 17 November, the northern force was further gutted when the four ships of the 6th Destroyer Flotilla sailed south. This left only *Scharnhorst* and the five destroyers of the 4th Flotilla available for operations.

With the German battlegroup depleted and the return of polar autumn, the British resumed the arctic convoys. In November JW54A, JW54B, and JW55A made the run to Murmansk without loss. However, German aircraft sighted JW55A, and this led both the German and British commands to begin thinking about a surface attack on the next convoy.

This development came at a time of disarray in the battlegroup's command structure. Vizeadmiral Kummetz departed in November for several months' convalescent leave, taking most of his staff. The Group Command appointed Führer der Zerstörer, Konteradmiral Erich Bey as his temporary replacement. The sight of a destroyer man flying his flag on a battleship assured officers and men they would not see action that winter. However, on 19 December, Dönitz told Hitler he would attack the next arctic convoy if a successful operation seemed certain.

On 22 December and again on 23 December aerial reconnaissance found JW55B. The escort seemed strong, but the aircraft saw no evidence of a heavy covering force. To Dönitz conditions seemed right for him to keep his word. But, although a year had gone by since the embarrassment of the Battle of the Barents Sea, little else had changed. The orders ultimately issued to Bey, while stressing the need for an offensive spirit to provide relief for the soldiers fighting on the Eastern front, cautioned him, as always, to avoid risk.

Battle of the North Cape, 26 December 1943

TIME: 0930–1945
TYPE: Interception
WEATHER: High winds SW force 6–7, overcast with rain and snow
               flurries
VISIBILITY: Dark, poor three to four miles with openings to ten miles
SEA STATE: Heavy SW swell
SURPRISE: Tactically Allies
MISSION: British—escort and transit, then interception based
               upon specific intelligence; German—interception based
               upon specific intelligence, then transit

JW55B sailed from Scotland's Loch Ewe on 20 December. It consisted of nineteen merchant ships escorted by ten destroyers. The British had three other groups at sea. Returning from Murmansk, convoy RA55A consisted of twenty-two ships and ten destroyers. Positioned to support both convoys during the most dangerous portion of their passage there was Force 1, under Vice Admiral R. L. Burnett, with the heavy cruiser *Norfolk* and the light cruisers *Belfast* and *Sheffield*. Finally, Force 2, under Admiral Sir Bruce Fraser, commander in chief of the Home Fleet, provided distant heavy cover with battleship *Duke of York*, light cruiser *Jamaica* and destroyers *Savage, Saumarez,* and the Norwegian *Stord*. The British learned German units were shadowing JW55B and took several actions to forestall an attack. At 1325 hours on 24 December, when it was only four hundred miles from Altenfjord and both covering forces far away, Fraser broke radio silence and ordered the convoy to reverse course for three hours. At the same time, he increased Force 2's speed to nineteen knots. On 25 December he broke radio silence again to order four destroyers from RA55A to reinforce JW55B and to send JW55B farther north.

Despite Fraser's broadcasts, Group North believed they had no concrete evidence of an enemy battleship at sea, at least in position to intercept *Scharnhorst*. They also believed they could achieve surprise, not knowing that London was receiving their sighting reports almost as quickly as Berlin. Accordingly, at 1415 hours on Christmas day Dönitz authorized operation Ostfront: *Scharnhorst* and the 4th Destroyer Flotilla's attack on convoy JW55B. "Practically all the staffs and commanders" on the spot received these orders with "grave reservations."[19] Bey asked Dönitz to reconsider because the weather would limit reconnaissance and severely handicap the destroyers, or at least to limit the sortie to *Scharnhorst* alone. The crew of *Scharnhorst* had opened their mail and Christmas parcels and the captain's rounds had been "an informal affair." The order at 1300 hours to prepare for sea came as an unwelcome surprise to most.[20]

At 1900 hours on Christmas day *Scharnhorst,* preceded by three minesweepers, sailed down the fjord for the open sea commanded by an admiral who had not sailed aboard a battleship since his days as a cadet. Z29 (Flotilla Commander Kapitän zur See Rolf Johannesson) led Z34 and Z38 while Z30 and Z33 sailed from Kaa Fjord to join him. The admiral, commander, captains, and staff had no opportunity to meet and formulate a plan or discuss tactics. The forecast for 26 December in the area south of Bear Island was grim: a heavy southwest swell, overcast with rain, wind gusting to forty knots and visibility limited to three to four miles. There would be no true day, just twilight for several hours with the sun reaching a zenith of 12 degrees below the horizon from 1122 to 1207.

At 2200 hours the Germans reached the open sea. The wind was blowing a moderate gale from the southwest with a heavy following sea. The warships worked up to twenty-five knots with the top-heavy destroyers laboring hard, heading north toward the expected position of the convoy. At 0423 hours on 26 December Bey altered course to 030 degrees. By this time JW55B was fifty miles south of Bear Island steering east-northeast at six to eight knots. The westbound RA55A was out of danger 220 miles west of Bear Island. Force 1 was 150 miles east of JW55B while Fraser and

Table 7.8. Battle of the North Cape, 26 December 1943

Allied Ships	TYP	YL	DFL	SPD	GUNS	TT	GF	DAM
Duke of York	BB	39	42,076	28	10×14/45 & 16×5.25/50		117	D1
Belfast	CL	38	13,175	32	12×6/50 & 12×4/45	6×21	33	
Sheffield	CL	36	12,190	32	12×6/50 & 8×4/45	6×21	29	
Norfolk	CA	28	14,600	32	8×8/50 & 8×4/45	8×21	32	D3
Jamaica	CL	40	11,090	31	12×6/50 & 8×4/45	6×21	29	
Musketeer	DD	41	2,810	36	6×4.7/50	8×21	8	
Opportune	DD	42	2,365	37	4×4/45	8×21	5	
Virago	DD	43	2,505	36	4×4.7/45	8×21	6	
Matchless	DD	41	2,810	36	6×4.7/50	8×21	8	
Savage	DD	42	2,505	36	4×4.7/45	8×21	6	
Saumarez	DD	42	2,505	36	4×4.7/45	8×21	6	D2
Scorpion	DD	42	2,505	36	4×4.7/45	8×21	6	
Stord (NO)	DD	43	2,505	36	4×4.7/45	8×21	6	
German Ships								
Scharnhorst	BB	36	38,900	32	9×11/54.5 & 12×5.9/55	6×21	79	Sunk
Z29	DD	40	3,597	38	4×5.9/50	8×21	8	
Z30	DD	40	3,597	38	4×5.9/50	8×21	8	
Z33	DD	41	3,691	38	5×5.9/50	8×21	9	
Z34	DD	42	3,691	38	5×5.9/50	8×21	9	
Z38	DD	41	3,691	38	5×5.9/50	8×21	9	

Force 2 were 210 miles southeast of the convoy, hurrying at twenty-four knots to close the distance. At 0339 hours on 26 December Fraser received the Admiralty's appreciation that *Scharnhorst* was at sea. But despite his preparations and dispositions, neither he nor Force 1 was in position to deflect an attack.

At 0700 hours Bey ordered his force into a reconnaissance formation with the destroyers in line abreast ten miles ahead of *Scharnhorst,* sweeping west-southwest at twelve knots, dead into the wind and sea. Although he had only a general idea of the convoy's location, Bey was doing well; he was east of his target and closing, neatly interposed between the two cover forces and in an excellent position to intercept. At 0814 he received a signal from U716 describing a contact she had made some hours earlier which seemed to place the convoy more to the northwest. At 0820, with the convoy forty miles west, Bey turned *Scharnhorst* north.[21] The destroyers, which were beyond visual range, continued clawing their way to the southwest, unaware the battleship was no longer following. In fact, because JW55B had turned north, they were sweeping past it to the south on a parallel, but reciprocal, course. Johannesson was out of the picture and, although he had his opportunities, he played no part in the coming battle.

Burnett was just barely in the picture. He had wandered too far ahead of the convoy despite Fraser's position broadcasts. However, he redeemed himself at 0834 hours when *Norfolk*'s radar picked up a blip at thirty-three thousand yards bearing 280 degrees. Over the next fifteen minutes *Belfast* and *Sheffield* also obtained contacts. By this time, the convoy was only thirty miles west of *Scharnhorst*. Bey was virtually groping in the dark. He brought his ship to the northeast and then at 0850 *Scharnhorst* altered course back to the southwest. Burnett, clinging to the contact, sailed in a line of bearing passing north of *Scharnhorst*'s stern to get between the battleship and the convoy.

At 0921 *Sheffield* sighted *Scharnhorst* sailing east-southeast thirteen thousand yards away. Three minutes later *Belfast* and then *Norfolk* fired star shells. The glaring pyrotechnics caught Bey by surprise; he altered course 30 degrees to port to a heading of 150 degrees. At 0930 *Norfolk* opened fire from ninety-eight hundred yards. She was south of the other cruisers blocking their line of fire. *Norfolk* shot six quick salvos while permitting *Belfast* to pull ahead, making a turn to port to course 265 degrees. Her fire was accurate, hitting twice on the second or third salvos. One shell destroyed *Scharnhorst*'s portside high angle director and the FuMo27 radar and the other penetrated the deck between a portside 5.9-inch gun and the torpedo tubes, but failed to explode. *Scharnhorst*'s Caesar turret replied as she worked up to thirty knots. At 0938 the British came to a heading of 105 degrees, completing their loop, but the range was opening rapidly because the heavy seas limited their speed to twenty-four knots.

The German destroyers, meanwhile, were thrashing about to the southwest. At 0855 Johannesson sent a sighting report to Bey and almost opened fire before he realized his contact was *Z38*, out of position to the north. Then, when the first engagement began, Johannesson saw flashes in the sky, but—strangely incurious—he continued sweeping southwest at ten knots for another hour.

At 1014 Burnett broke off chasing *Scharnhorst* and turned back to the convoy. Shortly after he was joined by the 36th Destroyer Flotilla, *Musketeer, Matchless, Opportune,* and *Virago* detached from convoy RA55A.

Burnett ordered them to screen his cruisers while he deployed ten miles east of JW55B.

Bey, meanwhile, complying with Dönitz's exhortations for an offensive spirit, returned north thinking to go for the convoy this time from the northeast. He was also trying strenuously to collect his destroyers. At 0925 he asked for their situation and at 1027 he sent them a signal telling them to come toward him. At 1135 he gave them his position. U277 sighted the convoy at 1000 and when Bey received this news, he signaled Johannesson again at 1158. The most important sighting report, however, failed to reach Bey. At 1012 a German aircraft flew over Force 2 and at 1135 reported five ships, one large. The senior air officer, however, deleted mention of the large ship (which would have caused Bey to immediately abort the operation), because the pilot had described it as probable. When the report was passed along, Group North interpreted it as five destroyers.

Admiral Fraser was displeased by Burnett's 1035 signal that he had let *Scharnhorst* get away. His destroyers were running low on fuel and Fraser believed there was a possibility *Scharnhorst* might break for the Atlantic to embark on anticommerce cruise. At 1058 he signaled Burnett that unless contact could be regained, he had no hope of finding the German battleship. Finally, he ordered Force 2 to reverse course.

At 1210 Force 1 was steering course 045 degrees in line abreast with *Belfast* farthest to port, *Sheffield* in the center, and *Norfolk* to starboard. The destroyers were in line ahead two miles east of the cruisers off Norfolk's starboard bow. Then *Sheffield*'s radar returned an echo from twelve miles away. Burnett had guessed right this time. He altered course east to intercept and, at 1221 with the range down to 11,000 yards, *Belfast* fired star shell and then a broadside. *Sheffield* also fired a full broadside, but *Norfolk* could only bring "A" and "B" turrets to bear. Once again enemy gunfire surprised Bey. Burnett ordered his destroyers to attack with torpedoes, but with *Scharnhorst* turning west, coming almost directly at them, this proved impossible; only *Musketeer* and *Virago* could engage with their 4.7-inch guns.

By 1225 the range had dropped to four thousand yards. Bey, nervous about rushing seven torpedo armed warships, turned south, southeast. He was shooting with some success, straddling *Virago* and *Sheffield*, spraying the latter with splinters. But *Norfolk*, whose gunpowder produced bright flashes with every salvo, attracted the most attention. At 1227 *Scharnhorst* hit her twice. The first shell hit exploded on "X" turret's barbette, producing a tall column of fire and disabling the guns. The second landed amidships; it failed to detonate, but knocked out all but one of the radar sets nonetheless. Seven men died and six more were seriously wounded. Although the British claimed several hits during this second action, it appears *Scharnhorst* went untouched. When *Norfolk* finally returned to harbor, she would be ten months undergoing repairs and a refit.

While *Scharnhorst* and the cruisers tangled, Johannesson's destroyers were navigating northwest following Bey's order of 1158. They passed within ten miles of the convoy by 0100, but failed to see it.

At 1241 with *Scharnhorst* opening the range the cruisers checked fire. Although it was just past the period of maximum twilight, visibility was only twelve thousand yards. The cruisers mostly relied on radar to aim their weapons. *Sheffield*, for example, only fired ninety-six 6-inch rounds in twenty minutes, the equivalent of just eight broadsides. The destroyers continued in action for six minutes longer. *Matchless* fired fifty-two salvos while *Virago* got off only six.

Rebuffed a second time, Bey judged he had followed orders sufficiently to justify a return to base. He continued south at twenty-eight knots altering to course 155 degrees. At 1343 he ordered the destroyers to break off and head for home as well. Burnett tagged along beyond visual range, shadowing by radar. *Duke of York* was sailing hard to intercept and Bey's course made it certain she would. Bey knew Burnett was behind him and doubtlessly believed the cruisers presented little threat. Had he known a battleship was bearing down, he could have turned into the teeth of the wind and heavy seas and run away. In any case, it would have seemed prudent to wonder why he was being followed.

Burnett's cruisers experienced some difficulties during their chase. At 1603 a fire flared up on *Norfolk* and just seven minutes later *Sheffield* stripped a shaft. With her speed reduced to eight knots, she fell far behind. Finally, at 1617 the first indication that *Duke of York*'s long run in to battle was almost over came when the battleship picked up a radar contact from 45,500 yards. It showed that she and *Scharnhorst* were on converging courses. The contact held firm and by 1636 Fraser was clearing for action. With *Jamaica* following a thousand yards astern of *Duke of York* he ordered *Savage* and *Saumarez* to take station to port while *Scorpion* and *Stord* stood to starboard. He instructed them to hold their torpedoes until he ordered otherwise. At 1644 *Duke of York* turned to starboard to bring her broadside to bear. Finally, at 1647 *Belfast* and *Duke of York* both fired star shell. *Belfast*'s shell failed to illuminate, but those from *Duke of York*'s 5.25-inch secondary battery silhouetted *Scharnhorst* in a harsh, white glare, clearly showing her turrets trained fore and aft. For the third time Bey was surprised.

Duke of York's first ten-gun broadside followed two minutes later from twelve thousand yards. She straddled *Scharnhorst* and scored a critical hit, jamming Anton turret. *Jamaica* commenced fire at 1652 and straddled with her third salvo, claiming one hit. *Scharnhorst* was slow to reply; she struggled to find her adversaries, firing star shell at 1653. The British pyrotechnics dazzled the German range finders and made their work extremely difficult and the German anti-air guns opened up trying to shoot down the drifting flares.[22] Then *Duke of York* struck again. A shell from her third salvo destroyed the aircraft hangar and killed many of the anti-aircraft gun crews. As *Scharnhorst* turned north at 1655 her captain, Kapitän zur See Fritz Hintze, ordered the remaining 4.1-inch crews to their shelters, an order he never countermanded. Fraser, concerned *Scharnhorst* might have fired torpedoes during her turn, altered course to the east-northeast to comb their tracks.

Initially *Scharnhorst*'s salvos were short, but her shooting quickly improved. She straddled *Duke of York* and her overs nearly hit *Jamaica*. One shell landed a half ship's length off *Jamaica*'s starboard side abreast "B" turret and the falling column of water drenched her bridge and deck. When British star shells inadvertently illuminated *Savage* and *Saumarez*, sailing south of *Scharnhorst* on a parallel course, the German battleship turned her guns on them, near-missing *Savage* and forcing the destroyers to sheer away. Fraser failed to order a torpedo attack and so lost an opportunity to bring the battle to an early conclusion.

As *Scharnhorst* ran north she encountered *Belfast* and *Norfolk* and they opened fire at 1657. *Scharnhorst* replied. Then, at 1708 Bey turned east to course 111 degrees. He had opened the range to seventeen thousand yards and continued to return fire with Caesar, occasionally turning to open Bruno's arc and firing six gun salvos. At 1715 Fraser belatedly ordered his destroyers to attack with torpedos, but they found it difficult to gain position in the heavy sea. *Duke of York*, however, continued to hit. A shell pierced Bruno's ventilation trunking and the turret was soon out of action because the poisonous fumes could not be extracted. Another 14-inch shell struck the foremost 5.9-inch turret on the starboard side, penetrated the deck and blew a hole three feet wide in the hull only two feet above the waterline. After these two blows, however, it would be more than an hour before *Duke of York* would score again. With her superior speed, *Scharnhorst* continued to pull away. She finally damaged *Duke of York*, although only slightly, when two shells passed through the British flagship's mainmast, destroying the aerial of the 281 air warning radar and putting the 273 surface warning set out of action.

By 1742 *Scharnhorst* was eighteen thousand yards away; *Jamaica*'s guns had fallen silent after only nineteen broadsides. By 1800 the destroyers were twelve thousand yards west of *Scharnhorst* and ten miles from *Duke of York*, low on fuel and careening wildly in the following sea. The cruisers of Force 1 were farther away to the north. The destroyers of the 36th Division were also to the north on a parallel converging course, trying to close. Twenty minutes later, *Scharnhorst* ceased fire. Bey signaled that the enemy was firing on him by radar from over eighteen thousand meters. He gave his position as grid square AC4965, his course as 110 degrees, and his speed as twenty-six knots.

It seemed *Scharnhorst* had escaped. Given her heading and the heavy seas, she was faster than anything chasing her. But this situation changed dramatically at 1822 when a shell fired from one of *Duke of York*'s last salvos penetrated *Scharnhorst*'s No. 1 boiler room and cut the high-pressure steam pipes. Suddenly her speed plummeted to ten knots. At first *Duke of York* didn't notice. At 1824 with the range at 21,400 yards Fraser ceased fire because the constant shock had disabled the 284 gunnery control radar. His ship had fired fifty-two salvos and registered five hits. Now he reluctantly concluded the German battleship had escaped and he advised Burnett he was going to turn back to the convoy. But before Fraser could do so, the destroyers signaled they were suddenly closing the enemy.

Damage control soon brought *Scharnhorst*'s speed back up to twenty-two knots, but Bey seemed to admit defeat at 1825, when he sent a disquieting signal that his ship would fight to the last shell. At 1840 *Savage* and *Saumarez* were astern of *Scharnhorst* approaching from her port quarter *Scorpion* and *Stord* were pulling ahead ten thousand yards off her starboard beam. The first two opened fire from seven thousand yards while the latter remained undetected. *Scharnhorst*'s return fire was rapid but erratic.

Hintze never ordered the 4.1-inch crews from their shelters although their guns might have been effective. Nonetheless, an 11-inch shell smashed through *Saumarez*'s director tower without exploding. Others exploded close around her and splinters perforated the destroyer cutting down a torpedo crew and damaging the starboard engine. She suffered eleven killed and another eleven wounded as her speed dropped to ten knots. Then German lookouts finally saw *Scorpion* and *Stord* coming in almost dead on.

Their torpedo solution was almost impossible, but whoever was ordering *Scharnhorst*'s helm seemed to panic; the battleship swung to starboard toward the southwest. This presented the destroyers a beam-on rather than a bow-on target and they launched full salvos, *Stord* from eighteen hundred yards and *Scorpion* from twenty-one hundred yards. At 1853 *Scharnhorst* swung back to comb the tracks of this barrage and *Saumarez* launched a half salvo of four torpedoes from eighteen hundred yards while *Savage* fired eight from thirty-five hundred yards. One of *Scorpion* and *Stord*'s sixteen torpedoes struck *Scharnhorst* to starboard just forward of the bridge while three of the twelve fired by *Savage* and *Saumarez* hit to port near the bow, in a boiler room, and aft. The battleship experienced serious flooding aft and her speed once again fell to ten knots. The destroyers also riddled the battleship's superstructure with 4.7-inch shells. Damage control soon restored speed to twenty-two knots, but *Duke of York* was closing minute by minute.

Norfolk fired two salvos, but it was *Duke of York,* her 284 radar back in action, that made the difference. At 1901 she and *Jamaica* opened fire from ten thousand four hundred yards. The British battleship's first salvo blasted *Scharnhorst*'s quarterdeck and the remains of the aircraft hangar, igniting a large fire. Caesar ineffectively shot back. By 1911 the German was listing to starboard and her speed had dropped back to ten knots. At 1915 *Belfast* joined the bombardment and registered two hits with her third broadside. One minute later *Scharnhorst*'s last 11-inch guns fell silent, although the British observed periodic flashes from a few 5.9-inchers that continued to shoot.

By 1919 *Duke of York* was standing only four thousand yards off her heavily damaged foe. Anxious to finish it, Fraser ordered *Jamaica* to fire torpedoes. At 1925 the cruiser launched two from thirty-five hundred yards, but missed because of bad visibility, and huge clouds of smoke caused her to miscalculate her target's speed. At 1927 *Belfast* came up and launched three torpedoes and claimed one hit, although this is not certain.

At 1928 *Duke of York* ceased fire. At about the same time Bey ordered his men to abandon ship. In twenty-seven minutes Fraser's ship had fired twenty-five 14-inch broadsides and forty-two 5.25-inch salvoes. Eight of her heavy shells hit their target.

As the German sailors were preparing to enter the icy water, or searching for life belts (according to survivors, life belts were not worn and were only used if they could be found at the last moment), the four destroyers of the 36th Flotilla closed to point-blank torpedo range.[23] At 1931 *Opportune* emptied four tubes from twenty-five hundred yards. Two minutes later *Musketeer* followed with four more and claimed three hits. As she turned away, she almost collided with *Matchless,* which didn't launch because of storm damage. *Opportune* then fired her last four torpedoes and claimed two hits. Finally at 1934 *Virago* discharged seven torpedoes from twenty-eight hundred yards and claimed two hits. The torpedo barrage continued when *Jamaica* came in at 1937 to use her starboard tubes. She claimed two possible hits.

Throughout this unequal finale, light guns aboard *Scharnhorst* continued to fire raggedly and without effect. On deck there were

> frightful scenes of carnage . . . with mangled bodies swilling round in a mixture of blood and sea water while stretcher parties picked their way through the damage with ever-increasing numbers of wounded. Most of the guns on the port side (were) out of action and their crews lay in grotesque attitudes all over the deck, slowly being washed overboard.[24]

Then at 1945, with the German ship obscured by a shroud of smoke, the British heard a large explosion, presumably her magazine exploding. When *Belfast* approached at 1948 to make yet another torpedo attack, there was nothing there.

Fraser sent *Belfast, Norfolk* and all the destroyers to rescue survivors. However, despite a long search, they only pulled thirty-six men from the frigid sea. Kapitän zur See Hintze made it to the water, but died before he could be picked up. Fregattenkapitän Ernst Dominik, the executive officer, had his hands on a line before he slipped back into the sea. (They had given their life belts to ratings.) The number of German sailors who perished was 1,932.

This action revealed that the 14-inch guns of the *King George V* class were still unreliable. *Duke of York* fired 80 broadsides, but because many of the guns malfunctioned, she only expended 446 rounds, a reduction in gunnery efficiency of 32 percent (compared to 26 percent for *Prince of Wales* and as much as 80 percent for *King George V* in their engagements against *Bismarck*).[25] She hit *Scharnhorst* 13 times with her heavy 1,950-pound shells. The British also expended 55 torpedoes and counted eleven hits. Like *Bismarck*, *Scharnhorst* withstood a tremendous battering by heavy weapons, but it was the torpedo which finally put her under.

German writers depict the results of this battle as a foregone conclusion—a suicide run—while for British authors "it was a very close-run thing."[26] *Scharnhorst* had opportunities. In both her engagements with the cruisers she could have fought more aggressively and perhaps swept them aside without incurring major damage, but what then? She would have encountered the convoy and a force of seven destroyers and three destroyer escorts. If history was any guide they would have protected the convoy with smoke and kept *Scharnhorst* at bay by threatening torpedo attacks. Even if she had not been hamstrung by the German doctrine of risk avoidance, the weather simply did not favor a decisive result.

British warships surprised Bey three times. Not many commanders survive a sea battle thus. Poor visibility coupled with superior British radar provides a partial explanation, but Bey feared to use his own radar, believing the British had powerful radar detection devices. German communications were faulty. German airplanes found *Duke of York*, but Bey never got the news. It is difficult to understand how Bey lost contact with his destroyers. British communications were better. Fraser broke radio silence when he felt he needed to, and the results justified his risks. Coupled with the advantages of Ultra intelligence and powerful radar, the British were able to overcome mistakes in deployment, Burnett's in particular, and achieve a decisive victory. Yet, perhaps it was a close-run thing. But for one shell fired at very long range at the very end of the chase, landing in the very wrong (right) place, *Scharnhorst* would have escaped.

8

THE EASTERN MEDITERRANEAN, August 1943–May 1945

This is the time to play high. Improvise and dare.

WINSTON CHURCHILL

On 8 September 1943 the Italian government abandoned the Axis. In his armistice address Field Marshal Pietro Badoglio (prime minister since the arrest of Mussolini in July) instructed his armed forces to cease fighting the Allies and to oppose attack from any quarter. The reaction of an American destroyer sailor off Sicily was typical: "This relaxed everyone. . . . We are headed for Italy, and the Italians have surrendered! The war is over!"[1] Such expectations—which went all the way to the top—proved naive. Germany had meticulously planned for Italy's exit from the alliance, and her reactions were swift and effective.

In September 1943 Germany controlled the Aegean islands of Milos, Lemnos, Chios, Skiros, Metelino, and nearly all of Crete. The German navy

Table 8.1. Actions in the Eastern Mediterranean 1943–44

Date	Location	Name	Opponent	Type
23-Sep-43	Aegean	Action South of Rhodes	British	Interception
17-Oct-43	Aegean	Attack on Atki Bay	British/GK	Harbor Attack
22-Sep-44	Adriatic	Encounter in Otranto Straits	British	Encounter
29-Feb-44	Adriatic	Battle off Ist	French	Convoy attack
7-Oct-44	Aegean	Action in the Gulf of Salonika	British	Convoy attack
19-Oct-44	Aegean	Action off Skíathos	British	Interception
1-Nov-44	Adriatic	Ambush off Pag Island	British	Interception

had improvised a scratch fleet to service and protect these isolated territories; by the summer of 1943 it consisted of the submarine chasers of the 21st Unterseebootsjäger (UJ) flotilla, at least seventeen vessels, including an ex-British minesweeper, Greek minelayers and converted fishing boats, yachts, and trawlers. There were the motor-minesweepers of the 12th Flotilla, Marinefährprahm (MFP) barges, S-boats, and a miscellaneous collection of smaller units serving as escorts, patrol boats, and mine-warfare vessels, along with five submarines. Italy contributed destroyers and torpedo boats supported by a contingent of thirty MAS and other light coastal types. The naval forces initially available to the British Eastern Mediterranean command consisted of a mixed destroyer flotilla with six fleet units and two Hunts, six submarines, MTBs, and sixteen motor launches.

The Italian navy emerged from the armistice with its morale, honor, and fleet largely intact, but not in the Aegean. Germany quickly seized the six Italian destroyers and torpedo boats, renaming them with a TA prefix (*Torpedoboote Ausländisch,* or ex-enemy torpedo boat). The captured ships included two destroyers at Piraeus, *Turbine* (TA14), *Crispi* (TA15); two torpedo-boats also at Piraeus, *San Martino* (TA17), *Calatafimi* (TA19); and two torpedo-boats at Suda, *Castelfidardo* (TA16) and *Solferino* (TA18). The transfer of command was routine. The Italian captain of *Turbine* marched down the gangplank of his ship, saluting and being saluted by German naval officers. These same officers marched aboard and that was that.

There was a strong strategic sense among the British leadership (beginning with Churchill) that Italy's surrender presented an opportunity to seize the Aegean with comparatively little effort, maybe bringing Turkey into the war and opening a shorter supply route to Russia, and perhaps precipitating the collapse of the entire German position in southeastern Europe. The Americans were focused on the Italian campaign, however, and did not share this vision. In the end, the British acted alone with the resources at hand. The result was a bitter air-land-sea campaign in the Aegean Sea as the British attempted to exploit a strategic opportunity that was not and were soundly defeated by the German navy's unexpected ability to wage amphibious warfare across disputed seas.

Rhodes was the real prize. The British parachuted a pair of SBS agents onto the island to convince the Italian governor to fight, but the seven thousand German soldiers on Rhodes did a better job convincing him to surrender. After this failure, the British flung scratch forces ashore on

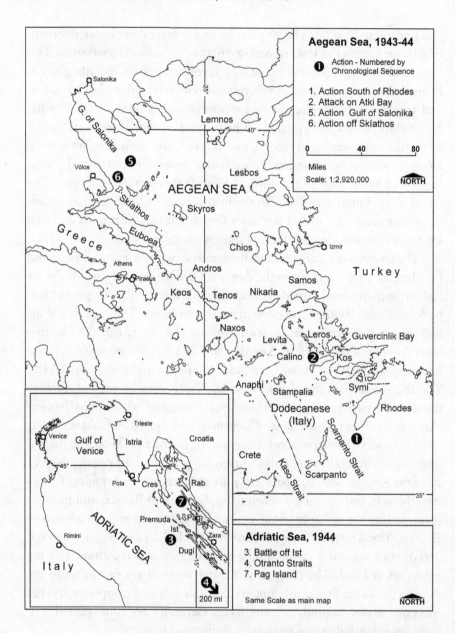

Aegean Sea, 1943–44

❶ Action - Numbered by Chronological Sequence

1. Action South of Rhodes
2. Attack on Atki Bay
5. Action Gulf of Salonika
6. Action off Skíathos

0   40   80

Miles
Scale: 1:2,920,000   NORTH

Adriatic Sea, 1944

3. Battle off Ist
4. Otranto Straits
7. Pag Island

Same Scale as main map   NORTH

Casteloriso on 11 September and then on the larger islands of Kos (the only airfield outside of Rhodes), Leros (site of a major Italian naval base), Calino, Samos, Symi, and Stampalia. According to Churchill's strategic concept, the British had pushed and it was now the turn of the Germans to topple. However, this was not to be the case.

After the German army secured Rhodes, they had to deal with 35,000 Italian prisoners. Thus, shipping came in with supplies and came out with human cargo destined for labor camps, or worse. Meanwhile, the British reinforced their Eastern Mediterranean fleet with the 8th Destroyer Flotilla; these warships ferried men and materials to the garrisons north of Rhodes and made the surrounding waters perilous for German shipping.

On the morning of 18 September a destroyer force under the command of Captain A. K. Moncrieff consisting of *Faulknor, Eclipse,* and the Greek *Vasilissa Olga* ran down a small convoy off Stampalia: the ex-Italian cargo ships *Pluto* (3,830 tons) and *Paula* (3,754 tons) and their escort, *UJ2104*. The Allied flotilla approached from down-moon at high speed and surprised the convoy at 0017 hours with a sudden barrage. The British destroyers quickly set *Paula* afire; she exploded and sank within five minutes. *UJ2104*, an ex-Norwegian whaler armed with an 88-mm gun forward and a pair of 20-mm guns aft, was outmatched and, lacking radar, practically blind; nonetheless, she turned toward the Allied warships. The British gunners aimed their guns on this threat and salvos of 4.7-inch shells slammed into the ex-whaler. She drifted off, barely afloat, and ran herself ashore where her crew was subsequently captured. *Vasilissa Olga* attacked *Pluto*. Her passengers and crew were abandoning ship when *Faulknor* came up and finished her off with a torpedo.

Action South of Rhodes, 23 September 1943

TIME: 0100
TYPE: Convoy attack
WEATHER:
VISIBILITY: Moon 71 percent, rise 0117
SEA STATE:
SURPRISE: Allies
MISSION: British—offensive and sea superiority patrol without specific intelligence; Germans—escort and transit

Despite British expectations of an easy victory, the Germans resisted their Dodecanese incursion and even began collecting forces for a counter-stroke. On the night of 22–23 September the destroyers *Eclipse, Faulknor,* and *Fury* carried twelve hundred troops to Kos, part of a hurried effort to reinforce the island before an expected German assault. Following this

Table 8.2. Action South of Rhodes, 23 September 1943

Allied Ship	TYP	YL	DFL	SPD	GUNS	TT	GF	DAM
Eclipse	DD	34	1,940	37	4×4.7/45	8×21	6	
German Ship								
TA10	TB	37	846	38	2×3.9/40	2×21	2	Sunk

mission, they returned south looking for trouble—*Eclipse* via the Scarpanto Strait and the other two via the Kaso Strait. Captained by Commander E. Mack, who had so aggressively hounded *Z26* to her destruction the winter before, *Eclipse* found trouble to make about ten miles south of Rhodes. She sighted *TA10*, the ex-French torpedo boat *La Pomone*, escorting the steamer *Donizetti* (2,428 tons) with 1,584 Italian prisoners aboard. *TA10* had been captured at Bizerta in April 1943 and transferred to the Aegean in July. The *Donizetti* operation was her first combat mission under the German flag. Attacking with gunfire shortly after 0100 hours, *Eclipse* set the steamer aflame, and she sank with no survivors, one of the larger maritime disasters suffered by Italy in the war. *Eclipse* also registered hits on *TA10*, destroying both of her engines and killing five of her crew. Rescue vessels towed the torpedo boat into Prassos Bay, Rhodes; there her crew judged the engines beyond repair and scuttled her. An Allied air attack two days later destroyed the wreck. *TA10* did not put up much of a fight as *Eclipse* only reported engaging a merchant ship.[2]

British naval victories could not protect isolated garrisons in the face of superior air power. The Aegean waters were dangerous for German shipping at night when the destroyers came out. They were dangerous for the Allied ships (British, Greek, Australian, French, Polish, and Italian) during the day when the Stuka divebombers came out. On 26 September the reinforced German air force attacked Leros and sank *Intrepid* and *Vasilissa Olga*. Nor could British naval victories forestall a German counteroffensive. On the first day of October Germany sent four convoys toward Kos. From Iraklion, Crete, sailed one transport and two MFPs, escorted by *UJ2111*; from Suda three transports and six MFPs, escorted by *UJ2101* and *UJ2102*; from Piraeus a transport, an MFP, the mineships *Drache* and *Bulgaria*, *UJ2110*, and *UJ2111*; and from Naxos three R-boats and six auxiliaries.

Every ship arrived. The troops disembarked intact; despite the wealth of targets, Allied destroyers were not in the right place at the right time. The large British garrison hardly resisted, and by the morning of 3 October Kos had fallen. Then the German navy began building up forces to take Leros, the main British holding. The British responded by upping the ante. Four light cruisers and three P class destroyers sailed for Alexandria on 4 October to reinforce the Eastern fleet.

On the evening of 7 October the British submarine *Unruly* sighted a major convoy: *Olympus* (5,216 tons) carrying a battalion of infantry, six MFPs (*F308, F327, F336, F494, F496, F532*), and *UJ2111*. Her torpedo attack failed, but she followed and later battle-surfaced and engaged *Olympus* and *F496* with gunfire. *UJ2111* drove her down again, but just over the horizon, the light cruisers *Sirius* and *Penelope* and the destroyers *Faulknor* and *Fury* picked up *Unruly*'s sighting report. They turned at full speed and forty minutes later, at 0450, hours intercepted the convoy south of Levita. The British ships closed to point-blank range and in only ten minutes they sank every enemy vessel except the straggler *F494*. Four hundred men perished.

Later that morning the German air force made it clear why British warships could not scourge all German shipping like this. They caught *Penelope* on her long run south and damaged her badly. Only the intervention of American Lightnings saved the cruiser from destruction. And, for the British, the situation was getting worse. By mid-October the Germans had concentrated over 350 first-line aircraft on Rhodes and Crete while the Lightnings, the only fighters capable of operating north of Rhodes, were needed to meet equally serious threats elsewhere.

Atki Bay, 17 October 1943

TIME:	Night
TYPE:	Harbor attack
WEATHER:	
VISIBILITY:	Moon 86 percent, set 1022
SEA STATE:	Calm
SURPRISE:	Allies
MISSION:	Allies—offensive and sea superiority patrol without specific intelligence; Germans—self-defense

Table 8.3. Atki Bay, 17 October 1944

Allied Ships	TYP	YL	DFL	SPD	GUNS	TT	GF	DAM
Jervis	DD	38	2,540	36	6×4.7/45 & 1×4/45	5x21	9	
Penn	DD	41	2,365	37	4×4/45	8x21	5	
Hursley	DE	41	1,625	27	6×4/45		6	
Miaoulis (GK)	DE	42	1,545	27	4×4/45	2x21	4	
German Ship								
UJ2109	DC	17	900	16	3×3.5		2	Sunk

On the night of 15–16 October British warships searched for a major convoy intelligence reported moving south, but found nothing; the next morning, however, the convoy fell afoul of the submarine *Torbay*. She sank the steamer *Kari* (1,925 tons) and damaged the modern German transport *Trapani* (1,855 tons). Alerted by this contact, a mixed destroyer force set out that evening from Guvercinlik Bay, the British navy's daytime hideout in neutral Turkey.

The convoy's survivors had taken refuge for the night in Atki Bay on the island of Calino. While the fleet destroyers *Jervis* and *Penn* stood off, the destroyer escorts *Hursley* and the Greek *Miaoulis* entered, illuminated the bay and found their quarry. In the ensuing bombardment they sank *F338* and *UJ2109*, the ex-British minesweeper *Widnes*, the largest vessel in the 21st UJ-Flotilla. They also hit *Trapani*, but she survived and was able to unload her cargo. The next night *Sirus* and *Penn* returned and shelled the transport until she capsized to port in shallow water. There is no mention of *UJ2109* offering any resistance. She was a large target and presumably surprised by the sudden onslaught.

After the destruction of yet another convoy the pace of operations picked up. Allied ships landed men and supplies by night and were attacked by day. The Germans also suffered, but the balance began to swing in their favor. By early November, German aircraft had bombed and disabled the cruisers *Carlisle, Sirus, Penelope,* and *Aurora*; there were only destroyers to confront the final invasion convoy. On 9 November intelligence indicated it was at sea and that night two mixed groups of destroyers and destroyer escorts lurked in the waters around Leros and Kos. When no ships appeared, they cleared the area at 0530 hours on 10 November. Five hours later, a Beaufighter sighted a portion of the invasion fleet. "The opportunity to attack, for which the Royal Navy had strained and sacrificed, had come but not one ship was within range of the elusive fleet."[3] Leros fell on 16 November after a long and bitter battle. The British navy could not prevent the invasion or its reinforcement.

The Aegean campaign cost the Allied navies dearly: The Germans sank six destroyers, two submarines, and ten smaller ships, damaged one cruiser beyond repair, and seriously damaged four cruisers, four destroyers, and eleven other ships. Although the Italian battle fleet lay at anchor in Malta's Grand Harbor, this campaign rudely taught the British that the naval war in the Middle Sea was not over.

Another naval campaign was under way in the Eastern Mediterranean during 1943 and 1944. This was in the Adriatic Sea. After Italy's surrender, the island-strewn east coast provided bases and seldom-used harbors where the Allies could smuggle supplies into the partisans. In late 1943 and January 1944 the Germans occupied most of the islands and began employing the coastal waterways to provision their Balkan armies. Although coastal forces saw most of the action, the Germans and Allies both maintained destroyer-sized warships in the theater.

Battle off Ist, 29 February 1944

Time:	2144
Type:	Convoy attack
Weather:	
Visibility:	Very dark, moon 21 percent, set 2313
Sea State:	
Surprise:	Allies
Mission:	Allies—interception based upon specific intelligence; Germans—escort and transit

In February 1944 the French navy finally came to grips with their original foe. Late that month the "super" destroyers *Le Terrible*, *Le Malin*, and *Le Fantasque* joined the ten ships of the British 24th destroyer Flotilla at Bari. Their speed allowed them to react to reconnaissance or intelligence to strike targets in the northern reaches of the Adriatic and still return before dawn. On 29 February they departed Manfredonia, a port fifty miles north of Bari, at 1345 hours, and headed up the Adriatic. A German convoy had sailed from Pola bound for Piraeus hardly an hour before. The convoy consisted of the freighter *Kapitän Diederichsen* (6,311 tons) and a strong escort: the ex-Italian *Ariete* class torpedo boats *TA36* (ex–*Stella Polare*) and *TA37* (ex-*Gladio*), the former Italian *Gabbiano* class corvettes *UJ201* (ex-*Egeria*) and *UJ205* (ex-*Colubrina*), and the motor minesweepers *R188, R190,* and *R191*. The torpedo boats had commissioned only the month before and were on their second operation. It proved difficult.

It was a very dark night and the new moon had just set. The French ships, under Capitaine de Frégate Pierre Lancelot, were sailing northwest at twenty-five knots and were passing Ist when, at 2135 hours, *Le Terrible*'s radar detected ships about 18,600 yards farther north. The French came to thirty knots and nine minutes later, the range down to 8,750 yards, both ships fired broadsides catching the Germans by surprise. *Le Terrible,* the leader, shelled the freighter while *Le Malin* targeted the nearest of the escorts. The Germans promptly returned fire, suggesting their lookouts had spotted shadows to the south, and also made smoke. But the French superdestroyers continued to close. Lancelot's flagship registered hits on *Kapitän Diederichsen* at 2148 when the range was down to 4,500 yards. She fired torpedoes several minutes later, and, at 2157, one exploded against its target. Burning fiercely, the stricken freighter drifted to a halt.

Le Malin continued northwest and encountered *UJ201*. She hit the escort several times with her 90-pound shells and then fired torpedoes.

Table 8.4. Battle off Ist, 29 February 1944

Allied Ships	TYP	YL	DFL	SPD	GUNS	TT	GF	DAM
Le Terrible	DD	33	3,400	40	5×5.45/50	6×21.7	9	
Le Malin	DD	33	3,400	40	5×5.45/50	6×21.7	9	
German Ships								
TA36	TB	44	1,110	28	2×3.9/47	6×17.7	2	D2
TA37	TB	43	1,110	28	2×3.9/47	5×17.7	2	D4
UJ201	DC	43	728	18	1×3.9/47	2×17.7	1	Sunk
UJ205	DC	43	728	18	1×3.9/47	2×17.7	1	
R188	MMS	42	126	23	1×37-mm		0	
R190	MMS	42	126	23	1×37-mm		0	
R191	MMS	42	126	23	1×37-mm		0	

One struck and detonated the corvette's magazine. The unfortunate ship exploded and quickly sank with all hands. During this period the destroyers also inflicted light damage on *TA36* and nearly disabled *TA37* with two well-placed salvos: one shell exploded in the latter's engine room and cut her speed to ten knots and others ignited fires. At this point, with the freighter and one escort burning and another sunk, Lancelot turned south and withdrew at high speed. He had noted the small motor minesweepers and, apparently believing they were MTBs, steamed off, afraid a torpedo might disable one of his ships deep in unfriendly waters.

TA36 and *UJ205* stood by the freighter and removed her crew. *Kapitän Diederichsen* remained afloat, but attempts to tow her to safety failed and she sank at 1145 the next morning. Only one man from her crew perished. *TA37*'s engine eventually failed and she required a tow to Pola.

Le Terrible and *Le Fantasque* attacked a small convoy of four Siebel Ferries (Siebel-Fähre) and an MFP on 19 March en route to Navarino. They sank *SF273* and *SF274* and crippled two others, suffering light damage from 20-mm return fire. After this mission, these useful vessels rotated to the Aegean and then back to French waters for the invasion of southern France.

Approximately one year after their embarrassing defeat in the Dodecanese, the British returned to the Aegean with enough muscle to do the job: seven escort carriers, seven cruisers, nine fleet destroyers, and eleven destroyer escorts. The Germans knew their dominance of the theater was nearly over because the Allies had signed an armistice with Romania and Soviet advances threatened to isolate Greece. On 5 September 1944, they began withdrawing from portions of Crete and some of the Aegean islands. For this task the German navy deployed fifty-two merchant ships, numerous small warships and naval auxiliaries, and more than two hundred caiques and landing craft. By the end of October, the navy had evacuated 37,138 troops for a loss of only 380 men.[4] The material costs were much higher: twenty-nine merchant ships, five torpedo boats, a minelayer, an R-boat, and three submarine hunters. Although aircraft sank the majority of these ships, the destroyers *Termagant* and *Tuscan* did their share of execution, twice running into German torpedo boats and twice destroying the opposition.

The ships of Force 120, Rear Adm. Thomas Troubridge's escort carrier fleet, began their rampage through the Aegean on 9 September 1944.

On 15 September the British seized Kithera off the Peloponnesus as an advance destroyer base. That same day the light cruiser *Royalist* and the destroyer *Teazer* found and sank the gunboat *KT26/Erpel* and *UJ2171* off Cape Spatha, Crete. (These were sister ships of a coastal freighter type meant for mass production, displacing 800 grt and capable of 14.5 knots.) Between 9 September and 24 September, aircraft from the escort carriers sank the warships *TA14, UJ2142, R178, Pelikan,* and *Drache,* and the steamers *Toni* and *Orion.*

In the face of this carnage, Naval Group South decided to reinforce the Aegean with three Adriatic torpedo boats. It would be difficult to insert ships into what was becoming a besieged sea. To escape after their job (to escort shipping and to lay minefields off Piraeus) was finished would be nearly impossible. Nevertheless, the torpedo boats *TA37, TA38,* and *TA39* (ex-Italian Ariete class torpedo boats *Gladio, Spada,* and *Daga*) sailed from Trieste on 20 September under the overall command of Kapitänleutnant Werner Lange. They had a relatively trouble-free transit down the Adriatic, except for some ineffective air attacks on *TA37,* when she fell behind with engine problems.

Encounter in the Strait of Otranto, 22 September 1944

TIME:	0550–0730
TYPE:	Encounter
WEATHER:	
VISIBILITY:	
SEA STATE:	
SURPRISE:	None
MISSION:	Allies—patrol and sea security; Germans—transit

Early on the morning of 22 September the German warships entered the Strait of Otranto and there a pair of patrolling British destroyer escorts, *Belvoir* and *Whaddon,* challenged them. At 0550 hours the British opened fire. The Germans were not interested in fighting and they enjoyed a three-knot advantage in speed. By 0630 hours they had escaped unharmed. At 0730 hours the three torpedo boats anchored in the safety of the Corfu Channel.

Table 8.5. Otranto Strait, 22 September 1944

Allied Ships	TYP	YL	DFL	SPD	GUNS	TT	GF	DAM
Belvoir	DE	41	1,590	27	4×4/45	2×21	4	
Whaddon	DE	40	1,450	28	4×4/45		4	
German Ships								
TA37	TB	43	1,110	31	2×3.9/47	5×17.7	2	
TA38	TB	43	1,110	31	2×3.9/47	3×17.7	2	
TA39	TB	43	1,110	31	2×3.9/47	3×17.7	2	

Lange's flotilla completed their odyssey (the transfer was code-named Odysseus) on the afternoon of 24 September when they dropped anchor at Piraeus. There, the real work would begin, and the new torpedo boats were quick to prove their worth escorting convoys and sowing mines on 30 September and 2, 3, and 5 October. *TA38* and *TA39* even fought a minor surface action on 6 October when they sank the British motor-launch *ML1227*. Their first encounter with British destroyers, however, did not go so well.

Action in the Gulf of Salonika, 7 October 1944

TIME: 0100
TYPE: Convoy attack
WEATHER:
VISIBILITY: Moon 71 percent, rise 2205
SEA STATE:
SURPRISE: Allies
MISSION: British—offensive and sea superiority patrol without specific intelligence; Germans—escort and transit

A principal evacuation corridor for the Germans led from Piraeus to Salonika. Most of the route followed inshore waters sheltered by the island of Euboea, but emerging from the inland waterway and rounding Skíathos at its mouth, there was the danger of a run over the open sea across the Gulf of Salonika. On the night of 7 October the well-used minelayer *Zeus* (the ex-Italian auxiliary cruiser *Francesco Morosini*) was crossing the mouth of the gulf, two and a half hours north of Skíathos; 1,125 evacuees crowded

Table 8.6. Action in the Gulf of Salonika, 7 October 1944

Allied Ships	TYP	YL	DFL	SPD	GUNS	TT	GF	DAM
Termagant	DD	43	2,505	36	4×4.7/45	8×21	6	
Tuscan	DD	42	2,505	36	4×4.7/45	8×21	6	
German Ships								
TA37	TB	43	1,110	31	2×3.9/47	5×17.7	2	Sunk
UJ2102	DC	?	?	?	1×3.5		1	Sunk
GK62	PB	?	?	?	?		0	Sunk
Zeus	ML	?	2,423	14	2×4.7/45		3	

the 2,423-ton ship. Befitting such an important cargo, she enjoyed a strong escort consisting of *TA37*, *UJ2102*, and the harbor patrol boat *GK62*. The British destroyers *Termagant* and *Tuscan* were patrolling the channel. They encountered the convoy shortly after midnight and launched a violent and effective attack. A flurry of gunfire sank all three escorts, but their sacrifice enabled *Zeus* to escape north. Losses aboard *TA37* were particularly heavy: two-thirds of her crew, 103 men, died.

Action off Skíathos, 19 October 1944

TIME: Night, 2340
TYPE: Interception
WEATHER:
VISIBILITY: Moon 3 percent, set 1914
SEA STATE:
SURPRISE: Allies
MISSION: British—offensive and sea superiority patrol without
               specific intelligence; Germans—transit

On 10 October troops of the Soviet 3rd Ukraine Front cut the rail line between Athens and Berlin near Nis, Yugoslavia. Germany evacuated Piraeus on 12 October. British paratroopers descended on Athens airport that same day. Although Germany maintained "fortress" garrisons on Crete, Rhodes, Leros, and Kos, the navy was nearly gone from the Aegean. *TA38* was scuttled following bomb damage and *TA39* was mined off Salonika, just three weeks and two days after her arrival in the Aegean. The

Table 8.7. Action off Skíathos, 19 October 1944

Allied Ships	TYP	YL	DFL	SPD	GUNS	TT	GF	DAM
Termagant	DD	43	2,505	36	4×4.7/45	8×21	6	
Tuscan	DD	42	2,505	36	4×4.7/45	8×21	6	
German Ship								
TA18	TB	20	1,076	31	4x4/45		3	Sunk

last major warship was *TA18*, the former Italian torpedo boat *Solferino*. She had only entered service on 25 July and was of doubtful combat value after being cannibalized for spare parts following her capture the year before.

On the evening of 19 October *TA18* entered the Gulf of Salonika and was still south of Vólos when *Termagant* and *Tuscan* found her. Well-practiced and efficient, the British destroyers severely damaged the German ship with their combined gunfire. *TA18* ran herself aground, but the British continued to bombard her until 2340. Most of the surviving crew were subsequently captured and shot by Greek partisans.

The remaining German ships in the Aegean, an S-boat, three R-boats, and three auxiliary minesweepers scuttled themselves at the end of the month when Germany evacuated Salonika. The garrisons of German troops scattered across the Aegean remained there, reduced, by the end of the war, to growing vegetables to feed themselves.

Although the Aegean campaign ended in October 1944, the naval battle to control the Adriatic and the Dalmatian coast continued. With the growing power of the Yugoslavian partisans the sea-lanes replaced the roads and railroads as supply routes for the beleaguered German army. British MTBs and MTGs supported by Hunt class destroyer escorts stalked these waters, preying on Germany's coastal shipping.

Ambush off Pag Island, 1 November 1944

TIME: 1950–2230
TYPE: Interception
WEATHER: Deteriorating
VISIBILITY: Moon 99.5 percent, rise 1751 set 0719
SEA STATE: Building swells

SURPRISE: Allies
MISSION: British—interception based upon general intelligence;
              Germans—self defense

On 26 October partisans advised Lieutenant Commander Morgan
Giles, commanding officer of the coastal forces operating in the northern
Adriatic, that two German destroyers were lying up during daytime cam-
ouflaged in a cove on the south coast of Rab Island. On 1 November two
Hunts, *Wheatland* and *Avon Vale* arrived to root them out. Placed under the
command of Giles, who sailed aboard *Wheatland,* they departed the British
base at Ist at 1700 hours accompanied by MTBs 295, 287, 274, MGBs 642,
638, 633, and *ML494.* The Hunts were to land a party of coast watchers on
the north end of Rab while the MTBs patrolled the waters between Rab and
Krk and the MGBs loitered to the southwest toward Premuda.

At 1950 the shore party had just cast off aboard a whaler when the
MTBs signaled two large ships were steaming south. These vessels were
the anticipated destroyers: *UJ202* (ex-*Melpómene*) and *UJ208* (ex-
Springarda), both Italian *Gabbiano* class corvettes. The Hunts abandoned
their boat and turned to the southwest. Twenty minutes later the radar-
equipped warships caught the Germans by surprise. Each focused on a
separate target and registered hits with their first salvos. Within minutes
Wheatland and *Avon Vale* had closed to point-blank range and were circling the unfortunate corvettes, all guns blazing away until both the German ships sank.

The British were rescuing survivors when radar detected another large
contact coming from the north. This was *TA20,* laid down in 1914 at
Yarrow for the Japanese and eventually commissioned by Italy as *Audace.*

Table 8.8. Ambush off Pag Island, 1 November 1944

Allied Ships	TYP	YL	DFL	SPD	GUNS	TT	GF	DAM
Wheatland	DE	41	1,625	27	6×4/45		6	
Avon Vale	DE	40	1,625	27	6×4/45		6	
German Ships								
TA20	TB	16	1,152	34	2×4/35		2	Sunk
UJ202	DC	43	728	18	1×3.9/47	2×17.7	1	Sunk
UJ208	DC	43	728	18	1×3.9/47	2×17.7	1	Sunk

The Hunts suspended their rescue work and turned to attack. Again their first salvos hit, this time on *TA20*'s bridge, slaughtering her officers and destroying the fire control systems. *TA20* sank at 2230, close inshore off Pag Island. The light craft, hampered by worsening weather, only pulled ninety Germans from the water. The two Hunts returned to Ist with empty magazines.

Hunt class destroyer escorts proved their effectiveness, particularly at night in close quarters. But while the Adriatic campaign continued to the end of the war, the Hunts did not again engage large German warships. This despite the fact the German navy was constantly launching and commissioning light destroyer types. On 31 October 1944, they had five destroyers (*TA20, TA40, TA41, TA44,* and *TA45*), and five corvettes (*UJ202, UJ205, UJ206, UJ208,* and *TA48*) operational in the northern Adriatic. On 1 January 1945 there were four destroyers (*TA40, TA41, TA44,* and *TA45*) and three corvettes (*UJ205, UJ206,* and *TA48*). Even as late as 1 April *TA43, TA45,* and *UJ206* were in commission and available to fight. These ships saw limited action. Allied aircraft sank four in port, during March and April; British MTBs torpedoed *TA45* in April, and four survived (two in damaged condition) to be scuttled when the German forces in Italy surrendered.

9

ACTIONS IN THE ENGLISH CHANNEL AND FRENCH WATERS 1943

> The continuous struggle in the western coastal waters was bitter and unrelenting.... These encounters had a grim significance to the men involved, yet were barely noticed by a world preoccupied with the fullness of greater events.
>
> VIZEADMIRAL FRIEDRICH RUGE

In the struggle for the English Channel 1943 was something of a forgotten year, but not because nothing happened. The British and the Germans attempted to dominate the coastal waters by waging war with mines and coastal forces and, in rare cases, with destroyers. The Germans believed if the Allies invaded Europe, they would cross the English Channel, and the channel was their first line of defense. To the south in the Bay of Biscay the British fought a fierce campaign to imperil the passage of German blockade runners and U-boats in and out of the Atlantic ports. In response, the German navy built up and maintained a strong destroyer and torpedo boat force to escort shipping and exert a degree of control over the bay's broad and often turbulent waters.

Every surface action fought in the English Channel during 1943 occurred off the rocky northern coast of Brittany (the Breton coast). Heavy traffic plied

Table 9.1. Actions in the English Channel 1943

Date	Location	Name	Opponent	Type
28-Apr-43	English Channel	Action in Morlaix Bay	British	Convoy attack
10-Jul-43	English Channel	First Action off Île de Batz	British/NO	Convoy attack
4-Oct-43	English Channel	Action off Les Triagoz	British	Interception
23-Oct-43	English Channel	Action off Les Sept Iles	British	Convoy attack
28-Dec-43	Bay of Biscay	Battle of Biscay	British	Interception

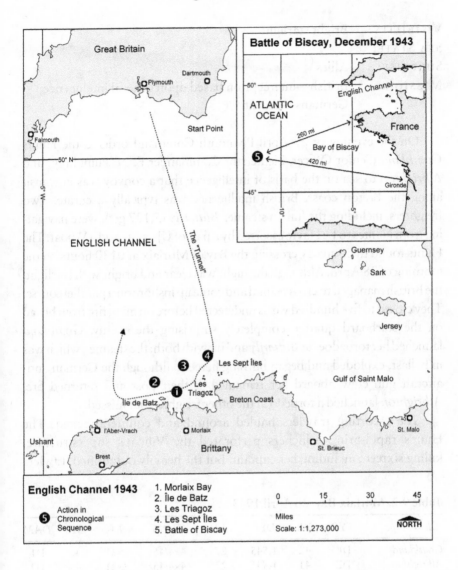

Great Britain

Dartmouth

Plymouth

Falmouth

Start Point

50° N

ENGLISH CHANNEL

The "Tunnel"

Battle of Biscay, December 1943

50°

English Channel

ATLANTIC
OCEAN

France

260 mi

Bay of Biscay

5

420 mi

Gironde

45°

Guernsey

Sark

Jersey

3   4   Les Sept Îles

2   Les
1   Triagoz

Gulf of Saint Malo

Île de Batz

Breton Coast

l'Aber-Vrach   Morlaix   St. Malo

Ushant   Brittany   St. Brieuc

Brest

English Channel 1943

5 Action in
   Chronological
   Sequence

1. Morlaix Bay
2. Île de Batz
3. Les Triagoz
4. Les Sept Îles
5. Battle of Biscay

0   15   30   45

Miles

Scale: 1:1,273,000

NORTH

these waters and they were too distant for the British to effectively interdict with coastal forces.

Action in Morlaix Bay, 28 April 1943

TIME: 0130
TYPE: Convoy attack
WEATHER: Clear

VISIBILITY: Bright starlight
SEA STATE:
SURPRISE: Allies
MISSION: British—interception based upon general intelligence;
               Germans—transit

On the evening of 27 April Plymouth Command ordered the Hunts *Goathland* (Senior Officer, Lieutenant Commander E. N. Pumphrey) and *Albrighton* to sea on the basis of intelligence that a convoy was in transit along the Breton coast. British intelligence was typically accurate. Two freighters, including the Italian steamer *Butterfly* (5,127 grt), were navigating from Nantes to Le Havre escorted by a pair of UJ-boats and a V-boat. The Hunts found their quarry crossing the Bay of Morlaix at 0130 hours on the morning of 28 April. Although the night was clear and bright with starlight, the British managed to cross behind and come up inshore on a parallel course. They closed to five hundred yards undetected before opening fire from broad on the starboard quarter, completely surprising the enemy. *Goathland* launched her torpedoes at *Butterfly* and hit with both; the steamer, which was in ballast, exploded and began burning fiercely, although the German anti-aircraft gun crew aboard her remained at their post and returned fire. *Albrighton* launched a torpedo at the other freighter, but missed.

The escorting trawlers hauled around and counterattacked. The Hunt's rapid-firing 4-inchers perforated the V-boat's superstructure, killing sixteen, including her captain. But the heavily outgunned trawlers

Table 9.2. Morlaix Bay, 28 April 1943

Allied Ships	TYP	YL	DFL	SPD	GUNS	TT	GF	DAM
Goathland	DE	42	1,545	27	4×4/45	2×21	4	D1
Albrighton	DE	41	1,545	27	4×4/45	2×21	4	D2
German Ships								
M??	MS	41?	775	17	1×4.1/45		1	
M??	MS	41?	775	17	1×4.1/45		1	
M??	MS	41?	775	17	1×4.1/45		1	
UJ1402	DC	?	?	?	?		?	Sunk
UJ??	DC	?	?	?	?		?	
V??	PB	?	?	?	?		?	D3

returned an intense fire of their own. Splinters sprayed *Goathland* and she broke off the fight. *Albrighton* could not follow, however, because shell fragments disabled her steering motor and she lost rudder control. She had no choice but to stay and slug it out.

The gunfire attracted three minesweepers of the 24th Flotilla. As *Albrighton* steamed unable to maneuver, they reinforced the trawlers, firing with all weapons. A British participant recalled:

> Our forward ammunition supply party had been wiped out by enemy fire so there was no more ammo reaching 'A' 4-inch mounting. The after 4-inch guns had taken a direct hit. . . . All our radio aerials had also been shot away by the intense fire so we could not communicate with SO.[1]

Finally, *Albrighton* managed to fix her steering and extract herself; she suffered two direct hits in addition to splinter damage and was under repair for ten days. In the fracas she severely punished *UJ1402*, ex-*Berlin*; the subchaser had three men killed and sank at 0900 hours the next morning. *Butterfly* was a total loss.

First Action off Île de Batz, 10 July 1943

TIME: Night
TYPE: Convoy attack
WEATHER:
VISIBILITY: Moon 43 percent
SEA STATE:
SURPRISE: Allies
MISSION: Allies—interception based upon general intelligence;
              Germans—escort and transit

Through the spring and summer of 1943 the Germans reinforced their torpedo boat flotilla at Brest. These useful ships escorted coastal convoys, shepherded U-boats and blockade runners in and out of port, and laid mines. The new torpedo boats *T24* and *T25* departed home waters on 3 July and by 9 July had reached St. Malo, repelling attacks by Dutch MTBs, the Dover batteries, and fighter-bombers en route.

While on the last leg of their perilous journey to join the 4th Torpedo Boat Flotilla at Brest, Naval Group West assigned these ships to cover the

2nd Minesweeper Flotilla, *M9*, *M10*, *M12*, *M84*, and *M153*, under the command of Korvettenkapitän H. Heydel, as they swept the shipping channel along the northern Breton coast.

Early in the morning of 10 July north of Île de Batz the British Hunts *Melbreak*, *Wensleydale*, and the Norwegian *Glaisdale* intercepted the minesweepers. An action lasting ninety minutes ensued. Rapid gunfire crippled *M153*, and damaged *M12*. However, "in spite of their great inferiority in arms and speed, the M-boats defended themselves well . . ."[2] Then *T24* and *T25* intervened and caught the Hunts unaware. In a confused and intense gunnery action they damaged all three Allied ships. A direct hit on *Melbreak* required eight days to repair while splinters laid up *Wensleydale* for seventeen and *Glaisdale* for six days. In return, a near miss perforated *T25*'s superstructure with more than a hundred holes. The British destroyers fired three torpedoes during this action and claimed one hit, presumably on *M153*.

A tug tried to tow *M153* to safety, but she capsized and sank at about 1800 hours that evening. Eighteen of her men perished. Except for *M12* the minesweepers suffered little damage.

T26 and *T27* joined *T24* and *T25* at Brest in early September. On 3 September and again on 29 September the torpedo boats sortied into the English Channel to sow mine fields. Stung by these activities, the British countered with offensive patrols using fleet destroyers combined with destroyer escorts. The Plymouth Command named these patrols Opera-

Table 9.3. First Île de Batz, 10 July 1943

Allied Ships	TYP	YL	DFL	SPD	GUNS	TT	GF	DAM
Melbreak	DE	42	1,545	27	4×4/45	2×21	4	D2
Wensleydale	DE	42	1,545	27	4×4/45	2×21	4	D2
Glaisdale (NO)	DE	42	1,545	27	4×4/45	2×21	4	D1
German Ships								
T24	TB	41	1,754	33	4×4.1/45	6×21	4	
T25	TB	41	1,754	33	4×4.1/45	6×21	4	D1
M9	MS	38	874	18	2×4.1/45		2	
M12	MS	38	874	18	2×4.1/45		2	D2
M10	MS	38	874	18	2×4.1/45		2	
M153	MS	39	878	18	2×4.1/45		2	Sunk
M84	MS	39	878	18	2×4.1/45		2	

tion Tunnel and, because Plymouth was a transit point, structured them to be modular, slotting in forces temporarily available like destroyers passing through on the way to their permanent station. The idea was to maximize resources, but there were flaws in the concept as became clear in execution.

Action off Les Triagoz, 4 October 1943

TIME: 0135–0240
TYPE: Convoy attack
WEATHER: High overcast, light wind from SW
VISIBILITY: Dark, moon 21 percent, set 2052
SEA STATE: Light swell
SURPRISE: None
MISSION: Allies—interception based upon general intelligence;
               Germans—escort and transit

On the evening of 3 October, the 4th Flotilla, *T23*, (flag of Korvettenkapitän Franz Kohlauf), *T22*, *T27*, and *T25* were at sea sailing east in line ahead formation along the Breton coast covering a small convoy. Shortly before 0130 hours intelligence notified Kohlauf that German shore based radar had detected enemy ships to the northeast.

That same evening commander in chief Plymouth sent a mixed group of destroyers, the Hunts *Limbourne* (flag Commander Hankey), *Wensleydale*, and *Tanatside* and the fleet destroyers *Ulster* and *Grenville* to patrol off the Breton coast in hopes of catching the German torpedo boats. The British had just reached the eastern point of their patrol zone, about seven miles north of Les Triagoz Islands, and had come about to the west southwest zigzagging in extended formation with twelve hundred yards between ships.

The Germans saw the British first silhouetted against the lighter northern horizon (remaining invisible themselves against the dark shore). Kohlauf decided to fight and brought his column about at 0129. At about 0137 *T25* fired one torpedo and *T27* four more, all of which missed. Both suffered malfunctions during the launch process as they had intended to empty their tubes.

Still unseen, the Germans crept back toward the Allied column, altering course from southwest to northwest. To obtain an accurate range, *T23* used her radar getting a reading of nearly four thousand yards.[3] With this

Table 9.4. Action off Les Triagoz Islands, 4 October 1943

Allied Ships	TYP	YL	DFL	SPD	GUNS	TT	GF	DAM
Grenville	DD	42	2,505	36	4×4.7/45	8×21	6	D2
Ulster	DD	42	2,505	36	4×4.7/45	8×21	6	D3
Tanatside	DE	42	1,590	27	4×4/45	2×21	4	
Wensleydale	DE	42	1,545	27	4×4/45	2×21	4	D1
Limbourne	DE	42	1,545	27	4×4/45	2×21	4	D1
German Ships								
T22	TB	41	1,754	33	4×4.1/45	6×21	4	
T23	TB	41	1,754	33	4×4.1/45	6×21	4	
T25	TB	42	1,754	33	4×4.1/45	6×21	4	
T27	TB	42	1,754	33	4×4.1/45	6×21	4	

information *T22* launched a full salvo of six torpedoes at 0202. However, *Tanatside* had picked up *T23*'s radar pulses and alerted the flag. Hankey ordered his ships to turn 40 degrees to port, but the two destroyers turned independently, while the Hunts followed their flagship around in line ahead. This resulted in a ragged British formation headed southeast led by *Grenville* followed in order by *Ulster, Limbourne, Tanatside,* and *Wensleydale.* One benefit of this maneuver: *T22*'s torpedoes churned uselessly ahead toward the old British course.

Hankey believed he had the drop on the Germans and held his speed to twelve knots to avoid making visible bow waves. At 0204 the 4th Flotilla responded to the British maneuver by ringing up twenty-eight knots and coming hard about 180 degrees to the northeast. About five minutes after both lines had steadied on their converging courses star shell and flares began bursting in the air—the German pyrotechnics "giving a 'daylight' lamp as compared to the yellowish-white of the British star shells."[4] The real things followed close behind and an intense running fight developed. The Germans concentrated on the nearer targets, the fleet destroyers. With the enemy in view, *Grenville* and *Ulster* quickly worked up to full speed trying to gain position ahead of the Germans. The Hunts increased speed to twenty-five knots, but that was barely sufficient to keep them in the battle.

When *Grenville* had closed to an estimated range of three thousand yards she fired a full salvo of eight torpedoes, but her captain had seriously underestimated the speed of the German column and these missed far astern. At about 0212 *T23* replied with a half salvo of three torpedoes, but these were off mark as well. The Germans did better with their guns—they hit *Grenville* shortly after she had emptied her tubes. One shell holed the fleet destroyer forward while the other struck her lattice mast. The blast cut down the crew of "X" gun and ignited a cordite bag and the ensuing fire quickly enveloped her quarterdeck. She dropped out of column as *Ulster* swept past. *Grenville* also suffered a number of splinter holes and had one man killed and seven wounded, although she was able to return to action after just one week.

This left *Ulster* alone to fight four opponents. She launched a half salvo of torpedoes at 0217 from thirty-five hundred yards, but at 0218 Kohlauf turned to the southeast, ensuring that all missed. Then, at 0230 two German shells struck *Ulster*, one on the waterline, flooding her forward magazine and the other just abaft her "A" turret. *Ulster* launched her final four torpedoes at 0232 and then turned away, done for the night. She returned to Plymouth independently with one killed and eleven wounded. She was out of commission for a month. *T23* chased her with her last three torpedoes as the Germans continued east. The Hunts were far behind and soon dropped out of sight.

In all, the Germans fired seventeen and the Allies sixteen torpedoes and missed with every one. The British claimed several hits on the enemy, and the flagship observed one ship turning away on fire. In fact, the Germans only suffered splinter damage; the ship *Limbourne* saw burning (and fired upon) was probably *Grenville*. Beside the harm done to the fleet destroyers, *Wensleydale* had splinter holes and two wounded while one direct hit on *Limbourne* caused light damage that required two days to repair.

This action was a rare occasion when German torpedo boats defeated British destroyers with gunfire alone. The British were in fact lucky that Kohlauf was not able to launch a mass torpedo attack. The lack of coordination between the British fleet destroyers (the temporarily available ships) and the Hunts (permanent members of Plymouth Command) in a fast night action, acting independently and being defeated independently, was an unsettling intimation of things to come.

Action off Les Sept Îles, 23 Oct 1943

TIME:	0129–0159
TYPE:	Convoy attack
WEATHER:	Low clouds, passing rain squalls

VISIBILITY: Poor, moon 32 percent, rise 0128 northeast
SEA STATE: Long, heavy swell
SURPRISE: None
MISSION: Allies—interception based upon specific intelligence;
               Germans—escort and transit

Overstated claims of damage inflicted on the Germans at Les Triagoz blinded Plymouth Command to Tunnel's structural defects: if a complete victory had eluded the British, it was simply a matter of applying more force, not better tactics, organization, and, above all, flotilla training.

The opportunity to prove Tunnel with a stronger force was not long delayed. The blockade runner *Münsterland* (6,408 grt) arrived in Brest on 9 October with a valuable cargo of rubber, tungsten, chromium, and other strategic materials. She had led a charmed existence since the beginning of the war, sailing from Panama to East Asia and eluding every effort of the Allied navies to hunt her down. She was on the final stage of her long voyage and the British, with the advantage of Ultra intelligence, were determined to make it the most perilous of all. Plymouth Command took advantage of the presence of a cruiser and some destroyers and ordered the execution of Tunnel. The operation had to meet a schedule set by the Germans and its organization and planning reflected this handicap.

The strike force consisted of the antiaircraft light cruiser *Charybdis* (senior officer, Captain G. A. W. Voelcker), recently arrived from much different duty supporting the Salerno landing, the fleet destroyers *Grenville* and *Rocket,* and the escort destroyers *Limbourne, Wensleydale, Talybont,* and *Stevenstone* (on loan from the 15th Flotilla). *Limbourne, Wensleydale,* and *Talybont* were the only ships from the same flotilla and their senior officer, Commander W. J. Phipps, had only been on the job two days. He wrote: ". . . didn't get to the conference on operation 'Tunnel' until 1130 (22 October). Very hurried show run by Voelcker. I hadn't the least idea of his intentions and could not get anything out of him."[5]

Münsterland departed Brest at 1500 hours on the 22nd; the British force weighed anchor four hours later. Six minesweepers of the 2nd Flotilla and the radar equipped patrol boats *V718* and *V719* guarded the blockade runner. The five torpedo boats of the 4th Flotilla, *T23* (Korvettenkapitän Franz Kohlauf), *T26, T27, T22,* and *T25* joined the escort that night and took up position northeast of the convoy.

Table 9.5. Action off Les Sept Îles, 23 October 1943

Allied Ships	TYP	YL	DFL	SPD	GUNS	TT	GF	DAM
Charybdis	CL	40	7,210	32	8×4.5/40	6×21	12	Sunk
Grenville	DD	42	2,505	36	4×4.7/45	8×21	6	
Rocket	DD	42	2,480	36	4×4.7/45	8×21	6	
Limbourne	DE	42	1,545	27	4×4/45	2×21	4	Sunk
Wensleydale	DE	42	1,545	27	4×4/45	2×21	4	
Talybont	DE	43	1,545	27	4×4/45	2×21	4	
Stevenstone	DE	42	1,545	27	4×4/45	2×21	4	
German Ships								
T22	TB	41	1,754	33	4×4.1/45	6×21	4	
T23	TB	41	1,754	33	4×4.1/45	6×21	4	
T25	TB	42	1,754	33	4×4.1/45	6×21	4	
T26	TB	42	1,754	33	4×4.1/45	6×21	4	
T27	TB	42	1,754	33	4×4.1/45	6×21	4	

The British force arrived off the Breton Coast near Les Heaux light on Île Rouzie (the most northerly of Les Sept Îles) shortly after midnight, 23 October and began sweeping west at thirteen knots. They navigated in the order: *Charybdis, Grenville, Rocket, Limbourne, Talybont, Stevenstone,* and *Wensleydale,* with seven hundred twenty yards between ships. Tunnel was very specific regarding times, headings, and speeds. Voelcker's fighting instructions, signaled while under way, called for the force to remain concentrated in a single line ahead formation; except for 271 and 272 10-centimeter surface search radar, other radar, Asdic, and hydrophone, would remain silent. He would close the enemy unobserved to six thousand yards and then fire star shell. The destroyers could engage with torpedoes individually as targets presented themselves. If he was seen first, he would commence action immediately.

The Germans had seen enough of Tunnel to know when and how the British would come. Voelcker was still five minutes from Les Heaux light when *T25*'s hydrophone detected ships to the northeast. Kohlauf turned toward the contact. Meanwhile, the British Hunts intercepted voice transmissions between the German ships and notified the flag, but Voelcker did not "appear to have appreciated their probable significance."[6]

At 0130 *Charybdis*'s radar detected the enemy fourteen thousand yards ahead. Kohlauf had just come to an easterly heading. Behind him a dark rain squall was moving in from the southwest. On opposite courses, the two groups of warships were rapidly converging toward a clash.

At 0135 Voelcker increased speed and reported the contact—now eighty-eight hundred yards and closing—to his destroyers. At 0141 the Germans intercepted messages indicating they had been sighted and Kohlauf concluded he had lost the opportunity to make a surprise torpedo attack. At 0142 Voelcker ordered his column to come 13 degrees to starboard and increase speed, but the only ship to receive his signal was *Stevenstone* at the rear. When Voelcker executed, *Limbourne,* for one, lost track of her flagship. The destroyers were picking up indications of enemy forces, ambiguous radar returns, and undecipherable signals—it was not a good time for the British formation to lose cohesion. Then, at 0143, Kohlauf saw the large silhouette of the cruiser illuminated against the lighter northern horizon only twenty-two hundred yards off. Believing, in fact, he had been surprised, he ordered an emergency turn 120 degrees to starboard. As they came about, *T23* followed by *T26* emptied their tubes in the direction of the enemy.

As Kohlauf launched and fled, Voelcker was still relying on radar. At 0145 *Charybdis* fired star shell, but they burst above the clouds and only brightened the bottom of the overcast. *Limbourne* plotted a contact four thousand yards off her port bow; she assumed it was hostile and fired rockets to illuminate. The fleet destroyers came to port and crossed *Limbourne*'s bow. Then lookouts aboard *Charybdis* reported the straight, white, foaming tracks of torpedoes.

The cruiser came hard to port, but it was too late. One torpedo "struck her on the port side under the torpedo tubes. . . . The ship took up a 20° list as she slewed to port and stopped."[7] The time was 0147. As this happened, the German column was still going through its evolution and between 0146 and 1050 both *T27* and *T22* fired full torpedo salvos as they came around. Only *T25* failed to launch because her new torpedo officer froze at the decisive moment (there was no substitute for experience in a rapidly developing night action). At 0151 the German column steadied on an easterly heading.

At 0151 another torpedo struck *Charybdis* to port; her list increased rapidly and within five minutes her deck on the port side was underwater. At 0152 a torpedo slammed into *Limbourne* and detonated her forward magazine. *Grenville,* and *Wensleydale* barely avoided falling victim to the massive and unexpected barrage by taking prompt evasive action.

The captain of *Grenville* (Lieutenant Commander Roger Hill) was now senior officer, but he failed to immediately appreciate this fact and until he did, no one was in charge. Finally, he withdrew north with *Talybont* and *Stevenstone* and then collected *Wensleydale* and *Rocket*. He assumed *Charybdis* had been torpedoed by S-boats and that he would be ambushed if he hurried back. Only when he learned that *Limbourne* was still afloat did he venture to the battle scene, arriving at 0330 hours. *Charybdis* had already sunk at 0230 hours. The destroyers crisscrossed through the wreckage and rescued 107 of *Charybdis*'s men, but 464 died in the icy water. Attempts to tow *Limbourne* failed and *Talybont* and *Rocket* were forced to torpedo her. She lost 42 members of her crew.

Kohlauf was content to monitor the British rescue operations with radar as *Münsterland* continued safely to St. Malo. Hitler subsequently awarded him the Knight's Cross of the Iron Cross for this action.

On 4 October the British lost control of their formation and assumed the enemy hadn't seen them first, but they were lucky and the cost was light; only two men died and two ships were moderately damaged. They repeated these mistakes two and a half weeks later with a much bigger force and were not lucky. They suffered over five hundred men killed and lost two ships. The difference was a massed torpedo salvo. This tactic was the result of years of study by the German navy in using shore radar to coordinate torpedo boat attacks. The British were probably lucky after all that they only lost two ships. Admiralty staff studied the action off Les Sept Îles intensely. They drew many of the right conclusions and, not coincidentally, it was the last clear victory German surface forces would win during the war.

The importance of blockade runners to the Axis economy increased after the invasion of the Soviet Union severed land access to essential raw materials such as rubber and tin. Between April 1941 and June 1942 sixteen vessels sailed from Japanese waters to France and twelve arrived safely. By the end of 1942, however, Ultra had revealed the safe lanes blockade runners were using and in August 1943 the Allies began to read the Enigma transmissions of the blockade runners themselves. In a second wave lasting between August 1942 and May 1943 only four of fifteen Axis blockade runners safely reached France.

Such heavy attrition forced the Germany navy to suspend further voyages while it reconsidered the problem. This was one of the major reasons the navy concentrated so many destroyers and torpedo boats on the French west coast. (It would have been a good reason to activate a light cruiser or two as well, but apparently this was never contemplated.) When *Münsterland* made port in France, her success encouraged Germany to order three loaded ships waiting in Saigon to set sail. However, the British knew full well what was afoot. They responded with increased aerial surveillance and a cruiser patrol based out of the Azores. Nonetheless *Osorno*, the first runner, eluded these forces to be met by the 8th Destroyer Flotilla, the 4th Torpedo Boat Flotilla, and an escort of long-range JU-88 fighters. They fought off air attacks on 25 December and *Osorno* delivered most of her cargo of raw rubber (ironically, after her long and dangerous journey, she struck a submerged wreck at the mouth of the Gironde).

After this successful mission the 8th and two ships of the 4th put into the Gironde while the rest of the 4th made for Brest. They were waiting for the next blockade runner, *Alsterufer* (2,729 tons), just a few days behind *Osorno*. However, Allied aircraft sighted *Alsterufer* on 27 December 1943 and sank her before she could signal. Meanwhile the British light cruisers remained at sea: *Glasgow* (Captain C. P. Clarke) had departed the Azores and *Enterprise* (Captain H. T. W. Grant, RCN) was sailing hard to join her while *Penelope*, *Gambia*, and *Mauritius* patrolled various locations in the western Atlantic.

On the morning of 27 December, having spent only a day in port, the two German flotillas set to sea once again to meet *Alsterufer*. Korvettenkapitän Kohlauf's 4th Flotilla sailed from Brest with *T23*, *T22*, *T24*, and *T26* while Kapitän zur See Hans Erdmenger's 8th Flotilla departed the Gironde with *Z27*, *Z23*, *Z24*, *Z32*, *Z37*, *T25*, and *T27*. The two flotillas united just after 1200 hours on 28 December and swept eastward toward the open Atlantic searching for *Alsterufer*.

There were three things Erdmenger did not know that morning. First, *Alsterufer* was at the bottom of the sea; second a USN aircraft had reported his presence two and a half hours before; and third, the *Glasgow* and *Enterprise* were south of his position and working north to intercept. Erdmenger expected air reconnaissance would give several hours forewarning of any enemy presence. At 1224 German aircraft found and attacked the British cruisers, but Erdmenger didn't get the news until a half hour later. He immediately turned due east and signaled for full speed, but the British had already worked around to the northeast of his position. It was a rough day in the outer bay with a strong easterly wind blowing spindrift from the wave tops; moreover, several German ships were experiencing mechanical difficulties. The German Type 36A destroyers were never good sea boats and conditions were particularly difficult heading into a high wind at high speed through high swells. It was even worse for the smaller torpedo boats as they plunged between crest and trough, green seas breaking over their bows and spray inundating their bridges. Erdmenger saw no profit in engaging British cruisers despite his superiority in ships, guns, and torpedoes.

The Battle of Biscay, 28 December 1943

TIME:	1346–1700
TYPE:	Interception
WEATHER:	Cloudy, wind building to thirty knots from the east
VISIBILITY:	Excellent
SEA STATE:	High swells, white foam crests
SURPRISE:	Tactical none, strategic British
MISSION:	Allies—interception based upon specific intelligence; Germans—escort and transit

Erdmenger had commanded the 8th Flotilla since March 1943, but his combat experience was limited. He captained *Z21 Wilhelm Heidkamp* when she torpedoed the antique Norwegian coast defense ship *Eidsvold,* but the next day British destroyers blew his ship from under him in a surprise torpedo attack. He commanded *Z28* from August 1941 through February 1943, but his vessel saw no action against enemy warships. His leadership during the Battle of Biscay was clouded by signaling difficulties, unrealistic orders, and questionable decisions. There was also evidence Kohlauf and Erdmenger didn't work well together. Before battle even began, Kohlauf ignored an order to conduct a torpedo attack he considered premature while Erdmenger disregarded Kohlauf's recommendations as to course and speed.

At 1332 hours lookouts aboard *Glasgow* reported ships sixteen miles to the southwest. Captain Clark sat down to dinner as he ordered full speed and altered course to put his cruisers between the German destroyers and the safety of the French coast. Eight minutes later lookouts aboard *Z23* reported the cruisers bearing down.

At this point Erdmenger was sailing south-southeast in three columns: *Z23* and *Z27* (1st Division, 8th Flotilla) to port and astern; the 4th Flotilla

Table 9.6. The Battle of Biscay, 28 December 1943

Allied Ships	TYP	YL	DFL	SPD	GUNS	TT	GF	DAM
Glasgow	CL	36	11,350	32	12×6/50 & 8×4/45	6×21	29	D1
Enterprise	CL	18	9,450	33	7×6/45 & 3×4/45	12×21	13	D1
German Ships								
Z23	DD	39	3,605	38	5×5.9/50	8×21	9	
Z24	DD	40	3,605	38	5×5.9/50	8×21	9	
Z27	DD	40	3,543	38	4×5.9/50	8×21	8	Sunk
Z32	DD	41	3,691	38	5×5.9/50	8×21	9	
Z37	DD	41	3,691	38	5×5.9/50	8×21	9	
T22	TB	42	1,754	33	4×4.1/45	6×21	4	
T23	TB	42	1,754	33	4×4.1/45	6×21	4	
T24	TB	42	1,754	33	4×4.1/45	6×21	4	
T25	TB	42	1,754	33	4×4.1/45	6×21	4	Sunk
T26	TB	42	1,754	33	4×4.1/45	6×21	4	Sunk
T27	TB	42	1,754	33	4×4.1/45	6×21	4	

in the center; and Z32, Z37, and Z24 (2nd Division, 8th Flotilla) on the starboard side. Almost immediately, he ordered a torpedo attack, but none of his ships could comply because of the range and rough seas. Meanwhile, with higher speeds and a converging course, the British closed rapidly. At 1346 Glasgow's forward turret fired the action's first salvo from eighteen thousand–plus yards.

The battle's initial phase lasted thirty-three minutes as both groups ran to the south southeast. Glasgow and Enterprise fired deliberate salvos at the nearest ships, Z23 and Z27. Complying with Erdmenger's order, Z23 launched six torpedoes from eighteen thousand six hundred yards (at least). The destroyers then returned fire and although both sides landed shells within one to two hundred yards of target, there were no hits. During this period Erdmenger again ordered the 4th Flotilla to conduct a torpedo attack. Kohlauf attempted to comply, but the seas inundating his range-finding equipment prevented him from acquiring a target, so he held his weapons and returned to line.

At 1356 Erdmenger ordered the 2nd Division to make a torpedo attack. They crossed ahead of the 1st Division, took station on the port flank, and edged toward the cruisers. Z32, the leading ship, opened gunfire at 1405 and even though her forward mount was unserviceable she registered a hit on *Glasgow*'s boiler room fan intake a minute later, killing two. Despite pitching decks and heavy spray, German salvos repeatedly straddled *Enterprise* and the British return fire was equally intense. Many shells landed close, but none hit. At 1415 *Z37*'s captain decided the range, now at fourteen thousand yards, was near enough and he fired four torpedoes.

While this futile barrage churned through seven miles of stormy water, Erdmenger decided to divide his force. (Kohlauf, for one, disagreed with this tactic and was unhappy to have his flotilla split.) The German fleet was strung out in a loose column, from north to south: *Z32, Z24, Z37, T23, T24, T27, T26, T22, T25, Z27,* and *Z23* (with *Z32* and *Z37* to port making their attack). It had been a long-range gunnery action and German shooting had been at least as good as the British. The situation was such that one decisive hit would cut the British force in half, while a decisive British hit would reduce the German fleet by a tenth. Nevertheless, Erdmenger apparently believed he could best preserve his command by splitting it in two and at 1419 ordered his five rear ships, *T26, T22, T25, Z27,* and *Z23,* to turn 180 degrees to starboard back to the north northwest. (The flagship came to port rather than starboard in making her turn, whether by mistake or because Erdmenger wanted his ship to act like a lightning rod for British gunfire is unknown.) In response *Enterprise* sheered out of line to starboard and headed west to engage this group.

Z32 covered Erdmenger's turn-away at 1423 by launching six torpedoes. *Z23* also put one torpedo into the water as she came about. *Z32* and *Z37* laid a smoke screen and joined *Z24, T23, T24,* and *T27* as they continued southeast. *Z32* was belching fire from her forward funnel, leading the British to believe she had been hit. Then lookouts aboard *Glasgow* reported tracks. At 1428 she maneuvered violently as one torpedo passed only thirty yards off her port quarter and two others down her port side.

Z27's turn to port separated her from the other ships in the northern group and brought her closer to *Enterprise*. At 1428 she launched four torpedoes. Then the flagship became the first German to suffer damage. A 6-inch shell from *Enterprise* penetrated her No. 2 boiler room, passed through an oil bunker, and ignited a huge fire. As *Z27* lost way she launched four more torpedoes toward *Enterprise*. The time was 1435 hours. The two ships were on a converging course and the range between them was dropping rapidly. The flagship was in trouble and her situation was about to get worse. Erdmenger signaled Korvettenkapitän R. von Berger of *Z32,* the senior officer, that he had command of the southern group. Berger led his ships southeast and out of the action. They would have crossed *Glasgow*'s bow except Clark came about to port at 1435 on an opposite heading.

As the Germans divided, the British concentrated. *Glasgow* steered west to join *Enterprise*. *T25*, *T22*, and *T26* were northwest of *Z27*'s position heading nearly due north while *Z23* was off on her own between *Z27* and *Glasgow*. *Glasgow* ranged her turrets on the three torpedo boats of the northern group. (Although *Z23* was nearer, she was obscured by smoke.) Blood had been spilled and British accuracy suddenly improved. The torpedo boats turned south to escape *Glasgow*'s salvos falling close around them. It was now 1440, exactly one hour since the Germans had first spotted the British cruisers. The powerful German formation, although it was still largely undamaged, had been shattered into three groups and was about to be defeated in detail.

T25 sailed at the rear of the torpedo boat column. At 1454 a flurry of shells hit her aft torpedo tubes and flak platforms. Severed oil lines caused her engines to stop. Then another projectile exploded near her forward funnel and blew it and her mast overboard. *T22* came about and tried to assist her sister. She fired six torpedoes toward the cruiser at 1458, but these were so far off target *Glasgow* never noticed their tracks. When *T22* saw geysers from 6-inch salvos ranging toward her, she made smoke and retreated southwest. Then *Glasgow* shifted fire to *T26* and hit her boiler room. *T22* passed *T26* and did what she could by laying another smoke screen before she turned to escape.

As Clark ravaged the torpedo boats, *Enterprise* was sailing north, busy with the two destroyers. *Z27* was in a bad way, slowly heading west-north-west. At 1506 *Enterprise* fired two torpedoes at her through a smoke screen laid by *Z23*. *Glasgow* navigated on the same course some distance behind until 1508 when she came about to the south. *Enterprise* continued north, temporarily disengaging to clear gun and fire control defects. *T25*, drifting slowly southwest and no doubt distressed to see the cruiser returning toward her, fired three torpedoes in *Glasgow*'s direction at 1510, but all missed. At this time *Z23* attempted to come alongside her leader, but Erdmenger ordered her to escape (supporting the theory he was most concerned with reducing the damage to his fleet and had assigned his ship the role of decoy).

With her problems resolved, *Enterprise* joined *Glasgow* as the two cruisers chased down *T26*, the most southerly of the three damaged ships.

They quickly caught her, and an *Enterprise* torpedo sank *T26* at 1620; only ninety of her men survived. As *Enterprise* sailed to catch up with *Glasgow* again, she encountered the heavily damaged *T25*. She closed to about thirty-three hundred yards and launched a single torpedo. This hit and *T25* sank at 1637; there were one hundred survivors. Finally, *Glasgow* operating to the north of *Enterprise* found *Z27* drifting with all guns silent. She closed to point-blank range and rapid salvos exploded the unfortunate destroyer's magazines. *Z27* sank at 1641; there were ninety-three survivors; Erdmenger and his staff were not among them.

Satisfied with their afternoon's work and with limited ammunition and fuel remaining, the British cruisers made for Plymouth. *Glasgow* had been hit once while *Enterprise* received minor splinter damage from numerous near misses.

The two survivors of the German northern group, *T22* and *Z23*, managed to reunite. They continued west and finally made port at St. Jean de Luz, a French harbor close to the Spanish border. At 1515 Berger sent the three torpedo boats of the southern group to Brest and turned back to reenter the battle. But *Z24* quickly developed engine defects and even though she still retained her full load of torpedoes, she had to rejoin Kohlauf's rump flotilla. *Z32* and *Z37* continued west and sighted the cruisers, but did not attack. They returned to the Gironde that night.

This battle makes an interesting comparison with the action on 23 October. In rough weather on the open sea with extended visibility, the better gun platform prevailed. In close waters at night, the better torpedo platform prevailed. But the reality was not so facile. Erdmenger's tactics are easy to question. He repeatedly ordered long-range torpedo attacks. The Germans fired thirty-four torpedoes in eight separate attacks; they never had the opportunity to make a mass torpedo attack. *Glasgow* had one close call and that was it. Erdmenger's fatal decision, however, was to divide his fleet. During the running engagement fought at long ranges, the British suffered light damage. After Erdmenger divided his force, ranges dropped and he quickly lost three ships and then his life. *Duke of York* sank *Scharnhorst* just two days before. December 1943 was a bad month for the German navy's surface forces.

10

ACTIONS IN THE ENGLISH CHANNEL

January–June 1944

In no other circumstances than in a night action at sea does the fog of war so completely descend to blind one to a true realization of what is happening.

ADMIRAL ANDREW CUNNINGHAM

The decisive year for the naval war in the English Channel was 1944. At first the nature of combat followed the pattern of 1943. Then came the long anticipated cross-channel invasion. The German navy threw its pitifully meager resources into the breach of the Atlantic Wall and surface clashes and encounters occurred almost nightly for a week. Finally, the Allies drove the larger German warships from the Chan-

Table 10.1. Actions in the English Channel, January–June 1944

Date	Location	Name	Opponent	Type
5-Feb-44	Breton Coast	Action off l'Aber-Vrach	British	Interception
26-Apr-44	Breton Coast	Second Action off Île de Batz	Brit/CDN	Interception
28-Apr-44	Breton Coast	Action off Île de Vierge	Canadian	Interception
6-Jun-44	English Channel	Attack off Sword Beach	British/PO/NO	Interception
7-Jun-44	English Channel	First Encounter off Le Havre	Ukn	Interception
9-Jun-44	English Channel	Second Encounter off Le Havre	Ukn	Interception
9-Jun-44	Breton Coast	Battle of Brittany	British/PO/CDN	Interception
10-Jun-44	English Channel	Third Encounter off Le Havre	British/PO/NO	Interception
13-Jun-44	English Channel	Fourth Encounter off Le Havre	Brit/NO	Interception

nel, although coastal forces and U-boats harassed Allied shipping until the end of the war.

Action off l'Aber-Vrach, 5 February 1944

TIME: Night
TYPE: Interception
WEATHER:
VISIBILITY: Moon 85 percent, set 0505
SEA STATE:
SURPRISE: Allies
MISSION: British—offensive and sea superiority patrol; Germans—escort and transit

Losses suffered in the Battle of Biscay debacle reduced the 4th Torpedo Boat Flotilla to four ships. *T28* and *T29* reinforced the flotilla from Germany, but *T22* and *T23* returned home for refit. *T29* got a taste of her new operational zone on the night of 5 February escorting *M156* and *M206* east along the Breton coast. The well-practiced Hunts of the Plymouth command were at sea as well that night, plying waters they knew far better.

Sweeping along the coast the four Hunts surprised the small German force and, in a sharp engagement, they hit *M156* eight times with 4-inch shells, disabling her engines and flooding three compartments. After the British broke off, she was taken under tow and brought to l'Aber-Vrach, a small port north of Brest. British Typhoons found her there the next morning. Their bombs finished the job and she capsized in shallow water.

Table 10.2. Action off l'Aber-Vrach, 5 February 1944

Allied Ships	TYP	YL	DFL	SPD	GUNS	TT	GF	DAM
Tanatside	DE	42	1,545	27	4×4/45	2×21	4	
Talybont	DE	42	1,545	27	4×4/45	2×21	4	
Brissenden	DE	42	1,750	26	6×4/45	3×21	6	
Wensleydale	DE	42	1,545	27	4×4/45	2×21	4	
German Ships								
T29	TB	41	1,754	33	4×4.1/45	6×21	4	
M156	MS	41	775	17	2×4.1/45		2	D4
M206	MS	41	775	17	2×4.1/45		2	

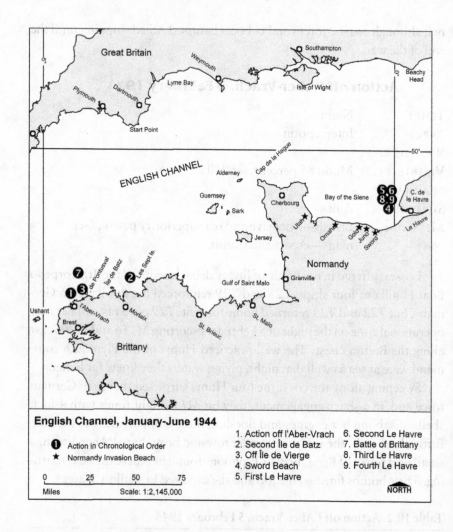

English Channel, January-June 1944

● Action in Chronological Order
★ Normandy Invasion Beach

0   25   50   75
Miles   Scale: 1:2,145,000   NORTH

1. Action off l'Aber-Vrach   6. Second Le Havre
2. Second Île de Batz   7. Battle of Brittany
3. Off Île de Vierge   8. Third Le Havre
4. Sword Beach   9. Fourth Le Havre
5. First Le Havre

Second Action off Île de Batz, 26 April 1944

TIME:	0220–0420
TYPE:	Interception
WEATHER:	Light breeze
VISIBILITY:	Dark, moon 13 percent, set 2335, 3,000 yards
SEA STATE:	Calm
SURPRISE:	None
MISSION:	Allied—interception based upon general intelligence; Germans—defensive mining and patrol

On the night of 25–26 April *T29*, *T24*, and *T27* of the 4th Torpedo Boat Flotilla under Korvettenkapitän Franz Kohlauf sortied from St. Malo to sow a mine barrage northwest of Les Sept Îles and then cover a convoy sailing toward Brest. After accomplishing the first portion of his mission, Kohlauf (by this time Germany's most combat-experienced destroyer leader) received word that British warships were in his area.

Commander in chief Plymouth, Vice Admiral Sir Ralph Leatham, ordered a Tunnel operation for the night of 25–26 April based on intelligence that German torpedo boats were sheltering in St. Malo. He dispatched a powerful British/Canadian group (Force 26) consisting of the light cruiser *Black Prince* (Captain D. M. Lees, senior officer), the destroyer *Ashanti*, and the Canadian destroyers *Haida* (Commander H. C. De Wolf, RCN, senior officer destroyers), *Athabaskan*, and *Huron* toward the Breton coast.

Having considered what went wrong on 23 October when the outnumbered Germans so easily sank *Charybdis*, the British were testing a new evolution of Tunnel. The destroyers were a homogeneous type—heavily armed Tribals—and they had trained together. Each ship had 360 degrees radar capability and the "Gee" radio navigation system. Rather than employing the venerable and vulnerable line-ahead formation, they deployed in subdivisions ahead of the cruiser (*Ashanti* and *Huron* to port, *Haida* and *Athabaskan* to starboard).

It was a dark, nearly moonless night with limited visibility, a light breeze, and a calm sea—perfect torpedo conditions. Force 26 swept west along the coast. When they reached Île de Batz, the crack of German shore

Table 10.3. Second Action off Île de Batz, 26 April 1944

Allied Ships	TYP	YL	DFL	SPD	GUNS	TT	GF	DAM
Black Prince	CL	42	7,410	32	8×5.25/50	6×21	11	
Ashanti	DD	37	2,710	36	6×4.7/45 & 2×4/45	4×21	11	D3
Athabaskan (CDN)	DD	41	2,745	36	6×4.7/45 & 2×4/45	4×21	11	D1
Haida (CDN)	DD	42	2,745	36	6×4.7/45 & 2×4/45	4×21	11	D1
Huron (CDN)	DD	42	2,745	36	6×4.7/45 & 2×4/45	4×21	11	D2
German Ships								
T24	TB	41	1,754	33	4×4.1/45	6×21	4	D2
T27	TB	41	1,754	33	4×4.1/45	6×21	4	D2
T29	TB	41	1,754	33	4×4.1/45	6×533	4	Sunk

batteries opening fire announced to Lees that he had lost the element of surprise. At 0130 hours he came about to the east northeast, thinking there would be no excitement that night.

Kohlauf sailed west cautiously, at medium speed, crews at action stations, probing for that vital first contact. But it turned out *Black Prince*, against her expectations, saw the Germans first at 0207 when her radar returned blips from twenty-one thousand yards. Lees, eschewing subtlety, turned toward the contact and ordered thirty knots. The Germans detected his approach shortly thereafter, reversed course, and fled. Force 26 followed for several minutes, then *Black Prince* fired star shell from "B" turret and Lees ordered the destroyers: "Engage bearing 090."[1] The time was 0220 hours and the range from the flagship thirteen thousand yards. *Haida* and *Athabaskan* were nearest the enemy. They opened fire from the German's starboard quarter from a range of eleven thousand yards. *Huron* and *Ashanti* chased to port. *Black Prince* hung back, periodically lobbing star shells overhead.

As they chased the Germans, the Allied destroyers shot with impressive accuracy, obtaining continuous straddles on *T24* and *T27*. *T24* replied with her aft guns and one of the torpedo boats jinked to bring her aft tubes to bear, firing a salvo back at the destroyers. Then, at 0231, just ten minutes into the action, a 4.7-inch shell struck *T27* astern and reduced her speed to twelve knots. At about the same time *Black Prince* maneuvered to avoid torpedoes; then her "B" turret jammed. Lees, seeing no reason to continue providing a large valuable target for a lucky torpedo, dropped out of the chase.

Kohlauf gave *T27* permission to turn inshore where the British lost her radar signature among the rocks of Morlaix Bay. *T24* and *T29* continued east at full speed, but the destroyers were the faster ships and continued to close. Then a shell exploded on *T24*'s range finder platform and another on her radio office. A fire erupted, which her crew quickly doused. Most importantly, these blows did not affect her speed. At 0254 she fired her forward torpedo tubes hoping to slow down her pursuers. Instead it was *T29* that was slowed when a shell struck her rudder and caused her to skew about back toward her pursuers. *Haida* and *Athabaskan* believed she was breaking back to Brest. While *Ashanti* and *Huron* continued chasing *T27*, they closed the German flagship firing full broadsides and torpedoes. The torpedoes missed; the guns did not. One shell detonated in *T29*'s aft funnel and sparked a series of secondary explosions. Others struck her forward boiler room, forward turbine room, after turrets, bridge, and torpedo tubes. The beleaguered torpedo boat fought back, but on this night the German gunners did not have the luck or skill they had shown on earlier occasions. (*T29* was a relatively new ship with little combat experience, but so were the Canadian destroyers.) By 0332, she was dead in the water and clearly doomed.

Shortly thereafter *Ashanti* and *Huron* returned having abandoned their pursuit of *T24* (she made it safely to St. Malo). As the other two destroyers withdrew north, they attempted to finish the drifting ship with torpedoes, but *Ashanti*'s signal said it all: "All torpedoes fired. They must have gone underneath."[2] In the smoke and darkness, the four destroyers had trouble sorting out who was who and where, and *T29* didn't help. One of her crew operating the aft 20-mm raked three of the four Allied ships when they got too close, causing some casualties aboard *Haida* and *Huron*. After this the destroyers circled *T29* from as near as seven hundred yards and ruthlessly blasted her. She rolled over and sank at 0420; 135 men, including the redoubtable Korvettenkapitän Franz Kohlauf died, but a German patrol boat later rescued 73 men. *Huron* and *Ashanti* collided near the end of the action and *Ashanti* suffered a nineteen-foot rip in her bow. She required three weeks in dry dock before she was again operational while *Huron*'s repairs lasted eleven days. *Haida* and *Athabaskan* were lightly damaged by 20-mm gunfire.

Admiralty staff criticized this action, particularly the failure to hit a drifting target with sixteen torpedoes and the concentration of all four Allied destroyers against a cripple while other damaged ships escaped. While these points were valid, the Tribals nevertheless turned in a good performance and their shooting had been outstanding.

Action off Île de Vierge, 28 April 1944

TIME:	0400–0450
TYPE:	Interception
WEATHER:	
VISIBILITY:	Dark, moon 30 percent, set 0032
SEA STATE:	
SURPRISE:	Allies
MISSION:	Allied—offensive mining and patrol; Germans—transit

Following the unhappy events of 26 April *T27* joined *T24* at St. Malo. There they patched up their damage and on the night of 27 April broke out for Brest. That same night a British coastal force of two MTBs and eight MLs laid an offensive minefield off Île de Batz, covered by the Canadian destroyers *Haida* (Commander Harry De Wolf, senior officer) and *Athabaskan*. After completing this mission the Canadians were in mid-Channel when coastal radar in Britain reported a very long-range contact. The time was 0313. The two destroyers turned southwest expecting to find the two German torpedo boats. Radar conditions were excellent and the Canadians obtained a contact of their own shortly after at a range of fourteen miles. De Wolf made a careful approach. He intended to engage using his ship's powerful gun batteries alone, mindful of how miserably the four Tribals had missed a stationary target with torpedoes just two nights earlier.

The German torpedo boats were about twelve miles north of Île de Vierge by 0400 hours. Their first intimation of danger came at 0412 when the yellow glare of star shell burst overhead. The Canadians were about seventy-two hundred yards northwest. Immediately the two torpedo boats made smoke and turned south-southeast. Each ship launched a salvo of six torpedoes as she came about, although, in the rush and confusion, *T24* discharged three to the wrong side. De Wolf turned 30 degrees to starboard. This course alteration presented a smaller target, but it wasn't so great that the aft 4-inch mount—which he needed to fire star shell—couldn't bear.

Athabaskan was just steadying on her new course when one of the three torpedoes *T24* fired in the right direction struck. "A great column of flame and white water rose from her port side aft. The ship coasted to a stop with considerable damage and no steering, turning slowly to port and settling aft."[3] The time was 0417 hours; the action was only five minutes old.

Table 10.4. Action off Île de Vierge, 28 April 1944

Allied Ships	TYP	YL	DFL	SPD	GUNS	TT	GF	DAM
Haida	DD	42	2,745	36	6×4.7/45 & 2×4/45	4×21	11	
Athabaskan	DD	41	2,745	36	6×4.7/45 & 2×4/45	4×21	11	Sunk
German Ships								
T24	TB	41	1,754	33	4×4.1/45	6×21	4	D2
T27	TB	41	1,754	33	4×4.1/45	6×21	4	Sunk

Haida cut across *Athabaskan*'s bow. De Wolf wasn't sure if the ship had been torpedoed or mined, but he was sure that duty required him to pursue the fleeing Germans. He paused only long enough to lay a curtain of smoke around his burning comrade. *Haida*'s gunners then proceeded to demonstrate that their accuracy of two nights before was no fluke. They hit *T27* as the German ship was still working up to full speed. In response the Germans separated—*T24* turned east while *T27* continued to the southeast. De Wolf followed *T27*. From the bridge he could see tracers from the torpedo boat's aft guns showing her return fire, and bright orange flashes indicating his guns were hitting. Then, at 0430, the sky behind the two ships erupted in a tremendous explosion that could be seen thirty miles away. *Athabaskan*'s men had been unable to control the fire and it detonated "Y" mount's magazine. Her captain, Lieutenant Commander John Stubbs, ordered abandon ship and the destroyer sank within twelve minutes.

Meanwhile *Haida* continued after *T27* hitting her six more times on her waterline, in the forward boiler room, the transmitting station, and the forward deck. Her captain, Kapitänleutnant W. Gotzmann tried to make l'Aber-Vrach, but he miscalculated his distance from the coast and ran his ship hard aground near Point Pontusval, nine miles east of his goal. *Haida* bombarded the stricken ship for a few minutes before withdrawing, setting off her ready ammunition and igniting a large fire. *T27* lost fourteen men. Salvage attempts were unsuccessful and British MTBs finally destroyed the wreck on 7 May. *Haida* returned to *Athabaskan*'s last position and, although she had only a quarter hour before she needed to clear the area, she rescued 38 men. The British rescued another 6 while *T24* (which also returned) and a pair of minesweepers pulled 86 men from the cold water. Captain Stubbs and 128 members of his crew perished.

In the after-action analysis, Admiralty staff faulted De Wolf for his failure to use torpedoes. They didn't note that this was the last action fought by the 4th Torpedo Boat Flotilla. De Wolf and the Canadians had eliminated a unit that had defeated the British repeatedly for more than a year.

Attack off Sword Beach, 6 June 1944

TIME: 0530–0540, British +1/2 hr
TYPE: Interception

WEATHER: Wind eighteen knots westerly, heavy overcast
VISIBILITY: Good
SEA STATE: Moderate swells
SURPRISE: Axis
MISSION: Allied—shore bombardment/amphibious attack; Germans—offensive and sea superiority patrol without specific intelligence

The largest amphibious assault of World War II (in terms of ships involved) crossed the war's most disputed body of water. After one false start, and in doubtful conditions, the 2,727 Allied vessels of the amphibious forces, the minesweepers, the transports, the auxiliaries, the screening forces, and the bombardment groups put to sea in seventy-five convoys—all to arrive at their appointed place, at their appointed time on the morning of 6 June 1944.[4]

This gigantic movement caught the German command by surprise. Naval Group West did not conclude the Allied invasion fleet was at sea until 0230 hours on the morning of 6 June. Given the evidence by his chief of staff, Vizeadmiral Theodor Krancke ordered the signal: "Mass landing in the Seine estuary." The German navy had no battleships, no cruisers, not even a destroyer available to challenge the Allied armada, but what it did have it threw into the fray. The largest warships were the three operational torpedo boats of the 5th Flotilla, based since 23 May at Le Havre: *T28* (Korvettenkapitän Heinrich Hoffman), just back from a four month refit, and the prewar ships *Möwe* and *Jaguar*. (*Kondor* and *Falke* were also present, but still under repair from damage suffered during their transit to Le Havre.) They cleared Le Havre's mole at 0442 hours, just behind the patrol boats of 15th Security (*Vorposten*) Flotilla and certainly before they had any clear idea what they were sailing into. Their specific mission was to attack landing craft reported in the western extremes of the Bay of the Seine (off the American beaches) but given the rough conditions, many doubted the Allies would be so stupid as to come on such a night

At 0505 hours the 5th Flotilla was entering the bay. At the same time the British/Polish/Norwegian "Sword" force had reached its bombardment position as near as eleven miles west of Le Havre and *Warspite* had just fired three blind ranging salvos. Allied aircraft were flying low across the group's flank dropping smoke bombs to hide the ships from the batteries at Cap de le Havre. Dawn was just breaking. The torpedo officer of

Table 10.5. Action off Sword Beach, 6 June 1944

Allied Ships	TYP	YL	DFL	SPD	GUNS	TT	GF	DAM
Warspite	BB	13	33,670	23	6×15/42 & 12×6/45		99	
Ramillies	BB	16	36,140	23	4×15/42 & 12×6/45		84	
Roberts	BM	41	9,150	12	2×15/42 & 8×4/45		63	
Mauritius	CL	39	11,090	31	12×6/50 & 8×4/45	6×21	29	
Arethusa	CL	34	7,400	32	6×6/50 & 8×4/45	6×21	20	
Frobisher	CA	20	12,190	30	7×7.5/45	6×21	19	
Danae	CL	18	5,780	29	5×6/45 & 2×4/45	12×21	11	
Dragon (PO)	CL	17	5,730	29	5×6/45 & 2×4/45	12×21	11	
Saumarez	DD	42	2,505	36	4×4.7/45	8×21	6	
Scorpion	DD	42	2,505	36	4×4.7/45	8×21	6	
Scourge	DD	42	2,505	36	4×4.7/45	8×21	6	
Serapis	DD	43	2,505	36	4×4.7/45	8×21	6	
Swift	DD	43	2,505	36	4×4.7/45	8×21	6	
Stord (NO)	DD	43	2,505	36	4×4.7/45	8×21	6	
Svenner (NO)	DD	43	2,505	36	4×4.7/45	8×21	6	Sunk
Verulam	DD	43	2,505	36	4×4.7/45	8×21	6	
Virago	DD	43	2,505	36	4×4.7/45	8×21	6	
Kelvin	DD	39	2,540	36	6×4.7/45 & 1×4/45	5×21	9	
Slazak (PO)	DE	41	1,625	27	6×4/45		6	
Middleton	DE	41	1,625	27	6×4/45		6	
Eglinton	DE	39	1,450	28	4×4/45		4	
German Ships								
T28	TB	41	1,754	33	4×4.1/45	6×21	4	D1
Möwe	TB	26	1,290	33	3×4.1/45	6×21	3	
Jaguar	TB	26	1,320	34	3×4.1/45	6×21	3	

Möwe, looking through his range finder, saw shapes on the western horizon. "He wiped his eyes . . . the apparition remained; there could be no doubt about it. Before them, less than 12 kilometers ahead, sailed a fleet of vast proportions which could only be that of the Allied invasion."[5]

The torpedo boats sailed in line ahead at twenty-eight knots undetected, thanks to the massive clouds of rolling smoke. Then, as they approached, aircraft began to buzz overhead. At 0531 a plane strafed T28 and damaged two of her torpedo tubes. However, the bombardment had begun and the attention of the Allied spotters and lookouts was focused ashore. Hoffman's ships reached the edge of the smoke curtain about seven thousand yards from Warspite at 0535 and began to turn, launching torpedoes one after the other. All sixteen were in the water before the Allied ships woke to their danger. *Warspite* and *Ramillies* turned their secondary batteries and *Mauritius* and *Arethusa* their main guns toward the intruders. Shells from forty radar-directed 6-inch guns began landing to either side of the torpedo boats, throwing columns of water into the sky as they fled back into the smoke, zigzagging at high speed.

Two torpedoes passed between the anchored battleships and the Landing Ship Headquarters (Large) *Largs* had to go emergency full astern to avoid another. The Norwegian destroyer *Svenner* was not so fortunate. A torpedo, near the limit of its range, hit her amidships; the force of the explosion broke her back and she quickly sank losing thirty-four men. Chased by salvos and strafing aircraft, Hoffman's flotilla made harbor again at 0615 hours. *Warspite* (whose log recorded engaging twelve destroyers and sinking one) registered a direct hit on *V1506* of the 15th Security Flotilla, sinking the small patrol boat.

Admiral Theodor Krancke noted in the Naval Group West War Diary: "It was only to be expected that no effective blow could be struck at such superior enemy forces with the limited forces at my disposal."[6] However, he may have missed the point. The attack of the torpedo boats cost the Allies a fleet destroyer (never a good thing). But, more importantly, it told the Allies that the German navy would fight with every weapon at its disposal, regardless of the odds—a point the German navy continued to make in the nights that followed.

First Encounter off Le Havre, 6–7 June, 1943

TIME:	Night
TYPE:	Encounter
WEATHER:	
VISIBILITY:	
SEA STATE:	
SURPRISE:	None
MISSION:	Allies—patrol and sea security; Germans—offensive and sea superiority patrol without specific intelligence

Every night thereafter the German navy tested the dangerous waters of the Bay of the Seine. S-boats did the most damage because they were hard to spot and available in greater numbers—this despite Ultra, which told the Allied command how many boats would be leaving what port as well as when and where they would be going. The torpedo boats of the 5th Flotilla that were available attempted to make their contribution as well, but found this nearly impossible in the face of Allied countermeasures.

After their Valkyrian thrust into the heart of the Allied fleet, the 5th Torpedo Boat Flotilla spent D-day in port, resting, refurbishing, and listening to battle news and rumors. *T28* entered dock to repair her damaged torpedo tubes. Then, after dark, Hoffman boarded *Jaguar* and, with *Möwe*, patrolled off Le Havre. He encountered two destroyers, part of the thick Allied screen guarding the invasion flank. The Germans made an unsuccessful attack and then returned to port.

Second Encounter off Le Havre, 9 June 1943

TIME: Night
TYPE: Encounter
WEATHER:
Visibility: Moon 94 percent, rise 2341
SEA STATE:
SURPRISE: None
MISSION: Allies—patrol and sea security; Germans—offensive and sea superiority patrol without specific intelligence

The 5th Flotilla sat out the next night, but by the evening of D+2 *T28* was ready to go again. Hoffman returned to his flagship and led *Jaguar* and *Möwe* on another patrol off Le Havre. They sighted a corvette from a convoy escort to their northwest and were stalking it when it fired star shell. The Germans counter-illuminated and opened fire. What neither knew, however, was that the four boats of the British 55th MTB Flotilla (Lieutenant Commander D. G. Bradford) were between them, approaching at low speed and nearly in position to launch their weapons.

In the white and yellow glare of the drifting flares, Hoffman's ships saw the MTBs. They immediately turned to the southwest and fired torpedoes at the corvette while the MTBs got six torpedoes into the water aimed at the Germans. Although Bradford claimed one of his weapons hit, all ships involved escaped undamaged.[7]

Battle of Brittany, 9 June 1944

TIME: 0122–0520
TYPE: Interception
WEATHER: Overcast, light southwesterly winds, intermittent rain
VISIBILITY: Limited 1–3 miles. Moon 94 percent, rise 2352
SEA STATE: Calm
SURPRISE: None
MISSION: Allies—interception based upon general intelligence;
               Germans—transit

On the morning of 6 June Vizeadmiral Krancke ordered the remnants of the 8th Destroyer Flotilla, ZH1, Z32, and Z24, under Kapitän zur See Theodor F. von Bechtolsheim, to leave the Gironde and make for Brest. The British quickly learned of this order and within an hour an Ultra alert was in the hands of the relevant commands. Coastal Command Canadian Beaufighters hit the destroyers en route and lightly damaged Z32.

The 8th Flotilla made Brest, where the two type 36A destroyers had their antiaircraft armament augmented. In company with T24, the 4th Torpedo Boat Flotilla's sole survivor, the Germans weighed anchor the evening of 8 June bound for Cherbourg where they would reinforce the defense and be in position to break east for home, if needed. They also carried extra torpedoes for the S-boats which were rapidly depleting their supplies in the target-rich waters off Normandy.

Ultra kept the British apprised of the 8th Flotilla's progress. That night the Allied 10th Destroyer Flotilla led by Captain Basil Jones in HMS *Tartar* put to sea patrolling twenty miles off the Breton coast. Jones deployed his flotilla in two divisions; the Polish *Blyskawica* (Captain Konrad Namiesniowski) led the northern unit (19th Division) which consisted of the newcomers to the flotilla, the Polish *Piorun,* and the British ships *Eskimo* and *Javelin. Tartar* led the southern group (20th Division) with *Ashanti* and the Canadians *Haida* and *Huron.*

The time was 0116 hours 9 June and the Allied flotilla had just steadied on a westerly course when *Tartar* picked up echoes on her radar about ten miles dead ahead. At 0122 Jones brought his division 35 degrees to starboard. At 0123 Bechtolsheim was about thirty miles west-northwest of Île de Batz heading nearly due east in order Z32, ZH1, Z24, and T24 when

Table 10.6. Battle of Brittany, 9 June 1944

Allied Ships	TYP	YL	DFL	SPD	GUNS	TT	GF	DAM
Blyskawica (PO)	DD	36	3,383	39	8×4/45	3×21	8	
Piorun (PO)	DD	40	2,330	36	6×4.7/45 & 1×4/45	5×21	9	
Eskimo	DD	37	2,710	36	6×4.7/45 & 2×4/45	4×21	11	D1
Javelin	DD	38	2,540	36	6×4.7/45 & 1×4/45	5×21	9	
Tartar	DD	37	2,710	36	6×4.7/45 & 2×4/45	4×21	11	D3
Ashanti	DD	37	2,710	36	6×4.7/45 & 2×4/45	4×21	11	
Haida (CDN)	DD	42	2,745	36	6×4.7/45 & 2×4/45	4×21	11	D1
Huron (CDN)	DD	42	2,745	36	6×4.7/45 & 2×4/45	4×21	11	
German Ships								
ZH1	DD	43	2,228	37	5×4.7/45	8×21	8	Sunk
Z24	DD	40	3,605	38	5×5.9/50	8×21	9	D3
Z32	DD	41	3,691	38	5×5.9/50	8×21	9	Sunk
T24	TB	42	1,754	33	4×4.1/45	6×21	4	

lookouts aboard the flagship picked out shadows to the northeast about five thousand yards away. He turned north to investigate. Then, the moon broke through a temporary rent in the thick overcast, allowing the Germans to recognize the silhouettes as British warships (perhaps cruisers).

Bechtolsheim was not looking for a fight, but, at 0125, when star shell began arcing into the sky, he knew he had one. He didn't hesitate: At 0126 his first three ships each launched four torpedoes forward from starboard with an estimated range to target of under five thousand yards. (T24 didn't see the enemy, so she held fire.) The British listening in on the German tactical radio net heard the order (los!) and Jones expected the attack in any case. The 19th Division had already turned 50 degrees to port. This put them in a staggered line abreast formation heading straight for the Germans in such a way the guns of every ship could bear while presenting a minimal torpedo target.

Making smoke, the German flotilla turned hard to port across the bows of the 19th division and a running fight developed. The "B" mount on each of the destroyers was used for star shell but the others fired for effect. And effect they achieved. Jones's four ships were veterans—some of more than two dozen night forays—on a steady heading, but even so their shooting was exceptionally good. They hit Z32 twice and forced her to the northwest. A flurry of six shells ravaged ZH1; one exploded in her turbine room and another flooded her boiler room. She lost engine power and drifted to a stop, smothered in escaping steam and smoke. Five shells struck Z24 and destroyed her wheelhouse and chart house and disabled her radio. German return fire was slow and ineffective, even though ranges dropped to the point where antiaircraft weapons opened fire. As ZH1 went dead in the water, Z24 sheered off to the southwest, losing contact with her flag. T24, the last ship in line followed.

In barely five minutes of action, the fury of the Allied bombardment had shattered the German formation, disabling one ship and damaging two others. As the Canadian ships chased Z24 and T24, Tartar and Ashanti hunted ZH1. Z32 was off by herself to the northwest. But she wasn't by herself for long because at 0132 she steamed directly into view of the 20th Division's four ships. As star shells burst overhead, trying to pin him in their yellow glare, Bechtolsheim turned to port and fired four torpedoes. The range was about seven thousand yards.

Blyskawica responded in the traditional manner, turning away from the enemy to the north and then east to avoid the German attack. Piorun, second ship in line, did not expect this maneuver and lost contact with her leader. Eskimo and Javelin thought Blyskawica was firing torpedoes so they turned as well, launching three and four torpedoes of their own before reforming on Blyskawica's lead. These maneuvers took the 20th Division to the north and effectively out of the fight. Before Z32 disappeared west into the smoke and dark, the gunners of the 20th claimed sixteen to twenty hits. This seems improbable, but if true, it did not slow Z32 down. For her part, Z32 registered one hit on the base of Eskimo's foremast that caused light damage.

Bechtolsheim had escaped a major threat, but where was his flotilla? He turned to the east once again hoping to reestablish contact, but instead he found Tartar and Ashanti. From around 0200 another running firefight ensued. Three shells hit Z32, forcing her to flood a magazine, disabling her after torpedo tubes and a gun mount, and destroying a pump-room and her sickbay. But the German's big 5.9-inch guns finally inflicted some harm in return. She landed four shells around Tartar's bridge and in the wheelhouse. The flagship's foremast toppled and splinters pierced her No. 1 boiler room, drastically reducing her speed. One crew member remembered:

Shrapnel rattled around in all directions and soon the small compartment filled with choking smoke. Pandemonium reigned for a few minutes on the bridge immediately above us, and from the wheelhouse adjoining our action station came the voice of the Coxswain shouting loudly, "Someone's been hit." ... Curling smoke swirled everywhere, and the stench of blood was sickening.[8]

Burning, she turned away wreathed in smoke.

At 0215 Z32 launched another salvo of torpedoes to the north, perhaps at the ships of the 20th Division, and then she retired south to reload her tubes. This gave *Tartar* time to control her fires and restore speed. *Ashanti* stood by the flagship. They were together when they encountered the drifting wreck of ZH1. ZH1 pugnaciously opened fire on *Tartar* and both destroyers replied. *Ashanti* then closed to point-blank range and launched two torpedoes. One hit, blowing off the German's bow. ZH1's captain, Korvettenkapitän Claus Barckow, ordered his crew to abandon ship, and then he had depth charges detonated below. At 0240 she exploded and sank. Thirty-nine men died, including Barckow; twenty-eight reached France in one of the ship's boats and the British 14th Escort Group saved 140.

The Canadians chased Z24 and T24 south until the Germans sailed across a British minefield, which forced them to detour and eventually lose contact. At 0214 De Wolf decided to reform on *Tartar.* When they saw they were no longer being followed, Z24 and T24 turned back as well and approached the battle to the point where they could see star shell in the distance. They then turned back to the west.

Z32 had so far demonstrated an impressive ability to take damage, having absorbed as many as twenty-five hits; unfortunately, she also proved easy to find. *Huron* and *Haida* returning from their unproductive chase sighted the German flagship at 0230 hours. She was approximately where they expected to find *Tartar* whereas Bechtolsheim was still looking for his lost flotilla. He noted:

Individual shadows are sighted. Exchanges of recognition signals by blinker gun, and even by night identification signal, do not lead to any identification. The fact that, despite German recognition signal interrogation, these shadows do not fire, however causes me to make the decision not to use my weapons.[9]

The Canadians were equally confused. ("Switch on Fighting Lights." "Where are you?" "What is enemy's position?" "Did you fire that star shell?")[10] But at 0254 when star shell finally established who was who, they opened fire and began to chase Z32 eastward with the rest of the 10th Flotilla following. Bechtolsheim eluded them at 0311 by sailing over the same British minefield.

At about 0400 hours Z24 finally restored communications and advised the flag of her location and damage, requesting permission to return to Brest with T24 (they were already under way). At 0415 Bechtolsheim, surprised they were so far to the west, granted her request, and these two ships took no further part in the action. T24 was the only German vessel to return to port undamaged.

At 0430 hours with hope of gathering his flotilla gone, Bechtolsheim turned west as well. "With a heavy heart I must therefore decide to break off the mission ordered. In this situation I cannot force a breakthrough to the east with Z32 alone."[11] He thought it likely he would encounter the enemy again and he was right. The Canadian destroyers were tracking him even as he turned. They sailed to cut him off and at 0444 opened fire. A running gun duel developed on parallel westerly courses. Z32 fired two torpedoes, but the Canadians declined to turn away. They came on firing steadily and at 0500 finally forced a decision when a 4.7-inch shell hit Z32's turbine room, reducing her speed to fifteen knots. Then three more shells hit her forward turret, leaving her with only No. 3 gun in action. But she was nearly out of ammunition in any case.

Bechtolsheim had reached the coast and now acted to save his men. At 0515 he turned toward the rocks off Île de Batz and ran his ship hard aground. The crew escaped under heavy fire. Despite all the punishment Z32 suffered, only thirty men died. The Canadians stayed offshore and shelled the wreck for ten minutes. At 0530 the destroyers of the 10th reformed and set course for Plymouth where cheering crowds greeted them.

The Battle of Brittany was unusual in that it lasted longer than most night actions and, with the Germans operating in three groups and the Allies in as many as four, it was more confused than most. Confronted with combat, Bechtolsheim used the same tactics the enemy had seen so often. Under the pressure of the 10th Flotilla's counterattack he quickly lost contact with his ships and control of the battle. This action demonstrated how the evolution of night combat tactics and technology had left Germany's first line units behind. Faced with the Allied first line, Germany lost her last effective destroyer force in the west.

Third Encounter off Le Havre, 9–10 June 1944

TIME: Night
TYPE: Encounter
WEATHER:
VISIBILITY: Moon 94 percent, rise 2341
SEA STATE:
SURPRISE: None
MISSION: Allies—patrol and sea security; Germans—offensive and
               sea superiority patrol without specific intelligence

The same night the 8th Destroyer Flotilla was destroyed for so little
return, the 5th Torpedo Boat Flotilla with *T28, Möwe*, and *Jaguar* sortied
from Le Havre again. They encountered a multinational force of Allied
warships, the Norwegian Hunt *Glaisdale,* the Polish Hunt *Krakowiak,*
and the British destroyer *Ursa.* The Allied force maneuvered around the
German attack and the Germans returned to port with no harm done on
either side.

Table 10.7. Third Encounter off Le Havre, 9/10 June 1944

Allied Ships	TYP	YL	DFL	SPD	GUNS	TT	GF	DAM
Glaisdale (NO)	DE	42	1,545	27	4×4/45	2×21	4	
Krakowiak (PO)	DE	40	1,625	27	6×4/45		6	
Ursa	DD	43	2,505	36	4×4/7/45	8×21	6	
German Ships								
T28	TB	41	1,754	33	4×4.1/45	6×21	4	
Möwe	TB	26	1,290	33	3×4.1/45	6×21	3	
Jaguar	TB	26	1,320	34	3×4.1/45	6×21	3	

Fourth Encounter off Le Havre, 12–13 June 1944

TIME: Night
TYPE: Encounter
WEATHER:
VISIBILITY: Moon 57 percent, rise 0129
SEA STATE:

SURPRISE: None

MISSION: Allies—patrol and sea security; Germans—offensive and
              sea superiority patrol without specific intelligence

The men of the 5th Torpedo Boat Flotilla could have had no illusions
regarding their ability to affect the outcome of the battle for the Normandy
beachheads. Yet, each night, they sortied again. On the night of 13 June
T28, Möwe, the recently repaired Falke, and Jaguar had an inconclusive
scuffle with the Norwegian destroyer Stord and her British sister Scorpion.
At 0237 hours T28 and Möwe fired torpedoes that the Allied destroyers
successfully avoided.

This was the 5th Flotilla's last surface action. They had sortied five
times in the week after the Allied invasion and made five torpedo attacks
against destroyer-sized warships. They had launched fifty-plus torpedoes
and expended large quantities of ammunition. Using low-risk launch-and-
run tactics, they had avoided damage and had been lucky to also avoid
being surprised and damaged themselves. For this effort they sank one
destroyer. The S-boats were more successful, accounting for five amphibious vessels, three merchant ships, a destroyer escort, a few coastal craft,
and a tug. They damaged others. This was trivial compared to the Allied
effort, but, nonetheless, Admiral Bertram Ramsey, naval commander of
the invasion forces, concluded he could no longer afford an operating German naval base so close to the beachhead.

On the evening of 14 June the British air force Bomber Command conducted a massive strike against Le Havre. More than twelve hundred tons
of bombs destroyed the harbor and sank Falke, Jaguar, and Möwe, fourteen
S-boats, and thirty-nine other craft and damaged most of the survivors.

Table 10.8. Fourth Encounter off Le Havre, 12–13 June 1944

Allied Ships	TYP	YL	DFL	SPD	GUNS	TT	GF	DAM
Stord (NO)	DD	43	2,505	36	4×4.7/45	8×21	6	
Scorpion	DD	42	2,505	36	4×4.7/45	8×21	6	
German Ships								
T28	TB	41	1,754	33	4×4.1/45	6×21	4	
Möwe	TB	26	1,290	33	3×4.1/45	6×21	3	

From this point, the naval war in the English Channel shifted to the isolated forces stranded to the west, at St. Malo, Brest, the Channel Islands, and along the Biscay coast. There, minesweepers reinforced by *T24* became the heavies of the German navy as it struggled to maintain a presence and keep the war effort alive.

11

FRENCH WATERS AFTER D-DAY
June–December 1944

I don't think any C.O. of the 10th Flotilla would prefer his sub-
division to have to fight four M-class minesweepers in lieu of
two enemy destroyers.

CAPTAIN BASIL JONES RN

Germany occupied coastal enclaves in western France through
the end of the war, in the Channel Islands and around
Lorient, St. Nazaire and La Pallice in Brittany, and La Rochelle and
the Gironde in Bordeaux. In all these areas the German navy maintained
a presence. When the Allies invaded, 146 minesweepers (from the large
M classes down to motor-minesweepers and converted trawlers and
fishing craft) and 59 patrol vessels operated out of the Atlantic ports.
The Channel coast had another 163 minesweepers and 57 patrol craft.
(This in addition to 5 destroyers, 6 torpedo boats, 38 S-Boats, and assorted
auxiliaries based along both coasts.)[1] The 1935/1939 M (Mob)-type

Table 11.1. Engagements in French Waters, June–December 1944

Date	Location	Name	Opponent	Type
14-Jun-44	English Channel	Battle in the Gulf of St. Malo	Polish/BR	Encounter
22-Jul-44	English Channel	Encounter off Fecamp	British	Encounter
6-Aug-44	Bay of Biscay	Attack off Île d'Yeu	British/CDN	Interception
7-Aug-44	English Channel	First Encounter off Jersey	U.S./French	Encounter
12-Aug-44	English Channel	Second Encounter off Jersey	U.S.	Encounter
14-Aug-44	English Channel	First Encounter off Guernsey	British/U.S.	Encounter
15-Aug-44	Bay of Biscay	Attack off Sables d'Olonne	British/CDN	Interception
19-Aug-44	English Channel	Second Encounter off Guernsey	Allied	Encounter

minesweepers were the workaday backbone of this fleet. They proved to be extremely well designed and suited to a variety of tasks, including escort, ASW, AA cover, and mine laying. Russian naval intelligence referred to them as "small M-type destroyers!"[2] They were stout and well-founded boats, and although never designed to take on destroyers, circumstances were such that they did exactly this, repeatedly, in the war's final months.

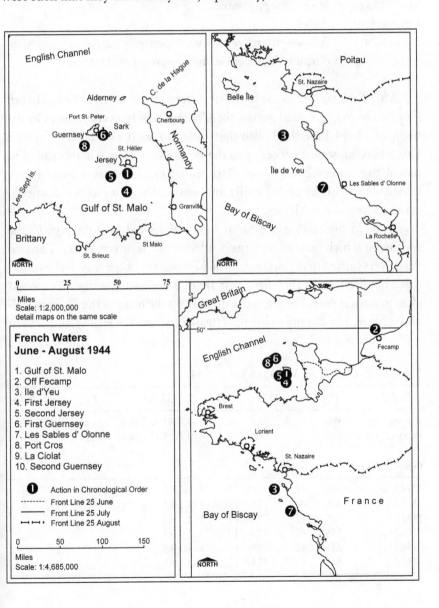

French Waters
June - August 1944

1. Gulf of St. Malo
2. Off Fecamp
3. Ile d'Yeu
4. First Jersey
5. Second Jersey
6. First Guernsey
7. Les Sables d' Olonne
8. Port Cros
9. La Ciolat
10. Second Guernsey

Action in Chronological Order
------- Front Line 25 June
——— Front Line 25 July
⊢⊢⊢⊷ Front Line 25 August

Battle in the Gulf of St. Malo, 14 June 1944

TIME:	Night 0037–0300
TYPE:	Convoy attack
WEATHER:	Wind twenty knots, heavy overcast
VISIBILITY:	Dark, moon 46 percent, rise 0203
SEA STATE:	Short, choppy waves
SURPRISE:	Allies
MISSION:	Allies—offensive and sea superiority patrol without specific intelligence; Germans—escort and transit

After their victory in the Battle of Brittany the ships of the Allied 10th Flotilla Destroyer raided across the Channel nearly every night. On the night of 13–14 June the Polish destroyer *Piorun* (Commander Tadeusz Gorazdowski, senior officer) and the British destroyer *Ashanti* sailed to patrol the waters from Île de Batz to Jersey. That same evening six minesweepers of the 24th Flotilla and assorted V-boats were escorting a small convoy toward Jersey.

At 0025 hours *Piorun*'s radar operator picked up four pips to the southwest which he read as ships headed north at fifteen knots. The two destroyers turned to investigate. At 0037 when the range was only twenty-three hundred yards they fired star shell, illuminating a line of three M class minesweepers. Their gunfire quickly set the head of the German column ablaze, but the minesweepers turned toward the enemy and fought

Table 11.2. Gulf of St. Malo, 14 June 1944

Allied Ships	TYP	YL	DFL	SPD	GUNS	TT	GF	DAM
Ashanti	DD	37	2,519	36	6×4.7/45 & 2×4/45	4×21	11	
Piorun (PO)	DD	40	2,330	36	6×4.7/45 & 1×4/45	5×21	9	D2
German Ships								
M343	MS	41	775	17	1×4.1/45		1	sunk
M412	MS	42	775	17	1×4.1/45		1	D3
M422	MS	42	775	17	1×4.1/45		1	D1
M432	MS	42	775	17	1×4.1/45		1	D1
M442	MS	42	775	17	1×4.1/45		1	D1
M452	MS	42	775	17	1×4.1/45		1	D1

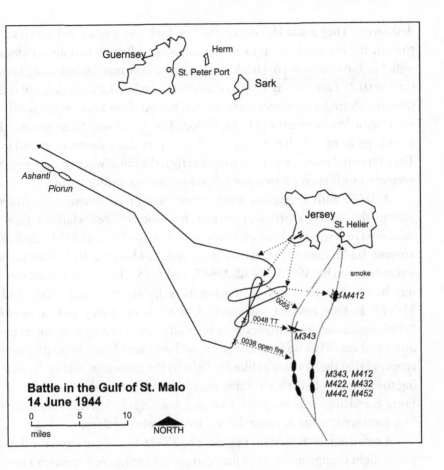

Guernsey

Herm

St. Peter Port

Sark

Ashanti
Piorun

Jersey
St. Heller

smoke

0055

0048 TT

M412

0038 open fire

M343

M343, M412
M422, M432
M442, M452

Battle in the Gulf of St. Malo
14 June 1944

0   5   10
miles   NORTH

back: "Their returning fire was both vigorous and, as always with the Germans, accurate."[3] They hit *Piorun* several times. One 4.1-inch shell struck near No. 4 gun and the explosion detonated some ammunition and wounded four, but her men quickly extinguished the fire. A second 4.1-inch shell damaged the destroyer's aft 20-mm mounting and wounded two. At 0048 the Polish destroyer responded by firing her full load of five torpedoes; one from this barrage exploded against *M343*.

At 0052 *Ashanti* spotted another group of three minesweepers about four thousand yards away and the destroyers turned to engage them, maintaining a speed of twenty-seven knots. The Germans made smoke and fled toward Jersey and the protection of the island's shore batteries. Then water spouts from heavy shells began erupting around the Allied destroyers. They made 180-degree turns at high speed away and then back toward the enemy. During these developments, *Piorun* had an accident with her gyroscope and fell back while *Ashanti* continued in action by herself. At 0125 *Piorun* caught up as the Allied warships came in range of the German shore battery once again which forced them back to the southwest. Shortly afterward *M343* exploded. The Allied warships continued to engage firing off all their star shell and after that, shooting by radar. They reported many targets on fire; in return the minesweepers registered several more hits on *Piorun,* but failed to cause significant harm.

At 0226 with magazines nearly empty and under renewed fire from *Jersey,* the Allied destroyers turned for home. They claimed three minesweepers sunk and one more severely damaged. In fact *M343* sank at around 0240 hours; the Allies damaged *M412* (she had four men wounded) and hit *M422, M432, M442,* and *M452,* but did not cause serious harm. The next day fighter-bombers lightly damaged *V203* and *M4615* as they rescued survivors. A witness on Jersey remembered: "Ambulances and charabancs were busy all of the morning bringing casualties and survivors up from the piers, and watchers from the south coast reported that the sky was lit like daylight by the numerous star shells during the action."[4] Shortly after this engagement a gale with winds of up to Force 8 and huge seas swept the Channel, limiting the activities of the surface forces, particularly coastal craft, for a number of days.

A small action fought on the night of 27–28 June illustrated the danger of night engagements, even for destroyers fighting converted trawlers. The 10th Flotilla ships *Eskimo* and *Huron* (Lieutenant Commander L. S. Rayner, senior officer) intercepted a minesweeper, *M4611* (ex–*Etienne Rimbert,* 197 tons), and two patrol boats, *V213* (ex–*Claus Bolten,* 282 tons) and *V203* (ex–*Carl Röver,* 390 tons), all formerly fishing trawlers—smaller, slower, and less capable boats than the six M class ships their flotilla mates had sparred with two weeks before.

The destroyers duly set *M4611* afire and, after maneuvering around and investigating a false contact, returned to finish off the two patrol boats. But *V213,* whose heaviest weapon was an 88-mm gun, fought back. She hit *Eskimo* twice. An 88-mm shell pierced the British destroyer's No. 1 boiler room and a 37-mm shell cut her main steam line in No. 3 boiler room. The powerful destroyer lost steering power and could only steam in circles at a top speed of six knots. She eventually made it back to Plymouth while the pesky *V213* escaped to St. Helier.

Encounter off Fecamp, 22 July 1944

TIME:	Night
TYPE:	Encounter
WEATHER:	
VISIBILITY:	Dark, moon 3 percent, set 2216
SEA STATE:	
SURPRISE:	
MISSION:	Allies—patrol and sea security; Germans—transit

T28 was the only ship of the 5th Torpedo Boat Flotilla to survive the mass bombing attack on Le Havre. During the night of July 21–22 she escaped the doomed port along with the S-boats *S90, S132,* and *S135.* On the way to Boulogne they had a brush with the British destroyer escort *Melbreak.* This indecisive encounter was the last engagement between destroyer-sized warships in the eastern English Channel.

Table 11.3. Encounter off Fecamp, 22 July 1944

Allied Ship	TYP	YL	DFL	SPD	GUNS	TT	GF	DAM
Melbreak	DE	42	1,545	27	4×4/45	2×21	4	
German Ship								
T28	TB	41	1,754	33	4×4.1/45	6×21	4	

St. Malo did not fall to the American army until 17 August and the Channel Islands remained in German hands until the end of the war. The Americans took over the job of policing the Breton coast and the British surface strike forces that formerly patrolled these waters began to operate farther south along the Biscay coast.

Attack off Île d'Yeu, 6 August 1944

TIME:	Night commence 0035
TYPE:	Convoy attack
WEATHER:	
VISIBILITY:	Good, moon 97 percent, rise 2207
SEA STATE:	
SURPRISE:	Allies
MISSION:	Allies—interception based upon specific intelligence; Germans—escort and transit

On 1 August 1944 the British initiated a combined offensive against German forces in the Bay of Biscay, employing Coastal Command patrols, Bomber Command raids, and cruiser/destroyer surface patrols following the tested Tunnel model.

Force 26, consisting of the light cruiser *Bellona*, the British destroyers *Tartar* and *Ashanti*, and the Canadian destroyers *Haida* and *Iroquois* sailed from Plymouth on 4 August as part of this offensive. On the night of 5 August they were heading southward, about thirty-five miles south of Belle Île off St. Nazaire, with the destroyers in a loose line abreast formation and the cruiser thirty-five hundred yards astern (the cruising order Plymouth Command had decided was best for joint cruiser/destroyer operations), when *Tartar*'s radar returned an echo from her starboard quarter.

That night the Germans had a convoy at sea proceeding south out of St. Nazaire: the large escort SG3, ex–*San Pareil*, the minesweepers *M263* and *M486*, the patrol boat *V414*, the coastal launch *Otto*, and assorted merchantmen.

The destroyers altered course to starboard and increased speed to twenty-five knots, crossing about fifteen miles in front of the convoy's route to take up a position along the coast while *Bellona* remained in the offing. At 0035 hours 6 August *Bellona* fired star shell, illuminating the German ships. Captain Basil Jones of *Tartar*, the senior destroyer officer, practiced his favorite tactic, altering course toward the enemy in a staggered formation, permitting all weapons to bear. He opened fire from nine thousand

Table 11.4. Attack off Île d'Yeu, 6 August 1944

Allied Ships	TYP	YL	DFL	SPD	GUNS	TT	GF	DAM
Bellona	CL	42	7,410	32	8×5.25/50	6×21	11	
Tartar	DD	37	2,710	36	6×4.7/45 & 2×4/45	4×21	11	
Ashanti	DD	37	2,710	36	6×4.7/45 & 2×4/45	4×21	11	
Haida (CDN)	DD	42	2,745	36	6×4.7/45 & 2×4/45	4×21	11	D1
Iroquois (CDN)	DD	42	2,745	36	6×4.7/45 & 2×4/45	4×21	11	
German Ships								
SG3	DC	42	1,372	16	3×4.1/45		3	D3
M263	MS	41	775	17	1×4.1/45		1	Sunk
M486	MS	42	775	17	1×4.1/45		1	Sunk
V414	PB	?	?	?	?		?	Sunk

yards as each Allied ship targeted her opposite number in the German line. The accuracy of the 10th Flotilla's gunfire maintained its usual high standards. 4.7-inch shells set *M486* ablaze almost immediately. The destroyers also launched torpedoes (perhaps to satisfy Admiralty staff critics).

Several ships were burning when the senior office aboard *Bellona* ordered the 10th to form up behind him. Jones's ships blasted the German column as they passed to rejoin the flag. *Haida* was the only ship damaged when a shell exploded prematurely disabling "Y" mount, killing two and wounding eight.

M486 sank at 0040 hours, north of Île d'Yeu. The 10th's gunnery also damaged *M263, V414, Otto,* and two other small ships in the convoy. *SG3* was badly damaged; British Beaufighters found her at Les Sables d'Olonne after dawn, and their rockets reduced her to a burned-out hulk.

The Gulf of St. Malo remained contested waters until the end of the war. Here operated the veteran 24th Minesweeper Flotilla led by Fregattenkapitän Fritz Breithaupt. By the beginning of August 1944, this unit included *M412, M422* (bombed and sunk on 4 August), *M432, M442, M452,* and *M475.* The 46th Minesweeper Flotilla under Kapitänleutnant Armin Zimmermann (converted trawlers numbered sequentially *M4600* through *M4628*) operated alongside the 24th. The battles in western Normandy and the campaign in Brittany were both American responsibilities and, after 2 August, so was the containment of this last vestige of German naval power in the western Channel. The United States Navy gave the job to destroyer escorts teamed with PT Squadron 30 (Lieutenant Commander Robert Searless with PTs *450–461*), and PT Squadron 34 (Lieutenant Allen Harris with PTs *498–509*), operating out of Cherbourg.

First Encounter off Jersey, 7 August 1944

TIME:	Night
TYPE:	Encounter
WEATHER:	
VISIBILITY:	Moon 97 percent, rise 2208
SEA STATE:	
SURPRISE:	
MISSION:	Allies—offensive and sea superiority patrol; Germans—transit

On the night of 6–7 August the surviving units of the 24th Minesweeper Flotilla, *M412*, *M432*, *M442*, and *M452*, evacuated St. Malo in the face of the advancing American army. Their destination was the Channel Islands. An Allied force consisting of two destroyers, supporting MTBs, intercepted Breithaupt's ships off Jersey. Heavy gunfire from this engagement was heard on the island, but the Allies only lightly damaged two of the minesweepers and could not prevent the Germans from fighting through to St. Helier on Jersey's southern shore.

With the German navy driven off the mainland, the Allies decided to quarantine rather than invade the Channel Islands. For this purpose the United States Navy, with assistance from the British and Free French, began to patrol the waters around the islands every night with PT boats supported by destroyers or destroyer escorts.

On the night of 8–9 August the American destroyer escort *Maloy* (Lieutenant H. J. Sherertz) in a support and control role accompanied *PT503*, *PT500*, *PT507*, *PT508*, and *PT509* to the waters west of Jersey. At 0530 hours on the morning of 9 August *Maloy*'s radar picked up contacts that proved to be six trawlers of the 46th Minesweeper Flotilla off St. Helier. In calm but foggy conditions the PT boats closed the contact. Two boats launched torpedoes by radar and missed. Then *Maloy* sent *PT508* and *PT509* roaring in at forty knots. They each fired a torpedo from four hundred yards, missed again, and circled to make a gunfire attack. But *PT509* entered a rent in the fog as she turned away and came under heavy fire. Aflame, she turned back and rammed one of the minesweepers. The German crew managed to crowbar her off; after that she sank—only one man survived to be taken prisoner. *PT503* and *PT507*, searching for the missing boat, engaged a minesweeper in St. Helier roadstead but were driven off with two killed.

Second Encounter off Jersey, 11–12 August 1944

TIME:	Night
TYPE:	Encounter
WEATHER:	
VISIBILITY:	Moon 51 percent, rise 0030
SEA STATE:	
SURPRISE:	

MISSION: Allies—offensive and sea superiority patrol; Germans—
             unknown

On 11–12 August the American destroyer escort *Borum* supporting
PT500 and *PT502* engaged two ships of the 24th Minesweeper Flotilla off
La Corbiere, the southwest coast of Jersey. The American PT boats fired two
torpedoes each, but failed to inflict any damage on the German vessels. The
Germans sent the Americans on their way with heavy gunfire that inflicted
light damage and wounded three men aboard *PT502* and one on *PT500*.

First Encounter off Guernsey, 13–14 August 1944

TIME: Night
TYPE: Encounter
WEATHER:
VISIBILITY: Moon 21 percent, rise 0142
SEA STATE:
SURPRISE:
MISSION: Allies—offensive and sea superiority patrol; Germans—
             unknown

On the night of 13–14 August the British destroyers *Onslaught* and
Saumarez, with the American destroyer escort *Borum*, *PT505*, *PT498*,
and two British MTBs, engaged *M412*, *M432*, *M442*, and *M452* and a
merchant vessel off St. Peter Port, Guernsey. The minesweepers inflicted

Table 11.5. First Encounter off Guernsey, 13–14 August 1944

Allied Ships	TYP	YL	DFL	SPD	GUNS	TT	GF	DAM
Onslaught	DD	41	2,430	36	4×4.7/45	8×21	6	
Saumarez	DD	42	2,505	36	4×4.7/45	8×21	6	
Borum (U.S.)	DE	43	1,823	23	3×3/50	3×21	2	
German Ships								
M412	MS	42	775	17	1×4.1/45		1	
M432	MS	42	775	17	1×4.1/45		1	
M442	MS	42	775	17	1×4.1/45		1	
M452	MS	42	775	17	1×4.1/45		1	

slight damage and some casualties on the destroyers and suffered light damage in return. *Borum* vectored the two American PT boats in toward the German flotilla. The Germans illuminated when the small boats were five thousand yards distant, but the PTs pressed on and launched two torpedoes each from fifteen hundred yards. *PT505* laid smoke as they turned away under heavy fire. The torpedoes all missed, but the PTs were able to retire undamaged.

Second Encounter Off Guernsey, 19 August 1944

TIME: Night
TYPE: Encounter
WEATHER:
VISIBILITY: Dark, no moon
SEA STATE:
SURPRISE:
MISSION: Allies—offensive and sea superiority patrol; Germans—
               transit

On 19 August there was an engagement between Allied forces and a convoy from Guernsey escorted by the 24th Flotilla, which lasted past dawn. The Allies heavily damaged *M432* and then harassed the German force "all the way from Grosnez [in northeastern Jersey] until it got into St. Aubin's Bay, and close enough inshore for the coast batteries to take a hand." *M432* sank near shore while the surviving minesweepers "came into harbour fastened abreast of each other and towed by a tug, their antics suggesting that the steering of one was deranged, whilst increasing smoke as they approached the pier clearly suggested that one of them was on fire."[5]

On 18 August the United States Army captured St. Malo and after that there was no reason for the German navy to hazard convoys between the mainland and the islands. With the 24th and 46th Flotillas keeping largely to port, the United States Navy discontinued offensive patrols. However, the German navy retained a sting. On the night of 8 March 1945 a small fleet under Kapitänleutnant Carl-Friedrich Mohr consisting of *M412*, *M432*, *M442*, and *M452*, a tug, three artillery lighters, three fast launches, and a pair of trawler minesweepers set sail from St. Helier. Shortly before midnight the U.S. submarine chaser *PC564* (463 tons, one 3-inch gun, and nineteen knots), which had been alerted by shore radar, confronted the German barges off Îles Chausey. She fired star shell, but after just one round, her gun jammed. The minesweepers then came up and hit the American ship four times, killing fourteen and wounding eleven. The captain ordered his ship abandoned, but after ten men had gone over the side, he decided to flee south. *PC564* grounded southwest of Pierre de Herpin Light on the western end of the Bay of Mont St. Michael. After this little victory the Germans assaulted Grandville, sinking shipping, freeing prisoners, capturing a collier, and getting away, although they had to blow up *M412* after she ran aground.

Attack off Sables d'Olonne, 15 August 1944

TIME: Night
TYPE: Convoy attack
WEATHER:
VISIBILITY: Moon 13 percent, rise 0239
SEA STATE:
SURPRISE: Allies
MISSION: Allies—interception based upon specific intelligence;
               Germans—escort and transit

The attack off Île d'Yeu on 6 August 1944 was the first blow in the Anglo-Canadian campaign to control the waters along the Biscay coast. A week later, on 12 August, Canadian and British destroyer escorts and frigates sank three armed trawlers south of Brest. The light cruiser *Diadem* and the destroyers *Onslow* and *Piorun* sank *Sperrbrecher 7* (7,078 tons) off La Rochelle that same night.

The light cruiser *Mauritius* (Captain W. W. Davis), accompanied by the destroyer *Ursa* and the Canadian destroyer *Iroquois*, were the hunters on the night of 14–15 August. Sweeping south along the coast, they encountered a German coastal convoy north of Sables d'Olonne. This included the aircraft repair ship *Richthofen, Sperrbrecher 157* (ex-*Tellus*, 1,495 grt), a small coaster escorted by *M385, M275*, and the veteran *T24*.

When star shell exploded overhead, the Germans knew exactly what they were in for; the convoy altered course and fled south toward the safety of the shore batteries in the vicinity of La Rochelle. However, they did not

Table 11.6. Attack off Sables d'Olonne, 15 August 1944

Allied Ships	TYP	YL	DFL	SPD	GUNS	TT	GF	DAM
Mauritius	CL	39	11,090	31	12×6/50 & 8×4/45	6×21	29	
Ursa	DD	43	2,505	36	4×4.7/45	8×21	6	
Iroquois (CDN)	DD	42	2,710	36	6×4.7/45 & 2×4/45	4×21	11	D1
German Ships								
T24	TB	42	1,754	33	4×4.1/45	6×21	4	D2
M275	MS	42	775	17	1×4.1/45		1	D3
M385	MS	42	775	17	1×4.1/45		1	Sunk

make it. By 0112 the Allies had sunk the coaster and heavily damaged both *Sp157* and *M385*. *T24* made smoke in an attempt to screen the cripples, but it was too late for *Sp157*, and she foundered from accumulated damage. *T24* then fired torpedoes at *Iroquois*, but her salvo missed ahead. In return *Iroquois* engaged *T24* and registered one hit. *Mauritius* and *Ursa* also claimed hits on the torpedo boat.

The British broke off when they came within range of the German shore batteries. *M385* was so heavily damaged she had to run herself ashore and was a total loss. *M275* barely reached La Pallice. *Richthofen* escaped. The British did not use torpedoes in this action, relying on gunfire alone. German resistance was described as "spirited" but ineffective, although they lightly damaged *Iroquois*.

On 23 August the same three Allied warships, lurking off Audierne in Brittany south of the invested fortress of Brest, detected vessels inshore at 0117 hours. They withdrew offshore to lure the Germans out. The ruse worked, and at 0209 the destroyers managed to close to four thousand yards and ambush a group of German patrol boats. They sank *V702* (ex–*Memel*, 444 tons), *V717* (ex–*Alfred III*, 1,000 tons), *V720*, *V729* (ex–*Marie Simone*, 282 tons), and *V730* (ex–*Michel Francois*, 535 tons). This was the last naval action of any significance to occur in French waters during the war.

12

THE WESTERN MEDITERRANEAN
September 1943–May 1945

> With a degree of determination and ingenuity, which may arouse even their adversaries' admiration, they improvised what they did not possess; and . . . managed to maintain a reasonably efficient coastal convoy service in the Ligurian Sea . . . almost to the end.
>
> STEPHEN ROSKILL

The Italian armistice signed in September 1943 transformed the balance of naval power in the western Mediterranean. With a simple signature the threat presented by Italy's six battleships, nine cruisers, eighty destroyers and escorts, and many smaller vessels disappeared from the naval balance sheet.[1] From October 1943 to June 1944 a reduced Axis, Germany and the Fascist Italian Social Republic, held the coastline from the Franco-Spanish border to the stalemated frontline south of Rome. Between June 1944 and August 1944 this coastline contracted drastically when the Allies finally drove through central Italy to the Gothic line in the north and then invaded southern France. From September 1944 through the collapse of German forces in late April 1945 Germany retained a portion of Italy's Ligurian coastline stretching from La Spezia to the French border. Despite the vast superiority of the Allied

Table 12.1. The Western Mediterranean

Date	Location	Name	Opponent	Type
15-Aug-44	South France	Action off Port Cros	U.S.	Interception
17-Aug-44	South France	Action off La Ciotat	U.S./British	Interception
02-Oct 44	Gulf of Genoa	Encounter off Imperia	U.S.	Encounter
18-Mar-45	Ligurian Sea	Battle of the Ligurian Sea	British	Interception

navies, German coastal convoys carried on a vital traffic in supplies, fuel, and ammunition. The Germany navy also laid extensive minefields and conducted offensive patrols; their torpedo boats and destroyers even shelled Allied ports and positions.

After the Armistice many small unit surface actions occurred in the western Mediterranean beginning on the morning of 9 September 1943. The German navy launched a surprise attack to capture the port of Bastia in northern Corsica. When this failed, a small flotilla consisting of *UJ2203*, *UJ2219*, five MFPs, and a rescue launch fled the harbor. The Italian torpedo boat *Aliseo* engaged them and sank all eight (with belated help from shore batteries and a corvette). Italian corvettes had several other skirmishes with German coastal craft and shore batteries at Piombino sank *TA11* before the Italian navy withdrew south in accordance with the terms of the armistice. The German navy then proceeded to evacuate more than six thousand men, three thousand vehicles, and five thousand tons of supplies from Corsica over the open sea without serious loss.

During the fall and winter of 1943 and into 1944 coastal forces fought the brunt of the naval war in the Tyrrhenian and Ligurian Seas while Germany rushed to press captured Italian warships into service. British MTBs sank the German minelayer *Juminda* (ex–*Elbano Gasperi*) on 29 October and USN PT boats sank *UJ2206* on 3 November. Larger Allied warships remained to the south, supporting the armies, maintaining the Anzio Beachhead (after January) and escorting convoys. Although Allied PTs, MTBs, MGBs, and improvised gunboats were very active, they could not shut down Germany's maritime traffic in the area. As Britain's official history noted: "Though the constant harassing of the German convoys by our coastal craft must have given them a good deal of trouble, the actual losses we inflicted were small in relation to the traffic carried on those routes."[2]

In October 1943 the German navy commissioned two captured Italian torpedo boats in the western Mediterranean. These TA-prefixed ships (*Torpedoboote ausländisch*) conducted their first operation in December, and by February 1944 there were enough to form the 10th Torpedo Boat Flotilla, under Korvettenkapitän W. von Gartzen, with *TA23*, *TA24*, *TA25*, *TA26*, *TA27*, *TA29*, *TA30*, *TA31*, and *TA32*. (Although ships entered and exited service between October 1943 and August 1944.) The 10th Flotilla operated almost nightly out of Genoa and La Spezia, laying minefields, patrolling, conducting coastal bombardments, and escorting

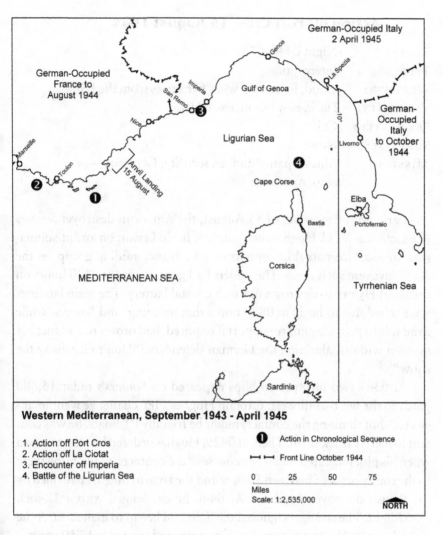

German-Occupied Italy
2 April 1945

German-Occupied
France to
August 1944

Genoa

Imperia

La Spezia

Gulf of Genoa

German-
Occupied
Italy
to October
1944

San Remo

Nice

Ligurian Sea

Livorno

Marseille

Toulon

Anvil Landing
15 August

Cape Corse

Elba

Bastia

Portoferraio

Corsica

MEDITERRANEAN SEA

Tyrrhenian Sea

Sardinia

Western Mediterranean, September 1943 - April 1945

1. Action off Port Cros
2. Action off La Ciotat
3. Encounter off Imperia
4. Battle of the Ligurian Sea

❶ Action in Chronological Sequence

⊢—⊣ Front Line October 1944

0   25   50   75

Miles
Scale: 1:2,535,000

NORTH

convoys. Mines sank *TA23* on 25 April 1944, PTs sank *TA26* and *TA30* on the night of 15 June 1944 and *TA25* on 21 June 1944, and American bombers destroyed *TA27* in port in June 1944. On 15 August 1944 the 10th Flotilla had four ships: *TA24*, *TA28*, *TA29*, and *TA31* with *TA32* about to enter service. On this day the Allies conducted their fifth major amphibious assault in the Mediterranean Sea on the Riviera coast of France. None of these vessels interfered with the Anvil landings, although the German navy did intervene with corvettes and fought two small but sharp battles against the United States Navy.

Action off Port Cros, 15 August 1944

TIME:	Night 0440–0722
TYPE:	Interception
WEATHER:	Good, light mist, wind five knots from the ESE
VISIBILITY:	Dark, new moon, rise 0216
SEA STATE:	Calm
SURPRISE:	None
MISSION:	Allies—patrol and sea security; Germans— reconnaissance

Early on the morning of 15 August, the American destroyer *Somers* (Commander W. C. Hughes) was south of Île du Levant on an antisubmarine, antisurface patrol in support of an advance raiding group on the Anvil invasion's left flank. The raiders had gone ashore at 0130 hours on the Îles d'Hyeres to destroy a 6.5-inch coastal battery. The main landings were scheduled to begin at 0830 hours that morning, and *Somers,* while available to provide gunfire support if required, had orders to conduct her mission without alarming the German defenders ("Don't give away the show").[3]

At 0347 two unexpected blips appeared on *Somers*'s radar 15,680 yards to the west-southwest. Captain Hughes's IFF challenge went unanswered, but thinking the contacts might be friendly PT boats, he was content to merely track them. Then, at 0429, Hughes ordered his ship forward when his plot indicated the steady course of the contacts would bring them to the transport area between *Somers* and the zone to the east patrolled by the British destroyer *Lookout.* At 0440 he challenged with a 12-inch searchlight. The strangers ignored the light and began to maneuver. As he passed astern, Hughes opened fire. The range to target was 4,750 yards.

Table 12.2. Action off Port Cros, 15 August 1944

Allied Ship	TYP	YL	DFL	SPD	GUNS	TT	GF	DAM
Somers	DD	37	2,767	37	6×5/38	8×21	13	
German Ships								
UJ6081	DC	42	728	18	1×3.9/47	2×17.7	1	Sunk
SG21	DC	39	917	20	2×4.1		2	Sunk

The two intruders were German warships: *UJ6081*, formerly the Italian corvette *Camoscio*, and *SG21*, a French aviso captured while being built and completed by the Germans. A shell from *Somers*'s first salvo struck *UJ6081*. She began jinking radically, altering course toward the north. *Somers* checked fire and swung to a parallel heading. *UJ6081*'s turn unmasked *SG21*, black smoke pouring from her funnel, and *Somers* shifted fire. "Our first salvo struck, causing a flash of flame the length of the target, immediately followed by numerous explosions forward and aft as ammunition began exploding."[4] An observer aboard *Augusta*, the flagship of Rear Admiral L. A. Davidson, off to the east saw these explosions lighting up the night "like a torch suddenly thrust over polished basalt."[5]

At 0450 *Somers* passed ahead of *SG21* and satisfied herself that the aviso was out of the fight. She then turned to pursue *UJ6081*, which was running southeast at eighteen knots. At 0505 she saw her quarry and three minutes later began firing deliberate salvos at a range of twenty-nine hundred yards. Despite the small target angle presented by the fleeing ship, *Somers* claimed hits with each broadside. The German's main armament was forward, and only her 20-mm antiaircraft guns could fire back. One

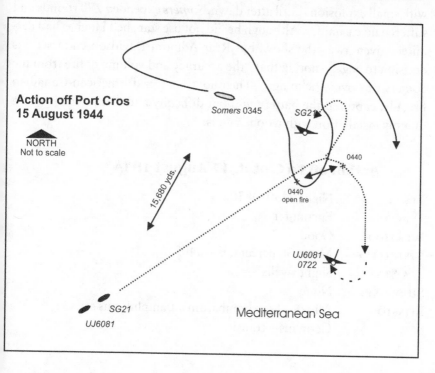

burst of white tracers passed fifty yards ahead and another fifty yards behind the American destroyer. At 0517 *Somers* fired ten rapid salvos and one minute later *UJ6081* began to circle to starboard and lose way. By 0520 she was dead in the water. *Somers* closed and when, five minutes later, her radar plot detected some motion from the enemy, she fired four more quick broadsides. When the corvette's crew began throwing rafts into the water Hughes ordered his gunners to cease fire. He cleared the scene to await daylight.

At 0620 *Somers* returned and rescued twenty-two survivors, including the ship's captain. At 0653 Hughes dispatched fourteen men in the whaler (along with the enemy captain) to board the smoking wreck. They found the topside nearly destroyed and estimated forty to fifty 5-inch shells had hit. "No section . . . was entirely free of damage from either direct hits or shrapnel."[6] The boarding party noted that the corvette's gunners had died at their stations. They quickly ransacked the ship and cast off at 0716 with papers ranging from a history of southeastern Europe to a partially destroyed list of radio messages, charts, and the ship's ensign. *UJ6081* rolled over and sank at 0722 hours. *SG21* burned and periodically erupted with small explosions until after dawn. *Somers* expended 270 rounds and suffered no casualties. Although he did not use star shell Hughes had definitely given away the show, but Rear Admiral Davidson endorsed his decision to engage noting that "the accuracy and volume of fire from the *Somers* was overwhelming."[7] The raiders, a mixed American-Canadian brigade, captured the battery without difficulty and discovered it was a dummy installation with wooden guns.

Action off La Ciotat, 17 August 1944

TIME:	Night 0430–0830
TYPE:	Encounter
WEATHER:	Good
VISIBILITY:	Moon 30 percent, rise 0409
SEA STATE:	Slight swells
SURPRISE:	None
MISSION:	Allies—shore bombardment/amphibious attack; Germans—transit.

Naval Special Operations Forces (SOF) acted on the flanks of the Anvil invasion, inserting raiders, simulating landings, and distracting attention from the real operation. On the invasion's second night, a mixed SOF flotilla consisting of the American destroyer *Endicott*, two British river gun boats, *Aphis* and *Scarab*, two PT boats, and four MLs of the 24th Motor Launch Flotilla appeared off La Ciotat, halfway between Marseilles and Toulon and sixty miles by sea west of the actual landing zone. They intended to feint a landing and thus, hopefully, tie down German troops. Lieutenant Commander Douglas Fairbanks, Jr., aboard *Aphis* (an SOF officer on an assignment that could have been conceived by one of his scriptwriters), commanded the British gunboats and the MLs. Beginning at 0300 hours they shelled the eastern half of the bay while the unstealthy MLs, "fitted with their strange radar devices, trailed their coats and waved their magic wands."[8] *Endicott*, *PT553*, and *PT554* with thirteen sixty-three-foot air-sea rescue craft (ASRC) preformed similar duty on the bay's western extremes, shelling the town of La Ciotat itself. German shore batteries ineffectively fired back with guns as large as 9.4-inch. During this attack the corvette, *UJ6082*, ex-Italian *Antilope* (Korvettenkapitän Hermann Polenz) and the large submarine chaser *UJ6073*, formerly the Khedive of Egypt's motor yacht *Nimet Allah*, departed Toulon en route to Marseilles.

After completing their shoot, the American division withdrew at 0430 hours without incident. *ASRC21* was lagging on her way to the rendezvous point when she picked up radar pips. She steered toward these, expecting to find friendly ships, but when she was only fifteen hundred yards away shells suddenly started falling around her. She had found German corvettes instead.

Endicott (Captain Harry C. Johnson, the section SOF naval commander, and Lieutenant Commander John D. Bulkeley, captain) was at the rendezvous point twenty-five miles south of La Ciotat when, at 0545, she received *ASRC21*'s urgent calls for help. Immediately Bulkeley rang up thirty-five knots and turned his ship north-northwest, followed by the PTs. However, the gunboats were closer. They arrived by 0555 only to find themselves outmatched. Low on ammunition and suffering gun, director, and electrical malfunctions, *Aphis* and *Scarab* fled southeast under heavy fire, pursued by the aggressive corvettes.

At 0620 *Endicott,* sighted the British gunboats off her port bow making smoke. Haze limited visibility to four thousand yards. However, believing the situation was critical and that one or both of the British ships were damaged, the American destroyer opened fire from fifteen thousand yards with her number three mount (the others had jammed breechblocks, caused by overheating from her rapid-fire bombardment of two hours earlier). After some minutes, *Endicott* sighted the German ships dead ahead, now steaming in line abreast to the west. She challenged with a flashing light and then engaged *UJ6073,* much the bigger target. In the first minutes two 5-inch shells detonated in the ex-yacht's engine room and she quickly lost way. The Germans returned fire with their main batteries and machine guns, and their shooting was nearly as good—they achieved numerous close misses and one shell struck the destroyer. It penetrated a forward compartment near the waterline, ignited a small fire, and caused minor flooding, but failed to explode.

Bringing other guns on line and using leather mallets to open and close the breech blocks (at no time was she able to fire a full four-gun broadside) *Endicott* continued to close range to three thousand yards, setting her sights on *UJ6082.* "When [*UJ6082*] had been hit several times, fire was shifted to [*UJ6073*]. Fire was then shifted back and forth between targets to prevent either from maneuvering radically or making their gunfire effective."[9]

UJ6073, listing heavily to port, began to explode at 0648 and her crew took to their rafts. But *UJ6082* was still very much in the fight; she launched two torpedoes, forcing *Endicott* to evade by looping southeast. The PT boats used this opportunity to attack, but the corvette's heavy barrage kept them at a distance; they launched their torpedoes fruitlessly from long range. *Endicott* returned, and at a range of thirty-two hundred yards,

Table 12.3. Action off La Ciotat, 17 August 1944

Allied Ships	TYP	YL	DFL	SPD	GUNS	TT	GF	DAM
Endicott	DD	42	2,395	35	4×5/38	5×21	8	D1
Aphis	GBR	15	645	14	2×6/40		4	
Scarab	GBR	15	645	14	2×6/40		4	
German Ships								
UJ6082	DC	42	728	18	1×3.9/47	2×17.7	1	Sunk
UJ6073	DC	34	1,710 grt?		1×3.5		1	Sunk

launched two torpedoes of her own. These also missed (by only ten yards astern and five yards ahead) but they did force *UJ6082* to comb their tracks, masking her main battery. *Endicott* closed to fifteen hundred yards. At 0702 her 20-mm and 40-mm guns raked the corvette's deck, scything down the gun crews at their unarmored stations. *UJ6082* gamely returned fire for a few minutes until direct hits exploded near her stack and bridge. The British gunboats had circled back and reengaged, but when their shells fell near *Endicott,* Bulkeley ordered them to cease fire, thinking they were targeting him by mistake.

UJ6073 sank at 0709 and *UJ6082*'s crew started abandoning ship at 0717, at which time *Endicott* ceased fire. The destroyer rescued 169 survivors while the gunboats pulled another 41 men from the water. *UJ6082* finally sank at 0830 hours, having fought hard against a greatly superior foe. Besides taking one hit *Endicott* suffered extensive splinter damage, particularly around her bridge and after battery; enemy action wounded 1 man.

In the weeks following these actions, the Allied armies overran southern France, but their resources did not permit an attack over the Alpine passes into the Italian Po Valley, and so the front line froze east of Monaco along the Franco-Italian border. This preserved the German enclave on the Ligurian Sea for another eight months. In October the Allies established a naval Flank Force, Mediterranean, largely consisting of French units and under French command to guard the western portions of this enclave while British and American destroyers and coastal craft based out of Livorno guarded the eastern flank of this miniature sea frontier. These naval forces supported Allied ground units, harassed German shipping, and were harassed in their turn by German coastal and small battle units. Throughout this campaign the 10th Torpedo Boat Flotilla continued in action, risking waters patrolled by Allied cruisers and destroyers with considerable luck and some success, as when they shelled Allied positions near the Arno estuary on the night of 30–31 August.

Encounter off Imperia, 2 October 1944

TIME: Night 0020–0035
TYPE: Encounter
WEATHER: Good

VISIBILITY: Good
SEA STATE:
SURPRISE: Germans
MISSION: Allied—patrol and sea security; German—offensive
               mining

On the evening of 1 October 1944, *TA24* (flag Korvettenkapitän von Gartzen), *TA29*, and *TA32*, the last two ships loaded with ninety-eight mines, sailed from Genoa along the coast toward San Remo as one third of an operation that included five MFPs and three R-boats, all of which were to lay a minefield off the Italian port. The night was bright and visibility good. At 2300 hours the torpedo boats joined the R-boats and they continued together with the small motor-minesweepers ahead, sailing west along the shoreline. At 2310 hours Gartzen received an urgent radio message that enemy warships had been observed in the exact zone he was to lay his mines.

Despite this intelligence, the small German force continued on course. They had just passed Imperia—shore based radio intelligence was continuing to send warnings of enemy ships—when lookouts aboard *TA24* spotted a large warship with two funnels at about eleven thousand yards to the southwest. In fact the German column had been intercepted by the USN destroyer *Gleaves* (Lieutenant Commander W. M. Klee). *Gleaves* was out that night patrolling the waters off San Remo because the weather was too threatening for the PT boats that normally did that duty. Like Gartzen, Klee was receiving reports of enemy activity. Allied aircraft had bombed three vessels off Porta Maurizio at 2107 hours. Klee decided to sail east toward Imperia to look for these intruders, and two hours later he was tracking a column of three ships heading west along the coast. At 2319

Table 12.4. Encounter off Imperia, 2 October 1944

Allied Ship	TYP	YL	DFL	SPD	GUNS	TT	GF	DAM
Gleaves	DD	39	2,395	35	4×5/38	5×21	8	
German Ships								
TA24	TB	43	1,110	31	2×3.9/47	6×17.7	2	D1
TA29	TB	43	1,110	31	2×3.9/47	6×17.7	2	D1
TA32	DD	31	2,000	37	4×4.1/45	3×21	4	

hours the American destroyer turned to a parallel course, rang up twenty knots, and opened fire at an estimated range of ten thousand nine hundred yards, concentrating on the center ship.

The Germans observed *Gleaves*'s threatening maneuvers, but continued west, hoping the mountainous shoreline immediately behind them would confuse enemy radar. However, at 2320 hours, geysers erupted around *TA24*, some shells landing only fifty yards off. The German torpedo boats maneuvered as the next salvo near missed *TA29*. They held fire, not wanting to give their position away.

At 2324, still fifteen thousand yards short of the drop zone, Gartzen decided it was time to scrub his mission. He ordered a simultaneous turn to starboard, but while executing this maneuver, *TA29*, her rudder control affected by her cargo of mines, rammed *TA24*. The two ships were locked for about a minute, but they managed to separate, and, after getting their formation straightened out, the Germans steamed back toward Genoa at full speed. The problem aboard *Gleaves* was that Klee never realized the nature of the targets he had under his guns. He saw the Germans come

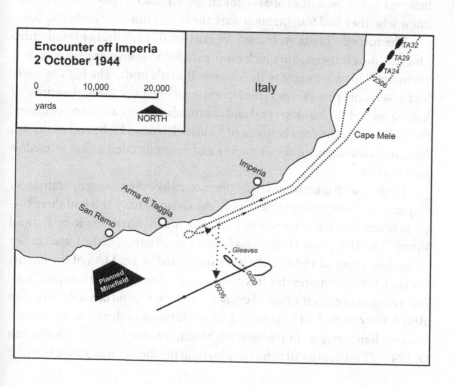

Encounter off Imperia
2 October 1944

0   10,000   20,000

yards

NORTH

Italy

TA32
TA29
TA24
2306

Cape Mele

Imperia

Arma di Taggia

San Remo

Gleaves

0020

0035

Planned Minefield

about, but, by 2329, he slowed to ten knots and checked fire as "the targets were now indistinct and situation was very obscure. Stars [shells] illuminated what appeared to be a dense cloud of smoke in area where targets had been circling."[10]

At 2334 *TA24*, now the rear ship, returned fire. She observed two shells hitting target, which was about thirteen thousand yards to the south southwest. However, her observers were mistaken. *Gleaves* thought shore batteries were attacking her, but only one shell splashed in her vicinity. American lookouts saw a large explosion where their targets had been. Then Klee received reports of unidentified aircraft. His radar was no longer able to distinguish the enemy ships against the coast, and he was very concerned about being attacked from the air by mistake. He ordered smoke and turned away. The Germans could clearly see *Gleaves,* and her sudden withdrawal completely mystified them. The Americans fired eighty rounds of 5-inch common and eight star shells. In his report Klee concluded he had bombarded three merchant ships. He observed two of them explode while under fire, and believed they were sunk or seriously damaged. Gartzen believed his ships had probably taken on a French cruiser. Neither side knew who they had fought: Such were the uncertainties of night combat.

The torpedo boats were back in port by 0215. *Gleaves* bombarded Oneglia, near Imperia, but much more exciting to the Americans was their encounter later that night with Axis small battle units. The big destroyer had several narrow escapes (the operator of one boat "was chagrined at having missed"),[11] sank several and captured one boat and two operators. For this action, the commanders of Cruiser Division Eight and of the 8th Fleet both commended the destroyer and recommended a slew of medals for her crew.

Despite such intense and risky operations like the mining operation off Imperia and heavy ongoing attrition, the German navy still had three torpedo boats, two minelayers, five UJ-boats, four V-boats, ten R-boats, and thirty-five MFPs, Siebel ferries, and other armed barges in the Ligurian Sea at the beginning of 1945. They were supported by six MAS of the Fascist Italian navy. To counter this force, the French, British, American, and Italian navies maintained a fleet of cruisers, destroyers, and coastal units. The British navy alone had forty-nine destroyers (most of them Hunts) and six modern light cruisers in the western Mediterranean Sea at the beginning of 1945. The disparity of forces deployed in the theater was a tribute to the

German navy's ability to tie down Allied warships that might have been better employed elsewhere.

Germany fought her final surface naval battle of the war involving large warships in the Gulf of Genoa. Her ships were engaged in an offensive mining operation, the same mission that had led to her first battle against the British navy in the North Sea sixty-four months before.

The Battle of the Ligurian Sea, 18 March 1945

TIME: 0300–0420
TYPE: Interception
WEATHER: Rain squalls and lighting
VISIBILITY: Moon 21 percent, set 0002
SEA STATE:
SURPRISE: None
MISSION: Allied—patrol and sea security; German—offensive mining

On the night of 17–18 March 1945 the last three operational ships of the 10th Torpedo Boat Flotilla conducted an offensive mining operation northwest of Corsica. Sailing out of Genoa, *TA24* and *TA29* successfully laid fifty-six mines south of Gorgona Island while *TA32* (the former Italian *Premuda*, and before that the Yugoslav *Dubrovnik*) placed seventy-six mines in another field north of Cape Corse. The flotilla then reunited for the return to Genoa with *TA24* and *TA29* preceding the larger *TA32*. They were about twenty miles north of Cape Corse when Allied shore radar at Livorno detected their presence. Four Allied destroyers were patrolling in

Table 12.5. Battle of the Ligurian Sea, 18 March 1945

Allied Ships	TYP	YL	DFL	SPD	GUNS	TT	GF	DAM
Meteor	DD	41	2,840	36	6×4.7/50	8×21	8	
Lookout	DD	40	2,840	36	6×4.7/50	8×21	8	D1
German Ships								
TA24	TB	43	1,110	31	2×3.9/47	6×17.7	2	Sunk
TA29	TB	43	1,110	31	2×3.9/47	6×17.7	2	Sunk
TA32	DD	31	2,000	37	4×4.1/45	3×21	4	D1

the vicinity: the French *Basque* and *Tempête*, and the British *Meteor* and *Lookout*. By 0145 all but *Meteor* had received Livorno's enemy report.

The senior officer, Captain A. Morazzani aboard *Tempête*, ordered the British ships to intercept the intruders while he led the older and slower French destroyers southeast to cover a convoy nearing Cape Corse, believing the Germans might double back in that direction. *Lookout* advised *Meteor* via TBS what was afoot and the British ships shaped separate courses northeast at full speed. By the time Morazzani determined the Germans were no threat to the convoy, he was too far away to join the action.

Lookout established radar contact with the enemy at 0301. The German column was sailing at twenty knots just west of north. The British destroyer approached at high speed from ahead and opened fire at 0310 from about five thousand yards. Two minutes later, she swung around on a heading similar to the Germans and launched torpedoes. This unexpected attack completely disrupted the German formation. *Lookout*'s radar-directed guns quickly scored hits on *TA24* and *TA29*. *TA29* dropped out of the line while the other two ships fled north. *Lookout* let them go, concentrating on the cripple. She circled *TA29* firing continuously from ranges as close as two thousand yards. *TA29* fought back; her gunners near missed the destroyer numerous times, but the only damage she inflicted on *Lookout* occurred when a burst of 20-mm shells hit some smoke-floats and ignited a small fire. *TA29* didn't sink until 0420, hours after being hit more than forty times. Fortunately, she only lost twenty men despite the intensity of *Lookout*'s bombardment.

Meteor, meanwhile, altered her course to south-southeast at 0328 to close the engagement. At 0352 she obtained radar contact on the other two German ships fleeing north from twelve thousand three hundred yards. Approaching, she opened fire at eight thousand yards and hit *TA24* almost immediately. She launched a salvo of torpedoes a few minutes later and one hit its target. *TA24* exploded and sank at 0405 hours. She lost thirty men. In just thirteen minutes *Meteor* developed her contact, attacked with guns and torpedoes, and sank her opponent. *TA32*, although also damaged, made good her escape. She participated in the engagement only briefly with a few broadsides and an ineffective torpedo barrage. *Meteor* rescued 119 survivors including the flotilla commander, Korvettenkapitän Burkart. Later that day Allied coastal forces and an LCI recovered another 125 of *TA29*'s men from boats and rafts.

After this German defeat, less than two more months of war remained. The German navy continued its struggle, but it was a struggle without hope. When the Axis armies in Italy surrendered on 2 May 1945, Germany "had lost virtually all its merchant shipping in the Mediterranean and practically all its warships. From the beginning of January 1945 up to the day of surrender, 112 warships and 118 small auxiliary vessels had been destroyed, more than half of these being scuttled to prevent capture."[12]

13

HOME WATERS: NORWAY AND THE BALTIC, 1944–1945

He who sees first lives longest.

CAPTAIN ABRAHAM VAN DER MOER, RNN

By November 1944 Allied offensives in France, Italy, the Soviet Union, and the Balkans had reduced Germany's sea frontiers to two enclaves of Italian coastline on the Mediterranean and Adriatic Seas, various islands in the Aegean, the North Sea coast from the Scheldt in Holland and the Baltic coastline to Memel and around the Courland pocket in Latvia. Germany's longest stretch of oceanic access was Norway's Arctic and Atlantic coastlines. Each of these areas still contained naval forces; they still carried maritime traffic, and Germany struggled to maintain her presence and dispute Allied use of the sea lanes up to the final day of the war.

Protecting Norway's long shoreline and the traffic in strategic ores that passed along it was a major concern of the German navy. Air power and mines alone were no longer able to keep larger Allied warships at a distance.

Table 13.1. Final Actions

Date	Location	Name	Opponent	Type
13-Nov-44	North Sea	Convoy Attack off Listerfjord	British/CDN	Convoy Attack
21-Nov-44	Baltic Sea	Action off Sworbe Peninsula	Soviet	Interception
11-Jan-45	North Sea	Attack off Egersund	British	Convoy Attack
28-Jan-45	Norwegian Sea	Action off Bergen	British	Interception

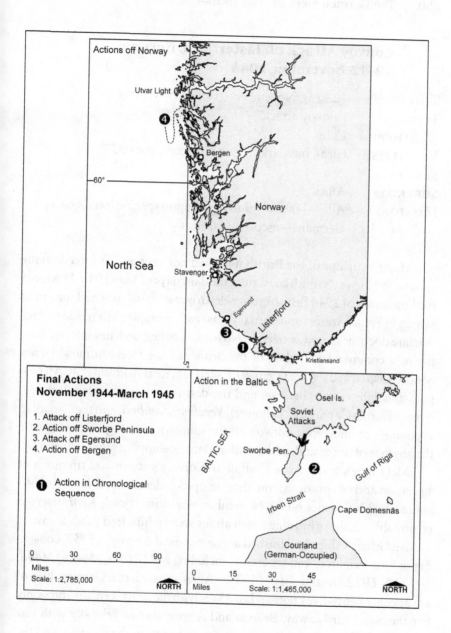

Actions off Norway

Utvar Light

❹

Bergen

60°

Norway

North Sea

Stavenger

Egersund

Listerfjord

❸

❶

Kristiansand

5°

Final Actions
November 1944–March 1945

1. Attack off Listerfjord
2. Action off Sworbe Peninsula
3. Attack off Egersund
4. Action off Bergen

❶ Action in Chronological
   Sequence

0   30   60   90

Miles
Scale: 1:2,785,000   NORTH

Action in the Baltic

Ösel Is.

Soviet
Attacks

BALTIC SEA

Sworbe Pen.

❷

Gulf of Riga

Irben Strait

Cape Domesnäs

Courland
(German-Occupied)

0   15   30   45

Miles   Scale: 1:1,465,000   NORTH

Convoy Attack off Listerfjord, Norway, 12–13 November 1944

TIME:	1230 12 November–0100 13 November
TYPE:	Convoy attack
WEATHER:	Calm
VISIBILITY:	Clear, but dark. Moon 8 percent, rise 0355
SEA STATE:	
SURPRISE:	Allies
MISSION:	Allies—interception based upon specific intelligence; Germans—escort and transit

Major warships of the British navy had not ventured in force into the waters off Norway's south coast since the dark days of May 1940. However, by the autumn of 1944 British cruiser-destroyer strike groups had run out of targets in French waters and the navy was ready to apply their tested surface warfare doctrine in new waters. In November, acting on Ultra information, the new commander in chief of the British Home Fleet, Admiral Henry Moore, dispatched the heavy cruiser *Kent* (Flag, Rear Admiral R. R. McGrigor), the light cruiser *Bellona,* and the destroyers *Myngs* (Flag 26th Destroyer Flotilla Captain M. L. Power), *Verulam, Zambesi,* and the Canadian *Algonquin* to intercept a convoy off the southern Norwegian coast where the absence of fjords and offshore islands made shipping more vulnerable.

McGrigor's force made landfall at Norway's southwest tip north of Egersund and swept south from there in open order, about seven miles offshore. At 2300 hours on 12 November, near Listerfjord, *Kent* detected enemy ships inshore heading north about sixteen hundred yards away.

McGrigor's ships had flushed a major coastal convoy, KS357, consisting of four freighters and six escorts including M427 (flag), M416, M446, UJ1221, UJ1223, and UJ1713. The Allies crossed the German line of advance at twenty-five knots and, at 2313, with the nearest enemy ships only five thousand yards away, *Bellona* and *Algonquin* filled the sky with star shell. The drifting pyrotechnics were very effective in the clear air, and the Allied ships could easily see their targets. UJ1221 and UJ1223 had the misfortune to be on the engaged side. They were new ships with inexperienced crews; their lookouts had just sighted the British force when they found themselves exposed and then, at 2314, deluged by gunfire. *Algonquin,* for one, claimed hits with her first salvo. The Allied destroyers overwhelmed

Table 13.2. Attack off Listerfjord, 12/13 November 1944

Allied Ships	TYP	YL	DFL	SPD	GUNS	TT	GF	DAM
Kent	CA	24	14,910	31	8×8/50 & 8×4/45	8×21	32	
Bellona	CL	42	7,410	32	8×5.25/50	6×21	11	
Myngs	DD	43	2,575	36	4×4.5/45	8×21	6	
Verulam	DD	43	2,505	36	4×4.7/45	8×21	6	D2
Zambesi	DD	43	2,575	36	4×4.5/45	8×21	6	D1
Algonquin (CDN)	DD	43	2,545	36	4×4.7/45	8×21	6	
German Ships								
M416	MS	43	775	17	1×4.1/45		1	Sunk
M446	MS	42	775	17	1×4.1/45		1	D3
M427	MS	42	775	17	1×4.1/45		1	D4
UJ1221	DC	43	970	12	1×3.5/45		1	Sunk
UJ1223	DC	44	970	12	1×3.5/45		1	Sunk
UJ1713	DC	43	970	12	1×3.5/45		1	Sunk

these two escorts as the other German vessels returned fire and fled toward the coast. Then shells detonated the ex-French freighter *Cornouaille*'s (3,324 grt) cargo of ammunition and she exploded violently. The British also sank *M416* at 2330 hours and then the freighter *Greif* (996 grt).

By midnight the battle had run into range of German shore batteries which counter-illuminated and returned fire with their large caliber guns. Despite this danger, McGrigor signaled: "Finish off the Enemy." The destroyers went in firing rapidly, turned and launched torpedoes, and came out firing rapidly. *UJ1713* escaped the initial slaughter, but when she lingered to assist survivors the destroyers caught and severely damaged her. They also hit *M446* and the freighter *Palermo*. *M427* was so shot up she had to be beached at Rekkefjord, nine miles south of Egersund, where she capsized and sank at 1300 hours on 13 November. *UJ1713* also sank the next morning. *Rosenberg* was the only German ship to escape unscathed.

Statistics reflect the intensity of this combat. *Algonquin* expended 315 4.7-inch rounds, 66 rounds of star shell, and 160 40-mm rounds. Twenty-two rounds of German 37-mm and 20-mm gunfire struck *Verulam*; she suffered two dead and five wounded and was out of action through February. Six 20-mm shells hit *Zambesi*, the only other Allied ship damaged. Satisfied with the results, McGrigor's force returned unmolested and anchored in Scapa Flow at 2030 hours on 13 November. For the Germans, who had enjoyed years of relative calm in this sector, the raid capped a very bad day because that morning the British air force finally managed to sink Germany's last battleship, *Tirpitz*.

Convoy Attack off Egersund, 11–12 January 1945

TIME:	2345
TYPE:	Convoy attack
WEATHER:	Clear, wind NW force 3
VISIBILITY:	Good, but dark. Moon 11 percent, rise 0617
SEA STATE:	Slight swells
SURPRISE:	None
MISSION:	British—interception based upon specific intelligence; Germans—escort and transit

Rear Admiral McGrigor returned to the waters of southwest Norway two months after his success off Listerfjord. In an operation codenamed Spellbinder, he led a strike force consisting of the heavy cruiser *Norfolk*, accompanied by *Bellona* and the destroyers *Onslow, Orwell,* and *Onslaught*, a minelaying force (minelayer *Apollo* and two destroyers), and a carrier force including the escort carriers *Premier* and *Trumpeter,* escorted by the light cruiser *Dido* and four destroyers. While *Apollo* laid mines, McGrigor led *Norfolk*'s group south in search of enemy shipping.

An important German convoy of three steamers carrying foodstuffs and coal escorted by five minesweepers (*M273, M253, M306, M436,* and *M456*) had left Kristiansand at dark that day bound for Stavanger. Shortly before midnight the escort commander received word that British ships had been spotted in the area; he ordered full speed, hoping to reach the safety of Egersund and the shore batteries there, but it was already too late. McGrigor's ships, just north of the convoy, fired star shell, which illuminated brilliantly. Aboard the transports it seemed the night was suddenly transformed into day and the erupting columns of water made them think they were under air attack. The opening salvos hit *Bahia Camerones* in the bridge and engine; fires broke out and the ship lost steering control. It was only from the twinkling flash of gunfire her crew realized surface ships were attacking, but the range was so great their small weapons were useless.

The minesweepers were closer to the action. The escort commander had sent two of them to port to stand between the convoy and the reported threat. Aboard *M273*:

Table 13.3. Attack off Egersund, 11–12 January 1945

Allied Ships	TYP	YL	DFL	SPD	GUNS	TT	GF	DAM
Norfolk	CA	28	14,600	32	6×8/50 & 8×4/45	8×21	27	
Bellona	CL	42	7,410	32	8×5.25/50	6×21	11	
Onslow	DD	41	2,430	37	4×4.7/45 & 1×45/45	4×21	7	
Orwell	DD	42	2,430	37	4×4/45	8×21	5	
Onslaught	DD	41	2,430	37	4×4.7/45 & 1×45/45	4×21	7	
German Ships								
M273	MS	43	775	17	1×4.1/45		1	Sunk
M253	MS	42	878	18	2×4.1/45		2	
M306	MS	42	775	17	1×4.1/45		1	D3
M436	MS	42	775	17	1×4.1/45		1	
M456	MS	42	775	17	1×4.1/45		1	

flashes were seen to port. Suddenly it was as bright as day as hundreds of fluorescent umbrellas illuminated the night. We opened up with all our guns, but the range was too great. There was a roar in the air and a column of water spouted to starboard; the impact of the hostile shells was precariously near. . . . Then a detonation caused us to all flinch together. We were hit. It killed our helmsman and we sailed out of control. The hostile gunfire slackened; an enemy destroyer dared to approach us and we poured our fire over her clearly observing hits. But, it was an unequal fight . . . we were hit again and again. Our ship shuddered from a heavy impact on the side and we began to rapidly list to starboard.[1]

M273 sank as did *Bahia Camarones* (8,551 grt) and *Charlotte* (4,404 grt). U427 was in the vicinity and she launched counterattacks at 0012 and 0045. Despite reporting explosions and breaking-up noises, her torpedoes all missed. German shore batteries at Egeröy and Egersund probed the battle sea with searchlights and opened fire. This caused McGrigor some difficulties, but no damage. However, the counter-bombardment kept the British at a distance and permitted the steamship *Wesermarsch* (1932 grt) and four of the escorts to escape, although M306 was heavily damaged. The Germans lost 142 men and another 38 were wounded. JU-88s attempted to bomb the withdrawing British, but fighters flying from the two escort carriers drove them away.

After the battle, Oslo's German-language newspaper *Osloer Zeitung* reported German shore batteries won a great victory and sank a cruiser and a destroyer.

Action off Bergen, 28 January 1945

TIME:	0048 to approximately 0230
TYPE:	Interception
WEATHER:	Clear and bright
VISIBILITY:	Excellent. Full moon, set 0839
SEA STATE:	Calm
SURPRISE:	None
MISSION:	British—interception based on specific intelligence; Germans—transit

In the year after the Battle of the North Cape, the destroyers of Germany's polar fleet, the 4th Flotilla (Kapitän zur See R. Johannesson and then Kapitän zur See H. F. von Wangenheim), saw little action other than a few summer training sorties (one with *Tirpitz*) toward Bear Island. In October 1944, Soviet attacks and Finland's exit from her German alliance led to some sea time escorting evacuation convoys from Kirkenes. Otherwise, the destroyers served as little more than floating antiaircraft batteries protecting *Tirpitz*. Finally, in January 1945, the 4th was ordered to vacate the arctic after a tour of duty that had lasted three and a half years. *Z31*, *Z34* and *Z38* sailed from Tromsö for Narvik on 25 January. Ultra informed the British of this movement and on 27 January Admiral Moore dispatched the light cruisers *Diadem* (Vice Admiral F. H. G. Dalrymple-Hamilton) and *Mauritius* to sweep the outer passage north from Bergen in case the German destroyers took that route. The cruisers sailed without destroyers, as they were all occupied in carrier operations and the British command considered it more likely the Germans would take the slower, but safer, inside passage.

In fact Wangenheim chose the faster route even though British aircraft had attacked that evening, which meant they knew he was at sea. The journey was quiet until three-quarters of an hour past midnight. He was about fifteen miles southwest of Utvar Light and thirty-five miles northwest of Bergen proceeding south in calm conditions under a bright full moon when lookouts picked out shadows about eleven miles to the west.

Table 13.4. Action off Bergen, 28 January 1945

Allied Ships	TYP	YL	DFL	SPD	GUNS	TT	GF	DAM
Diadem	CL	42	7,410	32	8×5.25/50	6×21	11	D1
Mauritius	CL	39	11,090	31	12×6/50 & 8×4/45	6×21	29	D1
German Ships								
Z31	DD	41	3,691	38	5×5.9/50	8×21	9	D3
Z34	DD	41	3,691	38	5×5.9/50	8×21	9	D1
Z38	DD	41	3,691	38	5×5.9/50	8×21	9	D1

Dalrymple-Hamilton's cruisers saw the Germans at about the same time, and they fired star shell almost immediately. The destroyers continued heading south as the cruisers swung to a parallel course. British long-range gunnery was initially on target. Seven 6-inch shells struck *Z31* early in the action leaving her on fire, her superstructure riddled with holes, her hydrophone compartment and torpedo transmitting stations knocked out, and her forward turret destroyed. Fifty-five men died and twenty-four more were wounded. Korvettenkapitän Karl Hetz, *Z34*'s captain, took command of the flotilla. He made two torpedo attacks in an effort to force the British to turn away. *Z38* tried to help, but first her funnel caught fire and then a boiler tube burst. After a shell hit *Z34* on her waterline, Hetz decided he could no longer continue south.

Z34 fired a third salvo of torpedoes as the flotilla made smoke and reversed course north. The cruisers avoided the torpedoes and gave chase. In a running fight, the destroyers returned fire with their stern guns and registered one hit on *Mauritius* on her port side forward. This did not cause any casualties. Six minutes later they hit *Diadem* on her boat deck amidships, inflicting slight damage, with one man killed and three wounded.

Using their superior speed the Germans gradually pulled away and by 0200 they reached the protection of German shore batteries. The cruisers disengaged and returned to Scapa Flow whereupon the destroyers resumed their voyage south. *Z31* docked in Bergen to repair her damage while *Z34* and *Z38* continued to Kiel. *Z31* moved to Oslo on 8 February for additional repairs and didn't return to Germany until 20 March.

The British were unhappy with the results of this action, considering they should have been able to force a more conclusive result. This expectation was

unrealistic given the superior speed of the German ships and their ability
run to the shelter of friendly shore batteries. However, British gunfire w
initially very effective and Z31 was fortunate: if any of the shells that hit h
had affected her speed, she would likely have been lost.

Action off Sworbe (Sõrve) Peninsula,
21 November 1944

TIME:	Night
TYPE:	Interception
WEATHER:	
VISIBILITY:	Moon 26 percent, set 2006
SEA STATE:	
SURPRISE:	
MISSION:	Soviets—shore bombardment; Germans—patrol and s security

The Baltic was a German lake from 1941 through the middle of 194
The Soviet summer offensive that year pushed the front line all the w
back to Poland and cut off a German army group in Courland, whereup
Hitler decreed the Latvian peninsula a fortress to be defended. And so
was. The German navy kept the army group supplied and continued
maintain sea superiority in the theater against a Soviet navy that foug
principally with submarines and coastal craft. The volume of German tr
fic between Courland and the homeland was significant: nearly 1.6 gr
registered tons in November and 1.1 million tons in December. But becau
the Soviets declined to deploy larger warships in the Baltic's narrow wate
surface battles involving large warships did not occur. The nearest thing
a sea battle happened on 21 November at the entrance to the Gulf of Rig
On 18 November the Soviet 8th Army launched an attack on t
Sworbe Peninsula, the southern extension of Ösel Island. They had be
trying to conquer the island since 5 October and needed to evict the Ge
mans in order to open the Irben Straits and the sea lanes to their armies fa
ther south. German naval support, including bombardments by Lützow
11-inch guns, helped the defenders hold their lines for five weeks.
For the final push Soviet naval forces penetrated into the Gulf of Rig
Three gunboats, Volga, Bureja, and Zeya, and eleven armored patrol boa

operated off the eastern side of the peninsula and supported the ground forces attacking the peninsula. German minesweepers and patrol boats did not let the Soviets have a free reign, however.

German and Soviet naval forces fought an engagement on 17–18 November when the Germans attacked the bombardment group. On the night of 19 November the torpedo boats *T23* and *T28* sailed into the gulf while the next day a task force, consisting of *Prinz Eugen, Z25, Z35, Z36, Z43, T13, T16, T19,* and *T21,* added their firepower to the defense from the west of the peninsula. On the night of 20–21 November *M328, M423,* and two patrol boats, *V306* (ex–*Fritz Hinke*) and *V1713* engaged a Soviet force of *Tral* class minesweepers, motor gunboats, and MTBs. *M328* sank the minesweeper *T207 Shpil* and damaged another armored gunboat, forcing her ashore. Soviet gunfire crippled patrol boat *V1713,* but the Germans were able to tow her to safety. The campaign ended when the Germans evacuated the last defenders from the peninsula on the night of 23–24 November.

The Baltic Sea continued to be a zone of intense naval conflict. Most of the surviving heavy ships, including *Lützow, Admiral Scheer, Prinz Eugen,* the light cruisers, destroyers, and torpedo boats, fought in the Baltic and lent the support of their big guns to the beleaguered German army (preventing the Soviet navy from assisting their own troops). They also maintained the Courland bridgehead to the very end of the war. In the final months the navy conducted one of the largest maritime evacuations in history when it lifted more than two million people out of the path of the advancing Soviet armies. There is no doubt that had Germany lost control

Table 13.5. Action off Sworbe Peninsula, 21 November 1944

Allied Ships	TYP	YL	DFL	SPD	GUNS	TT	GF	DAM
T207	MS	38	490	18	1×3.9/56		1	Sunk
Volga	GB	41	947	8	2×5.1		3	D4
Bureja	GB	41	947	8	2×5.1		3	
Zeya	GB	40	947	8	2×5.1		3	
German Ships								
M328	MS	43	775	17	2×4.1/45		2	
M423	MS	42	775	17	1×4.1/45		1	
V1713	PB	?	?	?	?		?	D4
V306	PB	?	?	?	?		?	

of the Baltic Sea in 1944 the war would have ended much sooner. Althoug
the Soviet Baltic Fleet consisted of a battleship, a pair of cruisers, and fi
teen flotilla leaders, destroyers, and torpedo boats by the end of the wa
the Soviet navy never seriously attempted to contest this control.

By 1 April 1945 the survivors of Germany's surface fleet included: *Lü
zow*. She was actively bombarding Soviet armies off Elbing. British aircra
damaged her on 16 April 1945, but she continued fighting as a floating ba
tery until May.

Admiral Scheer:	Her final actions occurred on 16 March. On 1 Apr she was docked at Kiel, changing her 11-inch bar rels. British aircraft bombed her on 9 April and sh capsized.
Admiral Hipper:	Her final mission was transporting refugees in Janu ary 1945. From 1 February she was docked at Kiel fo boiler work. British aircraft sunk her there on 3 Apri
Prinz Eugen:	She shelled Soviet forces off Hel until the middle o April and then sailed to Copenhagen where she sur rendered to the British.
Emden:	On 1 April she was inoperative at Kiel. British air craft disabled her during several attacks in April.
Köln:	British aircraft sunk her at Wilhelmshaven on 3 March.
Leipzig:	She conducted shore bombardments (firing 920 5.9 inch rounds between 14 and 24 March) until ammu nition ran out on 24 March. She carried refugee until 27 March and sat out the balance of the war i Denmark.
Nürnberg:	She remained in Copenhagen from 27 January to the end of the war.

There were also fourteen destroyers and fourteen torpedo boats in ser
vice on 1 April. To these larger units can be added hundreds of minesweep
ers, UJ-boats, V-boats, and S-boats still in action. The German navy'
surface fleet remained a significant force until Allied armies overran the
nation and finally ended the Nazi regime.

14

CONCLUSION

Thus was the once proud German Navy, built to challenge
Britain's sea supremacy, extinguished for the second time within
thirty years.

STEPHEN ROSKILL

This battle history of the German navy supports two quite dis-
parate conclusions. The first conclusion is that the record of
the navy's surface fleet is one of failure and lost opportunity beginning
with the harrying of *Graf Spee,* the destruction of *Bismarck,* and the failure of the fleet to significantly harm a single Arctic convoy. While it is true,
the navy fought a skilled and practiced opponent, its commanders repeatedly lost battles they could have won. The leadership of Bey at Narvik,
Stange at the Battle of the Barents Sea, or Erdmenger at the Battle of Biscay (even Lütjens at Denmark Strait) demonstrated a systemic problem
within the navy, evident in the way these commanders displayed excessive
caution in the face of the enemy and even let victory slip away. The question is, why?

The British did not hazard ships recklessly, but they were usually will-
ing to take chances because they could afford to and this is what their tradition expected. The Germans believed they could not afford losses and
their naval tradition did not approve of combat for the sake of combat.
Twelve years after the war *Prinz Eugen*'s former captain wrote:

The German Naval Command was never able to undertake an offensive
operation with the confidence that adequate replacements were immediately available or even on the building ways. On the contrary, losses

beyond destroyers were irreplaceable, and even destroyers could not be replaced at a faster rate than four a year. The effect? Simply that in our strategic planning risk played a greater role than is considered acceptable in war.[1]

Too often, especially after 1942, German commanders fought to avoid losing.

There were other factors that degraded German combat effectiveness. After the war one admiral reportedly remarked: "We Germans knew how to build outstanding freshwater ships."[2] U.S. sailors considered *Prinz Eugen* a yacht compared to their own cruisers. Overcomplicated machinery marked a design philosophy focused on theoretical possibility rather than everyday reliability. The destroyers only averaged 40 percent availability and German warships, from *Scharnhorst* down, had an unfortunate tendency to suffer boiler breakdowns in action.[3] German weapons were seriously flawed. They fixed their faulty torpedoes a year into the war, but continued to fire a high percentage of dud shells to the very end. German destroyers were no substitute for light cruisers and cramming 5.9-inch guns onto an undersized hull proved, in action, a complete failure. Finally, the navy's failure to achieve a lasting and effective working relationship with the German air force handicapped their surface operations in the English Channel, in the Bay of Biscay, and especially in the arctic.

From these facts it is easy to conclude that the German navy was roundly defeated by the British and that the only thing that mattered was the submarine war, echoed by Dönitz's famous postwar assertion that a realistic policy would have seen the German navy go to war with a thousand U-boats.

However, the details of the battle record also show that the German navy's surface forces fought a remarkably successful war to protect the nation's sea lanes, to project power over open water, to deny the enemy use of adjacent waters, and to disrupt enemy commerce under difficult, sometimes very adverse, conditions. The Norwegian and Aegean campaigns demonstrated that the German navy could seize territory in the face of a superior British fleet. The Channel Dash and the passage of the disguised raiders showed it could use England's coastal waters when needed despite her stiffest resistance. The Baltic and Mediterranean evacuations stand with Dunkirk as examples of armies rescued from destruction. The Arctic

Battlegroup's forays, and then its mere presence, was enough to deny an entire ocean to Allied shipping. The relentless courage of the minesweepers, the corvettes, and torpedo boats protecting little but vital convoys, or charging immense invasion armadas provided examples of the navy's resistance to Allied sea power up to the very end of the war wherever Germany retained a coastline.

This history supports the conclusion that, in fact, the surface fleet mattered greatly. When the navy's leadership and material problems are measured against its accomplishments—when all its battles are considered alongside its famous defeats—the surface fleet showed its potential as a war-winning weapon. The British navy was sorely stressed and, with its multitude of tasks and commitments and relative scarcity of resources, it was vulnerable to the type of pressure Germany's fleet could exert. The British themselves believed surface ships were the greatest threat. Just before the war Admiral Dudley Pound, the First Sea Lord, wrote: "Nothing would paralyse our supply system and seaborne trade so successfully as attack by surface raiders."[4] The 1941 cruise of *Gneisenau* and *Scharnhorst* provided a template on how to shut down the North Atlantic convoys. The long shadow cast by *Bismarck* was reflected in the exaggerated precautions the British took against *Tirpitz,* and demonstrated the fragility of Great Britain's mastery of the sea—at least until the problem of the Italian fleet was solved in September 1943. Thus the First Sea Lord's concern was no passing notion dispelled by German successes in the submarine campaign. The German navy's leadership failed to fully appreciate British fears and thus failed to identify the issues where risk was justified, with the exception of Norway.

The complete battle record shows that the German navy's surface fleet more than held its own during the first four years of the war. Up through the end of October 1943 the German navy fought thirty-seven surface actions against the Allied navies.[5] It sank or significantly damaged thirty-four Allied warships displacing 188,000 tons at a cost of twenty-three of its own ships displacing 167,500 tons. Germany either won or achieved a draw in twenty of these engagements. On 23 October 1943 off Les Sept Îles torpedo boats of the 4th Flotilla won Germany's most one-sided naval battle, sinking a light cruiser and destroyer escort at no cost to themselves. This defeat forced the British to question their training, tactics, and use of technology. Simultaneously, the Allies began to benefit from better use of intelligence and from greater material superiority with their victories over the U-boats and Italy.[6] Fighting units like the 10th Destroyer Flotilla emerged with the training and experience to defeat Germany's best, such as the 4th Torpedo Boat Flotilla. Meanwhile, the quality of the German surface fleet deteriorated from a lack of sea time (caused by a shortage of fuel oil), a reluctance to risk combat, and especially from policies that drafted the best human and material resources into the submarine branch in pursuit of the statistical chimera of the tonnage war.

After October 1943 the Allies sank or significantly damaged thirty-nine German warships displacing 87,600 tons in thirty-two naval battles at a cost of only seven of their own warships displacing 26,500 tons. The tide had turned. Many of the Allied naval victories of the war's last eighteen months were won by superior intelligence before ever a ship weighed anchor. The repeated ability of cruiser/destroyer groups to intercept and shoot up German convoys protected by coal-burning minesweepers and converted fishing trawlers was a product of intelligence. Intelligence enabled the Allies to concentrate overwhelming force at just the right place at just the right time; experience and battle-tested tactics enabled them to apply this force to obtain victory. But, even with their quantitative and, later, their qualitative advantages, the British and Allied navies never completely defeated Germany's surface fleet. The German navy dominated the Baltic Sea up to the very last days of the war. German shipping and warships plied the waters off Norway, and in the North, the Ligurian, and the Adriatic Seas. And, unlike in 1918, the morale of the *Matrosen*, the ordinary sailor, never broke.

Appendix A

Equivalents, Abbreviations, and Definitions of Terms

Equivalents

Ranks*

German Ranks/British Navy Ranks	German Ranks/U.S. Navy Ranks
Grossadmiral/Admiral of the Fleet	Grossadmiral/None
Generaladmiral/Admiral	Generaladmiral/Admiral
Admiral/None	Admiral/None
Vizeadmiral/Vice Admiral	Vizeadmiral/Vice Admiral
Konteradmiral/Rear Admiral	Konteradmiral/Rear Admiral
Kommodore/Commodore	Kommodore/Commodore
Kapitän zur See/Captain	Kapitän zur See/Captain
Fregattenkapitän/None	Fregattenkapitän/Commander
Korvettenkapitän/Commander	Korvettenkapitän/Lieutenant Commander
Kapitänleutnant/Lieutenant Commander	Kapitänleutnant/Lieutenant
Oberleutnant zur See/Lieutenant	Oberleutnant zur See/Lieutenant (Junior Grade)
Leutnant zur See/Sub-Lieutenant	Leutnant zur See/Ensign
Oberfähnrich zur See/None	Oberfähnrich zur See/None
Fähnrich zur See/Midshipman	Fähnrich zur See/None

The U.S. and British navies agree that their ranks are equivalent through lieutenant, but disagreed on their German equivalents. The Americans regarded Fregattenkapitän as the equivalent to commander while the British regarded it a junior captain rank between captain and commander with no Allied equivalent.

* Source for British equivalents: Naval Intelligence Division document (BR 634 G): "Dictionary of Naval Equivalents" (1943).
  Source for USN equivalents: *Naval Phraseology,* Annapolis: (1937) Table IV *Dienstgrade der Kriegsmarineoffiziere*

Metric Conversions

1 nautical mile = 2,205 yards, 1,852 meters, or 1.151 statute miles
1 knot = 1.852 km/hour or 1.151 mile/hour
1 meter = 1.094 yards
1 yard = .9144 meters
1 inch = 2.54 centimeters
1 centimeter = .3937 inches

Abbreviations

General

AA	antiaircraft
AP	armor-piercing
ASW	antisubmarine warfare
BR	British
CDN	Canadian
DP	dual purpose
FF	free French
FL	full load (displacement)
FR	French
FS	flagship
GE	German
GK	Greek
GRT	gross registered tons
HA	high angle
HE	high explosive (or high effect)
IFF	Identification Friend or Foe
IT	Italian
NO	Norwegian
NZ	New Zealand
PO	Polish
RCN	Royal Canadian Navy
RN	Royal Navy
RO	Romanian
SB	shore battery
SO	Soviet
US	United States
USN	United States Navy

Ship Types

AMC	armed merchant cruiser
ASRC	air-sea rescue craft
BB	battleship
BC	battle cruiser
BM	monitor
CA	heavy cruiser
CB	coastal battleship (obsolete)
CL	light cruiser
CLA	antiaircraft light cruiser
CV	aircraft carrier
CVE	escort aircraft carrier
DD	destroyer
DE	destroyer escort
DC	corvette/sloop
DF	frigate
GB	gunboat
GBR	river gunboat
HK	*Hilfskreuzer* (German disguised raider)
MAS	Italian motor-torpedo boat (*motoscafi armati siluranti* or *motoscafi anti sommergibili*)
MFP	*Marinefährprahm* (German armed barge or "F" lighter)
ML	minelayer or motor launch
MMS	motor minesweeper
MRS	*Minenraumschiff* (German minesweeper depot ship)
MTB	motor-torpedo boat
PB	patrol boat
PC	submarine chaser (USN)
PT	patrol torpedo boat (USN)
R-boat	*Raumboote* (German motor-mine sweeper)
S-boat	*Schnellboote* (German motor-torpedo boat or "E" boat)
SC	submarine chaser
SS	submarine
TA	*Torpedoboote ausländisch,* or ex-enemy torpedo boat
TB	torpedo boat
U-boat	*Unterseeboot* (German submarine)

UJ-boat   *Unterseebootsjäger* (German submarine chaser)
V-boat   *Vorpostenboote* (German patrol boat)

Gun Turret Nomenclature

	German	British
Forward	Anton	A
	Bruno	B
Aft	Caesar	X
	Dora	Y

Table Definitions

Missions:

Patrol and sea security. Patrolling friendly waters to deny their use by the enemy

Offensive mining and patrol. Engaged in a mining operation in enemy waters

Defensive mining and patrol. Engaged in a mining operation in friendly or disputed waters

Offensive and sea superiority commerce raiding. Attacked when engaged in a mission to sink enemy commerce in enemy or disputed waters

Interception based upon specific intelligence. At sea to attack a specific target whose movements are known

Interception based upon general intelligence. At sea to attack a specific target whose movements are inferred or estimated

Offensive and sea superiority patrol without specific intelligence. At sea in enemy or disputed waters to deny their use by the enemy

Transit. Attacked when in transit from one port or point to another

Escort and transit. Attacked while escorting other vessels in transit

Reconnaissance. At sea to obtain information regarding enemy dispositions or movements in enemy or disputed waters

Shore bombardment/amphibious attack. Attacked when engaged in bombarding targets or supporting the landing of troops on an enemy-controlled coast

Self defense. Unexpectedly attacked when not otherwise engaged on a mission

Damage

D1. Light or superficial damage, including splinter damage

D2. Moderate damage. One to four weeks to repair. Combat ability not significantly impaired

D3. Significant damage. Up to three months to repair. Combat and/or maneuvering ability somewhat impaired

D4. Major damage. More than three months to repair. Combat ability reduced significantly or eliminated. Maneuvering ability impaired or eliminated

Engagement types

Harbor Attack. Warships deliberately attack enemy warships in harbor. This is the least common cause, generally because ports are difficult to surprise and are usually protected by shore batteries.

Encounter. Warships at sea unexpectedly encounter enemy warships and a battle results.

Interception. Warships of one nation possess intelligence about the route or location of an enemy force and seek to bring that enemy force to battle.

Convoy Attack. This is a subset of Interception, except the primary objective of the mission is to sink merchant shipping, not warships.

Table Abbreviations

TYP. type of ship

YL. year launched

DLF. displacement full load in tons

SPD. maximum speed in knots (see comments)

GUNS. main and secondary gun batteries, size x number

TT. size of torpedo and number of tubes

GF. gun factor (see comments)

DAM. damaged suffered in action

The speed given is usually designed speed; operationally, most ships would have top speeds several knots less depending upon the condition of their machinery and the state of the sea and wind. The gunnery factor is calculated based on the weight of the individual shell, the rate of fire, and the pounds per minute the ship's guns were theoretically capable of delivering. This factor is consistently calculated, but it does not consider crucial elements like target-acquisition systems, training, tactics, doctrine, morale, fatigue, weather, gun condition (gun liners wear out and, toward the end of their life, accuracy is affected), or luck.

Appendix B

Organization of the German Navy

The German navy's organization consisted of area, fleet, security, and training commands. The relationship between these commands varied according to the war situation and as the navy acquired new responsibilities. This section briefly sketches the structure of German naval organization insofar as it affected the operations of the navy's surface forces.

In September 1939 there were four area commands under the Supreme Naval Command (*Oberkommando der Marine*). These were Naval Group Commands (*Marinegruppenkommandos*) East and West, with responsibility for directing the Fleet Command when operating in the Baltic and North Seas, respectively. There were also two Naval Commands (*Marineoberkommandos*) in charge of security and training in each of these areas.

Fighting ships were organized into a Fleet Command (*Flottenkommando*) under the command of the Fleet Commander (*Flottenchef*). The fighting units received their orders from the appropriate area command. Thus, in 1939, warships operating in the Baltic against Poland came under the aegis of Naval Group East. When the same ships helped lay the West Wall mine barrage in the North Sea, they did so under the command of Naval Group West.

In November 1939 the Fleet Commander had under him:

1. Commander of Armored Ships (*Befehlshaber der Panzerschiffe*)
2. Commander of Reconnaissance Forces (*B. d. Aufklärungsstreitkräfte*)
   a. Chief of Torpedo Boats (*Führer der Torpedoboote*)
   b. Chief of Destroyers (*F. d. Zerstörer*)
3. Commander of Submarines (*B. d. Unterseeboote*)

This structure underwent adjustments reflecting the state of the fleet. In August 1940 a major restructuring changed the organization to:

1. Commander of Cruisers (*B. d. Kreuzer*)
2. Chief of Destroyers
3. Chief of Torpedo Boats
4. Commander of Submarines.

The Commander of Cruisers was eliminated in October 1941. There was a Commander of Battleships (*B. d. Schlachtschiffe*) from June 1941 to May 1942. This was changed back to the Commander of Cruisers in June 1942, under Vizeadmiral Kummetz, who fought the Battle of the Barents Sea in December 1942, and then to the Battlegroup Commander (*B. d. Kampfgruppe*) in April 1943; Konteradmiral Bey was Kummetz's temporary fill-in when he fought the Battle of the North Cape in December 1943.

By January 1943, the area command structure of the German navy had evolved as follows:

1. Naval Group Command North (*Marinegruppenkommando Nord*)
   a. Naval Area Command Norway (*Marineoberkommando in Norwegen*)
      i. Admiral of the West Coast
      ii. Admiral of the North Coast
      iii. Admiral of the Polar Coast
   b. Naval Area Command Baltic
   c. Naval Area Command North Sea
   d. Admiral Denmark
2. Naval Group Command West
   a. Admiral Channel Coast
   b. Admiral Atlantic Coast
   c. Admiral South Coast
   d. Naval Area Command Italy
3. Naval Group Command South
   a. Admiral Adriatic
   b. Admiral Aegean
   c. Admiral Black Sea

Appendix C

Statistical Analysis

Statistical Analysis

Nearly half of the sixty-nine actions fought by the German navy resulted from warships intercepting enemy warships. Only one engagement in five resulted from an accidental encounter. Figure 2 shows how the four general causes compared to one another.

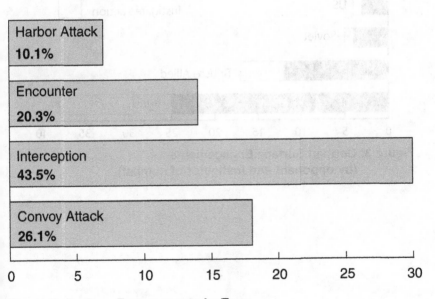

Figure 2: Surface Engagements by Type

Figure 3 lists the opponents of the German navy. The Germans fought sur
face engagements against the warships of eight Allied navies, but Grea
Britain was their greatest foe: they fought the British navy in thirty-eigh
engagements (55 percent of the total). These thirty-eight actions, fo
example, are represented by the bottom bar of this chart. The British initi
ated twenty-five (the black portion of the bar) while the Germans initiated
thirteen actions (the gray portion).

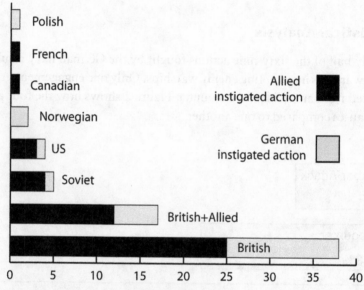

**Figure 3: German Surface Engagements
(by opponent and instigator of combat)**

Every significant body of water contiguous to Europe experienced at least one surface action, but Germany fought more than a third of all actions in the narrow waters of the English Channel. Figure 4 also shows where actions occurred in relation to land. The black portion of every bar represents engagements fought in open waters while the gray portion shows the number of actions fought in restricted wars, where land (or ice) influenced the events. For example, all five of the Atlantic Ocean's actions were open-water battles, while all four of the Baltic's actions occurred in restricted waters.

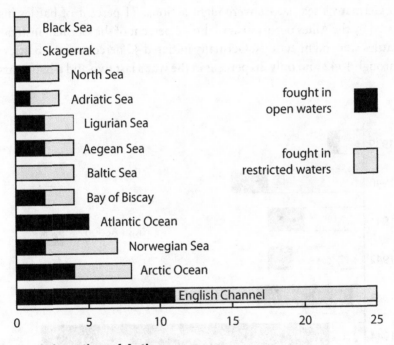

Figure 4: Location of Actions

Following the English Channel, Germany fought 24 percent of its actions in the far north (the Arctic Ocean, Norwegian Sea, and North Atlantic) and 16 percent in the Mediterranean Sea. Just over half of the battles were fought in restricted waters.

Figure 5 features a bar showing the number of battles fought in each of the war's seven years; the gray portion of the bar is the number of day actions while the black portion is the number of night actions; 41 percent of all actions took place in 1944. This shows the striking evolution of naval combat during the war: 70 percent of all battles were day actions through 1942, but from 1943, 90 percent were fought at night. Overall, 63 percent of Germany's sea battles were night actions; 71 percent of battles instigated by the Allies occurred at night; 48 percent of the German instigated battles were night actions. Germany initiated 43 percent of the battles up through 1942 and only 26 percent in the war's last two and a half years.

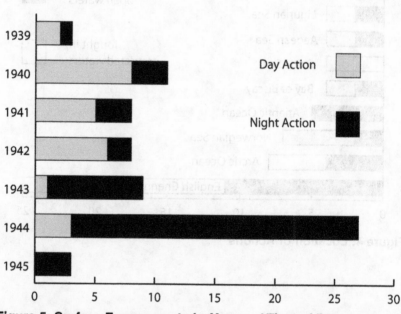

Figure 5: Surface Engagements by Year and Time of Day

Figure 6 shows the number of battles fought in each of the sixty-eight months that the war lasted. The two events that precipitated the most sea battles were the invasion of Norway in April 1940 and the invasions of France in June and August 1944.

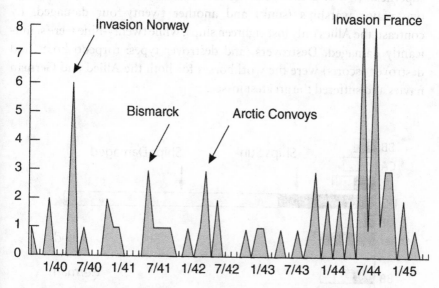

Figure 6: Surface Engagements by Month

An objective in most sea battles is to harm the enemy. Figure 7 shows the damage suffered by the German and Allied navies in the surface engagements described in this book. The abbreviation (BB, CA, etc.) identifies the type of warship shown in each bar. The black portion of the bar shows ships sunk while the gray portion represents ships suffering non-superficial (D2 or greater) damage. In these battles Germany lost forty-two major warships (sunk) and another twenty-four damaged. By contrast, the Allies only lost eighteen ships, while twenty-nine were significantly damaged. Destroyers (and destroyer types: torpedo boats and destroyer escorts) were the workhorses for both the Allied and German navies and suffered the greatest losses.

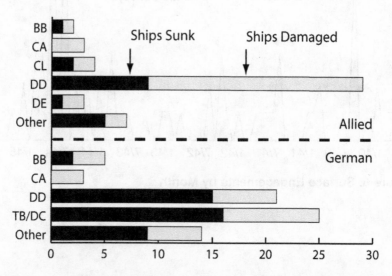

Figure 7: Large Warships Sunk and Damaged by Type in Naval Surface Engagements, 3 Septenber 39 – 18 March 45

In contrast to the Pacific, no heavy cruisers were lost in battles. Not one German light cruiser participated in a battle, again in contrast to Allied practice. The large German destroyers were intended to fill part of the role light cruisers occupied in the British navy. However, the Battle of Biscay and the Action off Bergen showed they were no match for Allied cruisers in practice.

Figure 8 identifies which weapons caused the damage shown in Figure 7. The black bars represent Allied warships and the gray bars German warships. Thus, 25 percent of the losses and damage suffered by Allied warships was caused by German torpedoes; Allied torpedoes, on the other hand, only inflicted 7 percent of all German losses and damage. The percent of damage inflicted by gunnery was nearly equal.

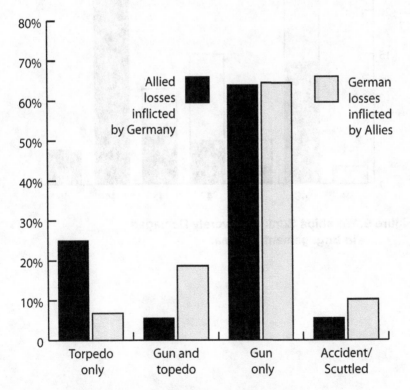

Figure 8: Percent of Warships Sunk or Severely Damaged during Engagements by Cause

Figure 9 provides a succinct summary of the naval war's progress. It shows the warships sunk and/or severely damaged in each year. The black portion of each bar represents German warships while the gray portion shows Allied warships. In the war's first three years Allied losses exceeded German losses. During the last three years this ratio was more than reversed.

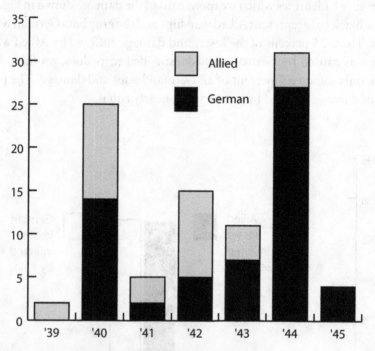

**Figure 9: Warships Sunk or Severely Damaged
in Engagements by Year**

Notes

Preface and Acknowledgments

1. Reinicke, "German Surface Force Strategy in World War II," 182.

Chapter 1

1. See Gardiner, *Conway's All the World's Fighting Ships, 1922–1946* and Gröner, *German Warships, 1815–1945*. The numbers vary depending on how "available" is defined and what ships are counted.

2. Ruge, "German Minesweepers in World War II," 996.

3. Peszke, *Poland's Navy, 1918–1945*, 37.

4. Raeder's directive to Marschall as quoted in Gray, *Hitler's Battleships*, 43.

5. Stephen, *Sea Battles in Close Up: World War II*, 16.

6. See Bekker, *Defeat at Sea*, 63; von der Porten, *The German Navy in World War II*, 49; and Whitley, *German Capital Ships of World War Two*, 96.

7. Grove, *German Capital Ships and Raiders in World War II*, Vol. 1, 1–43.

8. Harwood's action report stated that *Graf Spee* opened fire with one turret at *Exeter* and one at *Ajax*. However, difficulties with the fore turret "caused [Ascher] to continue in salvo firing for a time, giving Harwood the impression that he had succeeded in confusing the fire of the *Graf Spee*'s main armament." Grove, *The Price of Disobedience*, 68.

9. Ibid. However, the team which inspected *Graf Spee*'s wreck concluded that a 6-inch shell caused this damage.

10. Gray, *Hitler's Battleships*, 53.

11. Harwood's Report, paragraph 19, Supplement to the *London Gazette*, 19 June 1947.

12. Harker, *HMNZS Achilles*, Chapter 9.

13. Harwood's Report, paragraph 36.

14. Barnett, *Engage the Enemy More Closely*, 86.

15. Grove, *The Price of Disobedience*, 87.

Chapter 2

1. Whitworth seemed preoccupied with comfort. He noted in his report to the Admiralty on the Second Battle of Narvik that the transfer of his flag from *Renown* to *Warspite* was accomplished with "considerable difficulty, owing to the heavy swell." One of his reasons for not sending a landing party to occupy Narvik after his victory was that it had been "a long and strenuous day." See Whitworth's Report, paragraph 5 and paragraph 47, *London Gazette*, 3 July 1947.

2. Brown, *Naval Operations of the Campaign in Norway*, 15.

3. Ibid., 17.

4. Whitley, *German Capital Ships*, 115.

5. "The enemy's heavy guns were firing impressively fast and regularly by battery divisions. Until given the task of pursuit, the enemy maintained an intense fire and must have expended a large amount of ammunition." Koop and Schmolke, *Battleships of the Scharnhorst Class*, 101.

6. "Senkingen av PS Norge og Eidvoll." http://steinarweb.com/dykking/historie.htm.

7. Jones, *The World's Merchant Fleets*, 472, indicates *Skagerrak* was sunk 9 April 1940 by a British destroyer off Stockholm.

8. Brown, *Naval Operations*, 21.

9. Barnett, *Engage the Enemy*, 114.

10. Layman's Report, paragraph 7, *London Gazette*, 3 July 1947.

11. "Patrol against submarines in front of the harbour entrance until daylight." Dickens, *Narvik*, 56.

12. *Hotspur* Report, paragraph 14, *London Gazette*, 3 July 1947.

13. *Havock* Report, paragraph 10, *London Gazette*, 3 July 1947.

14. Grove, *Sea Battles in Close Up World War II*, Vol. 2, 18.

15. *Hotspur* Report, paragraph 22.

16. *Havock* Report, paragraph 22.

17. Koop and Schmolke, *German Destroyers of World War II*, 58–59.

18. Ibid., 62.

19. Brown, *Naval Operations*, 31.

20. Dickens, *Narvik*, 113.

21. Roskill, *War at Sea*, Vol. 1, 195; Kemp, *Key to Victory*, 65.

22. Quoted in the House of Commons Hansard Debates, 28 January 1999, Column 566. http://www.parliament.the-stationery-office.co.uk.

23. An alternative theory is that *Devonshire* understood *Glorious*'s message perfectly well. She was ferrying the King of Norway and his cabinet to Great Britain. "Five members of *Devonshire*'s crew have testified that the signals from

Glorious were far from unintelligible. Despite differing on the details, all five were adamant that the signal was sufficiently clear to cause considerable consternation on *Devonshire*'s bridge." Ibid., Column 568.

24. Howland, "The Loss of HMS Glorious," Note 6. This was arguably the longest range gunfire hit made on an enemy warship during the war.

25. Brown, *Naval Operations,* 129.

Chapter 3

1. World Vector Shoreline 1:250,000, http://earthtrends.wri.org/text/COA/variables/61.htm. Coastline lengths are difficult to estimate and vary over time.

2. Raeder, *Grand Admiral,* 326.

3. Smith, *Hold the Narrow Sea,* 121. There were a few survivors, according to this account.

4. Whitley, *German Destroyers of World War Two,* 111.

5. March, *British Destroyers,* 353.

Chapter 4

1. Rhys-Jones, "The Loss of Bismarck, Who was to Blame?" 27.

2. Roskill, *War at Sea,* Vol. 1, 400.

3. See Mulligan, "*Bismarck:* Not Ready For Action?" which argues that Raeder rushed *Bismarck* to action with an incompletely trained crew.

4. Whitley, *German Capital Ships,* 155.

5. von Müllenheim-Rechberg, *Battleship Bismarck,* 135.

6. Barnett, *Engage the Enemy,* 293.

7. Board of Inquiry Statements, Testimony of Captain John Leach. ADM 1/11726.

8. Kennedy, *Pursuit,* 87.

9. See von Müllenheim-Rechberg, *Battleship Bismarck,* 148–49, for example.

10. See the discussion in Roskill, *War at Sea,* Vol. 1, 404–5.

11. Mulligan, "Not Ready For Action." Cited as an example of inadequate training levels.

12. Kennedy, *Pursuit,* 128.

13. Tarrant, *King George V Class Battleships,* 74.

14. Stephen, *Sea Battles,* 97.

15. Satz, "I Escaped," 43.

16. Ibid., 44.

Chapter 5

1. Ruge, *The Soviets as Naval Opponents, 1941–1945*, 64.
2. Ibid., 12.
3. Ibid., 17.
4. This action is mentioned in Rohwer and Hummelchen, *Chronology of the War at Sea, 1939–1945*, 76. According to Meister (*Soviet Warships*, 228), *TKA 122* was not commissioned until 1942.
5. Huan, *La Marine Soviétique en Guerre I Arctique*, 17–18.
6. Whitley, *German Destroyers*, 124.
7. Daily War Situation telegram to Roosevelt from London, 8 September 1941.
8. Whitley, "Victim of Ultra? The Loss of the Bremse," 20–27.
9. Huan, *La Marine Soviétique*, 45.
10. Whitley, *German Destroyers*, 131.

Chapter 6

1. Stephen, *Sea Battles*, 129.
2. Grove, *German Capital Ships*, Vol. 2, 11–15.
3. Ibid., 11–16.
4. Smith, *Hold the Narrow Sea*, 142.
5. Roskill, *War at Sea*, Vol. 2, 168.
6. Dorrian, *Storming St. Nazaire*, 249.
7. Smith, *Hold the Narrow Sea*, 171.

Chapter 7

1. Barnett, *Engage the Enemy*, 703.
2. Whitley, *German Destroyers*, 136.
3. Roskill, *War at Sea*, Vol. 2, 127.
4. Ibid., 129.
5. The source of this torpedo is uncertain. Brown, *Warship Losses*, 61, says it was *Z24* and the time was 0657. Whitley, *German Destroyers*, 139, says it may have been *Z24* or *Z25*. Bekker, *Hitler's Naval War*, 270, credits *Z25*.
6. Barnett, *Engage the Enemy*, 706.
7. Bekker, *Hitler's Naval War*, 274.
8. Meister, *Soviet Warships*, 242.
9. Winton, *The War at Sea*, 267.
10. Bekker, *Hitler's Naval War*, 284. Visibility seemed much better in British than in German memories.

11. Roskill, *War at Sea,* Vol. 2, 296.

12. Pearson, Michael. *Red Sky in the Morning,* 67.

13. Bekker, *Hitler's Naval War,* 286.

14. Pearson, *Red Sky in the Morning,* 68.

15. Ibid., 76.

16. Ibid., 79.

17. Huan, *La Marine Soviétique,* 24; Gardiner, *Fighting Ships 1922–1946,* 321; Ruge, *Soviets as Naval Opponents,* 136. He writes that the Arctic fleet was "probably composed of 5 modern destroyers, 3 old destroyers, 3 torpedo boats, 21 submarines, 4 minelayers, 20 MTBs and 8 minesweepers."

18. Barnett, *Engage the Enemy,* 706.

19. Whitley, *German Capital Ships,* 201.

20. Grove, *German Capital Ships,* Vol. 2. German Battle Cruiser "Scharnhorst" Interrogation of Survivors, 12.

21. Whitley, *German Capital Ships,* 201, blames this on a "signaling problems." Stephen, *Sea Battles,* 204, speculates Bey changed course because "it may have been a fleeting radar contact . . . or it may have been the signal at 0814 from U716." Either way, Bey lost control before combat was joined.

22. Grove, *German Capital Ships,* Vol. 2, 14.

23. Ibid., 17.

24. Ibid.

25. Tarrant, *King George V Class Battleships,* 82.

26. Stephen, *Sea Battles,* 217.

Chapter 8

1. Beard, "Turning the Tide at Salerno," 35.

2. Brown, *Warship Losses of World War Two,* 93.

3. Lind, *Wine Dark Sea,* 147.

4. Schenk, *Kampf um die Ägäis,* 128.

Chapter 9

1. Smith, *Hold the Narrow Sea,* 175.

2. Ruge, "German Minesweepers," 1002.

3. Kohlauf's discretionary use of radar stands in contrast to Bey's total radar blackout two months later at the North Cape.

4. Smith, *Hold the Narrow Sea,* 178.

5. Ibid., 190.

6. Roskill, *War at Sea,* Vol. 3. Part I, 100.

7. Whitley, *German Destroyers,* 148.

Chapter 10

1. Darlington, *Canadian Naval Chronicle*, 140.
2. Ibid., 148.
3. Ibid., 143.
4. Morison, *Invasion of France and Germany*, 77 nb.
5. Bekker, *Defeat at Sea*, 136.
6. Tarrant, *Last Year*, 59.
7. Scott, *Hold the Narrow Sea*, 194–95.
8. Whitby, "Masters of the Channel Night."
9. Ibid.
10. Darlington, *Canadian Naval Chronicle*, 152.
11. Whitby, "Masters of the Channel Night."

Chapter 11

1. Tarrant, *Last Year*, 41.
2. Gardiner, *Fighting Ships, 1922–1946*, 245.
3. Peszke, *Poland's Navy*, 157.
4. Le Sauteur, *Jersey under the Swastika*, 12–13.
5. Ibid., 12–15.

Chapter 12

1. Dear, *The Oxford Companion to World War II*, 596, and Gardiner, *Fighting Ships 1922–1946*, 280–317.
2. Roskill, *War at Sea*, Vol. 3, Part 2, 83.
3. Morison, *Invasion*, 252.
4. Action Report, USS *Somers*, 5.
5. Morison, *Invasion*, 252.
6. Report of Boarding Party, USS *Somers*, 3.
7. Roscoe, *United States Destroyer Operations in World War II*, 377.
8. Pope, *Flag 4*, 238.
9. Action Report, USS *Endicott*, 3.
10. Action Report, USS *Gleaves*, 2.
11. Ibid., 4.
12. Tarrant, *Last Year*, 125.

Chapter 13

1. Letter from Felix Schirmer, quoted in http://www.klammi.de/Personen/ Page11095/Seegefecht/M273/m273.html.

Chapter 14

1. Reinicke, "German Surface Force Strategy," 182.

2. Koop and Schmolke, *German Destroyers*, 14.

3. Ibid., 16. The concept of "idiot proof" did not figure in German naval design calculations. For example: "Because the feedwater regulator is so inaccessible, two stokers have to be at the central stand at all times. One stoker has to be ready to shut off the water level and regulate the supercharger atomizer, while the other waits to close down the burn valve immediately should the Saacke burner flame go out since there is then a risk of explosion."

4. Roskill, *White Ensign*, 34.

5. This includes one action in the Black Sea in which German shore batteries assisted Romanian destroyers.

6. A similar process was under way in the Pacific. After outfighting the Allied navies for eighteen months, Japan's last significant victory in a surface engagement occurred in July 1943 at the battle of Kolombangara.

Bibliography

Primary Sources

Action Report, USS *Benson,* 2 October 1944, National Archives II, College Park, Md.

———. USS *Endicott,* 17 August 1944, National Archives II, College Park, Md.

———. USS *Gleaves,* 3 October 1944, National Archives II, College Park, Md.

———. USS *Somers,* 15 August 1944, National Archives II, College Park, Md.

Brown, David, ed. *Naval Operations of the Campaign in Norway.* London: Frank Cass, 2000.

Franklin D. Roosevelt Presidential Library and Museum, Great Britain Diplomatic Files, Box 36, War Situation Telegrams.

Grove, Eric, ed. *German Capital Ships and Raiders in World War II, Volume I: From* Graf Spee *to* Bismarck, *1939–1941.* London: Frank Cass, 2002.

———. *German Capital Ships and Raiders in World War II, Volume II: From* Scharnhorst *to* Tirpitz, *1942–1944.* London: Frank Cass, 2002.

London Gazette. "First and Second Battles of Narvik on 10th and 13th April 1940 Respectively." *Supplement.* 3 July 1947.

———. "The River Plate Battle." *Supplement.* 19 June 1947.

———. "Sinking of the German Battlecruiser *Scharnhorst* on the 26th December, 1943." *Supplement.* 7 August 1947.

———. "Sinking of the German Battleship *Bismarck* on 27th May, 1941." *Supplement.* 16 October 1947.

PRO ADM 234/444, H.M. *Ships sunk or damaged by enemy action 3rd September 1939 to 2nd September 1945.*

PRO *Battlefront: Sinking of the* Bismarck. Richmond, Surrey: PRO, 2001.

Secondary Sources

Achkasov, V. I., and N. B. Pavlovich. *Soviet Naval Operations in the Great Patriotic War 1941–1945.* Annapolis, Md.: Naval Institute Press, 1981.

Ansel, Walter. *Hitler and the Middle Sea.* Durham, N.C.: Duke University Press, 1972.

Auphan, Paul, and Jacques Mordal. *The French Navy in World War II.* Westport, Conn.: Greenwood Press, 1976.

Bagnasco, Erminio, and Enrico Cernuschi. *Le Navi da Guerra Italiani 1940–1945.* Parma, Italy: Ermanno Albertelli, 2003.

Barnett, Correlli. *Engage the Enemy More Closely: The Royal Navy in the Second World War.* New York: W. W. Norton, 1991.

Bekker, Cajus. *Defeat at Sea.* New York: Henry Holt, 1955.

———. *Hitler's Naval War.* New York: Bantam, 1974.

Bercuson, David J., and Holger H. Herwig. *The Destruction of the* Bismarck. Woodstock, N.Y.: Overlook Press, 2001.

Blair, Clay. *Hitler's U-Boat War: The Hunted, 1942–1945.* New York: Modern Library, 2000.

———. *Hitler's U-Boat War: The Hunters, 1939–1942.* New York: Modern Library, 2000.

Breyer, Siegfried. *Pocket Battleship* Admiral Graf Spee. West Chester, Penn.: Schiffer, 1989.

Brown, David. *Warship Loses of WWII.* Annapolis, Md.: Naval Institute Press, 1995.

Bulkley, Robert J., Jr. *At Close Quarters: PT Boats in the United States Navy.* Annapolis, Md.: Naval Institute Press, 2003.

Campbell, John. *Naval Weapons of World War II.* Annapolis, Md.: Naval Institute Press, 2002.

Churchill, Winston S. *The Second World War: Their Finest Hour.* Vol. 2. Boston: Houghton Mifflin, 1949.

———. *The Second World War: The Grand Alliance.* Vol. 3. Boston: Houghton Mifflin, 1950.

———. *The Second World War: The Hinge of Fate.* Vol. 4. Boston: Houghton Mifflin, 1950.

Cooper, Bryan. *The Battle of the Torpedo Boats.* New York: Stein and Day, 1970.

Cressman, Robert J. *The Official Chronology of the U.S. Navy in World War II.* Annapolis, Md.: Naval Institute Press, 2000.

Cunningham, Andrew Browne. *A Sailor's Odyssey.* London: Hutchinson, 1951.

Darlington, Robert, and Fraser McKee. *The Canadian Naval Chronicle, 1939–1945.* St. Catharines, Ontario: Vanwell, 1998.

Darrieus, Admiral Henri, and Jean Queguiner. *Historique de la Marine française 1922–1942.* St. Malo, France: l'Ancre de Marine, 1996.

Dear, I.C.B. *The Oxford Companion to World War II.* New York: Oxford University Press, 1995.

Derry, T. K. *The Campaign in Norway.* London: HMSO, 1952.

Dickens, Peter. *Narvik: Battles in the Fjords.* Annapolis, Md.: Naval Institute Press, 1997.

Dorrian, James G. *Storming St. Nazaire.* Annapolis, Md.: Naval Institute Press, 1998.

Dunn, John, and Donald Stoker. "Blood on the Baltic." *Naval History* 13, no. 2 (Mar/Apr 1999): 45.

Edwards, Bernard. *Salvo: Classical Naval Gun Actions.* Annapolis, Md.: Naval Institute Press, 1995.

Ellis, John. *World War II: A Statistical Survey.* New York: Facts on File, 1995.

Evans, Mark Llewellyn. *Great World War II Battles in the Arctic.* Westport, Conn.: Greenwood, 1999.

Friedman, Norman. *U.S. Naval Weapons.* London: Conway Maritime Press, 1983.

Gardiner, Robert, ed. *Conway's All the World's Fighting Ships, 1906–1921.* Annapolis, Md.: Naval Institute Press, 1986.

———. *Conway's All the World's Fighting Ships, 1922–1946.* New York: Mayflower, 1980.

Garrett, Richard. *Scharnhorst and Gneisenau.* New York: Hippocrene, 1978.

Garzke, William H., Jr., Robert O. Dulin, Jr., and David K. Brown. "Sinking of the *Bismarck*, an Analysis of the Damage" in *Warship 1994.* London: Conway Maritime Press, 1995.

German, Tony. *The Sea Is at Our Gates: The History of the Canadian Navy.* Toronto: McClelland & Stewart, 1990.

Gray, Edwyn. *Hitler's Battleships.* Annapolis, Md.: Naval Institute Press, 1999.

Gröner, Erich. *German Warships, 1815–1945.* Vol. 1. London: Conway Maritime Press, 1990.

———. *German Warships, 1815–1945.* Vol. 2. London: Conway Maritime Press, 1991.

Grove, Eric. *The Price of Disobedience: The Battle of the River Plate Reconsidered.* Annapolis, Md.: Naval Institute Press, 2000.

Harker, Jack. *HMNZS Achilles.* http://www.rnzncomms.net.nz/jackharker/achillesindex.html.

Hervieux, Pierre. "The Elbing Class Torpedo Boats at War" in *Warship.* Vol. 10. Annapolis, Md.: Naval Institute Press, 1986.

———. "German Auxiliaries at War 1939–45: Minesweepers, Submarine Chasers and Patrol Boats" in *Warship 1995.* London: Conway Maritime Press, 1995.

———. "German Destroyer Minelaying Operations off the English Coast (1940–1941)" in *Warship.* Vol. 4. Annapolis, Md.: Naval Institute Press, 1980.

———. "German TA Torpedo Boats at War" in *Warship 1997–1998*. London: Conway Maritime Press, 1997.

———. "German Torpedo Boats at War: The Möwe & Wolf Classes" in *Warship*. Vol. 7. Annapolis, Md.: Naval Institute Press, 1983.

———. "German Type 45, 40 and 43 Minesweepers at War" in *Warship 1996*. London: Conway Maritime Press, 1996.

———. "The Royal Romanian Navy at War 1941–1945" in *Warship 2001–2002*. London: Conway Maritime Press, 2001.

———. "War Operations of the German Types 35 and 37 Torpedo Boats" in *Warship 1994*. London: Conway Maritime Press, 1994.

Hague, Arnold. *The Allied Convoy System 1939–1945*. Annapolis, Md.: Naval Institute Press, 2000.

Howland, Vernon W. "The Loss of HMS *Glorious*. An Analysis of the Action." *Warship International*. http://www.warship.org/no11994.htm.

Huan, Claude. *La Marine Soviétique en Guerre I Arctique*. Paris: Economica, 1991.

Hughes, Terry, and John Costello. *The Battle of the Atlantic*. New York: Dial, 1977.

Jackson, Robert. *The German Navy in World War II*. London: Brown, 1999.

———. *The Royal Navy in World War II*. Annapolis, Md.: Naval Institute Press, 1997.

Jordan, Roger. *The World's Merchant Fleets, 1939*. Annapolis, Md.: Naval Institute Press, 1999.

Keegan, John. *The Times Atlas of the Second World War*. New York: Harper & Row, 1989.

Kemp, Paul. *Friend or Foe: Friendly Fire at Sea 1939–1945*. London: Leo Cooper, 1995.

Kemp, P. K. *Decision at Sea: The Convoy Escorts*. New York: E. P. Dutton, 1978.

———. *Key to Victory: The Triumph of British Sea Power in WWII*. Boston: Little, Brown, 1957.

Kennedy, Ludovic. *Pursuit: The Chase and Sinking of the* Bismarck. Annapolis, Md.: Naval Institute Press, 2000.

Kershaw, Andrew. *Battle of the Atlantic*. Avon, England: Purnell & Sons, 1975.

Kindell, Donald. "The 5th Destroyer Flotilla, Autumn 1940" in *Warship*. Vol. 4. Annapolis, Md.: Naval Institute Press, 1980.

Koburger, Charles, Jr. *Wine-Dark, Blood Red Sea: Naval Warfare in the Aegean, 1941–1946*. Westport, Conn.: Praeger, 1999.

Koop, Gerhard, and Klaus-Peter Schmolke. *Battleship* Tirpitz. London: Conway Maritime Press, 1998.

———. *Battleships of the Scharnhorst Class*. Annapolis, Md.: Naval Institute Press, 1999.

————. *German Destroyers of World War II*. Annapolis, Md.: Naval Institute Press, 2003.

————. *German Light Cruisers of World War II*. Annapolis, Md.: Naval Institute Press, 2002.

————. *Heavy Cruisers of the Hipper Class*. Annapolis, Md.: Naval Institute Press, 2001.

Langenberg, William H. "The Inglorious End of Glorious." *World War II*, July 1999, 30–36.

Langtree, Christopher. *The Kellys: British J, K & N Class Destroyers of World War II*. Annapolis, Md.: Naval Institute Press, 2002.

Le Sauteur, Philip Frederick. *Jersey under the Swastika*. http://tonylesauteur.com/arbre39.htm.

Levy, James. "Ready or Not? The Home Fleet at the Outset of World War II." *Naval War College Review*, Autumn 1999, 90–108.

Lind, Lew. *Battle of the Wine Dark Sea: The Aegean Campaign 1941–1945*. Kenthurst, Australia: Kangaroo Press, 1994.

Macintyre, Donald. *The Naval War Against Hitler*. New York: Charles Scribner's Sons, 1971.

March, Edgar J. *British Destroyers: A History of Development, 1892–1953*. Guildford, England: Billing & Sons, 1966.

Martienssen, Anthony. *Hitler and His Admirals*. New York: E. P. Dutton, 1949.

Meister, Jürg. *Soviet Warships of the Second World War*. New York: Acro, 1977.

Miller, Nathan. *The War at Sea: A Naval History of World War II*. New York: Scribner, 1995.

Mollo, Andrew. *The Armed Forces of World War II, Uniforms, Insignia and Organization*. New York: Crown, 1981.

Morison, Samuel Eliot. *The Atlantic Battle Won: May 1943–May 1945*. Vol. 10. Boston: Little, Brown, 1975.

————. *History of United States Naval Operations in World War II: The Battle of the Atlantic, 1939–1943*. Vol. 1. Boston: Little, Brown, 1984.

————. *The Invasion of France and Germany*. Vol. 11. Boston: Little, Brown, 1975.

————. *The Two Ocean War*. Boston: Little, Brown, 1963.

Müllenheim-Rechberg, Burkand Baron von. *Battleship* Bismarck: *A Survivor's Story*. Annapolis, Md.: Naval Institute Press, 1999.

Mulligan, Timothy P. "Bismarck: Not Ready for Action?" *Naval History* 15, no. 1 (Feb 2001): 20.

Pearce, Frank. *Last Call for HMS* Edinburgh. New York: Atheneum, 1982.

Pearson, Michael. *Red Sky in the Morning: The Battle of the Barents Sea, 1942*. Shrewsbury, England: Airlife, 2002.

Peszke, Michael Alfred. *Poland's Navy 1918–1945*. New York: Hippocrene Books, 1999.

Polmar, Norman, and Samuel Loring Morison. *PT Boats at War: World War II to Vietnam*. Osceola, Wis.: MBI, 1999.

Poolman, Kenneth. *The Winning Edge: Naval Technology in Action, 1939–1945*. Annapolis, Md.: Naval Institute Press, 1997.

Pope, Dudley. *The Battle of the River Plate*. Annapolis, Md.: Naval Institute Press, 1987.

———. *Flag 4—The Battle of the Coastal Forces in the Mediterranean, 1939–1945*. London: Chatham, 1998.

Potter, John Deane. *Fiasco*. New York: Stein and Day, 1970.

Powell, Michael. *Death in the South Atlantic: The Last Voyage of the Graf Spee*. New York: Rinehart & Co., 1956.

Preston, Anthony. "The Narvik Flotilla" in *Warship*. Vol. 1. Annapolis, Md.: Naval Institute Press, 1977.

———. *Navies of World War II*. London: Bison, 1976.

Raeder, Erich. *Grand Admiral*. Cambridge, Mass: Da Capo, 2001.

———. *Struggle for the Sea*. London: Kimber, 1959.

Reinicke, H. J. "German Surface Force Strategy in World War II." *Proceedings* 648 (February 1957): 181–87.

Reynolds, Leonard C. *Dog Boats at War: Royal Navy D Class MTBs and MGBs, 1939–1945*. Phoenix Mill, England: Sutton, 2000.

Rhys-Jones, Graham. "The Loss of *Bismarck*: Who Was to Blame?" *Naval War College Review*, Winter 1992, 25–44.

Roberts, John. "The Final Action—the Sinking of the *Bismarck*" in *Warship*. Vol. 7. Annapolis, Md.: Naval Institute Press, 1983.

Rohwer J., and G. Hummelchen. *Chronology of the War at Sea, 1939–1945*. Annapolis, Md.: Naval Institute Press, 1992.

Rohwer, Jergen. *Allied Submarine Attacks of World War II*. Annapolis, Md.: Naval Institute Press, 1997.

———. *Axis Submarine Successes of World War II*. Annapolis, Md.: Naval Institute Press, 1999.

———. *War at Sea 1939–1945*. Annapolis, Md.: Naval Institute Press, 1996.

Roscoe, Theodore. *United States Destroyer Operations in World War II*. Annapolis, Md.: Naval Institute Press, 1953.

Roskill, S.W. HMS *Warspite*. Annapolis, Md.: Naval Institute Press, 1997.

———. *The Offensive Part I*. Vol. 3. London: HMSO, 1960.

———. *The Offensive Part II*. Vol. 3. Nashville, Tenn.: Battery Press, 1994.

———. *The Period of Balance*. Vol. 2. London: HMSO, 1956.

———. *The War at Sea, 1939–1945: The Defensive*. Vol. 1. London: HMSO, 1954.

———. *White Ensign*. Annapolis, Md.: Naval Institute Press, 1960.

Ruge, Friedrich. *Der Seekrieg: The German Navy's Story 1939–1945*. Annapolis, Md.: Naval Institute Press, 1957.

———. "German Minesweepers in World War II." *Proceedings* 595 (September 1952): 995–1003.

———. *The Soviets as Naval Opponents*. Annapolis, Md.: Naval Institute Press, 1979.

Schenk, Peter. *Kampf um die Ägäis*. Hamburg, Germany: E.S. Mittler & Sohn, 2000.

Scott, Peter. *The Battle of the Narrow Sea*. London: Country Life, 1945.

Seegefecht vor Egersund 11.-12.011945. http://www.klammi.de/Personen/Page11095 /Seegefecht/seegefecht.html.

Showell, Jak. *The German Navy in World War II*. Annapolis, Md.: Naval Institute Press, 1979.

Smith, Peter C. *Hold the Narrow Sea: Naval Warfare in the English Channel, 1939–1945*. Ashbourne, England: Moorland Publishing, 1984.

Statz, Joseph. "I Escaped from *Bismarck*." *Naval History* 9, no. 1 (Jan 1995): 43–47.

Stephens, Martin. *Sea Battles in Close-up: World War 2*. Vol. 1. Edited by Eric Grove. Annapolis, Md.: Naval Institute Press, 1993.

Sweetman, Jack. "Great Sea Battles of World War II." *Naval History* 9, no. 3 (May 1995): 6–57.

Tarrant, V. E. *King George V Class Battleships*. London: Arms and Armour Press, 2000.

———. *The Last Year of the Kriegsmarine*. Annapolis, Md.: Naval Institute Press, 1994.

Tent, James F. *E-Boat Alert, Defending the Normandy Invasion Fleet*. Annapolis, Md.: Naval Institute Press, 1996.

Thompson, Julian. *The War at Sea: The Royal Navy in the Second World War*. Osceola, Wis.: Motorbooks International, 1996.

Uhlig, Frank, Jr. *How Navies Fight: The U.S. Navy and Its Allies*. Annapolis, Md.: Naval Institute Press, 1994.

Van der Vat, Dan. *The Atlantic Campaign*. New York: Harper Row, 1988.

Von Der Porten, Edward P. *The German Navy in World War II*. New York: Thomas Y. Crowell, 1969.

Whitby, Michael. "Masters of the Channel Night: The 10th Destroyer Flotilla's Victory off Ile De Batz, 9 June 1944." *Canadian Military History* 2, no. 1 (Spring 1993): 5–22.

Whitley, M. J. *Battleships of World War Two*. Annapolis, Md.: Naval Institute Press, 1998.

———. *Cruisers of World War Two*. Annapolis, Md.: Naval Institute Press, 1995.

———. *Destroyers of World War Two*. Annapolis, Md.: Naval Institute Press, 1988.

———. *German Capital Ships of World War Two*. London: Arms and Armour Press, 1989.

———. *German Cruisers of World War Two*. Annapolis, Md.: Naval Institute Press, 1987.

———. *German Destroyers of World War Two*. Annapolis, Md.: Naval Institute Press, 1991.

Whitley, Mike. "Victim of Ultra? The Loss of the *Bremse*" in *Warship*. Vol. 11. Annapolis, Md.: Naval Institute Press, 1987.

Winton, John. *Death of the* Scharnhorst. London: Cassell, 2000.

———. *The War at Sea—The British Navy in World War II*. New York: William Morrow, 1968.

Worth, Richard. *Fleets of World War II*. Cambridge, Mass.: Da Capo, 2001.

Zaloga, Steven, and Victor Madej. *The Polish Campaign, 1939*. New York: Hippocrene, 1985.

Ziemke, Earl F. *The German Northern Theater of Operations, 1941–1945*. Washington, D.C.: USGPO, 1976.

INDEX

VINCENT P. O'HARA was born and reared in San Diego, California, where he developed his lifelong enthusiasm for naval history. He holds a history degree from the University of California, Berkeley, and is a business consultant, researcher, and cartographer.

Mr. O'Hara's work has appeared in *Warship* and *World War II* and is forthcoming in other publications including *Naval History* and *MHQ*. *The German Fleet at War,* his first book, expresses his interest in a consistent examination of the surface naval engagements of the Second World War.

Mr. O'Hara resides in San Diego with his wife and son.